Political Graffiti in Critical Times

Protest, Culture & Society

General editors:
Kathrin Fahlenbrach, Institute for Media and Communication, University of Hamburg
Martin Klimke, New York University Abu Dhabi
Joachim Scharloth, Waseda University

Protest movements have been recognized as significant contributors to processes of political participation and transformations of culture and value systems, as well as to the development of both a national and transnational civil society. This series brings together the various innovative approaches to phenomena of social change, protest and dissent which have emerged in recent years, from an interdisciplinary perspective. It contextualizes social protest and cultures of dissent in larger political processes and socio-cultural transformations by examining the influence of historical trajectories and the response of various segments of social, political and legal institutions on a national and international level. In doing so, the series offers a more comprehensive and multi-dimensional view of historical and cultural change in the twentieth and twenty-first centuries.

Recent volumes:

Volume 28
Political Graffiti in Critical Times: The Aesthetics of Street Politics
Edited by Ricardo Campos, Andrea Pavoni and Yiannis Zaimakis

Volume 27
Protest, Youth and Precariousness: The Unfinished Fight against Austerity in Portugal
Edited by Renato Miguel Carmo and José Alberto Vasconcelos Simões

Volume 26
Party Responses to Social Movements: Challenges and Opportunities
Daniela R. Piccio

Volume 25
The Politics of Authenticity: Countercultures and Radical Movements across the Iron Curtain, 1968–1989
Edited by Joachim C. Häberlen, Mark Keck-Szajbel and Kate Mahoney

Volume 24
Taking on Technocracy: Nuclear Power in Germany, 1945 to the Present
Dolores L. Augustine

Volume 23
The Virago Story: Assessing the Impact of a Feminist Publishing Phenomenon
Catherine Riley

Volume 22
The Women's Liberation Movement: Impacts and Outcomes
Edited by Kristina Schulz

Volume 21
Hairy Hippies and Bloody Butchers: The Greenpeace Anti-Whaling Campaign in Norway
Juliane Riese

Volume 20
A Fragmented Landscape: Abortion Governance and Protest Logics in Europe
Edited by Silvia De Zordo, Joanna Mishtal and Lorena Anton

Volume 19
The Nuclear Crisis: The Arms Race, Cold War Anxiety, and the German Peace Movement of the 1980s
Edited by Christoph Becker-Schaum, Philipp Gassert, Wilfried Mausbach, Martin Klimke and Marianne Zepp

For a full volume listing, please see the series page on our website:
http://berghahnbooks.com/series/protest-culture-and-society

Political Graffiti in Critical Times

The Aesthetics of Street Politics

Edited by

Ricardo Campos, Andrea Pavoni
and Yiannis Zaimakis

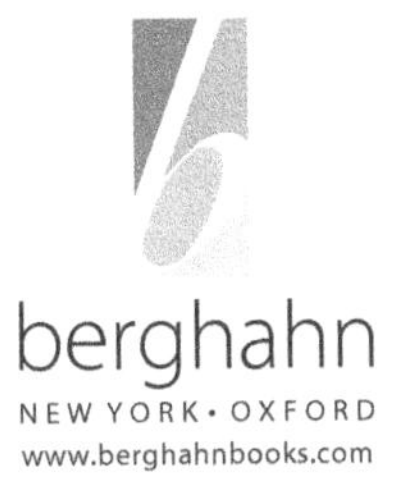

berghahn
NEW YORK · OXFORD
www.berghahnbooks.com

First published in 2021 by
Berghahn Books
www.berghahnbooks.com

Library of Congress Cataloging-in-Publication Data

Names: Campos, Ricardo (Marnoto de Oliveira Campos), editor. | Pavoni,
Andrea, editor. | Zaimakis, Yiannis, editor.
Title: Political graffiti in critical times : the aesthetics of street politics / edited
by Ricardo Campos, Andrea Pavoni and Yiannis Zaimakis.
Description: First Edition. | New York : Berghahn Books, 2021. | Series:
Protest, culture & society; 28 | Includes bibliographical references and
index.
Identifiers: LCCN 2020042160 (print) | LCCN 2020042161 (ebook) | ISBN
9781789209419 (hardback) | ISBN 9781789209426 (ebook)
Subjects: LCSH: Graffiti—Political aspects. | Street art. | Politics in art.
Classification: LCC GT3912 .P64 2021 (print) | LCC GT3912 (ebook) |
DDC 751.7/3—dc23
LC record available at https://lccn.loc.gov/2020042160
LC ebook record available at https://lccn.loc.gov/2020042161

British Library Cataloguing in Publication Data

A catalogue record for this book is available from the British Library

ISBN 978-1-78920-941-9 hardback
ISBN 978-1-80539-728-1 paperback
ISBN 978-1-80539-911-7 epub
ISBN 978-1-78920-942-6 web pdf

https://doi.org/10.3167/9781789209419

Contents

Illustrations

Figures

Tables

Political Graffiti in Critical Times

Andrea Pavoni, Yiannis Zaimakis and Ricardo Campos

Crisis

Crisis, today, is everywhere, or so we are told. From financial crisis to the refugee crisis, from the economic crisis to the crisis of representative democracy, and from the 'new urban crisis' (Florida 2017) to the crisis of political legitimation or the recent Covid-19 pandemic – our reality is framed as an endless series of crises. In the context of advanced capitalism, crises often justify as unavoidable the type of emergency 'solutions' that are crafted in response: militarization and commodification of space, economic austerity, suspension of rights, precarization of work... the list goes on. A permanent state of emergency, precariousness and uncertainty has seemingly become the white noise of our existence, as political systems are increasingly shaky, sociocultural bonds thinner, economics evermore unpredictable, and the global ecosystem off balance, while the overarching rhetoric, technology and normativity of security politics produce growing inequality, violence and fear.

Various excellent analyses have carefully dismantled the hegemonic discourses around such 'crises', showing to what extent they are indeed a by-product of the very systems (political, economic, financial, securitarian) that pretend to 'overcome' them (e.g. Arrighi 1978; Klein 2007; Harvey 2010). While much attention has (rightly) been given to demystifying the seemingly uncontroversial causal explanations of a given crisis, there has been less reflection on the notion of crisis itself, and the way it crystallizes as an uncontested framework through which we experience life under late capitalism (e.g. Mbembe and Roitman 1995; Lazzarato 2012). Crisis, in fact, also works as a filter through which reality is perceived, described, understood and, ultimately, contested (e.g. Koselleck 1988; Roitman 2013; Agamben 2015).

Originally referring to a medical condition – a *critical* tipping point oscillating between fatal danger and hopeful recovery – the etymology of 'crisis' points to a 'rupture' or a 'separation', as well as to the (critical) 'decision' that this rupture prompts.[1] Since the eighteenth century, the concept has undergone a significant translation. In the optimistic atmosphere of the belle époque, propelled by the industrial revolution and the nascent urbanization, as history began to be perceived as an arrow projected towards the future through the normative direction of progress, crisis came to signify a temporary interruption to the progressive temporality, and thus the normative injunction to act in order to restore progress and repair time (cf. Koselleck 2006). When translated onto the domain of politics, crisis has functioned as a mechanism of observation that suffocates the present, in the hopeful projections of a post-crisis future where the 'troubles' of this present will somehow be overcome.[2]

This reflection does not lead us to deny the reality of crisis, of course. More precisely, it highlights the functioning of crisis as an aesthetic and epistemological framework, and thus it strives 'to consider the ways in which it [crisis] regulates narrative constructions, the ways in which it allows certain questions to be asked while others are foreclosed' (Roitman 2013: 94). This volume takes inspiration from this observation, by diving within the reality of the polymorphous crises that encompass the contemporary existence, while at the same time assuming crisis as a frame – perhaps *the* frame – around (or against) which certain sociocultural and ethico-political imaginaries are produced, and others foreclosed. As an explicit or implicit indicator that something is not going as it should, 'crisis' increasingly appears as the framework around which contemporary politics is fought, in the shape of an aesthetic conflict over different ways to see, experience and act in the world.

As is very clear to anyone of us living in the present times, crisis works as a category that frames experience and provides it with a sense. The awareness of living in a crisis, or the experience of crisis, are the constitutive sites of a specific, precarious and uncertain subjectivity – an uncertainty and precariousness that at the same time speak of an inability to experience crisis itself, facing a world whose structural logics and logistics are increasingly alienated, dislocated, automated and imperceptible (Jameson 2007; Toscano and Kinkle 2015). One may simply think about the power that the TINA (There Is No Alternative) narrative has so far enjoyed in global politics; the extent to which crisis has become a background narrative of contemporary everyday life; or the role that technocratic narratives of the future (e.g. the smart city) play in shaping strategies of planning and governance. At the same time, we may also point to the seismic effects that times of crisis may have on taken-for-granted systems of values, understandings and normativities, letting alternative spaces of agency, political action and aesthetic intervention emerge. In fact, we believe it is not an overstatement to argue that *the* battleground of contemporary politics is a fundamentally aesthetic one, namely the task of *critically* re-imagining our present, and its relation to the future, away from the linear path that the narrative of crisis seemingly forces us into (Holmes 2008) – an aesthetic-political task that today, we add, is fundamentally *urban*.

Aesthetics, Visual Protest and Street-Level Micropolitics

During the twentieth century, the surfacing of a dominant visual culture with a gradual aestheticization and stylization of everyday life (Ewen 1988; Featherstone 1998) became remarkable, especially in the urban context. This is particularly evident vis-à-vis the contemporary rise of 'creative city' policies, today becoming a veritable 'meta-policy' shaping global urbanization dynamics (Peck 2012). As the sphere of entertainment has increasingly merged with those of economics, politics and security (e.g. Thrift 2011), aesthetics has become a key category of urban politics. This is all too evident to anyone living in contemporary cities, where urban branding has grown into a central development strategy, enrolling discourses and policies of planning, security, marketing and law in the production of safe, commodified and entertaining urban spaces, and functioning as a sort of lubricant that both propels and expedites this process of value extraction by mediating between the abstract and the concrete, the planetary and the local (Pavoni 2018). In this context, public art has gradually begun to play an important role in the process of place-valorization triggered by aesthetic capitalism (e.g. Deutsche 1996; Pinder 2008; Berry-Slater and Iles 2009; Guinard and Margier 2017). While it is not possible to even briefly sum up the complexity of this process – one that moreover is far from being linear and unilateral – what we are interested in emphasizing is the extent to which aesthetics has grown into a key context in which urban politics is expressed, repressed and fought.

To be sure, the city has always been a stage where power is manifested, and aesthetically so: from royal parades to contemporary mega events, from traditional monuments to certain forms of contemporary public art that extol heroes and emblematic historical episodes, as well as certain values cherished by governments. It is unsurprising, for instance, that after revolutions or violent processes of regime change there is often an energetic effort to remove symbols and artworks associated with the previous regime –

something that is buffered by propaganda, which also employs art as a medium. Political murals are perfect examples of this, as we can see from Soviet, Chinese, Mexican and Cuban murals. The instrumental use of art as a tool for propaganda, especially in the context of twentieth-century totalitarianisms, did foster a persistent suspicion for the aestheticization of politics, spelled out in different ways in the writings of Walter Benjamin, Theodor Adorno and Guy Debord, among others. This has cemented a belief in the pernicious effect that aestheticization may play vis-à-vis political expression, stemming from the assumption that 'the use of art for political action necessarily aestheticises this action, turns this action into a spectacle and, thus, neutralises the practical effect of this action' (Groys 2014).

While cautioning against such a decorative and 'distractive' danger, however, it is important to avoid over-deterministic approaches against the 'use' of aesthetics in politics. In fact, one may ask whether politics could actually exist without aesthetics or, following Jacques Rancière, whether aesthetics is to be *the* battleground of politics itself. According to Rancière (2015), politics has to do with the definition and framing of a *common*: a common space, relation, experience, with a given 'distribution of the sensible'; that is, the way in which certain ways of seeing, speaking and being are included, while others are excluded. The 'political', accordingly, is understood as the emergence of a dissensus within such a distribution of the sensible; or as the appearance of something, someone or some demand that cannot fit within this 'aesthetic' (from the root of *aisthēsis*, referring to the sphere of sensible, the perceptible) distribution, to the extent that forces it to change. In this sense, '[art] is political as it frames a specific space-time sensorium, as it redefines on this stage the power of speech or the coordinates of perception, shifts the places of the actor and the spectator, etc.' (Rancière 2006). In other words, art is not only political in so far as willingly and intentionally aimed a delivering a 'political' position, meaning or ideology. More profoundly, the encounter between art and politics is unavoidable, as both inhabit the common, aesthetic sphere of being together: at stake in this encounter is the relation between consensus and dissensus, compliance and contestation, and thus the consequent framing and reframing of the common (i.e. the public).

Lately the long-standing suspicion for aesthetics in activist circles has begun to be challenged, as the discourses, strategies and tactics of activist and artistic praxis have increasingly merged into visual forms of protest that challenge the hegemonic consensus, resignifying, reimagining and reshaping the urban landscape in significant ways. Stephen Duncombe argues that if 'every age creates a form of protest appropriate to its hegemonic power … artful protest is the response to a new regime of power: global Neoliberalism' (Duncombe 2016). If neoliberalism is sustained by global flows, which at their most essential may be understood as flows of information in which meanings, bodies, affects, technologies and money intersect and combine, then, it is argued, it is increasingly around the creation, legitimation and challenging of those meaningful and affective flows that politics will be articulated. This is all the more so vis-à-vis the current erosion of legitimation of the democratic system and its traditional actors, with the related breakdown of the formal political participation of citizens who, increasingly, seem to be looking for less conventional ways of participating politically (Loader 2007; Farthing 2010; Dahlgren 2013; Pitti 2018). In this context we have seen the surfacing of so-called 'new new social movements' (Langman 2013), characterized by various experimentations with novel codes and grammars which, although being significantly inspired and diffused via digital media (Juris 2012; Tremayne 2014; Simões et al. 2018), have the street as the privileged stage for its expression.

In fact, since its inception, the city has been a place of fluid normativity, political conflict and sociocultural vibrance; one in which official institutions overlap with informal networks and ways of life, and where strict and capillary apparatuses of regulation, governance and control coexist with extended patches of darkness, invisibility and resistance. It has been out of the vibrant and inspiring atmosphere of the city that public spheres have emerged, seditions have been plotted, public protests have been expressed, and revolutions have erupted. Here, social movements have deployed their tactics to try to win their battles; and here also more spontaneous and less structured groups or anonymous individuals have found a space for their political expression and participation. This has especially occurred in 'times of crisis', as urban landscapes are particularly affected in turbulent periods, marked by widening socio-economic imbalances, spatial exclusion and political turmoil, and, as a consequence, by intense citizen mobilization that brings novel politically and aesthetically creative responses onto the streets.

In the last decades, in fact, different incidents, events, and social movements challenging the ruling political powers have had the epicentre of their political struggle on urban streets, where new strategies of mobilization and communication have suddenly germinated. This includes the various forms taken by the so-called 'Arab Spring'; the protests against increases in public transport ticket prices, and against Brazil hosting the football World Cup ('Anti-Cup'); the expression of the Occupy movement around the world; and the anti-austerity demonstrations in Greece, Spain, Portugal, and elsewhere. Not only have the majority of recent protests across the world occurred in cities, but most of the issues being protested against have also been distinctively urban: the privatization and commodification of public space, the intensification of surveillance and social control, housing crises, social exclusion, austerity politics, and so on. In many of these protests, the 'right to the city' has often been upheld, providing a global dimension to the local discontents of the protesters (Sugranyes and Mathivet 2010; Brenner 2013; Harvey 2013). As the world's urban populations grow, in fact, it is the right to the city itself that is increasingly unobtainable for their inhabitants, as the way in which cities are built, managed and lived in appears to be determined by global forces that escape our understanding, perception and control.

A naturally democratic – although not necessarily legal – means of expression, urban streets, spaces and surfaces have always been a potential stage for the expression of more informal, vernacular, transgressive and counter-institutional forms of communication. Across the decades, writers, crews, activists, political groups and street artists have been using various strategies and tactics to disseminate marks of artistic experimentation, signs of existential quest, piercing sarcasm, idiosyncratic exhilaration and political dissent around the city surfaces. Lately, many authors have been highlighting novel forms of creativity and aesthetic creation, whether in exercise of everyday life micropolitics, or in the more episodic actions of contentious politics, in particular when these are manifested in the context of social movements or collective activism: for example, hybrid forms of protest combining both the street and the internet (Castells 2012; Juris 2012; Tremayne 2014); the development of new grammars of communication and protest (Flesher Fominaya and Cox 2013; Baumgarten 2015; Díez Garcia 2017); and the emergence of new non-institutional and horizontal collective actors (Castells 2012; Dahlgren 2013; Flesher Fominaya and Cox 2013; Tejerina et al. 2013; Pickerill et al. 2014; Ancelovici, Dufour and Nez 2016). The analysis of these different ways of conceiving and practising politics has given rise to novel notions such as 'creative democracy' (Hankins 2017), 'creative citizen' (Hargreaves and Hartley 2016), 'creative activism' (Harrebye 2015), 'artivism' (Sandoval and Latorre 2008), 'aesthetics of protest' (Buser et al. 2013), and 'carnival of protest' (St John 2003).

It is surely not a coincidence that this outburst of creativity, at the intersection of aesthetics, politics and the urban space, has coincided with the current 'times of crisis'. If crisis, as argued above, is first of all a frame through which the world is perceived, it will be when the urban landscapes are more explicitly immersed within 'crisis' that aesthetic efforts to challenge, resignify, reimagine, and indeed dismantle this imaginary will multiply in quantity and quality. Challenging the rhetoric, aesthetics and thus the reality of crisis means first of all to imagine and express valuable alternatives to its taken-for-granted reality; a precise aesthetic task is to find ways and channels to express sociopolitical dissent and critique, as well as anger, in the face of a political system that is increasingly unable to represent social demands.

It is in this complex situation that this edited collection is situated: at the point of encounter between crisis (and the construction thereof), urban space, and the visual expression of protest. This is the battleground that this volume intends to explore. It is an attempt to understand how the politics and aesthetics of the urban *in* crisis are experienced, engaged with and reworked, by looking at the way forms of artistic visual production from the street are engaging with, and challenging, the current 'times of crisis'. How to turn the passive enduring of these times of crisis into the active imagining of alternative *critical times*? Inspired by this question, the volume gathers various contributions reflecting on the relation between urban space and visual protest across both geographical and historical axes. In order to navigate through this vast variety, we chose to focus on graffiti, a form of expression that continues to be relevant, accompanying and complementing other novel forms of visual political expression (e.g. performance, pranksterism, occupation) emerging in the streets. In particular, the contributions gathered in this volume focus on what we define as 'political graffiti', and the various forms this practice has evolved in contemporary urban space.

Political Graffiti in Critical Times

Graffiti is a complex, mark-making phenomenon; a specific form of writing that usually occurs 'out of place', produced by the use of simple writing instruments, such as spray paint and marker pens. It is unofficial, informal and, frequently, illegal. Modern graffiti is said to have emerged in the 1970s, together with hip-hop music and breakdance, out of the underground culture of deprived US East Coast inner cities (Castleman 1982; Cooper and Chalfant 1984; Phillips 1999; Austin 2001; Macdonald 2001).[3] 'Classic' signature graffiti, or tagging, is mostly concerned with the act of marking a presence and a territory with a self-referential claim (the tag), the meaning of which is often fully resolved within an internal language that for the most part remains obscure to the outsider. Born as being, by definition, excessive to the social, legal and aesthetic normativity of the urban, graffiti was immediately perceived as an assault on urban morality and decor, thus attracting social stigmatization and legal persecution. At the same time, its subversive aura, literally incorporating a transgression to the aesthetic regime of the contemporary city, and especially to its normative utopia of order, safety and cleanliness, provided it with a unique capacity to redraw the perception, experience and meaning of public space, allowing for hitherto subdued expressions, claims, narratives and conflicts to publicly appear (Ferrell 1996; McAuliffe and Iveson 2011: 133). With time, the rupturing quality of some forms of graffiti has to some extent waned, as the aesthetic of contemporary capitalism gradually attuned to the 'gritty', 'edgy' and subversive allure of this, as well as other, countercultural spaces, styles and practices, consistently with its tendency to co-opt and ingest radical artistic practices by turning them into marketable lifestyles (cf. Boltanski and Chiapello 2007; Moses 2013; Bohme 2017). Most importantly, to significantly alter the sociocultural, legal and economic status of this practice has been the surfacing of street art, or 'post-graffiti' as it is sometimes called (Waclawek 2011).

Despite the wide range of definitions that attempt to capture the differences between graffiti and street art, the debate is far from being settled (McAuliffe 2012; Blanché 2015; Ross 2016; Avramides and Tsilimpounidi 2017). Norms and definitions change with time, and it may thus be more productive to focus on common evolving trends and shared features, rather than attempting strict categorizations. Street art emerged in the late 1990s at the intersection between graffiti subculture and art market, adding new techniques (e.g. collage, stencilling, posters, stickers, throwing-up, pasting-up of drawings, airbrushing) to the traditional spray can, and gradually moving from the cryptic language of tagging to the pictorial image. Street artists have fewer ties with conventions of the subculture scene of graffiti, and their work 'is less likely to be considered vandalism, because it is more easily understood and accessible for the greater public than graffiti' (Blanché 2015: 35). Its 'shift from the typographic to the iconographic' (Manco 2004: 16), together with a greater attention to the political content of the message, has provided street art with 'a more universal, democratic aesthetic' (Dickens 2010: 77), as well as with a more comfortable relation with the art world and market (Bengtsen 2014; Wells 2016; Molnár 2018). To be sure, this evolution has been, and is, far from linear or smooth. In the contemporary city, graffiti and street art take different forms and produce different effects that are transversal to, and differently affected by, ongoing phenomena of commodification and securitization of the urban space. In many contexts, street art is undergoing a remarkable institutionalization, the result of often becoming, intentionally or not, a tool in the context of creative city politics and urban branding strategies (cf. Schacter 2014, 2016a, 2016b; Guinard and Margier 2017; Campos and Sequeira 2019). At the same time, graffiti continue to be criminalized, writers fined or arrested, and walls cleaned by generously loaded brushes of moral outrage and grey paint (McAuliffe 2012). Simultaneously, there are other artistic forms using urban surfaces as a means of expression, such as muralism, which underwent a rather different stylistic and conceptual evolution, and cannot simply be explained via the graffiti–street art dichotomy.

The dynamics and contested geographies of graffiti (here taken in its widest sense) are, in other words, complex and multifaceted, and their boundaries remain porous (Kramer 2010; McAuliffe and Iveson 2011). Policymakers, local authorities and practitioners alike constantly negotiate with the constitutive ambivalence of a practice that remains unamenable to strict stylistic, moral and even legal categorizations. This is most crucially dependent on the fact that graffiti are unavoidably public: 'by *taking place*', Chmielewska (2007: 161) explains, graffiti 'makes itself public'. As a consequence, their role, existence and 'social life' are never static or stable, but always dynamically immersed in the complex structures, power relations and 'distribution of the sensible' of a given space and a given time. On the one hand, this highlights the necessity of exploring theses spaces and times with transcultural, historical and ethnographic sensibility; on the other, this makes explicit that the political quality of graffiti resides in its capacity to question not simply a given notion or theme but, first of all, 'the definition of the nature and the limits of public space *qua* public' (Brighenti 2010: 328).

Intentionally or not, graffiti have always to do with negotiating and reworking the spatial and aesthetic normativity of urban space and experience. In this sense, they may be said to constitute a veritable site of crisis in its most profound sense, as well as a *critical* site in itself: that is, a site in which the conditions of possibility of urban space, publicness and experience are potentially subjected to radical reformulation, and so are put *in crisis*. Even prior to conveying any critical 'message' or aesthetic 'form', graffiti are critical – and thus *in nuce* political – in so far as materializing a *rupture* with respect to the sociocultural and aesthetic normativity of the street, and thus of everyday urban life at large, thereby embodying a challenge to the given order and its aesthetic, legal and moral consensus (Campos 2015; Light 2018).

While graffiti always incorporate a political quality, this volume is particularly interested in 'political graffiti'. In crafting this definition, we refer to the wide understanding of graffiti encapsulated in the Oxford dictionary definition, namely as 'writing or drawings scribbled, scratched or sprayed illicitly on a wall or other surface in a public place' – with a specification, however, that we do not assume political graffiti to be only the 'illicit' ones. Regardless of their legal status, we use 'political graffiti' as an umbrella term (e.g. Lynn and Lea 2005; Carrington 2009) that includes various styles and forms of visual expression (e.g. marker and pencil markings, drawings, slogans, stencils, street art, murals) that forge a relationship between the graffitist and the citizen over current sociopolitical issues and social change.

We recognize this is an extremely broad concept that encompasses different techniques, languages and styles, belonging to various social and geographical backgrounds.

There are many different traditions of street visual communication that can be framed within this field: from the graffiti produced during the French 'May 68' to the political muralism of Northern Ireland and of the Bolshevik revolution in Russia; from the Brazilian *pixação* to contemporary stencils (e.g. Banksy) and the revolutionary graffiti produced in the context of the Arab Spring and beyond. In fact, all these examples share something in common. Unlike other forms of graffiti and street art, political graffiti have, of course, an explicitly political content; and they engage in a less conventional yet more effective political struggle that is designed to resist particular constellations of legal, political and religious authority inscribed in social institutions and materialized in socio-spatial relations (Ferrell 1995: 34; Waldner and Dobratz 2013: 379). Especially in contested areas, such as Northern Ireland (Goalwin 2013; Rolston 2013) or the Spanish-Basque region (Chaffee 1988, 1993; Rolston and Berastegi 2016), political graffiti may figure prominently as an alternative means of communication and political mobilization among rival political groups negotiating conflicting political identities. This collective dimension is worth stressing.

While graffiti have often been tied to an individualist subculture, political graffiti are usually produced through collective action, at the coming together of writers, artistic collectives, activists. Working together on the graffiti-making, urban activists may produce a sense of creative community, solidify social bonds and enhance collectively perceived sentiments of solidarity. Contemporary scholarship has recognized the contribution of the visual to the expression of social movements, and its role in the effort to confirm and empower a collective, often marginalized or excluded, identity (Doerr and Teune 2012; Philips 2012; Rolston and Berastegi 2016), and there is indeed consistent awareness among social movements as regards the value of political graffiti as an autonomous and independent form of aesthetic production that is able to link art and politics by bringing together the public, the partial and the intimate (Schuster 2015; Schachter 2014, 2016b). Graffiti may serve as a catalyst in the effort of social movements to release imagination, explore innovative politico-aesthetic practices and express their identities and political claims in a creative way. Social movements may deploy them as part of their repertoires of collective action and micro-level political activism constituting an expressive resistance strategy in struggles against politically powerful actors (Awad and Wagoner 2017; Ryan 2018). Political graffiti may serve to frame sociopolitical issues by employing visual frames which are often exercised at the emotional, affective and aesthetic level (Doerr and Teune 2012: 161; Rolston and Berastegi 2016: 34), by acting as a pedagogical tool and interactive avenue for creative expression and engagement in community dialogue and political debate (Harris 2006: 97), or even by working to subvert and deface billboard advertising, as in the case of BUGA UP activists in Sydney and Street Advertising Takeovers in New York and Madrid (Iveson 2013; Deitz 2016). Particularly significant is the case of Latin America, with its long tradition of graffitists framing the contentious politics of divergent political actors by drawing political slogans and iconic symbols, memorializing remarkable events of the past, and depicting desired trajectories of future change (Chaffee 1993; Paento 1999; Campbell 2003; Borland and Sutton 2007; Kane 2009; Burdick and Vicencio 2016; Ryan 2018).

To be sure, the political use of graffiti as a means of self-expression and critique, especially in contexts of reduced freedom of expression, has been documented over many centuries, from the Roman and Umayyad empires to Franco's Spain and Chile's Pinochet dictatorships; from the antifascist graffiti written in the Milan subway by Italian fighters (Fabbri 2007: 418), in Rome's Nazi prison by political detainees (Pugliese 2002) during the Second World War, and in Berlin's Reichstag by Soviet soldiers in 1945 (Baker 2002; Burdick and Vicencio 2016) to those employed as a means of communication among exiles on isolated Greek islands during post-civil war Greece (Mamoulaki 2013). This is unsurprising, as political graffiti are particularly appropriate to produce counter-hegemonic discourses used by marginalized people and political actors who lack access to institutionalized forms of political participation, or who believe that, as usual, politics will not bring about the desired change (Waldner and Dobratz 2013: 387). Much fieldwork suggests that political graffiti may become a site of resistance against authoritarianism, oppression and injustice during periods of social and political upheaval (Chaffee 1988, 1993; Borland and Sutton 2007; Hanauer 2011; Marche 2012; Waldner and Dobratz 2013; Zaimakis 2015, 2016; Rolston and Berastegi 2016; Campos 2016; Ryan 2018). It is in fact especially during periods of authoritarianism and extreme oppression that they are employed by counter-establishment social forces in 'hit and run' visual protest expressing opposition to the regime, as well as by governmental organizations in attempting to mobilize popular support (Bushnell 1990; Johnston 2006; Ryan 2018). A striking example are the intifada graffiti (Peteet 1996; Hanauer 2011), where Palestinians 'without access to a national media [or] political assembly' take advantage of graffiti activism to transgress the censorship and to visualize opinions (Toenjes 2015: 57), sometimes encouraging the continuance of the intifada and its tactics of civil disobedience, 'sometimes asserting the dominance of a particular political faction in an area, and still other times expressing Palestinian national identity'. Likewise, political graffiti became an empowering tool of revolutionary communication and public mobilization in the different contexts of the so-called Arab Spring (Elias 2014; Lenon 2014; Nicoarea 2014; Werbner, Webb and Spellman-Roots 2014; Toenjes 2015; Abaza 2016), as well as within the aesthetic protest that emerged across the anti-austerity mobilizations in Southern Europe and beyond (Tsilimpounidi and Walsh 2010; Tsilimpounidi 2015; Zaimakis 2015, 2016, 2018; Campos 2016; Tolonen 2016; Serafis, Kitis and Archakis 2018). At the same time, graffiti may take a more problematic ultra-nationalist, xenophobic and racist nuance, becoming a tool to denigrate and attack minorities (Wilson 2008; Nayak 2010; Zaimakis 2015). In fact, graffiti are always embedded in delicate dialectics, which see them being at the same time a tool employed, or exploited, both by those who champion 'right to the city' politics, and by those who impair them by engendering processes of commodification, gentrification and touristification, using graffiti themselves, directly and indirectly, to do so. Such dialectics, moreover, are increasingly global in scope. Being an eminently urban phenomenon, graffiti are unavoidably prolonged by the planetary dimension of the contemporary process of urbanization (see Brenner 2013). This is also a result of new technologies, as digital mediatization allows graffiti writers to achieve international visibility by overcoming the physical boundaries of their site, in this way taking advantage of the multileveled potentials of graffiti themselves to put screen and street cultures into complex negotiation and self-reflexive reappropriation (Elias 2014: 89; Davies 2017: 7). While they have been for the most part examined as rooted, place-based practices, today graffiti increasingly need to be explored and conceptualized as a global phenomenon (Avramidis and Drakopoulou 2015; Hannerz 2016; Ross 2016).

In sum, if social and political turbulence (thus when the common *doxa* is fragmented into contested imaginaries) has always been a particularly fertile ground for the surfacing of graffiti, it is especially in the current 'times of crisis' that political graffiti are an important source for understanding how people experience the conditions of undesirable social change and the structures of feeling that lie behind a crisis-ridden world, capturing issues of oppression, unveiling social inequalities, and expressing passionate and affective responses (e.g. Argenti 2007; Knight 2015). Political graffiti may reveal the politics of public visibility (Campbell 2003) used by new social movements and protesters in their efforts to maintain, empower and materialize their own identities, narratives and aesthetics, perform contentious politics and influence social experience (Zaimakis 2016: 80). This edited collection emerges out of this promising complexity, at the encounter between crisis, urban space, and the visual expression of protest.

Contributions

The contributions to this volume form a variegated and yet coherent assemblage of voices within, against and beyond the present (of) crisis, across different geographies and temporalities, by engaging with diverse times of crisis and their dense imaginaries, practices and problematics. Through differently addressing the way in which the narratives and realities of crisis affect and modify the social worlds of street art and graffiti, they provide readers with a 'bottom-up' attention to the reality of the place-specific forms of visual protest in times of crisis, allowing an understanding of the dynamics of political mobilization and the diffusion of symbols and ideas inside and outside urban social movements, and in the urban environment at large. Albeit the themes explored in the different chapters often overlap, mirroring the manifold aesthetics and sociopolitical complexities of the urban in times of crisis, we have organized them in three main parts.

In the first part, we gather contributions exploring the relation between street activism and visual protest in the contemporary city. We begin with Konstantinos Avramidis and Myrto Tsilimpounidi who, employing the method of *periegisis* – the act of showing around – in five graffiti pieces in the Exarchia district of downtown Athens, reveal the complex relation between graffiti and political tension in the current turbulent times that city is living through. Developing in the form of a playful dialogue between a graffiti practitioner/architect and a sociologist/photographer, the text also reflects on how to cross the boundaries between doing and studying graffiti, art and social sciences, moving from praxis to theory, and back. Through five stops, the authors offer critical reflection on the multiple and contradictory narratives of practising graffiti and street art in times of crisis: the small and mundane visual expressions against fascism; the imported graffiti and the process of touristification of space; the divergent meaning of depoliticized colourful street art and its use as a tool for gentrification; the socio-spatial contrasts in the city and the crisis of representation of particular groups, such as the poor; the reuse of space in occupied public parks and the meaningful street artists' spatial politics as a counter-response to the monopoly of state-run or commercially driven messages in the urban fabric.

The next chapter, by Jonna Tolonen, is similarly set in the context of the 2008 financial crisis and the consequent austerity policies that plagued several countries in southern Europe. In this context, various organized and unorganized forms of protests took place, with large demonstrations and strong spontaneous movements like the 15M in Spain, who carried out several prolonged occupations of public space, or *acampadas*. Unsurprisingly in a country that had experienced a long period of dictatorship, during which political graffiti were often one of the few key devices of political communication in public, the context of this crisis proved to be fertile for this kind of political expression. Political graffiti played a prominent role in the urban visual landscape, as the street became a showcase of the anguish and problems being experienced by ordinary people. Drawing from an ethnographic research, Tolonen focuses on ways in which the crisis affected the personal narratives, political commitments, and artistic practices of Spanish street artists. With the help of insightful interviews, she shows how the crisis pushed artists into a different creative mode, prompting them to produce more politicized works on the street, and politicizing the street itself in the process.

The question of the intersection between alternative ways of doing politics and the transnational visual language of graffiti in critical times is the focus of the contribution by Yiannis Zaimakis and Leonidas Oikonomakis, which unfolds via a comparative analysis based in four exemplary countries, two in South America (Argentina and Bolivia) and two in Southern Europe (Greece and Spain). Despite the significant differences, common in these countries is the use of street art and political graffiti as an aesthetic and affective tool of communication and mobilization. During the last few decades, in the context of economic hardships, politicized graffiti collectives enacted their 'right to the city' by connecting small-scale tactical interventions in cityscapes with social movement struggles, in this way producing performative spaces of resistance and active participation with novel, playful and sometimes carnivalesque forms of visual protest. Exploring different examples, the authors show that, while the crisis also facilitated the rise of some xenophobic and racist graffiti, the vast majority have been embedded within various anti-capitalist movements through which they have expressed various forms of visual protest. At the same time, the latter may easily turn into spectacle, and critical graffiti can unintentionally become tools of urban commodification, thus showing the inherent ambivalence of the relation between graffiti and the urban landscape of crisis.

The next chapter looks at another country that experienced a dramatic dictatorship: Chile. While in this context muralism has been an important and well-researched political role, the focus of Javiera Manzi, Matías Marambio DLF, Isidro Parraguez and María Yaksic is another visual praxis, serigraphy, explored both as a technique of production tied to the artisanal and the collective, and as a tool of urban political intervention. Focusing on the recent cycle of social protest, the authors look at a decade (2008–2018) of graphic activism in the context of the student movement and its protest against neoliberalism and post-dictatorship politics. This is done via an analysis of posters made by student collectives and propaganda brigades, complementing a focus on their 'images, languages and materiality', with attention on 'the complex fabric of social relations that enable their production, reproduction and circulation in urban public space'. The authors, themselves located 'between the archive and the streets', reconstruct the historical trajectory of the intersection between graphic production and urban politics, exploring the circulation of images in urban public space as a peculiar form of visual imagination and reappropriation of the urban imaginary. In this way they provide an insightful reflection on visual protest in critical times, at the intersection between visual techniques, activism and urban space.

The next contribution by Jeffrey Ian Ross brings us to the United States in the times of Donald Trump. The latter's 2016 election has become one of the most debated topics in the media and among ordinary citizens, generating a number of diverse reactions. Trump's controversial proposals and poorly polished comments have generated strong reactions at the national and international level, while his right-wing conservative and populist politics have made him a target for various progressive groups and social movements worldwide, often materialising in various forms of visual protest. Trump has indeed become an iconic protagonist of criticism, satire and humour. In his chapter, Ross sets out to analyse the amount, distribution and content of political graffiti against Trump by focusing on the city of Washington, DC, the nation's capital and home of the presidential residence. This exploration draws an interesting relation between a powerful figure whose impact on culture is seemingly global and deterritorialized, and the contingency of his embeddedness in the US capital, where he lives and works. Exploring different districts of the city, Ross provides an insightful snapshot of the visual landscape of protest in a city that hosts the most controversial president in American history.

We conclude this section by going to Bologna, Italy, and specifically looking at an (in)famous event that took place in the city in March 2016, when the renowned street artist Blu took the drastic decision to erase all his murals from the city's walls. Prior to this event, various graffiti, included some by Blu, had been removed from the city's walls to populate the exhibition 'Street Art. Banksy & Co.' Taking inspiration from Blu's iconoclastic protest, Andrea Pavoni develops a theoretical discussion that intersects notions of art, heritage and vandalism, exploring the contemporary obsession with physical preservation and the way it surreptitiously seeped through the lively public debate that followed Blu's decision to erase his murals. Pointing towards a notion of urban commons that is dynamic, conflictual and in becoming, Pavoni shows the potential of Blu's gesture in the context of the ongoing co-optation of street art and, more generally, vis-à-vis the complex relation between street politics, public art and urban commons.

The second part focuses more specifically on anti-gentrification protests in the context of cities characterized by political, socio-economic and spatial divisions. It begins with Betty Dobratz and Lisa Waldner who, looking at Berlin, Germany, over a long period of recent history (1945–2018), explore the intersection between political graffiti and the major political crises that the city has undergone: the division and reunification; the Cold War that saw Berlin as the epicentre; its contemporary neoliberal urbanization; and the concomitant growth of anti-immigrant and xenophobic right-wing politics. Such an ambitious historical gaze is held together by a piercing analysis of selected key examples of political graffiti, which are treated both as a precious archive to gain insight into turbulent times, as well as explored as veritable actors in the public sphere, often conveying alternative counternarratives able to provide a contingent as well as a long-term impact. The second part shows the extent to which the political force of graffiti tends to be entangled in a contradictory ambivalence, as street art critical of neoliberal urbanization and at times used to actively sustain squatters and poorer neighbourhoods, often ends up contributing to the economic valorization of urban space and, consequently, to those very processes of gentrification and touristification that it had contested in the first place.

Another temporality of crisis is explored by Pafsanias Karathanasis in the context of Nicosia, Cyprus, the last divided capital in Europe. Here, in contrast to other 'cities-in-crisis' like Athens, where the proliferation of political graffiti has been a direct response to the dystopian conditions of crisis, the content of visual protest mainly refers back to the initial '1974 crisis', caused by the Turkish invasion in the island, and the traumatic experience of the prolonged territorial and sociocultural division of the country. In this context, drawing upon ethnographically informed semiotic and spatial analysis of relevant political street art pieces, the chapter investigates the city's wall as a visual landscape marked by the material remains of division, and its street activists' interventions. In the midst of a process of gentrification, with a concomitant rise in leisure activities, nightlife and tourist business that normalize and invisibilize the materiality of the division, Karathanasis focuses on the opening of the Green Line crossings in 2008, which transformed the Old Town into a zone of 'prolonged crisis' or 'permanent liminality', in which grass-roots movements have the chance of contesting dominant narratives and questioning established identities and separations via political stencils, often transforming the conditions of crisis into an opportunity for critical intervention.

The relation between visual aesthetics, street politics and gentrification in the context of creative city strategies is the context of the next chapter, written by Anna Giulia Della Puppa. It is also set in Bologna, a city with a strong tradition of left-wing activism, one of Italy's most important student communities, and Europe's oldest university. This vibrant cultural scene, however, is slowly but persistently being neutralized of its most diverse, underground and informal quality, due to the interconnected action of the municipal forces and the market. On the one hand, Bologna is undergoing a widespread process of gentrification, twinned by the touristification of the city centre, where the revamping of whole streets and neighbourhoods via a cool 'creative city' aesthetics is complemented by its aggressive rebranding as the 'city of food'. On the other hand, ever-stricter social control regulations, consistent with the nationwide obsession with the notion of *decoro*, increasingly deprive the city of its most culturally active, diverse and non-commercial spaces, evicting squatted social centres, removing free access to libraries, and so on. Della Puppa explores the atmosphere of sociocultural and political crisis in which the city is seemingly immersed via a series of ethnographic perambulations through its 'contested spaces and surfaces', exploring the ambivalent relationship between the street art and graffiti, the current sociopolitical climate, and the urban space.

The third part addresses visual activism and protest in the context of political turmoil, regime transformations and revolutions. Cláudia Madeira, Cristina Pratas Cruzeiro and Ricardo Campos explore the Portuguese revolutionary murals of the 1970s and 1980s. The revolution, which occurred on 25 April 1974, overthrowing four decades of dictatorship, gave rise to intense and volatile political dynamics. The fragmentation of the political field and the eruption of citizen participation converted the public space into a privileged arena for debate and political propaganda. During these turbulent and vibrant decades, murals, mainly executed by left-wing movements, both official and unofficial, marked the landscape of the largest Portuguese cities, becoming emblematic of this period of renewed freedom of expression and democratization of public access to art, following decades of repression and silencing. Although they have now disappeared, they are still remembered as a legacy of the revolution and the democratization of Portuguese society, and they constitute an invaluable archive to explore the relation between political graffiti, public space and the political sphere in the fluid, critical post-revolutionary times. Analysing key examples, the authors unpack the role played by these murals in the crucial political and symbolic struggles that ensued from the revolution.

The next chapter moves to one of the youngest nations in the world, East Timor, which gained its independence in 2002 after about three decades of Indonesian occupation. The ensuing political and social process has been turbulent, marked by several critical and violent episodes, including the violence that followed the 2012 parliamentary elections, which is the period that Catherine Arthur explores. As in the other contributions, here we find the capacity of street art to give political expression to marginalized groups in turbulent times. In this context, Arthur focuses on the so-called Geração Foun, the 'New Generation', that grew up under Indonesian occupation, assimilating various aspects of Indonesian culture, and for this very reason found itself marginalized from the nascent state's political sphere. Young artists from the Geração Foun countered this marginalization by employing street art as a tool of communication and representation, using the public space as a means to invoke indigenous, ethno-cultural symbolism, referring to a precolonial, indigenous identity that would precede and transcend current social divisions, and expressing an alternative and peaceful vision to the dominant, exclusionary ones.

The part ends with an in-depth immersion in the war-torn landscape of contemporary Syria, where the revolution of 2011 has been followed by an enormously destructive war that is still ongoing, albeit barely noticed by the global media. The revolution released a powerful will to express, after decades of systematic suppression of alternative political voices, including graffiti and street art, and provided a liberatory form of expression, communication and protest against both the regime of Bashar al-Assad and the occupying force of Daesh. In their contribution, Hend Alawadhi and Julia Tulke interview Abu Malek al-Shami, a self-taught muralist and rebel fighter in the Free Syrian Army, by tracing his involvement in the revolutionary struggle, and the effect that the siege of Darayya had on the development of his creative practice. The latter unfolds as a participatory and collective endeavour which repurposes the ruined landscape of the war-torn city into a tool of national and global communication, via digital media, by showing that 'crises and struggles are not isolated events but connected across space and time through acts of solidarity and collective resistance'. Piercing the cloak of invisibility that covers the reality of Syria to those outside, this is a particularly valuable account on the relation between street art practice, political engagement, and war.

We conclude with Rafael Schacter's engaging Afterword. Written 'from lockdown', it provides a topical complement to the volume's central *problématique*, namely the relation between politics, street art and public space, by exploring what occurs when this very relation is drastically severed as a result of a global pandemic. The latter ushered in 'a crisis of publicness, a crisis in which the quintessential site of protest, of debate, of urban life, has been (necessarily) evacuated', and 'our very ability to articulate dissent has thus been sharply curtailed'. While the exceptionality of this situation is evident, overlooking its continuity with the 'normality of crisis' would be naive, as many of the other contributions show. Thus, the significance of Schacter's question: 'If the crisis has evacuated the city, absenting us of the traditional space of protest, where is the site of reimagination, where is the site for activity today?' From 'hyperlocal' grass-roots solidarity to 'hypermediated' digitally formed groups, the text speculates on the creative and resilient ways in which the commons are reproduced, concluding by asking what this situation may tell us about the future of political graffiti – the question remains open.

Acknowledgements

Andrea Pavoni's research is funded by FCT/MCTES under CEEC Individual contract [CEECINST/00066/2018/CP1496/CT0001]. Ricardo Campos's research is funded by FCT/MCTES (IF/01592/2015, PTDC/SOC-SOC/ 28655/2017). This book was partially supported (image subvention) by FCT/ MCTES (IF/01592/2015).

Andrea Pavoni is Research Fellow at DINAMIA'CET [Centre for Socio-economic and Territorial Studies], ISCTE-IUL – Instituto Universitário de Lisboa, Portugal. Drawing from various areas such as critical geography, urban studies, legal theory, sociology and philosophy, his research explores the relation between materiality, normativity and aesthetics in the urban context. He is Associate Editor at *Lo Squaderno, Explorations in Space and Society,* and co-editor of the Law and the Senses Series [University of Westminster Press]. His book, *Controlling Urban Events: Law, Ethics and the Material,* has been published with Routledge.

Yiannis Zaimakis is Professor of Sociology of Culture and Local Societies, and Director of the Social Analysis and Applied Social Research Laboratory at the University of Crete. He publishes in the areas of sociology of popular music and rebetika, street activism and political graffiti, sport cultures and fandom identities, social and solidarity economy, and the politics of the commons. He coordinated the research programme 'Political and existential graffiti and voices of protest on urban landscapes in times of crises – Greece' and currently coordinates two research projects ('The many faces of "Trouba": A socio-cultural study of prostitution in Piraeus' red-light district in the Post-War years-Greece' and 'Need assessment and local value-system in Lasithi highland plateau – Crete').

Ricardo Campos holds a Masters' degree in sociology and a PhD in visual anthropology. He is a researcher at CICS.NOVA – Interdisciplinary Centre of Social Sciences, Portugal. He currently coordinates two research projects: 'Artcitizenship – Young people and the arts of citizenship: Activism, participatory culture and creative practices' (2019–2021), and 'TransUrbArts – Emergent Urban Arts in Lisbon and São Paulo' (2016–2020), both financed by FCT/MCTES. He is also a co-coordinator of the Visual Culture Group of the Portuguese Association of Communication Studies, and of the Luso-Brasilian Network for the Study of Urban Arts and Interventions (RAIU).

Notes

1. The Greek *Krisis* from *krinein* (to separate, decide, judge), from PIE root **krei-* (to sieve, discriminate). See also the Greek *krinesthai* (to explain).
2. Post-political theory has extensively dissected this point: 'crisis' is evoked as a mode of justification that opens a post-political sphere of action prompted by a moral imperative to act to reinstate a given norm (Zizek 1999; Rancière 2001; Mouffe 2005).
3. Other modes of graffiti associated with alternative ways of doing politics or even 'everyday resistance' also emerged in many Latin American and South European countries. As Ryan underlines, the rich tradition of political graffiti and street art in Latin America seems to have been neglected by contemporary literature, which has centred more on Anglo-American experience and focused on a very short time frame (Ryan 2018: 7).

References

Abaza, M. 2016. 'The Field of Graffiti and Street Art in post-January 2011 Egypt', in J.I. Ross (ed.), *Routledge Handbook of Graffiti and Street Art*. London: Routledge, pp. 318–32.

Agamben, G. 2015. *Pilate and Jesus. Stanford, CA: Stanford University Press.*

Ancelovici, M., P. Dufour and H. Nez. 2016. *Street Politics in the Age of Austerity: From Indignados to Occupy.* Amsterdam: Amsterdam University Press.

Argenti, N. 2007. *Intestines of the State: Youth, Violence, and Belated Histories in the Cameroon Grassfields.* Chicago: University of Chicago Press.

Arrighi, G. 1978. 'Towards a Theory of Capitalist Crisis'. *New Left Review* 111(3): 3–24.

Austin J. 2001. *Taking the Train: How Graffiti Became an Urban Crisis in New York.* New York: Columbia University Press.

Avramidis, K., and K. Drakopoulou. 2015. 'Moving From Urban to Virtual Spaces and Back: Learning In/From Signature Graffiti Subculture',.in P. Jandrić and D. Boras (eds), *Critical Learning in Digital Networks*. New York: Springer, pp. 133–160.

Avramides, K., and M. Tsilimpounidi. 2017. 'Graffiti and Street Art: Reading, Writing and Representing the City', in K. Avramides and M. Tsilimpounidi (eds), *Graffiti and Street Art: Reading, Writing and Representing the City*. New York: Routledge, pp. 1–24.

Awad, S., and B. Wagoner (eds). 2017. *Street Art of Resistance*. Cham, Switzerland: Palgrave Macmillan.

Baker, F. 2002. 'The Red Army Graffiti in the Reichstag, Berlin: Politics of Rock-Art in a Contemporary Urban Landscape', in G. Nash and C.C. Chippindale (eds), *European Landscapes of Rock-Art*. London: Routledge, pp. 20–38.

Baumgarten, B. 2015. 'Culture and Activism across Borders', in B. Baumgarten, P. Daphi and P. Ullrich (eds), *Conceptualizing Culture in Social Movement Research*. Basingstoke: Palgrave Macmillan.

Bengtsen, P. 2014. *The Street Art World*. Lund: Almendros de Granada Press.

Berry-Slater, J., and A. Iles. 2009. 'No Room to Move: Radical Art and the Regenerate City'. *Mute*, 24 November. Retrieved 10 August 2020 from http://www.metamute .org/editorial/articles/no-room-to-move-radical-art-and-regenerate-city#.

Blanché, U. 2015. 'Street Art and Related Terms: Discussion and Working Definitions'. *Street Art and Urban Creativity Scientific Journal* 1(1): 32–39.

Bohme, G. 2017. *Critique of Aesthetic Capitalism*. Milan: Mimesis.

Boltanski, L., and E. Chiapello. 2007. *The New Spirit of Capitalism*. London: Verso.

Borland, E., and B. Sutton. 2007. 'Quotidian Disruption and Women's Activism in Times of Crisis, Argentina, 2002–2003'. *Gender and Society* 21(5): 700–722.

Brenner, N. 2013. 'Theses on Urbanization'. *Public Culture* 25(1): 85–114.

Brighenti, A.M. 2010. 'At the Wall: Graffiti Writers, Urban Territoriality, and the Public Domain'. *Space and Culture* 13(3): 315–32.

Burdick, C., and F.C. Vicencio. 2016. 'Popular Demands Do Not Fit in Ballot Boxes': Graffiti as Intangible Heritage at the Iglesia De San Francisco, Santiago?' *International Journal of Heritage Studies* 21(8): 735–56.

Buser, M., C. Bonura, M. Fannin and K. Boyer. 2013. 'Cultural Activism and the Politics of Place-Making'. *City* 17(5): 606–27.

Bushnell, J. 1990. *Moscow Graffiti: Language and Subculture*. Boston: Unwin Hyman.

Campbell, B. 2003. *Mexican Murals in Times of Crisis*. Tucson: University of Arizona Press.

Campos, R. 2015. 'Graffiti, Street Art and the Aestheticization of Transgression'. *Social Analysis* 59(3): 17–40.

———. 2016. 'From Marx to Merkel: Political Muralism and Street Art in Lisbon', in J.I. Ross (ed.), *Routledge Handbook of Graffiti and Street Art*. New York: Routledge, pp. 301–17.

Campos, R., and Á. Sequeira. 2019. 'Urban Art Touristification: The Case of Lisbon', *Tourist Studies*. Retrieved 10 August 2020 from https://doi.org/10.1177/1468797 619873108.

Carrington, V. 2009. 'I Write, Therefore I Am: Texts in the City'. *Visual Communication* 8(4): 409–25.

Castells, M. 2012. *Networks of Outrage and Hope: Social Movements in the Internet Age*. Malden, MA: Polity Press.

Castleman, C. 1982. *Getting Up: Subway Graffiti in New York*. Cambridge, MA: MIT Press.

Chaffee, L.G. 1988. 'Social Conflict and Alternative Mass Communications: Public Art and Politics in the Service of Spanish-Basque Nationalism'. *European Journal of Political Research* 16: 545–72.

———. 1993. *Political Protest and Street Art: Popular Tools for Democratization in Hispanic Countries*. Westport, CT: Greenwood Press.

Chmielewska, E. 2007. 'Framing [Con]text: Graffiti and Place'. *Space and Culture* 10(2): 145–69.

Cooper, M., and H. Chalfant. 1984. *Subway Art*. London: Thames & Hudson.

Dahlgren, P. 2013. *The Political Web: Media, Participation and Alternative Democracy*. London: Palgrave Macmillan.

Davies, D. 2017. 'Walls of Freedom: Street Art and Structural Violence in the Global City'. *Rupkatha Journal of Interdisciplinary Studies in Humanities* 9(2): 6–18.

Deitz, M. 2016. 'Cut and Paste: Australia's Original Culture Jammers, BUGA UP'. *Global Media Journal* (Australian Edition) 8(1): 1–10.

Deutsche, R. 1996. *Evictions: Art and Spatial Politics*. Cambridge, MA: MIT Press.

Dickens, L. 2010. 'Pictures of Walls? Producing, Pricing and Collecting the Street Art Screen Print'. *City* 14: 63–81.

Díez Garcia, R.D. 2017. 'The Spanish 15M Movement in Space and Time'. *Global Society* 31(1): 43–64.

Doerr, N., and S. Teune. 2012. 'The Imagery of Power Facing the Power of Imagery: Towards a Visual Analysis of Social Movements', in K. Fahlenbrach, M. Klimke, J. Scharloth and L. Wong (eds), *The 'Establishment' Responds: Power, Politics and Protest since 1945*. New York: Palgrave, pp. 43–55.

Duncombe, S. 2016. 'Does It Work?: The Æffect of Activist Art'. *Social Research: An International Quarterly* 83(1): 115–34.

Elias, C. 2014. 'Graffiti, Social Media and the Public Life of Images in the Egyptian Revolution', in H. Basma and K. Don (eds), *Walls of Freedom: Street Art of the Egyptian Revolution*. Berlin: From Here to Fame Publishing, pp. 89–91.

Ewen, S. 1988. *All Consuming Images: The Politics of Style in Contemporary Culture*. New York: Basic Books.

Fabbri, F. 2007. 'Orchestral Manoeuvres in the 1970s: L'Orchestra Co-operative 1974–1983'. *Popular Music* 26(3): 409–27.

Farthing, R. 2010. 'The Politics of Youthful Antipolitics: Representing the "Issue" of Youth Participation in Politics'. *Journal of Youth Studies* 13(2): 181–95.

Featherstone, M. 1998. 'Postmodernism and the Aestheticization of Everyday Life', in S. Lash and J. Friedman (eds), *Modernity and Identity*. Oxford: Blackwell, pp. 265–90.

Ferrell, J. 1995. 'Urban Graffiti: Crime, Control, and Resistance'. *Youth and Society* 27: 73–92.

———. 1996. *Crimes of Style: Urban Graffiti and the Politics of Criminality*. Boston, MA: Northeastern University Press.

Flesher Fominaya, C., and L. Cox (eds). 2013. *Understanding European Movements: New Social Movements, Global Justice Struggles*. New York: Routledge.

Florida, R. 2017. *The New Urban Crisis: How Our Cities are Increasing Inequality, Deepening Segregation, and Failing the Middle Class, and What We Can Do About It*. New York: Basic Books.

Goalwin, G. 2013. 'The Art of War: Instability, Insecurity, and Ideological Imagery in Northern Ireland Political Murals, 1979–1998'. *International Journal of Politics, Culture and Society* 26(3): 189–215.

Groys, B. 2014. 'On Art Activism'. *e-flux journal* 56. Retrieved 10 August 2020 from http://www.e-flux.com/journal/56/60343/on-art-activism/.

Guinard, P., and A. Margier. 2017. 'Art as a New Urban Norm: Between Normalization of the City through Art and Normalization of Art through the City in Montreal and Johannesburg'. *Cities* (77): 13–20.

Hanauer, D. 2011. 'The Discursive Construction of the Separation Wall at Abu Dis: Graffiti as Political Discourse'. *Journal of Language and Politics* 10(3): 301–21.

Hankins, K. 2017. 'Creative Democracy and the Quiet Politics of the Everyday'. *Urban Geography* 38(4): 502–6.

Hannerz, E. 2016. 'Scrolling Down the Line: A Few Notes on Using Instagram as a Point of Access for Graffiti Research'. *Street Art and Urban Creativity Scientific Journal* 2(2): 37–40.

Hargreaves, I., and J. Hartley (eds). 2016. *The Creative Citizen Unbound: How Social Media and DIY Culture Contribute to Democracy, Communities and the Creative Economy*. Bristol: Policy Press.

Harris, K.B. 2006. 'Graffiti as Public Pedagogy: The Educative Potential of Street Art', in J. Kincheloe and K. Hayes (eds), *Metropedagogy: Power, Justice and the Urban Classroom*. Rotterdam: Sense Publishers, pp. 97–114.

Harrebye, S. 2015. 'The Ambivalence of Creative Activism as a Reorganization of Critique'. *Culture and Organization* 21(2): 126–46.

Harvey, D. 2010. *The Enigma of Capital: And the Crises of Capitalism*. Oxford: Oxford University Press.

———. 2013. *Rebel Cities: From the Right to the City to the Urban Revolution*. London: Verso.

Holmes, B. 2008. *Unleashing the Collective Phantoms: Essays in Reverse Imagineering*. New York: Autonomedia.

Iveson, K. 2013. 'Cities Within the City: Do It Yourself Urbanism and the Right to City'. *City* 37(3): 941–56.

Jameson, F. 2007. 'Modernism and Imperialism', in F. Jameson, *The Modernist Papers*. London: Verso.

Johnston, H. 2006. 'Let's Get Small: The Dynamic of (Small) Contention in Repressive States'. *Mobilization: An International Journal* 11(2): 195–212.

Juris, J. 2012. 'Reflections on #Occupy Everywhere: Social Media, Public Space, and Emerging Logics of Aggregation'. *American Ethnologist* 39: 259–79.

Kane, S. 2009. 'Stencil Graffiti in Urban Waterscapes of Buenos Aires and Rosario, Argentina'. *Crime Media Culture* 5(1): 9–28.

Klein, N. 2007. *The Shock Doctrine: The Rise of Disaster Capitalism*. New York: Metropolitan Books.

Knight, D.M. 2015. 'Wit and Greece's Economic Crisis: Ironic Slogans, Food, and Anti-austerity Sentiments'. *American Ethnologist* 42(2): 230–46.

Koselleck, R. (1959) 1988. *Critique and Crisis: Enlightenment and the Pathogenesis of Modern Society*. Cambridge, MA: Berg Publishers.

———. 2006. 'Crisis'. *Journal of the History of Ideas* 67(2): 357–400.

Langman, L. 2013. 'Occupy: A New New Social Movement'. *Current Sociology* 61(4): 510– 524.

Lazzarato, M. 2012. *The Making of the Indebted Man: An Essay on the Neoliberal Condition*. Los Angeles: Semiotext(e).

Lenon, J. 2014. 'Assembling a Revolution: Graffiti, Cairo and the Arab Spring'. *Cultural Studies Review* 20(1): 237–75.

Light, E. 2018. 'Aesthetic Ruptures: Viewing Graffiti as the Emplaced Vernacular'. *Communication and Critical/Cultural Studies* 15(2): 179–95.

Loader, B.D. (ed.). 2007. *Young Citizens in the Digital Age: Political Engagement, Young People and New Media*. New York: Routledge.

Lynn, N., and S.J. Lea. 2005. 'Racist Graffiti: Text, Context and Social Comment'. *Visual Communication* 4(1): 39–63.

Macdonald, N. 2001. *The Graffiti Subculture: Youth, Masculinity and Identity in London and New York*. Basingstoke: Palgrave Macmillan.

Mamoulaki, E. 2013. 'An Unexpected Hospitality: Narratives, Practices and Materialities of the Memory of Exile and Cohabitation on the Island of Ikaria'. Unpublished doctoral dissertation, University of Barcelona.

Manco, T. 2004. *Street Logos*. London: Thames and Hudson.

Marche, G. 2012. 'Expressivism and Resistance: Graffiti as an Infrapolitical Form of Protest Against the War on Terror'. *Revue Française d'Etudes Américaines* 131: 78–97.

Mbembe, A., and J. Roitman. 1995. 'Figures of the Subject in Times of Crisis'. *Public Culture* 7: 323–52.

McAuliffe, C. 2012. 'Graffiti or Street Art? Negotiating the Moral Geographies of the Creative City'. *Journal of Urban Affairs* 34(2): 189–206.

McAuliffe, C., and K. Iveson. 2011. 'Art and Crime (and Other Things Besides...): Conceptualising Graffiti in the City'. *Geography Compass* 5(3): 128–43.

Molnár, V. 2018. 'The Business of Urban Coolness: Emerging Markets for Street Art'. *Poetics* 71: 43–54.

Moses, J. 2013. 'Byron, Brewdog, and the Recuperation of Radical Aesthetics'. *openDemocracy*. Retrieved 10 August 2020 from https://www.opendemocracy.net/ourkingdom/jonathan-moses/byron-brewdog-and-recuperation-of-radical-aesthetics.

Mouffe, C. 2005. *On the Political*. New York: Routledge.

Nayak, A. 2010. 'Race, Affect, and Emotion: Young People, Racism, and Graffiti in the Postcolonial English Suburbs'. *Environment and Planning A* 42: 2370–92.

Nicoarea, G. 2014. 'Cairo's New Colors: Rethinking Identity in the Graffiti of the Egyptian Revolution', in G. Grigore and L. Sitaru (eds), *Romano-Arabica XIV*. Bucharest: Editura Universității din București, pp. 247–62.

Paento, P. 1999. 'Political Mobilisation and Place Specificity: Radical Nationalist Street Campaigning in the Spanish Basque Country'. *Space & Polity* 1(2): 191–204.

Pavoni, A. 2018. *Controlling Urban Events: Law, Ethics and the Material*. Abingdon: Routledge.

Peck, J. 2012. 'Recreative city: Amsterdam, vehicular ideas and the adaptive spaces of creativity policy'. *International Journal of Urban and Regional Research* 36(3): 462-85

Peteet, J. 1996. 'The Writing on the Walls: The Graffiti of the Intifada'. *Cultural Anthropology* 11(2): 139–59.

Philips, A. 2012. 'Visual Protest Material as Empirical Data'. *Visual Communication* 11(1): 3–21.

Phillips, S. 1999. *Wallbangin': Graffiti and Gangs in L.A.* Chicago: University of Chicago Press.

Pickerill, J., J. Krinsky, G. Hayes, K. Gillan and B. Doherty. 2014. *Occupy! A Global Movement.* New York: Routledge.

Pinder, D. 2008. 'Urban Interventions: Art, Politics and Pedagogy'. *International Journal of Urban and Regional Research* 32: 730–36.

Pitti, I. 2018. *Youth and Unconventional Political Engagement.* Basingstoke: Palgrave: Macmillan.

Pugliese, S.G. 2002. *Desperate Inscriptions: Graffiti from the Nazi Prison of Rome, 1943–1944.* Boca Raton: Bordighera Press.

Rancière, J. 2001. 'Ten Theses on Politics'. *Theory and Event* 5(3): 1–21.

———. 2006. 'Aesthetics and Politics: Rethinking the Link'. Lecture given at the University of California, Berkeley, 6 May 2006. Transcript available at https://web.archive.org/web/20131005022500/http://www.16beavergroup.org/monday/archives/001881.php (last accessed 29 September 2020).

———. 2015. *Dissensus: On Politics and Aesthetics.* London: Bloomsbury Publishing.

Roitman, J. 2013. *Anti-crisis.* Durham, NC: Duke University Press.

Rolston B. 2013. 'Prison as a Liberated Zone: The Murals of Long Kesh, Northern Ireland', *State Crime Journal* 2(2): 149–172.

Rolston, B., and A.A. Berastegi. 2016. 'Taking Murals Seriously: Basque Murals and Mobilisation'. *International Journal of Politics, Culture and Society* 29: 33–56.

Ross, I. (ed.). 2016. *Routledge Handbook of Graffiti and Street Art.* London: Routledge.

Ryan, H. 2018. *Political Street Art: Communication, Culture and Resistance in Latin America.* London: Routledge.

Sandoval, C., and G. Latorre. 2008 'Chicana/o Artivism: Judy Baca's Digital Work with Youth of Color', in A. Everett (ed.), *Learning Race and Ethnicity: Youth and Digital Media.* Cambridge, MA: MIT Press, pp. 81–108.

Schacter, R. 2014. 'The Ugly Truth: Street Art Graffiti and Creative City'. *Art & the Public Sphere* 3(2): 161–76.

———. 2016a. 'Street Art is a Period, PERIOD: Or, Classificatory Confusion and Intermural Art', in K. Avramidis and M. Tsilimpounidi (eds), *Graffiti and Street Art: Reading, Writing and Representing the City.* Abingdon: Routledge.

———. 2016b. *Ornament and Order: Graffiti, Street Art and Parergon.* London: Routledge.

Schuster, G. 2015. 'The Concept of the Visible between Art and Politics'. *Latin America Perspectives* 42(1): 84–94.

Serafis, D., D. Kitis and A. Archakis. 2018. 'Graffiti Slogans and the Construction of Collective Identity: Evidence from the Anti-austerity Protests in Greece'. *Text and Talk* 38(6): 184–200.

Simões, J.A., R. Campos, I. Pereira, M. Esteves and J. Nofre. 2018. 'Digital Activism, Political Participation and Social Movements in Times of Crisis', in I. David (ed.), *Crisis, Austerity, and Transformation: How Disciplinary Neoliberalism Is Changing Portugal.* Lanham, MD: Lexington Books, pp. 71–90.

St John, G. 2003. 'Post-Rave Thecnotribalism and the Carnival of Protest', in I.D. Muggleton and R. Weinzierl (eds), *The Post-Subcultures Reader.* New York: Berg.

Sugranyes, A., and C. Mathivet. 2010. *Cities for All: Proposals and Experiences towards the Right to the City*. Santiago, Chile: Habitat International Coalition.

Tejerina, B., I. Perugorría, T. Benski and L. Langman. 2013. 'From Indignation to Occupation: A New Wave of Global Mobilization'. *Current Sociology* 61(4): 377–92.

Thrift, N. 2011. 'Lifeworld Inc – and What to Do About It'. *Environment and Planning D: Society and Space* 29(1): 5–26.

Toenjes, A. 2015. 'This Wall Speaks: Graffiti and Transnational Networks in Palestine'. *Jerusalem Quarterly* 61: 55–68.

Tolonen, J. 2016. 'Visage of Madrid: Illegal Graffiti as a Part of Spanish 15-M Protests'. PhD thesis, University of Helsinki.

Toscano, A., and J. Kinkle. 2015. *Cartographies of the Absolute: An Aesthetics of the Economy for the Twenty-First Century*. Winchester: Zero Books [e-book].

Tremayne, M. 2014. 'Anatomy of Protest in the Digital Era: A Network Analysis of Twitter and Occupy Wall Street'. *Social Movement Studies* 13(1): 110–26.

Tsilimpounidi, M. 2015. 'If These Walls Could Talk': Street Art and Urban Belonging in the Athens of Crisis'. *Laboratorium* 7(2): 18–35.

Tsilimpounidi, M., and A. Walsh. 2010. 'Painting Human Rights: Mapping Street Art in Athens'. *Journal of Arts and Communities* 2(2): 11–122.

Waclawek, A. 2011. *Graffiti and Street Art*. London: Thames & Hudson.

Waldner, L., and B. Dobratz. 2013. 'Graffiti as a Form of Contentious Political Participation'. *Sociology Compass* 7(5): 377–89.

Wells, M. 2016. 'Graffiti, Street Art, and the Evolution of the Art Market', in J. Ross (ed.), *Routledge Handbook of Graffiti and Street Art*. New York: Routledge.

Werbner, P., M. Webb and K. Spellman-Roots (eds). 2014. *Political Aesthetics of Global Protest: The Arab Spring and Beyond*. Edinburgh: Edinburgh University Press.

Wilson, J. 2008. 'Racist and Political Extremist Graffiti in Australian Prisons, 1970s to 1990s'. *The Howard Journal* (47)1: 52–66.

Zaimakis, Y. 2015. '"Welcome to the Civilization of Fear": On Political Graffiti Heterotopias in Greece in Times of Crisis'. *Visual Communication* 14(4): 373–96.

———. 2016. 'Youth Precariat Worlds and Protest Graffiti in the Dystopia of the Greek Economic Crisis: A Cross-Disciplinary Perspective'. *Punctum* 2(2): 66–84.

———. 2018. '"No Surveillance Streets": Young People, Bodies and Depictions of Crisis on Political Graffiti', in Y. Zaimakis (ed.), *Research Journeys in Social Sciences: Theoretical/Methodological Contributions and Case Studies* (in Greek). Herakleion: University of Crete / Social Analysis and Applied Social Research Laboratory, pp. 391–413.

Zizek, S. 1999. *The Ticklish Subject: The Absent Centre of Political Ontology*. London: Verso.

Part I

Street Activism and Visual Protest in Contemporary Cities

Chapter 1

A Periegesis through the Greek Crisis in Five Graffiti Acts

Cartographic and Photographic Dialogues

Konstantinos Avramidis and Myrto Tsilimpounidi

This chapter takes the form of a dialogue between the authors: one a graffiti practitioner and an architectural designer who is interested in writing in space and how we write about writing in space (Konstantinos), and a sociologist and photographer who investigates different forms of visual markers on urban walls and is interested in the subversive politics behind graffiti and street art (Myrto). More specifically, it is a dialogue between: (a) the means that the two authors use as their key research modes in their respective disciplines: cartographic drawing and photographic documentation; (b) the different ways that graffiti and street art have disciplined them to view and research urban environments; and (c) the border-crossing experience as practitioners/insiders and researchers/outsiders of the graffiti and street art scene in Athens. As such, the multiple aspects of our identities both as insiders of the graffiti and street art scene in Athens, and at the same time as scholars researching the scene from the outside, provide valuable tools with which we unpack the multiple and contradictory narratives of practising, researching and teaching graffiti and street art in times of crisis. In particular, we are interested in the ways we shape knowledge and the tension between the epistemological and the ontological ways of knowing, seeing and sensing the city through graffiti and street art practices. In other words, by moving from praxis to theory and back, we are attempting to reconcile the problem of knowing, and the problem of being part of, a specific cultural practice (Avramidis and Tsilimpounidi 2017).

This work sprang from an urban walk that the authors were asked to prepare in the context of a Masters' students field trip to Athens.[1] The purpose of this walk was distinctly different from street art tours that make a profit from the art on the streets, reduce walking to prescribed routes and restricting the conversation to particular pieces and topics (Bengtsen 2014; Young 2016; Andron 2018). Contrary to street art tours that build an image of authenticity, locality and authority to promote their product to tourists (cf. Ioannides, Leventis and Petridou 2016), we do not consider ourselves as the knowledgeable subjects who share their expertise. This does not mean, however, that there are no 'curatorial' decisions made. What we hope to avoid is to 'aestheticise transgression' (Campos 2015) and to make ourselves part of an economy that contributes to the depoliticization of our walls, streets and squares. The walk was limited to the district of Exarchia[2] – an area in Athens city centre saturated with graffiti, known as the stronghold of the anti-authoritarian movement – and had five stops in front of key graffiti pieces that we consider characteristic. When studied together, they are able to offer a comprehensive – albeit subjective and partial – narrative of the Greek crisis. In what follows we first provide a short account of crisis and its manifestations on Athenian walls, then we move into a discussion of the chosen method of periegesis in order to carve the way for the five acts presented in this chapter.

Crisis of Representation and Representations of Crisis

Is there such thing as the Greek crisis? And if so, what crisis and whose crisis is it? Post-2008, the word 'crisis' has been introduced in our lives with a clear reference to the financial stagnation and economic impoverishment of certain strands of the European populace. The European periphery, and Greece in particular, have been characterized as the epicentres of this 'crisis'. For many thinkers (Harvey 2012), what distinguishes the post-2008 crisis from other historical examples of financial shocks and instabilities is its relation to a particular model of urban growth. Globalization and the concomitant flows of populace to urban areas mean that the biggest proportion of people nowadays live in cities. Yet, as Andy Merrifield (2014) suggests, this incessant expert hype about exploding urban populations is closer to a type of Malthusian fear-mongering that obfuscates the class and power questions surrounding our current urban conditions. Historically, this is not the first time we have witnessed the relationship between the increased investment in urban areas and the explosion of financial bubbles able to shake the foundation of the global economy. The difference now is the reference to a particular neoliberal model of urban life. According to Laura Burkhalter and Manuel Castells (2009), the urban crisis has much deeper implications and social effects, such as the deterioration of everyday life, the rise of fear and the concomitant culture of violence and mistrust, and as a result, urban space has been abandoned to the dynamics of real estate. Moreover, cities are the central stages of the expression of civic reactions against the crisis and the resulting austerity policies. As Merrifield suggests, these kinds of civic reactions are 'contesting our hyper-exploitative undemocratic system of global urbanism' (Merrifield 2014: ix).

Athens had it all: patterns of uneven but spectacular development related to the hosting of the Olympic Games; real estate and Airbnb bubbles; xenophobic fear-mongering; and last but not least, fierce, massive and explosive patterns and tactics of resistance to austerity, racism and exploitation, to name a few. More recently, in the summer of 2015, Athens became the epicentre of another European 'crisis' – what was called the refugee crisis of Europe – and was characterized as the 'entrance gate to Europe' and managed as the European hotspot of Fortress Europe (Carastathis, Spathopoulou and Tsilimpounidi 2018). In other words, Athens has been the epicentre of two concomitant crises, or as Anna Carastathis argues, the place of 'intersecting, nesting crises' (Carastathis 2017). In this context, we witness a crisis of representation of particular groups in the public realm. The representations of crisis, such as those in the graffiti studied here, come as responses to the crisis of representation. We have theorized the rhetorical tropes, etymological schemas and after-effects of the notion of crisis elsewhere (Tsilimpounidi 2017), yet in this chapter we want to focus on its urban manifestations on the Athenian city walls.

Street art and wall writing is hardly a new phenomenon in Athens. A short walk in the city centre reveals writings on ancient columns, poems on marble signs, and names and quotations of ancient philosophers on marble monuments, with some of the inscriptions going back to classical antiquity. Next to the ancient ruins lie the modern ruins of the crisis. Given that the current layers of the city intersect with the old city centre, the passer-by experiences a visual bombing of ancient inscriptions, Byzantine signs and contemporary graffiti and slogan writing. As graffiti historian Orestis Pangalos (2014) and anthropologist Pausanias Karathanasis (2014) suggest, there was a proliferation of graffiti and street art even before the crisis in Athens, which intensified during the first crisis for two reasons: firstly, because it is very expensive and difficult for the municipality to sustain an active anti-graffiti programme, as the funds needed for that cannot be found in the era of financial austerity; and secondly, because both crises – the financial and the refugee – experienced by Greece were quickly transformed into a political and social crisis in which marginal groups of the population were silenced by the mainstream media. Simultaneously, protests and uprisings resulted in the creation of a highly politicized public. Thus, more people were participating in political street art, graffiti and slogan writing as one more means of autonomous expression and reclamation of public space.

Graffiti in the Athens of memoranda has been studied through various means and disciplines. Mainly through ethnographic studies, sociologists explore graffiti as a visual indicator and product of social change as well as a means of resistance in an urban environment characterized by rapid degradation, or else they see it as a counter-hegemonic response to the crisis (Tsilimpounidi and Walsh 2011; Zaimakis 2015; Tsilimpounidi 2015a). Literature and linguistics analyses focus on the role of language in recent graffiti production (Boletsi 2016; Stampoulidis 2016), while visual culture scholars address issues related to urban aesthetics (Kim and Flores 2017; Tulke 2017). Architects have approached the subject focusing on the urban processes that affect graffiti (Leventis 2013; Stavrides 2017), map the places where writings acquire particular meanings (Avramidis 2012, 2014a) or, by design means, attempt to decipher and narrate the spatial, social and material conditions in which graffiti signify (Avramidis 2015, 2019, 2020a, 2020b; Leventis 2017).

Building upon the aforementioned works, and in order to (a) navigate through the deeply performative, situated and embodied practices of graffiti and street art, (b) map the social, political and urban context of Athens, and (c) transcend discursive borders between social sciences and the arts, we introduce the notion 'periegesis'. This concept has a long association with travellers, and has had a particular meaning in the context of Athens since ancient times. The word *periegesis* (< peri- 'around' + hegesis 'lead') means 'the act of showing around', denoting a tour and a geographical description. As such, it connotes movement. This sense of movement – whether this is a movement from one site to another or in and through a particular site – we attempt to capture through cartographic and photographic gestures. The way each site is described and/or (re)presented is a demonstration of our understanding of it.

Of course, we never complete the whole picture of 'Athenian crisis graffiti' because we are dealing with only five situations, but we are going to show how they can be interconnected through history and place, which are key in the understanding of each situation. As we have argued elsewhere (Avramidis 2018), the situation is the *context* in which graffiti is undertaken as well as the *action* of graffiti itself, the timeframe within it. This is the reason why we talk about five 'acts' of graffiti, referring to the time and space, action and context of the gesture of writing.

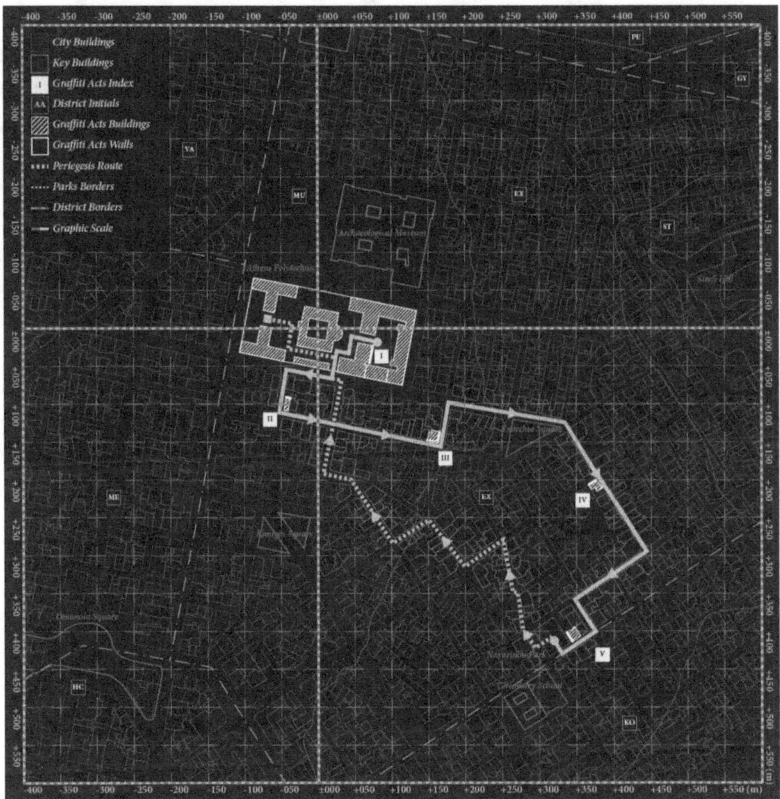

Figure 1.1 Periegesis map: A square kilometre in Athens city centre. ©
Konstantinos Avramidis, 2018.

A Map of the Periegesis and a
Periegesis through our Mappings

As is evident in the etymology of the Greek word *theoria*, theory is the establishment of a point of view; it involves the act of looking from a particular
place, and from there making a leap into analysis of the wider interrela-
tionships of events. If, as John Berger (1977) famously stated, seeing comes
before words, then there is a fundamental connection between visualization
and our being in the world. However, our ways of seeing are dependent not
only on our positionality but also on the available discursive *framings*. The
common denominator of 'cartography' (< carte 'map' + graphy 'writing')
and 'photography' (< phos 'light' + graphy 'writing') is 'graphy', i.e. writing.

This is also the etymological root of graffiti (cf. Avramidis 2014b). Another shared characteristic of cartography and photography is *framing*: they frame realities, include and exclude, and in the process transform the realities they represent whilst creating new realities. In other words, photography and cartography frame and are being framed by our thoughts and writing, and so this chapter is about frameworks and how frames work. In so doing, it engages with the framing of subjectivity and chance, exposing the circumstantial constraints that affect the situated nature of graffiti execution and perception (Avramidis 2014c).

Are the following framings an act of subjectivity and chance? And if so, what can we learn about chance and positionality in our urban explorations? The sequence of our documentation/periegesis might reveal not only temporal but also spatial correlations. The restrictions that physical elements impose (parked cars, trees, etc.) designate how we make the periegesis and record the pieces. These frames expose the situated nature of graffiti, street art, and urban scholarship. What is excluded from our frames might provide valuable information about what is included. In many instances, the absence of a focal point reveals the focus of the frame. To be more precise, we invoke a multimodality of framings in this paper: photographic frame, cartographic frame, the urban frames used by the artists, and the framing in academic writing and thought. In doing so, we want to challenge the borders between seeing, visualizing, imagining and writing.

This periegesis is framed as a dialogue between visual representations and social theories. In doing so, it attempts to treat them both as equal partners in the knowledge-producing process, and as such dissolves scientific over-reliance on text and numbers. Thus, it moves away from traditional approaches on visual methods that tend to treat photographs as another source of data. Rather, it is informed by the postmodern turn in visual studies (Knowles and Sweetman 2004; Pink 2013), in which the possibilities of the visual itself as empirical knowledge and critical text should inform our approaches and methodologies. To put it differently, the use of photography to construct visual aspects of events adds another dimension to the research sources, thus fighting the tendency to reduce all social phenomena into text. This approach by no means signifies a treatment of images as true representations of reality, but rather points towards the possibilities of multiple forms of portrayal of social realities. Cartography not only measures but remakes territories. James Corner (1999) claims that maps have agency due to their both 'analogous and abstract' nature. Their analogous character – having the ability to measure sites through geometric projection – makes them feel neutral. Yet, maps are always a result of a series of choices, such as framing, scaling, orientation, and so on. This abstractness, together with their analogous character, transforms maps into 'operating tables' where the cartographer 'discovers new worlds within past and present ones' (ibid.: 214). By collecting and combining seemingly unrelated elements, making new or breaking existing connections, and generally disrupting pre-existing spatial and temporal sequences, cartography reveals relationships and constructs reality anew.

Many years ago, Vilem Flusser stated that photographs 'are meant to be maps, and they become screens' (Flusser 1983: 10), meaning that in the beginning photography was supposed to act as a map that would introduce new worlds and provide navigation capacities to the ways we understand everyday life in these new worlds. According to Flusser, what ended up happening was that photography became a screen hiding from our gaze the world out there. He refers to the multiple mechanical and digital reproduction of images that in the speed of the modern world have become our way of seeing the world, and thus our way of understanding it. In a way, by combining photography and cartography, we wish to return to the potential of photography to act as a map, a map rich in revealing surfaces. Les Back argues that there is always a relationship between 'portrayal and betrayal' (Back 2009), by which he suggests that the fluidity and complexity of the real world is very difficult to capture in a representation. This is not, of course, a claim to abandon analysis or the representation of 'real life', but rather to re-examine our modes of writing and representing. As such, in what follows we acknowledge that the portrayal of these five specific acts also includes the notion of betrayal of the complexities and the multimodalities in which crisis is affecting the Athenian urban landscape. To put it differently, since this periegesis was initially designed as a student field trip to Exarchia, we move away from a didactic approach, which would portray 'us' as the experts. Rather, we engage with the daily, soft, embodied experiences of crisis in a model of collective 'meaning-making'.

Act I: 'Pavlos Fyssas' in Athens Polytechnic

We are inside the Polytechnic University of Athens, a building that has never ceased being a space of resistance and has gradually become a symbol of freedom in the modern history of the country. During the Axis Occupation, the Athens Polytechnic was a student centre that cultivated resistance spirit and liberation morale. In 1973, while Greece was under a military junta, students gathered at the premises of the Polytechnic University and after several days of occupation they were brutality dispersed by tanks and bullets. This resulted in the death of twenty-four students, and since then the Athens

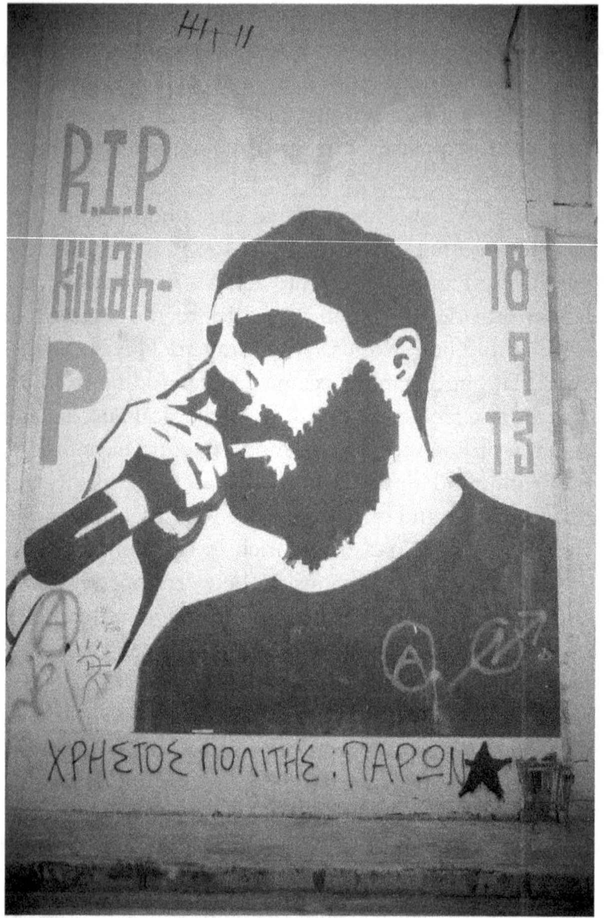

Figure 1.2 Act I: 'Pavlos Fyssas' in Athens Polytechnic by university students. © Myrto Tsilimpounidi, 2018.

Polytechnic has epitomised the struggles against dictatorship, fascism and totalitarianism in the country. This also explains the asylum policy implemented in Greek universities after the overthrow of the military junta, transforming these spaces into democratic resorts in potentially repressive times, and bases from which to fight against and avoid any repetition of another junta.[3] Due to its history and its geographical position, the Athens Polytechnic can be considered to be a symbol of student politicization and, at the same time, as the gate of Exarchia neighbourhood, contributing to the politicized image of the whole area.

We stand in front of the big mural that commemorates Pavlos Fyssas, an antifascist rapper and activist with the artistic pseudonym 'Killah P', who was stabbed to death on 13 September 2013 by members of the extreme far-right organization – albeit officially elected political party – Golden Dawn. The piece was produced by university students and remained unsigned/anonymous, as its focus is on the murdered rapper Killah P and not on the individual or crew who painted the mural. This is a piece about memory and commemoration, not about the personal 'fame' of the artists, which is usually a key notion among practitioners of the graffiti subculture. We start with this act because we want to talk about violence and crisis; not only the kind of normalized and canonical (at least by now) violence that living in the milieu of crisis entails – which is, for example, extreme cuts in salary, massive increases in unemployment rates, collapse of the health-care system, and a rise in suicides and antidepressants – but rather, the violence that comes as a repercussion of the resistance from those who refuse to accept the rising xenophobia, racism and fascism that go hand in hand with the milieu of crisis. We want to move away from the romantic portrayal of Exarchia as the 'last anarchic village in Europe' and talk about the daily struggles, the pain, and the loss in the years of intensified brutality, intimidation and social cannibalism. Since we are still awaiting the outcome of the trial for the murder, this first stop is a reminder of how history is inscribed on the walls. In 2017, the Athens Polytechnic, a space usually overwhelmingly full of graffiti and street art, underwent a refurbishment that included the repainting of the walls. This mural was left untouched as it was seen as a reminder of the struggles against fascism and, as such, it had become an integral part of the building. To live in the era of crisis translates into being able to cope with unpredictable shifts on a daily basis. Public/collective memory is being distorted as crisis breaks the linear contract of time (Tsilimpounidi 2017). In that sense this mural, made by the students of the institution, is an important reminder of the antifascist movement in a place where fighting fascism in all its historical appearances has always been paramount.

The piece depicts Pavlos Fyssas, in black on a white background, rapping and comes from a particular, widely distributed photograph. His nickname and date of the incident appear sideways in red. On the top, the white colour that serves as the background follows the pre-existing piece on the wall. Due to the antennas on the top of the mural, this looks like a typical Athenian skyline view. This unintentionally conveys a very familiar urban scene, where the hip-hop practitioner appears as the protagonist who represents the city with his singing. This part of the mural also refers to the Greek expression 'keep your antennas open', which can translate to 'keep an eye out for' or 'keep your ear to the ground', or being alert and engaged with the social realities around you; it is the opposite of the disconnected, individualized life in this era of uncertainty. The struggle against fascism is not only connected to the spectacular moments of the Antifa protests, rallies and marches. It is an everyday battle with the small and mundane expressions of oppression that get normalized if 'we', the public, remain silent. It is with this top part of the mural that Pavlos Fyssas reminds us what it means to keep our antennas open against fascism.

Act II: 'Athens is the New Berlin' in Kaniggos Street

Our second act is in Kaniggos Street, just a few metres away from the Athens Polytechnic. The blind facade of a typical 1960s multistorey building is full of pixação-like letters, introducing the aesthetics of Latin American slums in the Athenian urban landscape.[4] The texts read 'Pharao' and 'Suton', and are written twice, vertically, covering the whole facade. The supernatural size of the intervention suggests that it was made possible by the use of rappelling gear and hanging equipment. The whole composition is signed by 1UP crew, a notoriously prolific graffiti collective from Berlin. The writers make no effort to hide their origin; they repeatedly sign as 'Berlin Kidz' and even dedicate their piece to the citizens of Athens: 'From Neukölln [Berlin district] with Love'. In contrast with our first act, this is a piece about 'fame' and subcultural credentials. What does it mean for an art form to travel such a distance from Berlin's boroughs to the centre of Athens? And what does it mean to appropriate a highly politicized form of protest art like pixação in order to convey hegemonic messages?

The piece reads 'Athens is the New Berlin'. This refers to the blossoming of the arts in Berlin during the 1990s, and links it to the recent artistic renaissance of Athens during the crisis. Athens is considered to be so culturally vibrant at this moment that it is capable of replacing Berlin as Europe's new arts capital. The slogan is not new, nor is this its first appearance in Athens.[5] It has been on the walls of the city for some years now, igniting social debate. Yet, it is different when this comes from Berliners, because when discussed in a historical perspective we are able to appreciate the multiple meanings this might afford in the context of Athens. Given that the very first king of the newborn Greek state in early nineteenth century was Bavarian, any sort of 'colonialist' attitudes cannot be taken lightly. But except for the distant past, the recent past examples like the mega art event 'documenta 14', under the title 'Learning from Athens',[6] show how Athens' recent urban ruination and social degradation have been glorified by the arts establishment and exoticized to such an extent that it has becomes an exemplar case to (l)earn

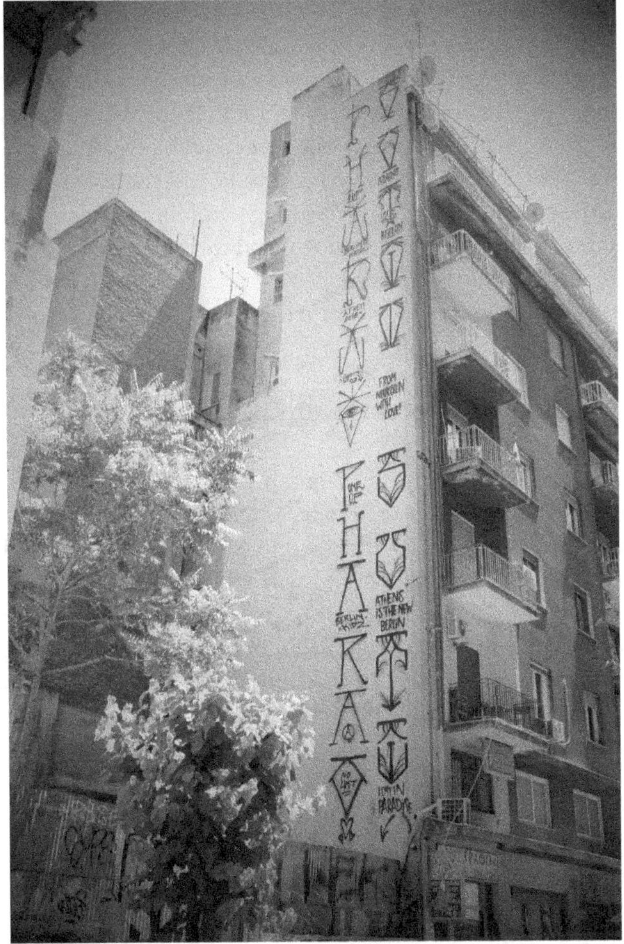

Figure 1.3 Act II: 'Athens is the New Berlin' in Kaniggos Street by 1UP crew. © Myrto Tsilimpounidi, 2018.

from. The guinea pig of Europe is turned into an ideal arty destination with cheap rents and an inviting underground atmosphere – a result of the closure of many industries and shops during the past decade.

Athens, often called the 'graffiti Mecca of Europe' (Bicanski 2014), and especially Exarchia district, despite the neighbourhood's politicized history, have turned into a graffiti Disneyland where the global graffiti and street art superstars can party in front of the walls without worrying about being caught.[7] This kind of intervention evinces the touristification of graffiti and Exarchia; it is the '#crisisporn' at its best. It emphatically demonstrates the appeal, or rather 'sexiness', of urban decay caused in recent years. This 'imported' graffiti – regardless of its artistic value or subcultural significance – clearly ignores the local issues at stake, reproduces particular narcissistic stereotypes, and largely contributes to the perpetuation of particular attitudes, turning the counter-hegemonic into hegemonic (cf. Vamvakas 2019). At the same time the placement of this piece is highly problematic as it ignores the politicized history of the neighbourhood, and treats it as just the ideal canvas for the 'fame' of the artist and the crew – perhaps an excellent Instagram opportunity for the graffiti and street art tours of Athens.

Act III: 'Urban Jungle' in Soultani Street

We are now at the intersection of Soultani and Solomou streets. Here, the lower part of a typical interwar modernist residential building is covered with a large and visually compelling commissioned mural by the US-born graffiti artist (with Greek and Mexican ancestry) Alex Martinez. The piece introduces – with the trademark style of its producer – a tropical iconography depicting a scene rich in vegetation, full of big trees, colourful exotic birds and animals enjoying the other wildlife. The mural feels as if it is trying to focus on the positive image of the 'jungle', a nickname often assigned to the city of Athens. This piece is an exemplar product of contemporary crisis, but for completely different reasons from the rest examined here. It is not representing or referring to crisis scenes. On the contrary, it a representation that allows us to escape from what has been named as the 'aesthetics of crisis' (Tulke 2017).

The mural is a response to the intensification, both in numbers and content, of the graffiti phenomenon in the area during the crisis. It is used here to deter 'negative' graffiti with its 'positive' image (cf. Craw et al. 2006). The cute aesthetics and neutral content of the mural makes it very pleasant, in stark contrast to the aggressive, crisis-related iconography in the streets around it. Another important aspect of this piece – which often passes unnoticed – is its commemorative nature. Alex Martinez, when invited to create his artwork on this wall, found there was already a piece there by late Barns, a prolific 23-year-old Athenian graffiti writer who lost his life from electrocution in September 2008 while writing on subway cars. The respectful incorporation of Barns's piece into the jungle composition by Martinez speaks volumes to the values and practices of the subculture. The commemorative nature of the piece, coupled with the unwritten rules of graffiti artists to avoid writing over somebody else's work that is of a high standard, turns

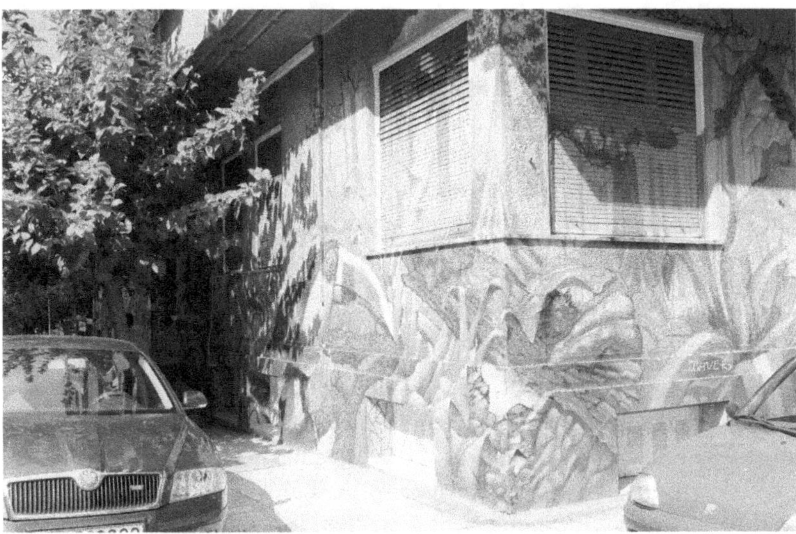

Figure 1.4 Act III: 'Urban Jungle' in Soultani Street by Alex Martinez.
© Myrto Tsilimpounidi, 2018.

the mural into an effective anti-graffiti tool. These kinds of strategies are frequently adopted by building owners in order to keep unwelcome graffiti (e.g. tags, bombs, slogans) away from their surfaces, while at the same time giving them a cool look and, often, extra value.

Historically in many urban environments, the signs of (usually politicized) graffiti and street art were associated with conditions of sociopolitical crisis. As an indicative example, in New York the numerous attempts of 'war on graffiti' between 1980 and 1983 succeeded not in eliminating graffiti but in 'repositioning graffiti not only as a crime, but also as a metaphor for New York's crisis' (Wacławek 2011: 54). Looking at this piece, we are recalling the statement of the adviser of the municipality's programme to permit graffiti and street art in Athens: 'When a city collapses, and has been tagged everywhere, we have an obligation to stop it … Once graffiti becomes commissioned art, it is a signal of the beginning of the end of the financial or social crisis that the city has gone through' (cited in Alderman 2014). This statement could not reveal more emphatically the deterministic association of graffiti and crisis in Athens. It elaborates, in the clearest possible manner, the disturbance and revolutionary potential of political street art in Athens. When Athens is 'clean' the crisis is going to end. Furthermore, the adviser recognizes that it is only when illegal and political street art becomes commissioned art that the aesthetic effects it has on the city will cease to counteract the hegemonic narratives. This is a piece that points towards the potential to depoliticize graffiti and street art, and instead to transform it into a colourful facade. It would then add to the value of the area, and since apolitical graffiti and street art are hype and cool, can enter galleries and are being sold at highly expensive prices, they can be used as a tool for gentrification. We feel that we need to clarify here that we have nothing against colourful facades; our critique is against the insidious ways that aesthetics, imagination and desires are hijacked – a subcultural appropriation from within.

Act IV: 'No Land for the Poor' in Benaki Street

Our fourth act is the piece 'No Land for the Poor', made in 2015 by street artist WD from Bali who has lived and painted in Greece for the past decade. As WD explains, the piece 'is inspired by the Eurozone crisis and its impact on Greek people. This mural, as it is written, is dedicated to the Poor and Homeless in Greece and around the Globe. Why our society always ignores Poor or Homeless people? They are not invisible, they are there… on our way home' (WD, 2015). Currently crisis has its tenth anniversary in Greece and, as expected in the last decade, it has produced a new class of urban poor – more than one in three Greeks now live below the poverty threshold (Traynor 2013). If we add the statistically invisible suffering of 'sans-papier' migrants and refugees, we could visualize how it feels to practise a periegesis in a city where numerous people are sleeping rough.

WD's statement and artwork touch upon a set of contested questions, such as the notion of visibility and invisibility in public space in the era of crisis. Which civic performances are allowed to be visible, whose suffering should be made public, and who has the right to decide? While in the last decade financial stagnation has produced a new strand of urban poor, the municipality of Athens has been particularly aggressive in making sure that homeless people are not seen in the streets – for example, through the installation of 'anti-homeless spikes' and uncomfortable benches, which make it impossible for people to sleep on them. Indeed, as explained in our previous acts, Athens is one of the most popular destinations in Europe, and the touristification and gentrification of the city centre leaves no room for any civic realities that could spoil the enjoyment of the tourists. Yet, as one street encounter informed us, the neighbourhood of Exarchia is one the safest places for men to sleep rough; but if you are a woman, things can be very difficult. Perhaps this could explain the visibility of certain bodies in the area and, as evident in the image, underneath WD's street art piece

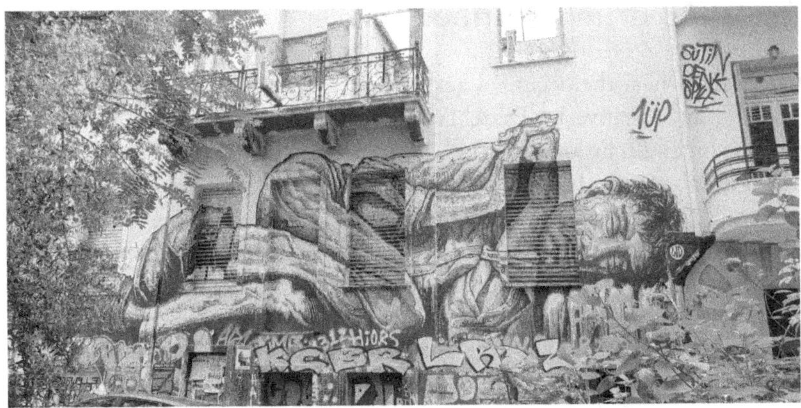

Figure 1.5 Act IV: 'No Land for the Poor' in Benaki Street by WD. © Myrto Tsilimpounidi and Konstantinos Avramidis, 2018.

our street encounter is trying to set up his small 'store' for the day selling untaxed tobacco and cigarettes, which is part of a black market economy that is flourishing in the years of the crisis (Tsilimpounidi 2015b).

As we are trying to frame the picture for this act, our encounter is willing to explain to us that this piece is very beautiful, and that it has received international recognition and appeared in many newspapers. We ask his permission to frame his 'store' as part of this image. Our encounter feels that he is finally being represented in the city, making his life visible and as such perhaps meaningful. As we walk away, we talk about the paradox of beautification and consumption of certain suffering bodies. By appearing in many newspapers, and on blogs and travel websites, this piece has attracted an international audience of art enthusiasts.[8] What probes a self-proclaimed 'homeless' person to set up a black-market shop underneath this piece? We are astonished by the capacity of street art pieces to be inscribed not only on the surface of the urban landscape – in other words, to present an alternative (or not) visual representation on the urban walls – but, most importantly, its capacity to form social and spatial relationships. This corner is going to be recognized as the monument to homeless people by residents of the area, tourists, the tour guides of Athens, the international media, and by homeless people themselves. The spatial contract of this corner is, from the moment of recognition onwards, informed by this knowledge; or, to put it differently, street art has the capacity to create public monuments and spatial contracts in the city.

Act V: 'Seeds' in Navarinou Park

Our last act is at the occupied and self-managed Navarinou Park. It is the result of an initiative by Exarchia residents, who occupied an abandoned parking lot and transformed it into a park, which opened on 7 March 2009. This took a spectacular as well as festive character of collective claim for more open and green spaces. The happening, however, takes places at a very particular and sensitive historical and geographical point: it was three months after the assassination of 15-year-old Alexandros Grigoropoulos on 6 December 2008 – which should considered as the prelude of the current crisis – and only a few metres away from that spot, on the very borders of Exarchia neighbourhood with the bourgeois Kolonaki district. The 2008 Uprising bequeathed a spatial activist ethos, the momentum of which is evident in the creation of the Navarinou Park. This space is an exemplar of what Stavros Stavrides identifies as 'commoning' tactics 'in the prospect of reappropriating the city', as for him 'common spaces are the spatial nodes through which the metropolis once again becomes the site of politics' (Stavrides 2015: 11). In that sense, the park is a common space and, as such, different from both public and private space. We chose this as our last stop as we wanted to open up questions of what it means practically and politically to create an artwork at a common space, and what messages and aesthetics need to be in common between the artist and the community of the park.[9] If our line of argumentation is that there is too much hegemonic visual noise in public space, and street art becomes a counter-response to the visual monopoly, then what is its function in a place that has already been reappropriated by a certain community?

On a blank facade overlooking the park, the internationally renowned and politically active Italian street artist Blu painted an impressive, non-commissioned mural in 2012. Blu became very enthusiastic about the idea of reuse of public space and the creation of a common park. According to him, Navarinou Park was an 'ugly parking lot and it has been occupied and transformed in 2009 in opposition to the urbanistic plans to build an office building there' (Blu 2017). This piece, as with much of Blu's work, is a site-specific work that speaks to the values and issues raised by the people who had occupied and were managing the park. It is an artistic interpretation of the Navarinou Park manifesto, which speaks about the omnipresence of concrete and the absence of green spaces in the neighbourhood. As we can see in the image underneath the roots of the trees, people are reading, meeting, playing and using the space of the new occupied park. The piece is complemented by a slogan written underneath in Greek, indicating that 'You did everything to bury me, but you forgot that I was a seed' – a celebration

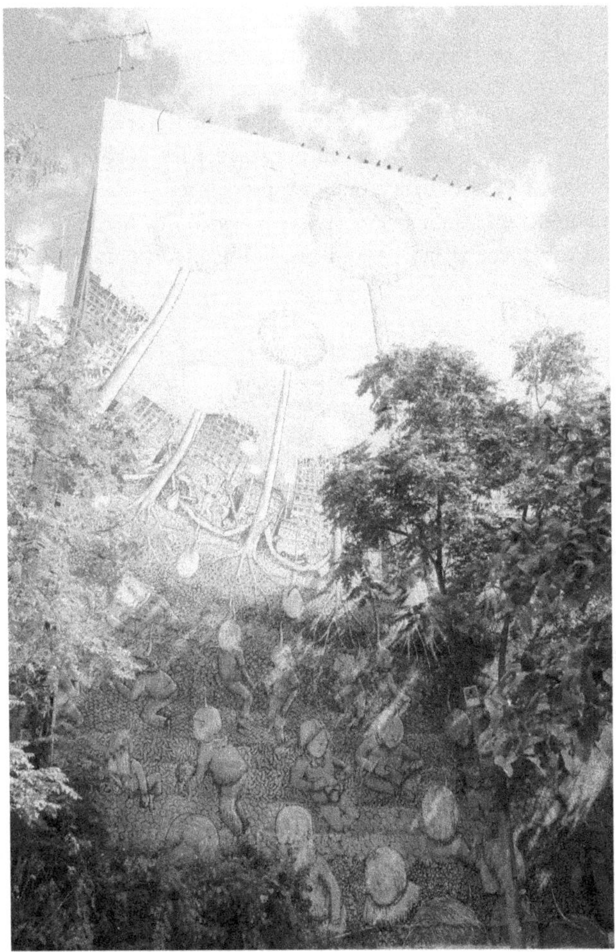

Figure 1.6 Act V: 'Seeds' in Navarinou Park by Blu. © Myrto Tsilimpounidi, 2018.

of community resilience.[10] This piece is an excellent example of subcultural advertisement, as it serves as the perfect visualization of the common philosophy and ethos of the occupied Navarinou Park. Here, a world-acclaimed artist used his skills and engaged with the concerns of the community in order to create his piece.

We stand in front of the slightly discoloured mural, trying to capture the piece which is also covered by the rich leaves of the adjacent tall trees, the living proof of the residents' initiative to create the park. Currently the space is transformed into a big playground, as the community agreed that one of the biggest problems of their neighbourhood was the absence of green spaces and children's playgrounds. Street art and an occupied park share the same notion of ephemerality in the sense that one never knows when a piece is going to be destroyed or when an occupied park is going to be evicted. Moreover, they are also in a perpetual process of metamorphosis, as the park is changing uses (allotment space, playground, reading area, cinema space), and the piece is fading and becoming incorporated into its urban environment.

Final Act: Returning and Reflecting

After some time in the park, and with the aforementioned thoughts in mind, we start descending towards the centre of Exarchia. We pass by and leave behind some emblematic pieces that we have not included in this periegesis – such as the portrait and toponymic sign of Alexandros Grigoropoulos on Messologiou Street, the 'Welcome to Athens' by WD on Tzavela Street, and the 'Welcome to the Dark Side' a few metres farther on – we acknowledge how these inform the ones we are discussing; they are present in their absence. As we move in space, the different temporalities of the pieces come together. The periegesis becomes the 'act' of the different graffiti 'acts' in present tense.

After a few minutes we reach the Athens Polytechnic, the institution that taught us some of the methods we used here, that equipped us with critical thinking and an appreciation of the political nuances in modern Greek history. We now sit at the Rector's building and look at our digital photographs whilst sketching our map. Which are the new monuments that we actualized in our periegesis? How long will they last? Can the coordinates and cardinal points of our periegesis map be the same as the ones tradition-ally found on the maps of this city? Does cartography, in a similar way to photography, frame and set up a different cardinality whilst introducing a preferred axis of reading the city? Ultimately, we wonder what our means of representation have to offer back to Athens in this moment of crisis of representation. Is representation the answer, or is it yet another way to frame the question?

Konstantinos Avramidis is a Lecturer in Architecture and Landscapes at the University of Cyprus. He holds a DipArch from the AUTh, an MSc in Architecture and Spatial Design from the NTUA with distinction, and a PhD in Architecture by Design from the University of Edinburgh. He has extensively taught at various institutions in Greece and the UK, most recently at Drury University and the University of Portsmouth. He co-founded the architectural design research journal *Drawing On*, and is the principal editor of *Graffiti and Street Art: Reading, Writing and Representing the City* (Routledge, 2017).

Myrto Tsilimpounidi is a social researcher and photographer. Her research focuses on the interface between urbanism, culture, and innovative methodologies. She is the author of *Reproducing Refugees: Photographia of a Crisis* (Roman & Littlefield, 2020); *Sociology of Crisis: Visualising Urban Austerity* (Routledge, 2017); and the editor of *Graffiti and Street Art: Reading, Writing and Representing the City* (Routledge, 2017). She is the co-director of the Feminist Autonomous Centre for Research in Athens, Greece.

Notes

1. The field trip (15–19 May 2018) was organized by cultural geographer Penny Travlou, who also serves as the programme director of the MSc in Cultural Landscapes at the University of Edinburgh. The walk took place on the third day of the field trip under the theme 'Weaving narratives of presences and absences on the city fabric: From writings on walls to emerging networks of locals and newcomers'.
2. Recently the district of Exarchia was characterized as an anarchist neighbourhood on Google maps, and is listed in expensive guided tours of Athens as the last anarchist village in Europe, while at the same time whole apartment blocks and houses are being sold to 'foreign investors'. The pervasive presence of graffiti in the area contributes to its 'rebellious' image (for more on Exarchia graffiti, see Spyropoulos 2013).
3. The Academic Asylum Law (AAL) was founded after the end of the dictatorship in order to ensure that spaces where uncensored thought and free circulation of ideas are protected would exist in the future. According to the AAL, all university spaces in the country are to be guaranteed freedom of speech and research. Everyone working, teaching or learning in academic premises has the legitimate right of academic freedom. The contemporary – sometimes distorted – usage of the AAL has turned it into a subject of controversy in the public discourse. The Greek state repealed the law in 2011 to try to deal with riotous demonstrations. Even today, the AAL remains a taboo subject, with strong supporters and strong opponents.
4. Pixação is a very unique graffiti genre originating from São Paulo in Brazil, which is associated with and born from the slums of the city. For more details on this writing type, see Chastenet 2007 and Lamazares 2017.
5. Famous Greek street artist Cacao Rocks has frequently written this motto on various walls around Athens city centre. The catchy nature of the slogan and its proliferation in the city attracted the attention of the media, leading to its overconsumption. This led local artists like Cacao Rocks to declare that 'Berlin is the New Athens', 'This is not Berlin', and 'Athens is the New Athens'.
6. The documenta art exhibition, as the name suggests, documents and promotes art since its foundation. Started in the 1950s, it takes place in Kassel, Germany, every

five years. In 2017, the event was hosted for the first time in two cities: Kassel and Athens. This unprecedented decision was largely welcomed by the local art establishment because it put Greece at the centre of the art world. Of course, it caused controversy, and concerns were raised regarding the potential exploitation of the local cultural scene (Scourta 2018).

7. The drone film 'Graffiti Olympics' by 1UP documents the crew's illicit interventions in the city of Athens in 2018. Available at: https://www.youtube.com/watch?v=tcLY9T_Vtew (last accessed 18 August 2020).

8. As we have argued elsewhere (Avramidis 2015; Avramidis and Drakopoulou 2015), the physical graffiti surfaces are often turned into hyper-surfaces through their online dissemination.

9. As Stavrides explains: 'Common spaces are those spaces produced by people in their effort to establish a common world that houses, supports and expresses the community they participate in. Therefore, common spaces should be distinguished from both public spaces and private ones. Public spaces are primarily created by a specific authority (local, regional or state), which controls them and establishes the rules under which people may use them. Private spaces belong to and are controlled by specific individuals or economic entities that have the right to establish the conditions under which others may use them' (Stavrides 2015: 10–11).

10. These lyrics are from a 1978 poem of the late Greek poet Dinos Christianopoulos (1931–2020). Interestingly, they have been translated in many languages and turned into a slogan that was used in protests around the globe, most recently in the US as part of the #blacklivesmatter movement.

References

Alderman, L. 2014. 'Across Athens, Graffiti Worth a Thousand Worlds of Malaise', *New York Times*, 15 April 2014. Retrieved 18 August 2020 from http://www.nytimes.com/2014/04/16/world/europe/across-athens-graffiti-worth-a-thousand-words-of-malaise.html?_r=0.

Andron, S. 2018. 'Selling Streetness as Experience: The Role of Street Art Tours in Branding the Creative City'. *The Sociological Review* 66(5): 1036–57.

Avramidis, K. 2012. 'Live your Greece in Myths': Reading the Crisis on Athens' Walls'. Professional Dreamers, working paper no.8. Retrieved on 20 August 2018 from http://www.professionaldreamers.net/_prowp/wp-content/uploads/Avramides-Reading-the-Crisis-on-Athens-walls-fld.pdf.

———. 2014a. 'Mapping the Geographical and Spatial Characteristics of Politicized Urban Art in the Athens of Crisis', in M. Tsilimpounidi and A. Walsh (eds), *Remapping 'Crisis': A Guide to Athens*. London: Zero Books, pp. 183–203.

———. 2014b. 'Public [Ypo]graphy: Notes on Materiality and Placement', in M. Karra (ed.), *No Respect*. Athens: Onassis Cultural Centre, pp. 21–34, 85–96.

———. 2014c. 'The Agency of Space on the Scene of Encounter: Thoughts on the Situational Nature of Perception', in K. Drakopoulou and A. Fakis (eds), *Meta*. Athens: Futura, pp. 47–54.

———. 2015. 'Reading an Instance of Contemporary Urban Iconoclash: A Design Report from Athens'. *The Design Journal* 18(4): 513–34.

———. 2018. 'An Atlas of Athenian Inscriptions: A Book of Drawings of Writings and Writings on Drawings' (PhD thesis). Edinburgh: University of Edinburgh.

———. 2019. 'Tagging a WWII Detention Centre in Athens: Drawing Biographies on/ of the Walls'. *Lo Squaderno* 54: 31–35.

———. 2020a forthcoming. 'Crises and/of Representations: The Sites of Drawings and/ of Writings in Athens'. *City* 24(6).

———. 2020b. 'An Architectural Palimpsest: [Re]Writing Crisis-ridden Athens'. *Journal of Urban Cultural Studies* 7(2/3): 243–62.

Avramidis, K., and K. Drakopoulou. 2015. 'Moving from Urban to Virtual Spaces and Back: Learning In/From Signature Graffiti Subculture', in P. Jandrić and D. Boras (eds), *Critical Learning in Digital Networks*. New York: Springer, pp. 133–60.

Avramidis, K., and M. Tsilimpounidi (eds). 2017. *Graffiti and Street Art: Reading, Writing and Representing the City*. London: Routledge.

Back, L. 2009. 'Portrayal and Betrayal: Bourdieu, Photography and Sociological Life'. *The Sociological Review* 57(3): 471–90.

Bengtsen, P. 2014. *The Street Art World*. Lund: Almendros de Granada Press.

Berger, J. 1977. *Ways of Seeing*. London: Penguin Books.

Bicanski, M. 2014. 'Contemporary Graffiti Art on the Walls of Athens'. *Guardian*, 11 November. Retrieved 24 October 2018 from https://www.theguardian.com/world/ gallery/2014/nov/11/contemporary-graffiti-art-on-the-walls-of-athens-in-pictures.

Blu. 2017. *Navarinou Park*. Retrieved 16 October 2018 from http://blublu.org/sito/ walls/2017/001.html.

Boletsi, M. 2016. 'From the Subject of the Crisis to the Subject in Crisis: Middle Voice on Greek Walls'. *Journal of Greek Media and Culture* 2(1): 3–28.

Burkhalter, L., and M. Castells. 2009. *Beyond the Crisis: Towards a New Urban Paradigm*. Retrieved 15 October 2018 from http://files.archinect.com/uploads/ai/aiu_Beyond_ the_Crisis_-_Towards_a_New_Urban_Paradigm-2nd_Edition.pdf.

Campos, R. 2015. 'Youth, Graffiti, and the Aestheticisation of Transgression'. *Social Analysis* 59(3): 17–40.

Carastathis, A. 2017. 'Nesting Crises'. *Women's Studies International Forum* 68: 142–48.

Carstathis, A., A. Spathopoulou and M. Tsilimpounidi. 2018. 'Crisis, What Crisis? Immigrants, Refugees, and Invisible Struggles'. *Refugee: Canada's Journal on Refugees* 34(1): 29–38.

Chastanet, F. 2007. *Pixação: São Paulo Signature*. Paris: XG Press.

Corner, J. 1999. 'The Agency of Mapping: Speculation, Critique and Invention', in D.E. Cosgrove (ed.), *Mappings*. London: Reaktion Books, pp. 213–52.

Craw, P., et al. 2006. 'The Mural as Graffiti Deterrence'. *Environment and Behavior* 38(3): 422–34.

Flusser, V. (1983) 2000. *Towards a Philosophy of Photography*. London: Reaktion Books.

Harvey, D. 2012. *Rebel Cities: From the Right to the City to the Urban Revolution*. London: Verso.

Ioannides, D., P. Leventis and E. Petridou. 2016. 'Urban Resistance Tourism Initiatives in Stressed Cities: The Case of Athens', in A.P. Russo and G. Richards (eds), *Reinventing the Local in Tourism*. Bristol: Channel View Publications, pp. 229–50.

Karathanasis, P. 2014. Re-image-ing and Re-imagining the City: Overpainted Landscapes of Central Athens', in M. Tsilimpounidi and A. Walsh (eds), *Remapping 'Crisis': A Guide to Athens*. London: Zero Books, pp. 177–83.

Kim, A.M., and T. Flores. 2017. 'Overwriting the City: Graffiti, Communication, and Urban Contestation in Athens'. *Defence Strategic Communications* 3: 9–40.

Knowles, C., and P. Sweetman (eds). 2004. *Picturing the Social Landscape: Visual Methods and the Sociological Imagination*. London: Routledge.

Lamazares, A. 2017. 'São Paulo's Pixação and Street Art: Representations of or Responses to Brazilian Modernism?', in K. Avramidis and M. Tsilimpounidi (eds), *Graffiti and Street Art: Reading, Writing and Representing the City*. London: Routledge, pp. 198–215.

Leventis, P. 2013. 'Walls of Crisis: Street Art and Urban Fabric in Central Athens, 2000–2012'. *Architectural Histories* 1(1): 1–10.

———. 2017. 'Dead Ends and Urban Insignias: Writing Graffiti and Street Art (Hi) stories along the UN Buffer Zone in Nicosia, 2010–2014', in K. Avramidis and M. Tsilimpounidi (eds), *Graffiti and Street Art: Reading, Writing and Representing the City*. London: Routledge, pp. 135–63.

Merrifield, A. 2014. *The New Urban Question*. London: Pluto Press.

Pangalos, O. 2014. 'Testimonies and Appraisals on Athens Graffiti, Before and After the Crisis', in M. Tsilimpounidi and A. Walsh (eds), *Remapping 'Crisis': A Guide to Athens*. London: Zero Books, pp. 154–77.

Pink, S. 2013. *Doing Visual Ethnography*. London: Sage.

Scourta, T. 2018. 'Give Me Athens to Stand On, and I Can Move the Art World': A Reading of *documenta 14* in Athens, 8 April – 16 July 2017'. *Journal of Modern Greek Studies* 36(1): 210–15.

Spyropoulos, T. 2013. *EX-ARCHEIA Uncensored: The Slogans and Graffiti of Exarcheia, 2009–2013*, trans. by D. Zakynthinou. Athens: Rakosyllektis.

Stampoulidis, G. 2016. 'Rethinking Athens as Text: The Linguistic Context of Athenian Graffiti during the Crisis'. *Journal of Language* 1(1): 10–23.

Stavrides, S. 2015. 'Common Space as Threshold Space: Urban Commoning in Struggles to Re-appropriate Public Space'. *Footprint* 9(1): 9–20.

———. 2017. 'The December 2008 Uprising's Stencil Images in Athens: Writing or Inventing Traces of the Future?', in K. Avramidis and M. Tsilimpounidi (eds), *Graffiti and Street Art: Reading, Writing and Representing the City*. London: Routledge, pp. 164–76.

Traynor, I. 2013. 'Crisis Over in the Eurozone? Not in the Real World', *Guardian*, 9 October 2013. Retrieved 16 October 2018 from: www.theguardian.com/business/2013/oct/09/crisis-over-eurozone-not-real-world.

Tsilimpounidi, M. 2015a. '"If These Walls Could Talk": Street Art and Urban Belonging in the Athens of Crisis'. *Laboratorium* 7(2): 71–91.

———. 2015b. 'Topographies of Illicit Markets: Trolleys, Rickshaws and *Yiusurum*', in M. Zaroulia and P. Hager (eds), *Inside/Outside Europe: Performances of Capitalism, Crises and Resistance*. London: Palgrave, pp. 56–74.

———. 2017. *Sociology of Crisis: Visualising Urban Austerity*. London: Routledge.

Tsilimpounidi, M., and A. Walsh. 2011. 'Painting Human Rights: Mapping Street Art in Athens'. *Journal of Arts and Communities* 2(2): 111–22.

Tulke, J. 2017. 'Visual Encounters with Crisis and Austerity: Reflections on the Cultural Politics of Street Art in Contemporary Athens', in D. Tziovas (ed.), *Greece in Crisis: The Cultural Politics of Austerity*. London: I.B. Tauris, pp. 201–19.

Vamvakas, V. 2019. 'Athens, an Alternative City: Graffiti and Radical Tourism', in P. Panagiotopoulos and D. Sotiropoulos (eds), *Political and Cultural Aspects of Greek Exoticism*. London: Palgrave, pp. 153–66.

Wacławek, A. 2011. *Graffiti and Street Art*. New York: Thames & Hudson.

WD. 2015. *WD Street Art Blog*. Retrieved 16 October 2018 from http://wdstreetart.com/blog/20-wild-drawing-paints-a-new-mural-in-athens-no land-for-the-poor.html.

Young, A. 2016. *Street Art World*. London: Reaktion.

Zaimakis, Y. 2015. '"Welcome to the Civilization of Fear": On Political Graffiti Heterotopias in Greece in Times of Crisis'. *Visual Communication* 14(4): 373–96.

Chapter 2

'Whatever I Can Do to Put Those People in Jail'

Crisis Turns Spanish Artists to Street Activism

Jonna Tolonen

Drawing the Sketch:
Street Art in Spain during Political Unrest

It is Thursday afternoon at siesta time and I am photographing street art in the neighbourhood of Lavapiés in Madrid, Spain. From a distance, I spot a piece by Madrid-born street artist Ze Carrion. The work is painted on a door and it illustrates a policeman forcefully twisting a young man's arm behind his back (see Figure 2.1). When I later talk with the artist himself, he explains, 'I only paint about things that are personally important to me. Reminding people of the brutality of the Spanish police forces during demonstrations is one of them' (Ze Carrion. Interview with the artist, Madrid, October 2017).

During the nine years that I have studied the Spanish street art scene, I have been inspired by the boldness and braveness of the artists to paint direct and uncensored political messages on the walls. Some of them have been fined, arrested or even incarcerated for painting without permission, but that has not stopped them. As Por Favor, who has been fined several times, explains, 'I have an urge to show my disgust for the Spanish politicians who hurt us' (Por Favor. Interview with the artist, Madrid, October 2017, author's translation).

Political street interventions in Spain have a long history. For much of the twentieth century, the Spanish people were controlled by a dictatorship that left a permanent mark on Spanish society. Franco's forty years of repression and censorship turned city space into a device for political communication:

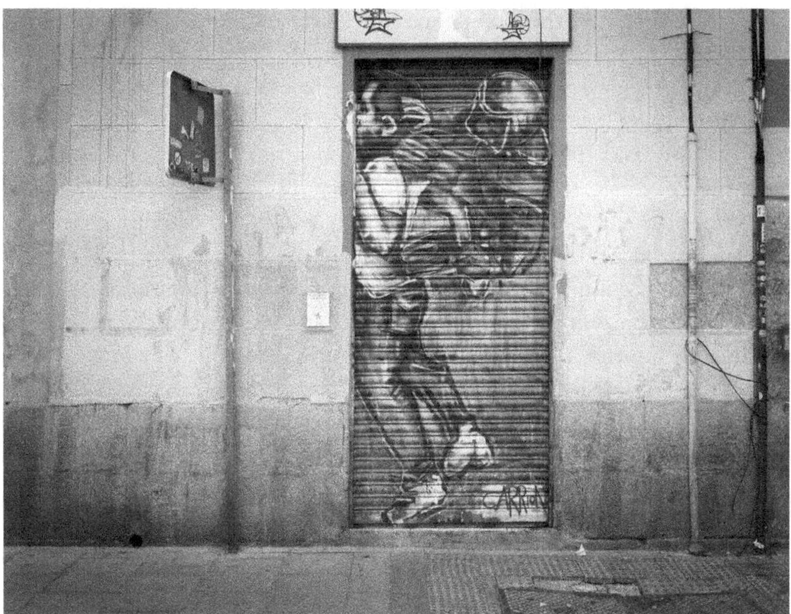

Figure 2.1 Piece by artist Ze Carrion. Photographed in Madrid, Spain, 2017. © Jonna Tolonen.

Franco's own regiment utilized streets for propaganda messaging, the opposition groups spoke out against Franco, and citizens wrote spontaneous outbursts on walls. There are many scholars who study and write about political street art, yet definitions of the term are surprisingly infrequent. Therefore, one must appreciate Ryan's contribution, that states that political street art is

> a loose category for interventions whose creative and material use of street is some way tied to their political meaning. The definition is deliberately broad, and seeks to make space for the consideration of overt and non-overt forms of politics that manifest *in and around* street art. In other words, it holds that to be *political* is not just to express political opinions but rather to be oriented toward society and to engage with its variegated terrains of power. (Ryan 2017: 5. Italics in original)

In Spain, during the economic crisis, political street art and wall writings were reborn (see Tolonen 2016). The Spanish economy, which had been rising since 1997, was severely curtailed by the end of 2008. Both the Spanish and the international media reported on the overheated construction sector, the high levels of indebtedness of households and companies, bank credit losses and the fall in house prices. Like Greece and Ireland, Spain faced a large-scale economic crisis, and it quickly felt the effects: unemployment rates grew swiftly, payment difficulties increased, and public services were cut back. Citizens were angry, as they did not feel responsible for the crisis and nor did they know how they could improve the situation. This frustration gave rise to the political and social instability that culminated in the spring of 2011 as the Spanish Revolution, with demonstrations, strikes, riots and the occupation of Madrid's Puerta del Sol square. On 15 May 2011 (15M), tens of thousands of Spaniards gathered in the Puerta del Sol in a huge demonstration to show their mistrust of the institutions of representative democracy (for a detailed analysis of 15M, see Fuster Morell 2012). People were dissatisfied with the neoliberalism of the European Union and the government's policy response to the crisis. The demonstrators protested against the growth of unemployment and the non-transparency of politics, and demanded 'real' democracy in which every citizen could have an influence. The walls were saturated with spontaneous outbursts against the politicians, and included slogans like *Lo llaman democracia* [They call this democracy], *El problema es el sistema* [The problem is the system] and *No es crisis: es estafa!* [It's not crisis: it's fraud!] (Tolonen 2016).

Spain experienced an extremely long and paralysing social, political and economic breakdown, which has not yet come to an end. Even today, Spain's unemployment rate is one of the highest in Europe. The Spanish government is still implementing austerity-based politics and actions, and this is prompting much political unrest. One of the most controversial laws that the government implemented was *Ley de Seguridad Ciudadana* [Citizen Security Law], which was soon nicknamed *Ley Mordaza* [The Gag Law]. According to the law, for example, permission to demonstrate cannot be assumed, and filming a policeman without his permission can result in fines up to 30,000 euros (Freedom House 2020). In addition, the law prohibits citizens from gathering in front of Congress House, the Senate and Parliament House, and allows police to have their own black list of protesters, activists and alternative media. By closing certain significant places for gatherings, the government gives the impression that 'public' space is only intended for certain people and for certain activities, and only those voices can be heard in those places. According to the new law, some of these fines can be imposed without a trial (Pen International 2015). The government stated that the law was drafted to improve public security and to fight against terrorism, but human rights experts and organizations regard the law as unconstitutional and non-democratic. The Spaniards feel that it aims to limit activism, collective action and the mobilization of the people. It also restricts freedom of expression – authorities have applied this law to song lyrics, tweets, comic strips and artworks. Rappers with adverse political messages have been jailed, and artworks critical of Spanish society have been removed from art exhibitions (Amnesty International 2018). The number of political street art pieces, however, increased during the crisis, not only because of the anger and frustration of people, but because municipalities had difficulties sustaining a proper anti-graffiti programme after their funding levels had been cut. As the economic crisis quickly expanded into a social and political crisis, in which many marginalized groups were excluded from the mainstream media, many saw this as an opportunity to utilize political street art as a means of communication and resistance (Tolonen 2016). The same kind of explosion of political street art during the crisis has been reported as happening in Athens (Tsilimpounidi 2015: 74–75) and Egypt (Smith 2015: 39). Political street art has become an eye-catching feature of many Spanish cities, creating new political spaces where artists can exhibit their opinions and thoughts. Street art pieces build alternative political narratives that debate about the concerns of the crisis.

The Spanish artists I interviewed for this chapter[1] had all been personally affected by the economic crisis. Its impact came up in every interview, even if I had not directly asked about it. Most of artists had graduated from university at the peak of the crisis, and so had barely any hope of supporting themselves financially. There was hardly any demand for buying art at the time, and many galleries were closing down. In addition, many of them experienced the impacts of the crisis through their family and friends. As political mistrust and socio-economic rights were at the heart of the Spanish crisis, and because young people were amongst those who were suffering the most from the economic and social collapse, it is unsurprising that the artists began to protest. This unexpected situation motivated artists to engage in resistance through their art on the Spanish streets. As DosJotas, one of the artists I interviewed, reflected on his own situation in the midst of the crisis:

> I was without a steady job for two years. I had economic problems, my parents had problems, my brother, and my friends. I did any shitty job with maybe 50 euros for 40 hours of work. … It was really bad time for me. … Some point I thought 'Shit! – I consider myself a political person, interested in the issues of the society, and here I am painting [classical] flower paintings. No, no! This is not okay!' So, I started doing political pieces. (DosJotas. Interview with the artist, Madrid, October 2017)

As argued by Judith Butler, hegemonic comprehension of politics is accomplished in part through restraining what will and will not be admissible as part of the public sphere itself:

> To produce what will constitute the public sphere … it is necessary to control the way in which people see, how they hear, what they see. The constraints are not only on content … but on what 'can' be heard, read, felt, seen and known. The public sphere is constituted in part by what can appear. (Butler 2004: xx)

Drawing on Butler's framework, my research focus lies on illegal street art as forms of artistic creation that challenge political hegemony by articulating alternative narratives in the public sphere. Many researchers have taken a closer look at the relationship between public sphere, crises and street. Most prominently, Holly Eva Ryan's *Political Street Art: Communication, Culture and Resistance in Latin America* (2017), and 'Affect's Effects: Considering Art-Activism and the 2001 Crisis in Argentina' (2015), both of which provide insights into crisis-driven art. Others who have studied graffiti and street art during political or economic unrest include: Mona Abaza (2015, 2016) and Christine Smith (2015) about the Egyptian uprising; Julie Peteet (2016) about Palestine; and Myrto Tsilimpounidi (2012, 2015) about the situation in Greece.

Building on this vein, along with my visual ethnographical research in Spain, which was carried out from September 2017 to January 2018, my analysis here seeks to show that the crisis has moved artists in new directions, transforming their thinking and therefore their art. The Spanish cities of Madrid and Valencia have a particularly rich tradition of political street art and wall writings. Data collection methods included large-scale still photographing and video recording (especially in inner city areas and working-class neighbourhoods where the presence of political street art is evident), field notes, and interviewing eight street artists. Drawing conclusions mainly from the excerpts from the artists' interviews, and exemplifying them with selected artworks, this chapter attempts to point out the ways in which the crisis has impacted on artists, and how they have creatively responded.

The Politicization of Street Artists

Many artists that I interviewed, like Por Favor (2017) and Vinz Feel Free (2017), emphasized the importance of the crisis, and especially the 2011 Spanish Indignados movement that followed, as a starting point for their street activism:

> On 15M I went out onto the street to participate in the demonstrations. I was there in the first line. (Por Favor, 2017)

Crisis really was an important point for the [political street art] scene, many people started doing works that time. Clearly. I started in 2011, during the crisis. I went onto the street because everyone went onto the streets. There were demonstrations, strikes, a lot of riots. … It was a movement that nobody orchestrated. We all just went onto the streets to scream. I went there with others, there were thousands, and I decided to take a space [for my art]. (Vinz Feel Free. Interview with the artist, Valencia, November 2017)

There are many parallels between the reasons artists state, and the motives that social psychologists have given, for street activism. Social psychological studies have shown that the most strongly motivated individuals who take to the streets experience shared grievances, feelings of injustice, unexpected threat upon people's rights or feel that important values are being violated (Kelly and Breinlinger 1995; van Stekelenburg and Klandermans 2013; Youkhana 2014). When asked why artists paint political artworks, the artists gave diverse answers:

First, I use the public space that is for everyone and [open] to everyone to use. It is in my responsibility to utilize it for common good: it is my role to protest, communicate and say the things out loud. Second, I use the city as if it was my sketchbook about the issues that I worry and think about. (El Rey de la Ruina. Interview with the artist, Madrid, November 2017, author's translation)

I want to give a voice to the people who are not heard in the society, like LGBT and anarchist groups. I believe in changes, and from my experience, if you fight enough, you can reach what you want. I am *siempre en lucha* [always fighting]. (Vinz Feel Free, 2017)

I paint political pieces because I have empathy for other people. I use the skill I have, and I want to make myself feel better, which is of course a very egoistic reason. (Noaz. Interview with the artist, Madrid, November 2017, author's translation)

Interestingly, Noaz here emphasizes the remedial benefits of the act of painting. Most of the artists understood street art creation as an affective process. Many of them reflected that 'painting does something' to their bodies, and reported experiencing intense physical and emotional sensations during the process of creating street art, as Por Favor describes here:

I need to paint as much as I need to breathe. The current political situation in Spain is horrible. They've been cutting our freedom of expression and civil rights. This affects everyone – we are all suffering. I would go crazy from the frustration if I didn't release my anger by painting. (Por Favor, 2017)

Artists also mentioned the importance of bringing to the streets the things that are ignored and often left out in mass media reports, as Ze Carrion (2017) explained: 'People forget things easily. With my works, I am exposing people to see, and reminding them of what has happened'. Motivations for painting political street art seem to have some variation between artists but the majority focus on civil rights (see also della Porta 2015: 24, 93).

The street intervention seen in Figure 2.2, *La dignidad siempre es lucha, La lucha siempre es dignidad* [Dignity is always a fight, Fight is always dignity], is an example of an artist highlighting civil rights. The stencil illustrates Ascensión Mendieta, and is a work by Por Favor. Mendieta became a famous *luchadora* (fighter) against the Spanish state. Mendieta's father was a victim of political violence and was buried in a mass grave. The search for her father's remains marks the first instance of graves being dug on the orders of an Argentinian judge in a lawsuit seeking redress for crimes committed during the 1936–39 Spanish Civil War, and the nearly four-decade dictatorship of Francisco Franco that followed. After Franco died, Spain passed a law prohibiting investigations of political crimes committed in his era. This has meant that the court cases had to be opened abroad. Mendieta took her case to Argentina, and in 2017 the court ordered that her father's grave be exhumed, and for the first time, a Spanish judge allowed it. Thus Mendieta, at the age of 91, was able to re-bury her father nearly seventy-eight years after he was killed in 1939. It is estimated that there still are hundreds of thousands of people in mass graves, and tens of thousands of Spaniards are fighting to get their relatives identified and then buried with dignity (see e.g. Junquera 2017). Mendieta became a hero for the victims of the Franco's regime, and anyone following the Spanish media can easily recognize her from the stencil (see Figure 2.2).

When I asked the artist himself to explain the motive for painting this particular work, Por Favor explained:

It is a case that I have followed for a long time. A case that reveals what Spain really is made of. We have an image of a modern and democratic country, but in reality, we are slaves of the past. Our judicial system is very antiquated. ... This woman, after so many years of fighting, finally buried her father, and for me this is an example of a fight that has not been useless. Our systems are oppressors, but with time, you can find a crack in them – she proved it. ... And my stencil, a tribute to her and

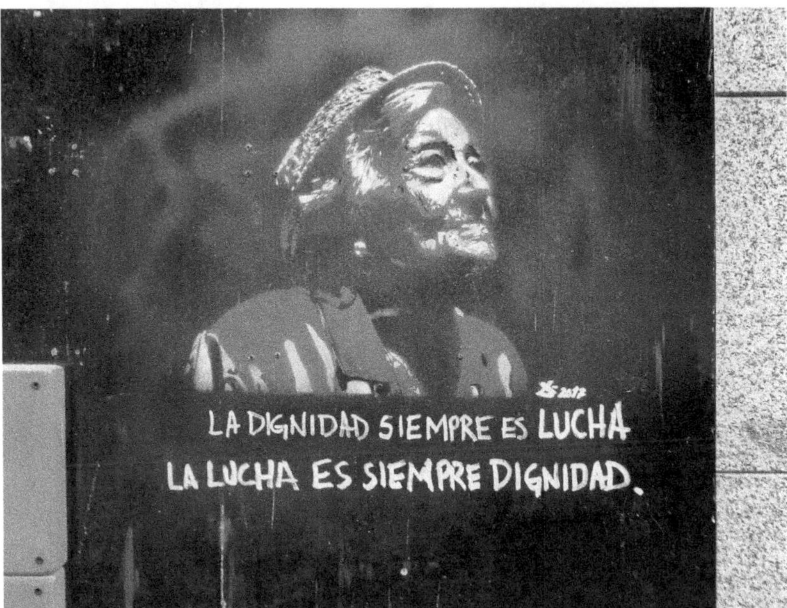

Figure 2.2 Stencil by artist Por Favor. Photographed in Madrid, Spain, 2017. © Jonna Tolonen.

her father, I painted it just a few days after the burial [of the remains]. For me, it is a great pleasure to do such a work, because it has a very powerful meaning: she is a fighter who has changed the system. She is without any resources or money, and they accomplished this only with the solidarity of people. Imagine what we all could achieve together? (Por Favor, 2017)

By painting the stencil of Mendieta (Figure 2.2), Por Favor shows his appreciation for her long and victorious fight with the state; but for him it is also a proof of collective power. Por Favor's work, painted in Madrid, is a reminder for passers-by of the strength in people. The piece communicates on many levels. It invites reflection on attitudes with a view to a social change, it brings pleasure over Mendieta's victory, and it seeks the viewer's interaction with the work. Por Favor labels himself as 'an activist rather than artist', and because of his deep resentment over the current state of affairs in Spain, he believes it is his 'responsibility to keep fighting with paint'.

Por Favor is not alone in his feelings of responsibility. Flug reflected that he has 'a responsibility to create political artworks because, I'm committed

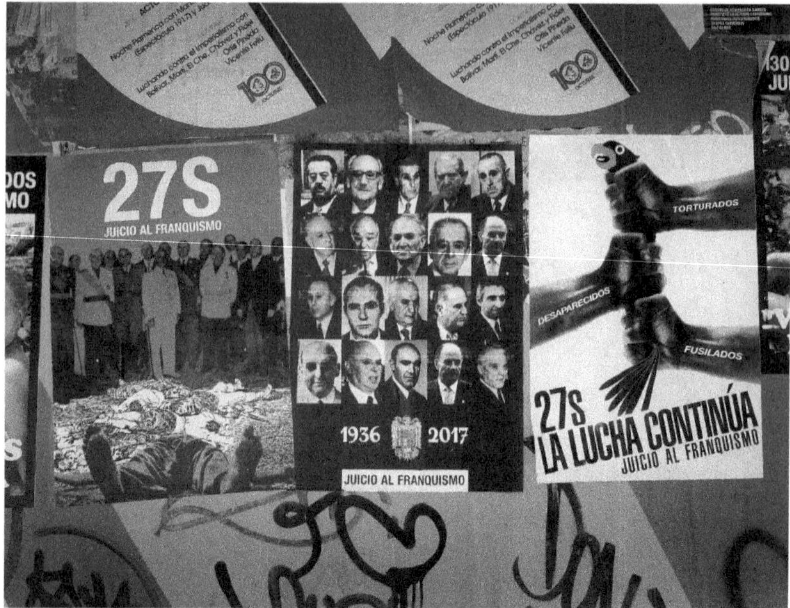

Figure 2.3 Series of posters (27 September 2017 in Spain marked 42 years since the last death penalties ordered by Franco and excecuted by shooting). From left to right: '*27S. Juicio al franquismo*' [27 September. Conviction to Francoism]; '*1936–2017. Juicio al franquismo*' [1936–2017. Conviction to Francoism]; '*Torturados. Desaparecidos. Fusilados. 27S. La lucha continúa. Juicio al franquismo*' [Tortured. Disappeared. Shot to death. 27 September. The fight continues. Conviction to Francoism]. Poster in the middle by Noaz. Photographed in Madrid, Spain, 2017. © Jonna Tolonen.

both to society and art' (Interview with the artist, Las Palmas, January 2018, author's translation). Also, Noaz (2017) described his latest co-project, a series of posters about the crimes of the Franco regime, as a 'responsibility of a citizen', and added, 'whatever I can do to put those people in jail' (see Figure 2.3).

In times of crisis, political participation rises. The Spanish Indignados increased the participation of Spanish people in demonstrations, social movements and activist groups. Social participation in activism became the strongest since the late 1970s. Spaniards began to feel that representative politics no longer cared for citizens. Many new communities and activist groups were formed (Tolonen 2016). The original Spanish Indignados that united together against state politics and corruption is still alive today, but it has fragmented into various activist groups. Some fight against gentrification, others for a fair minimum wage, others – like the two examples above – for justice for Franco's victims (see figures 2.2 and 2.3). They might be fighting for different issues but they have one thing in common: all actively aim to transform relationships of power.

The dialogues presented here, which focus on artists' motivations for making political street-based interventions, reveal insights into the artists' creation of their art. The comments of the artists tend to support the argument that political street art is often motivated by a feeling that constitutional politics will not bring desired change. Therefore, they decide to take illegal actions such as painting without permission, and believe in grass-roots political action. They see it as being more powerful and purposeful than the usual and more restrictive formal rights of citizenship. As the examples here show, their artistic practice offers a particularly intriguing lens through which to analyse grass-roots citizenship. As El Rey de la Ruina (2017) stated, 'I think it is in my responsibility not just to vote every four years, but also to paint political works'. Most of the artists consider their works as being 'against something' or as 'oppositional'. Two-thirds of those interviewed mentioned their concern over basic human rights. The artists also reported feeling anger, a sense of unfairness, and a shared group identity – which are all affect-based responses for protesting and taking action (della Porta 2015: 64). Their visual contentious politics is driven by collective participation, critical engagement, and deep feelings of solidarity.

Political Artworks Generate Career Drawbacks and Censorship

Street art has evolved from a small underground activity to a trendy mainstream phenomenon in just a few decades, and the number of artists and festivals that focus on street art has grown. Nevertheless, the number of political street artists has not changed much, and nor are there any street art festivals that exhibit primarily political works. It seems that artworks with a political message might not be a profitable career move for a street artist. When I raised this with DosJotas (2017), his experiences confirm my thoughts:

JT: Do you often get asked to paint murals at festivals?

DosJotas: No, they know me already. I have been labelled as a political street artist, and nowadays I don't even get asked.

> JT: But would you like to paint political murals?

> DosJotas: Yes, I have few good ideas in my head.

It seems that some artists have already dropped out from the artist list of festivals due to their political profile. Although some artists do get invited to participate, they are sometimes clearly reminded about the content they are allowed to paint, as Ze Carrion (2017) affirmed:

> JT: Your art has a very political tone, right? The issues you paint about are, for example, slavery, hunger and police violence. I wonder, do you get invited to street art festivals?

> Ze Carrion: Well, yes, but in some street art festivals I've been told to ease down with my political message.

These comments raise questions about the limitations of commissioned street art. For example, street art festivals, urban projects, mural competitions and neighbourhood regeneration processes are often led by city officials or private investors, and they need authorization from property owners and city councils. Therefore, the aim for the artworks often seems to emphasize an aesthetic perspective, and so permission for political artwork is seldom given. Flug (2018) called these restrictions of artwork 'total censorship', and Por Favor (2017) mentioned that 'very rarely am I allowed to paint what I really want to'.

Many artists stated that festivals and urban regeneration projects are not the only administrators that seem to impose selection or censorship. The crisis has made different kinds of art grants very desirable. When I asked DosJotas (2017) about his willingness to apply for a scholarship, he replied: 'The *becas* [grants] are difficult for me, because my projects are with hard content and they want more comfortable ideas than what I have. It's difficult to get scholarships for my kind of art'. Owing to the crisis, the number of state grants have also been cut down, which nowadays means that the most profitable grants are awarded by commercial actors. This often creates a conflict of interest for political street artists, as Noaz (2017) explained: 'Many scholarships, as well as festivals, are now sponsored by Spanish banks that are at the same time evicting people from their homes because they can't pay the mortgage'. According to Vinz Feel Free (2017), who mainly creates nude human figures with animal heads, censorship has increased in almost every sector during recent years:

> Nudity is not accepted, either in social media or in the streets. People don't see it as acceptable anymore. I had my social media accounts

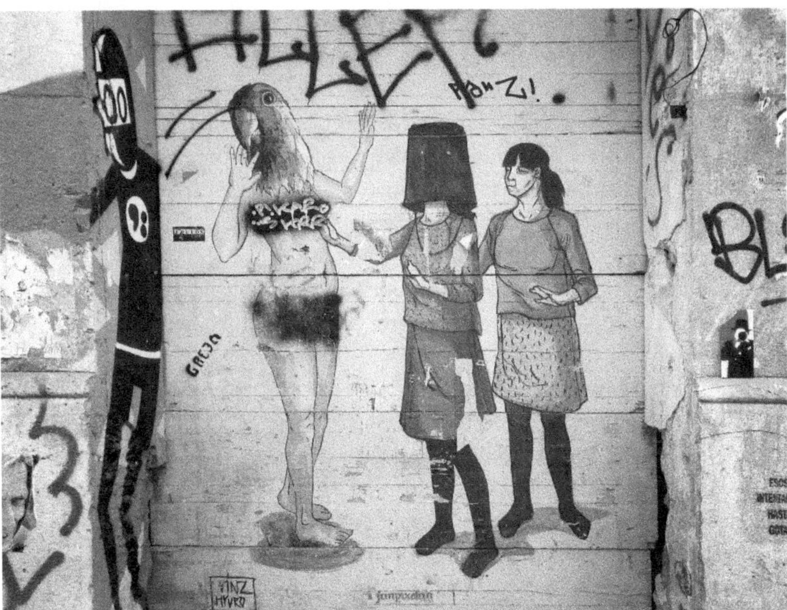

Figure 2.4 Artwork by artist Vinz Feel Free. Photographed in Valencia, Spain, 2017. © Jonna Tolonen.

removed because there were nipples in my works. Now I have to put pixels instead of nipples. In the street people remove or paint over the nipples and genitals from my paste-ups. … So nudity is allowed only in private space, unless it's an advertisement. One magazine declined to promote my art exhibition because I had a nude person in the picture, because the advertisers of the magazine don't want any nudity in the magazine. And these advertisers were like tobacco, alcohol and weapon companies. A lot of companies that kill people, right? So, they don't want to promote nudity or breast feeding which is life, they prefer promoting death. So, all that is death is allowed, but not life! … Even the museums, for example when promoting my exhibitions, they don't want any nudity, not even nipples. Even if in my works the nude people are doing normal things, they mainly just stand still, there is nothing sexual about them. Each year the museums are getting stricter about this.

Vinz Feel Free's artwork in Figure 2.4, which is painted together with another Valencian street artist Hyuro, illustrates a nude person with a bird's head. The bird in Vinz Feel Free's works is associated with freedom. The nipples and genitals have been painted over in black paint, but the rest of the piece has been left untouched.

There are more of Vinz Feel Free's works in galleries and museums than in the streets, and therefore he is able to making a living from his art, but this is exceptional among the artists I spoke to. Another artist who is able to support himself with his artwork is Ze Carrion, who also uses a lot of nude figures in his work, but he often paints them on recycled materials, like old wooden doors or used chipboards, making his art not as attractive or manageable as Vinz Feel Free's printed or canvas-based works. As Ze Carrion (2017) himself reflected: 'I'm not much for galleries. My work is not a sellable product. I used to be bothered about this, but I don't mind it anymore, it is not my thing. I'm more for collectors, social projects and streets'.

The artists I interviewed were all very conscious of the fact that street is not only for protesting and communicating but is also a place to exhibit and promote art. By painting illegal pieces around the city, it becomes a framework within the artist's identity that is made visible and accessible to the rest of the world (Wacklawek 2001: 106). The street is also considered a cost-free place for creating and exhibiting art, as the following artists' comments underline:

Museum is not the only place for people. Street is a democratic museum. (Disneylexia. Interview with the artist, Valencia, November 2017, author's translation)

Many more people come to the streets than to museums. (Por Favor, 2017)

In the streets, there are no timetables, you don't have to think about the sales. It's cheap to do what I do, even cheaper for the public to see what I do, and they don't need to pay to see it. (Vinz Feel Free, 2017)

Walls are canvases to me. I make them richer and improve them. Street must be a big canvas. (Ze Carrion, 2017)

Among the artists, the street was basically seen as a 'free place for everyone' in many aspects. It is a free place to exhibit art, and it is free for people to see it. It is also free from having to please the gallery owners' taste, and the artist is free to paint whatever s/he wants. Nevertheless, many artists showed their concern with the perceived democratic nature of the street (see Young 2014: 27), and almost all of them criticized the advertising industry for displaying commercial imagery: 'Street should be a free place for everybody, but the laws forbid this. Street should be more democratic, and more for the people who live in the area, more for the neighbourhood – we don't need

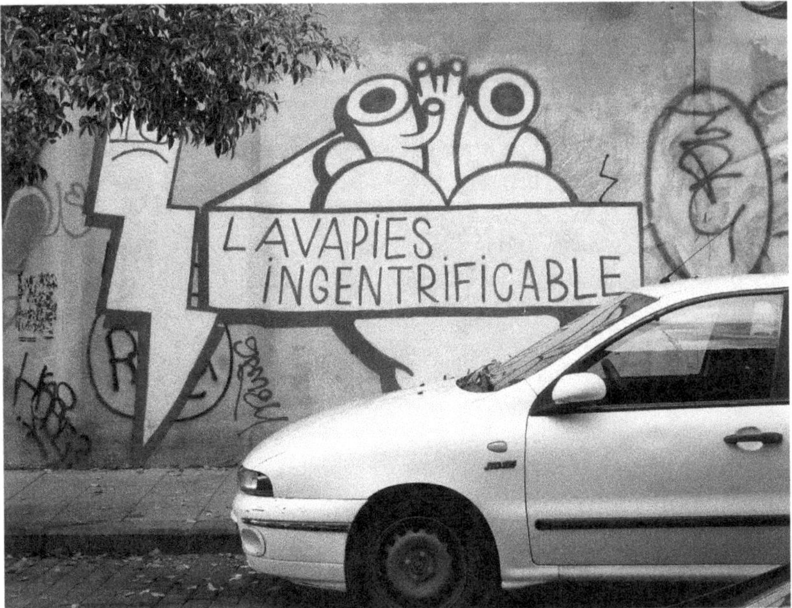

Figure 2.5 *'Lavapiés Ingentrificable'* [Lavapiés is impossible to gentrify].
Artwork by artist El Rey de la Ruina. Photographed in Madrid, Spain, 2017.
© Jonna Tolonen.

to see the Nike ads' (Flug, 2018). At the same time, advertisers are increasingly interested in using street art in their advertisements, and some of the artists had received offers from companies to cooperate. For a consciously political artist, it is difficult to work with huge corporations, as Vinz Feel Free (2017) stated: 'I have had some big offers from some brands, but no, I can't sell myself, I couldn't sleep after that'. Some artists, like El Rey de la Ruina (2017), revealed that their works had been used for commercial purposes without their permission. Since the most recognizable piece of El Rey de la Ruina is the shape of the heart in which he writes his messages, he admits that he 'probably doesn't own the copyright of heart', but he felt disappointed that researchers had used his artwork on the cover of a book about gentrification without asking his permission or mentioning his name in the credits (see Figure 2.5).

According to my interviews, creating artworks with political messages has an influence on artists' careers. Firstly, most of the artists pointed out that they do not like to paint 'decorative illustrations' for festivals because it is not what they want to do – they like painting without limitations or censorship.

Secondly, these artists prefer to create illegal works in the street, with the content and the location of their choice. Thirdly, the artists appreciated that in the street their political street art is freely accessible to all passers-by. Their work is visible to all ages and all classes of society, not just groups of gallery or museum visitors. Political street art was seen as a citizen's dialogue, as Vinz Feel Free (2017) highlights:

> Public space is *public* and it should mean it is for everyone to use. I love to do interventions in public space. I don't mind if people comment on or alter my works. It means the city is alive, in constant movement, and people are sharing their thoughts. Legal murals – they are like cute huge postcards with a sign: '*Please do not touch, do not disturb*'. (Author's italics)

The Impact of Political Street Art

I was meeting up with a friend for a run in Retiro Park, and was waiting for him in the square in front of Madrid's El Reina de Sofia museum, where Picasso's *Guernica* is the most visited artwork. The square was packed with tourists, as the museum was about to open in ten minutes. It was a beautiful and exceptionally warm October day, and I was trying to find some shade from the sun, in which to do my leg stretching. I noticed a tourist information centre on the left side of the entrance of the museum, and took a few steps to get into the corner of it. It looked like it had not been in use for a while because it was covered with tags, posters and wall writings. On one side of the tourist information centre I spotted a Madrid City information leaflet with its familiar typography and official colours of blue and white. As I began to read it, I realized that it could not be an official city information leaflet – I was looking at a piece by DosJotas (see Figure 2.6).

When I talked with the artist himself, I asked DosJotas (2017) about the impact he had wished to achieve with this particular street intervention:

> This work near the museum... Well, my works are very often camouflages: my idea is to go inside the system, *to use the language of power against the power*. I changed the typical tourist information into typical problems that tourists cause and do in the streets when they party. I have put these up in Madrid, Barcelona and Valencia. ... And as you were surprised reading it and realizing it was a camouflage, so will others. ... My works don't work like murals or advertisements: it's

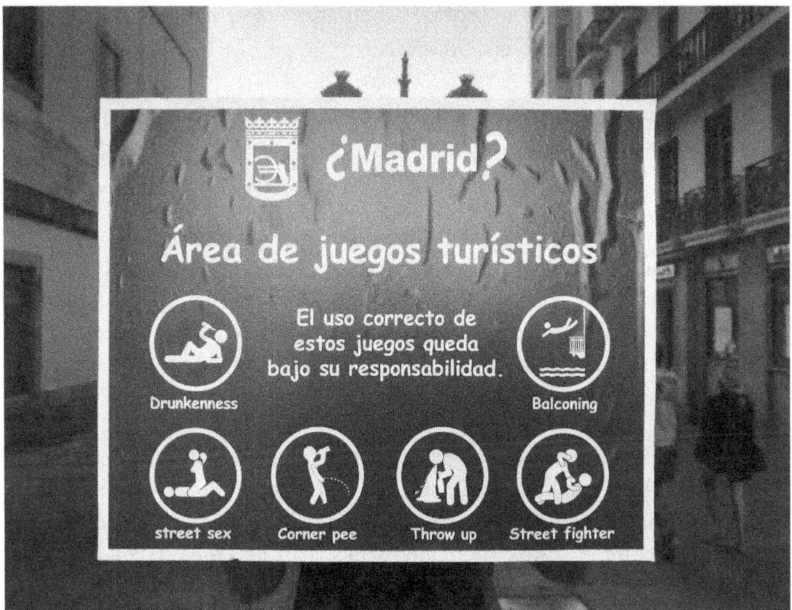

Figure 2.6 '*¿Madrid? Área de juegos turísticos. El uso correcto de estos juegos queda bajo su responsabilidad*' [Madrid? Area for tourist games. The correct use of these games is your own responsibility]. Artwork by artist DosJotas. Photographed in Madrid, Spain, 2017. © Jonna Tolonen.

a more like a personal conversation with a viewer. That's why my works have an impact on people. (Author's italics)

The potential influence of artworks that express sociopolitical dissent is hard to measure (Ryan 2017: 37). There are some researchers attempting to analyse the wider-scale impacts of political graffiti and street art. For example, Tolonen (2016, 2017) analyses the communicative effects of political pieces, and Waldner and Dobratz (2013) study graffiti as part of political participation. The artists I spoke with all declared that they had made a conscious decision to act both creatively and politically in turbulent times. They also stated that they believed in the possibilities of achieving social change through street activism. They are motivated to create artworks in the streets because they think their pieces will have an influence on people. As El Rey de la Ruina (2017) stated, 'I'm convinced that my works have an impact on people'. When other artists were asked, 'What *kind* of impact would you like to achieve with your works?', their answers varied from pedagogical influence to changing viewers' opinions:

> To make people to go out and push them to make art in the streets. (Disneylexia, 2017)

> I try to be actual and take part in the discussion in our society. In twenty years from now the historians will be looking back and talking about what happened in Valencia's street art scene. (Vinz Feel Free, 2017)

> There is a difference between social media and street. Both are equally okay, but street is impacting more – it's more annoying, and affects people of all ages. (Flug, 2018)

> People wake up when they look at my works. They come and tell me, like, 'You have totally changed my point of view', or 'It's true, I hadn't really thought about it, but the government is stealing from us'. ... I prefer people to think about my works than like them. (Por Favor, 2017)

As the comments above show, the artists are performing street activism hoping to impact on a political or social situation. The idea is to create artwork that communicates with passers-by, both aesthetically and with their message. Artists tend to rely on the emotional response that art creates because it has the power to engage passers-by with issues that are often difficult to grasp. Many of the artists emphasized their desire to make old buildings and walls 'richer' or 'more interesting' with their works. Artists also sought to give aesthetic pleasure. Almost all of the artists I interviewed have a graffiti writer background, but they no longer see any point in bombing the city. Instead, they carefully look for a perfect spot for their unique and often once-only artworks.

The political street art the artists create is an expressive resistance tactic that challenges power relations (Waldner and Dobratz 2013: 379), and 'sensitizes for problems related to socio-spatial transformation in the city' (Youkhana 2014: 174). As I talked with the artists and asked if they see their political street art as a form of resistance, some of them were hesitant, like El Rey de la Ruina (2017): 'Resistance? Against system? Maybe not, I think it's more like a dialogue with somebody'. Yet, Vinz Feel Free (2017) thinks strongly the opposite: 'My works are resistance, totally! I have resistance in my mind all the time'. Others, like DosJotas (2017), see the 'act of painting illegally' itself as resistance. While Por Favor (2017) hopes that his artworks, which he sees as a form of resistance, will make people think more about the political system, because 'at the moment there is nobody criticizing the government, because they control the media'. Intriguingly, Flug (2018) and Noaz (2017) both emphasized the instrumental resistance value of street art. Noaz saw 'art as tool for activism', and Flug stated that 'through art, I'm able to set my protest free into the street'.

'They Are the Same Dogs with Different Collars'

The task of this chapter has been to look more closely at the ways in which the crisis has affected street artists. It has analysed both selected artworks and excerpts from the artists' interviews. Four specific findings are worth emphasizing.

The first is that the crisis and the austerity politics that followed pushed artists to turn to a different creative mode. They deliberately shifted their artistic practice to address political and social issues. For many artists, this was due to concretely experiencing the crisis in their own lives. Artists and their closest ones lost their jobs, the government cut their rights to freedom of expression, and their friends got beaten up by policemen in peaceful demonstrations. People became politically active because they felt something profoundly – a wide spectrum of affective stimuli, such as injustice, drove artists to protest. Many years of economic growth and democracy had 'blinded us from the reality', DosJotas (2017) told me, and continued: 'Franco never really died, because most of our politicians are the relatives of the Franco-era power elite'.

The second finding relates to the political system. None of the artists I talked to belonged to a political party, and they all had a very similar view of politicians; as Flug (2018) described it, 'They are the same dogs with different collars'.[2] Some of the artists vote, and many of them cooperate and work with various neighbourhood anarchistic or charity groups. The artists seem to have lost their trust in representative politics and tend to invest their efforts in bottom-up activism. The illegal political street art the artists create is also a form of bottom-up street activism. Their artworks emphasize the ethical-social-political problems that exist today in Spanish society. The artists felt that with representative politics, there is no hope for positive change, and therefore they have decided to act. According to my interviews, street art is a part of artists' grass-roots political participation. Artists are protesting by means of artistic expression. Political street art pieces, as illegally produced works in publicly accessible places, are expressing political views, social observations, beliefs or rejections, with the hope of changes in society, referring to the political climate of the time.

The third finding is the capacity of street art to function as an alternative form of political communication. Researchers like Waldner and Dobratz (2013) and Young (2014) have studied artists' reflections on their street activism. The results of this study are similar and substantial in that they reveal the artists' aim to use art to engage passers-by in political communication. My findings clearly resonate with Alison Young's insight that 'street art partakes in a conversation with the city by making marks within it' (Young 2014: 26). Artists see the street as a place to visually address controversial, forgotten or ignored issues. They harness their artistic creativity for a social purpose and it becomes a tool for political dialogue. Like any other form of communication, communication through art has objectives. The interviews revealed that artists aim to change political decision-making processes, for example by preventing legislative reform or by reducing corruption. Artists believe that street politics can influence the political agenda and decision-making processes. Their ideological, political communication does not result in an aesthetical void – on the contrary, as I have illustrated in this chapter. There are artists who do prefer that passers-by 'get bothered' rather than just 'like and take a picture for Instagram' of their artworks, but their art school background tends to guarantee the quality of their pieces. Artists are also fully aware of the influence of images. Ryan's comment (2017: 141) reflects well to this study: 'Street art production and reception sometimes connects with the feelings of practitioners, activists and audiences in ways that words and text cannot'.

The fourth finding worth highlighting is the dimension of the spatial politics. The link between space and politics is a studied topic in graffiti and street art (for more, see e.g. Chmielewska 2007; Carrington 2009; Young 2014; Ryan 2017). For example, Margaret Kohn emphasizes the relation of space and politics by stating that 'space is not just a tool for social control – spatial practices can contribute to transformative politics – as they employ language, symbols, ideas and incentives' (Kohn 2003: 7). By manifesting contentious messages to passers-by, political artworks politicize public space. Artworks claiming and occupying public space are spatial contestations within the public sphere, and illuminate the complexities currently facing Spanish society. It does not automatically mean that artworks themselves make or effect political change, but artists have an ability to communicate issues, and to try to convey to passers-by their emotions, ideas and solidarities (Smith 2015: 26). Political street art also has a potential to engage passers-by for interaction and debates with each other in that public space. Therefore, it is a medium to invite people to think about and discuss political questions. The new political spaces that emerge out of artists' artworks challenge the power relations. Crisis launched new political spaces and groomed a new generation of street activists with a heightened sense of political aware-ness. Producing street artworks, as Chmielewska (2007: 161) states, art is 'marking a spatial entity with individual trace', and 'by taking place, it makes itself public, taking position within a larger visual sphere and its immediate discourse'. Spatial politics allow artists to transform material dimensions of public place into purposeful visual expression.

When an interview with an artist was coming to an end, and if I felt the artist was not in a hurry, I asked about the future of political street art in Spain. All the artists I talked with were between thirty and forty years old, and I had been unable to find artists in their twenties for my research. So, I asked why there were no younger Spanish artists creating political street art. The answer was invariably, 'the crisis', as Noaz and Vinz Feel Free concluded:

> There are no young political street artists because the crisis killed the social and youth centres that were the places to meet other young people. People are nowadays very fragmented. ... Also because of the new law [Citizen Security Law] that was passed during the crisis, you can get really big fines for painting illegally. Some of the people are afraid to do political artworks. (Noaz, 2017)

> We are really old who are doing activism through art. The new genera-tion is not interested in political issues. It really was the last time in the beginning of the crisis that people were really angry about things. If the new generation is angry, they just make a Facebook update: 'Oh, I'm so angry'. But they don't go onto the streets and burn a car if necessary. (Vinz Feel Free, 2017)

Acknowledgements

The research for this chapter involved talking to street artists who create artworks without permission. For a number of reasons (e.g. risk of self-incrimination), I would like to express my deepest thanks to the following interviewees: Disneylexia, DosJotas, El Rey de la Ruina, Flug, Noaz, Por Favor, Vinz Feel Free and Ze Carrion.

Jonna Tolonen (Doctor of Arts) is a photographer and a postdoctoral researcher at the Faculty of Art and Design at the University of Lapland, Finland. Her thesis was titled 'Visage of Madrid – Illegal Graffiti as a Part of Spanish 15-M Protests'. She has written widely about street art and gentrification, and is a member of INDAGUE, the Spanish Association of Researchers of Graffiti and Urban Art. Her current research interests deal with visual culture, socio-environmental justice and artivism (www. streetwalker.fi).

Notes

1. Interviewees were selected based on their reputation as political street artists, and social networks were used to find those who would like to talk about their art. The eight interviewees of this case study are well-known street artists, and all the interviews were done in person. In each interview, the conversation covered certain questions: the artist's insights on the artworks they create; why the artist had decided to create political street art; and what kind of impact they wanted to achieve with their work. Interviews lasted for anything between 45 minutes and 3 hours 20 minutes, and were held in Spanish or English, whichever language the artist preferred. Interviews held in English have been transcribed as they were originally spoken, including grammar mistakes.
2. The word 'dog' in Spanish language is *perro*, and is used as a negative description of a person – for example, a worthless, spineless or rotten person.

References

Abaza, M. 2015. 'Graffiti and the Reshaping of the Public Space in Cairo: Tensions between Political Struggles and Commercialisation', in E. Youkhana and L. Förster (eds), *Grafficity: Visual Practices and Contestations in Urban Space*. Cologne: Morphomata, pp. 267–94.

———. 2016. 'The Field of Graffiti and Street Art in Post-January 2011 Egypt', in Jeffrey I. Ross (ed.), *Routledge Handbook of Graffiti and Street Art*. Abingdon: Routledge, pp. 318–33.

Amnesty International. 2018. 'Tweet… If You Dare: How Counter-Terrorism Laws Restrict Freedom of Expression in Spain'. Retrieved 24 August 2020 from https://www.amnesty.org/download/Documents/EUR4179242018ENGLISH.PDF.

Butler, J. 2004. *Precarious Life: The Powers of Mourning and Violence*. London: Verso.

Carrington, V. 2009. 'I Write, Therefore I Am: Texts in the City'. *Visual Communication* 8(4): 409–25.

Chmielewska, E. 2007. 'Framing [Con]text: Graffiti and Place'. *Space and Culture* 10(2): 145–69.

Della Porta, D. 2015. *Social Movements in Times of Austerity*. Cambridge: Polity Press.

Freedom House. 2020. 'Freedom in the World 2019: Spain'. Retrieved 23 August 2020 from https://freedomhouse.org/country/spain/freedom-world/2019.

Fuster Morell, M. 2012. 'The Free Culture and 15M Movements in Spain: Composition, Social Networks and Synergies'. *Social Movements Studies* 11(3–4): 386–92.

Junquera, N. 2017. 'Ascensión Mendieta recupera a los 91 años los restos de su padre, fusilado en 1939'. *El País*, 11 June. Retrieved 11 November 2018 from https://politica.elpais.com/politica/2017/06/09/actualidad/1497026126_358165.html.

Kelly, C., and S. Breinlinger. 1995. 'Identity and Injustice: Exploring Women's Participation in Collective Action'. *Journal of Community and Applied Social Psychology* 5(1): 41–57.

Kohn, M. 2003. *Radical Space*. New York: Cornell University Press.

Pen International. 2015. 'Spain: New "Gag Law" Is a Serious Attack on Freedom of Expression'. Retrieved 21 August 2018 from https://pen-international.org/news/spain-new-gag-law-is-a-serious-attack-on-freedom-of-expression.

Peteet, J. 2016. 'Wall Talk: Palestinian Graffiti', in Jeffrey I. Ross (ed.), *Routledge Handbook of Graffiti and Street Art*. Abingdon: Routledge, pp. 334–44.

Ryan, H.E. 2015. 'Affect's Effects: Considering Art-Activism and the 2001 Crisis in Argentina'. *Social Movement Studies* 14(1): 42–57.

———. 2017. *Political Street Art: Communication, Culture and Resistance in Latin America*. Abingdon: Routledge.

Smith, C. 2015. 'Art as a Diagnostic: Assessing Social and Political Transformation through Public Art in Cairo, Egypt'. *Social & Cultural Geography* 16(1): 22–42.

Stekelenburg, J. van, and B. Klandermans. 2013. 'The Social Psychology of Protest'. *Current Sociology Review* 61(5–6): 886–905.

Tolonen, J. 2016. 'Madridin katujen kasvot: laiton graffiti osana Espanjan 15M-protesteja' [in Finnish] [Visage of Madrid: Illegal graffiti as a part of Spanish 15-M protests]. PhD dissertation. Lahti, Finland: Acta Universitatis Lapponiensis.

———. 2017. 'Power of Paint: Political Street Art Confronts the Authorities', in P. Soares Neves (ed.), *Street Art & Urban Creativity Scientific Journal: Knowledge Transfer* (Vol. 3, No. 2). Lisbon: Urban Creativity, pp. 20–29.

Tsilimpounidi, M. 2012. 'Performances "in Crisis" or What Happens When a City Goes Soft?' *City* 16(5): 546–56.

———. 2015. 'If These Walls Could Talk: Street Art and Urban Belonging in the Athens of Crisis'. *Laboratorium* 7(2): 71–91.

Wacklawek, A. 2001. *Graffiti and Street Art*. London: Thames & Hudson.

Waldner, L.K., and B.A. Dobratz. 2013. 'Graffiti as a Form of Contentious Political Participation'. *Sociology Compass* 7(5): 377–89.

Youkhana, E. 2014. 'Creative Activism and Art against Urban Renaissance and Social Exclusion: Space Sensitive Approaches to the Study of Collective Action and Belonging'. *Sociology Compass* 8(2): 172–86.

Young, A. 2014. *Street Art, Public Art: Law, Crime and Urban Imagination*. Abingdon: Routledge.

Chapter 3

Walls of Resistance in Critical Times

A Reflection on Political Graffiti and Visual Protest in Southern Europe and Latin America

Yiannis Zaimakis and Leonidas Oikonomakis

Introduction

The devastating experience of the economic crisis in countries of Latin America since the 1980s, and in Southern Europe during the recent global financial recession, gave rise to massive mobilizations, new forms of visual protest and grass-roots activism in urban spaces. In this context, the street-level language of political graffiti transformed the palimpsest of urban landscape into a platform for political dialogue, creating counter-public zones of alternative ordering and sites of resistance.

Although there is a great deal of research on the social mobilizations, it mostly focuses on the traditional repertoires of protest such as roadblocks, marches, sit-ins, strikes, civil disobedience, and big-protest-event mapping, whereas little attention has been placed on more subtle and creative forms of visual protest employing street art and graffiti in contentious politics.[1] Moreover, graffiti literature tends to reproduce uncritically repeated stereotypical views about the emergence of modern graffiti within the hip-hop movement of the 1970s, ignoring the rich tradition of political graffiti and its ties with social movements in countries outside the Anglo-American world (Ryan 2018: 7).

This chapter employs a comparative analysis of visual politics in four exemplary countries of South America (Argentina and Bolivia) and Southern Europe (Greece and Spain), all with long-standing traditions of political graffiti during turbulent times. From the Second World War era to the recent decades, all these countries have experienced civilian and military rebellions, dramatic political upheavals, social tensions and significant crises that have led to the de-alignment of political systems. Despite the differences in terms of political setting and the forms of visual protest, what is common among these countries is the use of street art and graffiti as an aesthetically affective tool of communication by multiple political actors in efforts to mobilize popular support and make their voices heard. In this sense, these countries constitute a fertile ground for scholarly investigation into infrapolitical forms of expression and visual protest in struggles over authority and recognition during periods of social tension. Drawing from existing literature on political graffiti and selective fieldwork material, we offer an empirically grounded understanding of graffiti activism used by emerging social movements in these countries.

The chapter examines the evolving role of political graffiti in alternative ways of doing politics and in change-oriented struggles by divergent political actors in critical times. Then, it addresses the genealogy of political graffiti in each of our four countries and, employing a socio-spatial analysis of key examples, focuses on protest, revolt and anti-austerity graffiti employed by social movements struggling against austerity and the politics of enclosure in the context of economic crisis. It concludes with some critical reflections on wider cultural struggles associated with urban social movements' tactical repertoires and discourses in which political graffiti is immersed.

Political Graffiti, Resistance and Social Movement's Politics of Visibility in Turbulent Times

In the contemporary process of capitalist urbanization around the globe there is an increasing mobilization of cultural producers, including street artists, graffitists and muralists, in oppositional movements and grass-roots collectives against the wholesale instrumentalization of culture, art and creativity (Novy and Colomb 2013). Urban social movements activism emerged against the increasing commoditization, polarization and the enclosures of the urban commons. Seeking visibility, they handle graffiti as an infrapolitical mode of protest (Marche 2012), in which collective action is directed towards altering power relations in social institutions and everyday cultural practices (Waldner and Dobratz 2013: 379).

We use graffiti as an umbrella term to describe various forms of 'unsanctioned texts' (Carrington 2009) on walls, ranging from slogans and tags to representational forms of illicit public art (murals, stencils, characters). They serve as a means for communicating a variety of sociopolitical issues relevant to the claims of urban social movements, expressing political demands, social commentaries, criticism, protest, and rejection of, or agreement with, social changes (Zaimakis 2015: 375). For many street activists, the act of doing graffiti stems from the imperative of the right to the city, which is, in Harvey's terms, 'to imagine and reconstitute a totally different kind of city out of the disgusting mess of a globalizing, urbanizing capital run amok', challenging the unpleasant social and environmental consequences of the endless and sprawling urban growth (Harvey 2013: xvi). Employing the creative potential of graffiti, grass-roots collectives build counter-publics and reclaim the right to the city for all citizens – and particularly for the oppressed, the vulnerable and the poor.

Political graffiti may employ linguistic and iconic elements in everyday stories. It not only works at the intellectual level, but also stirs up emotions, feelings or passions for the members of the social movements constituting a form of political-aesthetic intervention in the city. As Rolston and Berastegi point out, murals (and also stencils) convey messages that are profoundly political and intellectual, concerning justice, inequality and democracy, but they work mainly at the emotional level: 'The heart warms to the sight of the flag, the back straightens to the portrayal of the hero and the eyes tear to the representation of injustice' (Rolston and Berastegi 2016: 54). Playful graffiti has a potential for triggering aesthetic emotions in their audience by associating the deployment of an oppositional conscience with pleasure (Marche 2012), and by generating 'spaces of hope', in which one can think and feel outside existing normative, aesthetic and conceptual frameworks (Levitas 2003; Johnson 2006).

Street activists create a minimal organizational structure through which they transmit information, use strategies of political mobilization, and produce more or less alternative views of public space expressing their opposition to the prevailing power and the social and urban enclosures (Bassets 2008). They employ a small-scale do-it-yourself urbanism, explore and sometimes reveal the alternative cities within the existing city, injecting spaces with novel forms of visibility and identification, reinforcing solidarity, affective and emotional engagement, and producing new meanings (Iveson 2013: 943).

Within the diverse urban landscapes, activists tend to create, in Lefebvre's terms, heterotopian spaces that call for alternative authority, charting the paths towards post-capitalist forms of urbanization and the possibility for a radical or revolutionary response to crisis (Lefebvre 2003). Resistance here is stimulated by people's feelings of discontent within the high uncertainty context of crisis in which activists employ the playful potential of graffiti to question dominant cultural conventions and political discourses. In such a way, they are getting involved in a constant process of adaptation, subversion and reinscription of dominant discourses of crisis (Thomas and Davies 2005: 687).

Political graffiti were developed in countries of Latin America and in Southern Europe at times of political instability, and used by divergent actors in attempts to mobilize popular support and to visualize popular discontent and political disaffection (Chaffee 1993; Bassets 2008; Rolston and Berastegi 2016; Ryan 2018). Over the last few decades, graffiti micropolitics have often been performed by actors who feel they have been disenfranchised from the political process and feel the necessity to react aesthetically to the unfavourable conditions of crisis. They have used the power of graffiti in raising political claims, attacking austerity, calling people into action and propagandizing alternative forms of social organization and, sometimes, utopian thinking towards desired future societies. Politicized grass-roots collectives use graffiti as part of their ritualized protest strategies dealing with issues of collective suffering, resilience, democracy, inequality and injustice. They challenge the conventional political imagery and perform resistance on a more subtle, day-to-day level by rejecting and transgressing the 'law-wall infrastructures of cityscapes' (Marche 2012: 87).

Protest Graffiti and Anti-austerity Sentiments in Southern Europe

Greece

Greece has a long-standing tradition of political graffiti that dates back to the years of the German Occupation of the country (1941–44) and the following bloody civil war (1944–49). Slogans and revolutionary symbols appeared in urban areas as means of communication for guerrilla organizations under communist leadership to cultivate a resistance spirit and a socialist ethos.[2] During the junta or the 'Regime of the Colonels' (1967–74), and in the following period of the restoration of democracy, political graffiti were employed by left-wing groups propagandizing party politics and labour movement claims. Gradually, graffiti by anarchist groups came into play, demonstrating a deliberately playful and provocative critique of capitalism and authoritarian socialism through sarcastic and ironic slogans.

Starting in the mid-1990s, a new wave of radical urbanism emerged in the aftermath of the neoliberal urban development introduced by market-oriented restructuring polices of privatization and commodification. This was followed by the advent of millions of immigrants from ex-communist

Balkan countries, which gave rise to a xenophobic discourse by ultra-right groups. Social movement activists utilized graffiti to visualize their fight against homophobia, sexism, racism and the politics of neoliberal enclosures of urban spaces. Strong graffiti activism resurged in 2008 during massive demonstrations and riots throughout the country against the assassination of 15-year-old student Alexis Grigoropoulos by a policeman in downtown Athens. Protest graffiti served as a street diary, providing passers-by with a candid insight into youth feelings, opinions and frustrations.

Political graffiti in Greece reached its peak during the period of the global economic crisis, which had started in 2008. The deterioration in the standard of living for most people, and the collapse of the traditional political system, shattered traditional beliefs and created a cross-class and cross-generational alliance of protesters (Diani and Kousis 2012; Sotirakopoulos and Sotiropoulos 2013; Roos and Oikonomakis 2014; Knight and Stewart 2016). Under these circumstances new forms of contentious politics emerged, including visual protest through alternative media opposing the mainstream discourses and neoliberal 'normalcy' of the crisis. Social movements built fluid and multifarious painted zones in appropriated urban spaces as part of the collective experience of emerging 'common spaces', which reclaimed the city as a potentially liberating space (Stavrides 2014: 546).

In this context, visual protest moved towards political and materialistic claims concerning inequality, poverty and collective suffering. Graffiti activists visualized the anti-austerity spirit in working-class and industrial areas, and around illegally squatted housing across the country with protest slogans such as 'Our lives cannot fit in a world full of hunger, poverty, unemployment', 'With 500 Euros, you can't live. Rise up!' 'I am dead broken'. At the same time, more existentialist graffiti, imbued with melancholic sentiment, commented on ordinary people's everyday lives and illustrated precarious subjectivities representing feelings of vulnerability, despair and fear, embedded in the experience of living with risk and uncertainty (e.g. 'Abasement, loneliness, desperation'; 'Wretchedness, misery, depression'; 'Fear is rising everywhere') (Zaimakis 2016: 73).

Discontented street artists, often living in precarious conditions, expressed their solidarity with the deprived people by articulating figures of suffering bodies in crisis, making the urban palimpsest more emotionally and politically vibrant and stimulating. Specific locales are used by street artists to excite the curiosity of the passer-by; elaborated stencils and murals depict young people wandering in the streets, stateless young refugees lying down on pavements, immobile bodies of juvenile immigrants with painful faces and tearful eyes, and wretched homeless people. In this vein, the closed door of a derelict house in downtown Athens became the natural decor of an inventive piece by street artist Gnor, depicting a muzzy elderly figure with a painful face saying: 'Don't underestimate hunger'. Meanwhile, on a nearby surface, a graffiti by WD[3] offers a meaningful visual commentary on the everyday life of homeless people through a huge mural covering the forefront of a central building in Exarchia. It depicts a grotesque homeless figure lying in the street, with a tag in the left corner saying 'Dedicated to the poor and homeless here and around the globe'.

The rich iconography of the suffering and stateless body speaks of a political praxis, a cry for justice that brings to mind the invisible bodies of those people who find themselves excluded from the welfare state's protective services and who exist outside the hegemonic system of political representation (Fieni 2016: 351). Body depictions have been used not only in a metaphoric sense as mark of the cultural other, but also as an 'ostentatious materiality' (Flemming 2001: 320) of the body as a material being in the real world: the body that protests and asserts justice and a respectable human life.

The painted façade of VIOME factory – a cooperative and solidarity economy venture run by self-organized workers in Thessaloniki – is exemplary of street activism's spatial politics. The wall is partly covered with a mural by Skitsofrenis, a well-known street artist, illustrating the melancholic face of a young refugee wearing a work helmet. A line from the song 'It rains in the slum'[4] by left-wing poet Tasos Leivaditis, saying 'You are little and you can't fit into my groan', brings to mind the social suffering of Greek refugees from Asia Minor after the catastrophe of Smyrna in 1923. The dark face of the child in semiotic contrast with the open coloured symbols of a ship at sea signify the controversy between the hope for a better future in the developed world and the frustration of vision in a crisis-ridden country. On the right side of the wall, local activists illustrate a red-and-black coach-wheel and two funnels, symbolizing traditional working-class culture, accompanied by a fighting slogan reading: 'The factories belong to those who run them'. The mural offers a visual expression of solidarity with the present-day refugees, employing past memory in an affective way, and at the same time visualizes the imperative of another classless society in which people would take the products of their labour into their own hands, thus echoing Emiliano Zapata's (borrowed from Flores Magón) legendary slogan 'The land belongs to those who work it'. As Knight and Stewart point out, ordinary people in Southern Europe 'telescope specific pasts and futures into the present, temporally condensing moments that light on the rupture in everyday routines'. It is a strategy for resolving the *aporia* of crises: an affective response to the crisis and a desire to express creatively not only protests but also dreams and visions (Knight and Stewart 2016: 4).

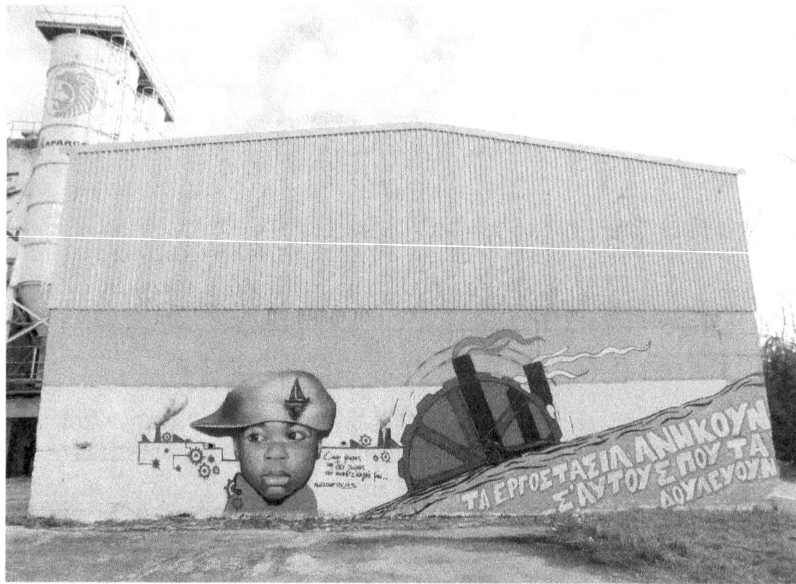

Figure 3.1 Mural on a wall of the self-run factory of VIOME, Thessaloniki. © Antonis Drakonakis.

Other graffiti express a strong opposition to the country's patronage under the Troika, and target the blame for the austerity onto puppet governments, powerful politicians and the power games taking place within the global capitalist economy. Graffitists criticized state authoritarianism and the zero-tolerance policies of successive governments during the anti-austerity mass mobilizations. Public spaces across the country were adorned with iconic figures of tear-gassed street fighters with protective masks holding weapons of street-level struggles (catapults, stones and sometimes Molotov cocktails), echoing the anti-globalization movement, Zapatistas and anarchist Black Blocks tactics of resistance. They have employed the mask as a powerful symbol, a 'soft weapon' reflecting and empowering those who have been excluded from the public domain (Ruiz 2013: 264, 275).

Revolt graffiti draw inspiration from the revolutionary past, creating an imaginary link with older social movements' materialistic claims and calling people throughout the country onto the streets with militant slogans, such as 'When injustice becomes law, resistance becomes duty' (Volos), 'Come on, get the freedom with songs, arms and swords' (Heraklion). In the same vein, activists visualize their solidarity with the Spanish Indignatos movement ('Solidarity with 15-M') and foreground the Latin American revolutionary

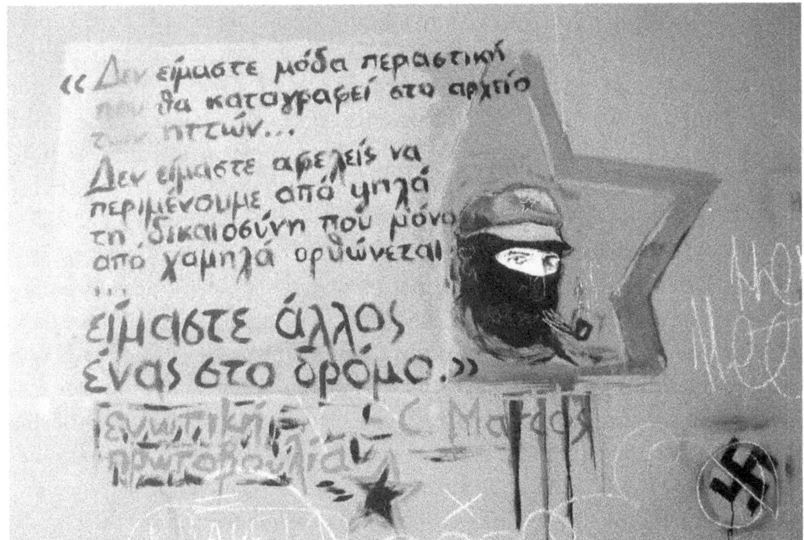

Figure 3.2 Graffiti by a left-wing student group depicting Subcomandante Marcos calling people onto the streets, Chania, Greece. © Yiannis Zaimakis.

spirit through militant slogans: 'From Chile to Thessaloniki the youth is on the streets [heading] to victory' (Thessaloniki); '25 years of autonomy, Zapatistas without state or bosses' (Archanes); and murals depicting historical Latin American rebels accompanied by relevant catchphrases. A striking example of this form of solidarity activism is a piece by a left-wing student organization at the Polytechnic University of Crete (Chania), which illustrates the portrait of Zapatistas' Subcomandante Marcos calling people onto the streets with a militant tag: 'We are not a passing fashion that will be recorded in the archives of defeats, we are not gullible to expect justice from above that only stands up from the bottom... we are another one [coming] onto the streets'.

Similarly, a stencil in downtown Athens materializes a popular slogan chanted by the Movement of the Squares during mass demonstrations in Athens in June 2011, thus bringing to mind the 2001 revolt in Argentina, when rebels forced the head of state Fernando de la Rua to escape from the country in a helicopter: 'One magic night, like in the case of Argentina, we will see which one [of the leaders] will get into the helicopter first' (Zaimakis 2016: 386).

Crisis gave rise to hybrid forms of street activism, evident in the counterpublics of the newly emerged self-organized Antifa sports teams fighting commercialized modern football and austerity (Zaimakis 2018) and, in parallel, sparked pre-existing forms of visual protest associated with antifascism, veganism, anti-speciesism, feminism and the LGBTQ movement. In this vein, feminist groups displayed iconic figures of girls with anti-conformist style accompanied by transgressive slogans full of irony and sarcasm, reading, for example, 'Lesbians, trans, priestesses of shame, we are proudly the disgrace of the nation'.

On the other side of the political spectrum, crisis-ridden Greek society became fertile ground for promoting an openly nationalist, xenophobic, homophobic agenda by extreme-right political formations (Zaimakis 2015: 378). It was the first time that the ultra-nationalist party of Golden Dawn had systematically employed graffiti as part of its tactic to disseminate the politics of fear against immigrants, racial others, homosexuals, and politicians in urban neighbourhoods. Its activists employed prosaic, racist and populist catchphrases (e.g. 'Politicians are tramps, ruffians, traitors'; and 'We need jobs, not immigrants'), sometimes recalling historical evidence of the bloody Greek civil war through graffiti depicting nationalist and fascist symbols and politically provocative catchphrases. This development incited a strong reaction from antifascist, leftist, anarchist and queer collectivities, which have diachronically attained a hegemonic position in the political graffiti scene, and given rise to a symbolic war on the walls among controversial groups, illustrating aggressive and competitive graffiti battling, erasing and replacing one another (Zaimakis 2015: 378, 389). Since the domestic scene of crisis graffiti eventually attracted international attention, a global international network of communication has been developed between foreign and domestic graffitists, contributing to the evolution of a 'graffi-tourism', which allows eminent foreign street artists to exhibit their works on Greek urban surfaces, and sometimes at street art festivals in Athens and Thessaloniki.

Spain

Similar to Greece, creative protest in Spain has flourished during turbulent times (civil war, dictatorship, financial crisis), accompanying the relevant social struggles that adopted it as part of their repertoires. During the most recent cycle of protest (2010–15) references to the Latin American anti-neoliberal struggles, which took place almost a decade earlier, appeared. During the Spanish civil war (1936–39), painted graffiti logos and slogans were used by anarchist, communist and socialist groups claiming recognition and visibility. At the same time, Franco nationalists often demarcated democratic villages with offensive and sexist graffiti, such as 'Your women will give birth to Fascists' (Chaffee, 1988: 570, 559; 1993, 18). During the dictatorship, political graffiti were used by dissident groups visualizing anti-regime protest. After a period of 'visual silence' during Franco's early dictatorship, several Basque country streets were transformed into a centre of affective political expression. In this context, the nascent Basque separatist group ETA employed graffiti as an effective means of informing Basque society and the Spanish government of its active, and even armed, resistance against Franco, distancing these forms of mobilization from the more subtle ones used by the moderate nationalist factions of the movement (Chaffee 1988: 550–51; Paento 1997: 196).

The regime tried to control this form of political communication and imprisoned many street artists and graffitists (Payne 1987; Chaffee 1988). Towards the end of the 1960s the regime grew weaker, which led to a weakening of the control of media and politicized public art. As a result, new organizations and cycles of protest were articulated and a culture of underground resistance was developed employing street activism, which was particularly evident in radical circles within the ETA movement (Chaffee 1988: 570; Basset 2008: 27). They conveyed political messages with anti-capitalist spirit (e.g. 'There is no independence without socialism'; and 'Expropriate the banks and the large landowners'), turning the independence struggle towards a fight for the socialist transformation of Spanish society (Chaffee 1988: 550–51). Public art revitalized during the early post-Franco era. A resurgence of previously forbidden visual forms of protest in the streets carried out by militant political groups criticized the established reality, the authoritarian nature of the state, and its weakness in not fulfilling people's emancipatory visions in the context of democracy (Chaffee 1988; Labrador Méntez 2015).

Creative protest resurged in Spain during the recent financial crisis, which accelerated the bursting of the financial bubble in the country, with devastating effects for its economy. Austerity led Spain to lower economic activity, higher unemployment, increased inequality, deteriorated personal economic well-being, expanded low-wages, and precarious conditions of employment (Halvorsen 2014; Zamora-Kapoor and Coller 2014). Responding to austerity politics, an explosion of grass-roots movements, such as the Indignados, precarious youth, solidarity economy groups and counterculture networks, emerged contesting neoliberal austerity politics through large-scale mobilizations and demonstrations (Martin García 2014; Sitrin and Azzelini 2014; Roos and Oikonomakis 2014; Gerbaudo 2017). The squares in major cities were occupied by a multitude of citizens who discussed in assemblies about their demands for the return of popular sovereignty, criticizing neoliberal capitalism and the distance between the 'original' spirit of democracy and its denaturalization as an effect of financial powers over politics, which was crystallized in the logo DRY (Democrácia Real Ya [Real democracy now]) (Labrador Méntez 2015: 118).

Activists used political graffiti to disseminate their opinion and feelings, endow them with an epochal performative language (real democracy, revolution, citizen, representation and utopia), reflecting both the negation to accept the known real and the vision towards desirable post-capitalist worlds. Creative protest was actually a strategic repertoire of 15M (Indignados); they organized workshops (usually in squats) for the creation of placards, just as had happened in Argentina a decade earlier. Members of the movement were in charge of coming up with militant slogans. They were called 'Los Creativos' (the creative ones) and they were normally advertising professionals or graphic designers (Romanos 2016: 5). Paolo Gerbaudo notes that even the logo DRY, extensively used by the 15M, was written in a stencil form echoing 'the subversive language of graffiti and street art, thus giving the group's identity a youthful while studiously unobtrusive creative edge' (Gerbaudo 2012: 85).

In the context of the anti-austerity movement, visual forms of protest moved from the cultural and identity agenda of new social movements back to more bread-and-butter, redistributive concerns (della Porta 2015). Tolonen (2017) points out that, since austerity, politics and corruption scandals have shaken the credibility of Spanish political representation, street art has become central for Spanish activists to produce a more democratic environment by reclaiming space and visually expressing dissent, dissatisfaction and justice demands. Street activists have created their own 'performance spaces' to reach out to a wider audience and to protest about their exclusion by mainstream media, as conveyed by a slogan reported by Jonathan Blitzer on the Madrid streets in 2011, which read: 'While the media outlets keep lying, the walls keep speaking' (Blitzer 2012). During the latest protest cycle, social demands concerning work, health, housing, and pension rights returned to the political forefront, and so do they on the walls of resistance: references to impoverishment, unemployment, and house confiscations by the banks are regularly seen in the streets of the Spanish cities. In Valencia, even direct Marx quotations have reappeared on the walls: 'There is nothing to lose but the chains' reads the mural recently prepared by an association of unemployed workers.

Many slogans express opposition to the labour reforms that were demanded as part of the austerity measures. They highlight the political climate of the new temporality, in which trade unions and political parties are seen as part of the system and, as such, are considered untrustworthy, as slogans in the Huertas neighbourhood emphasize: 'Labour Unions Traitors'; and 'Partido Popular Fascist' [Fascist Popular Party]. Other slogans, such as 'Closed for revolution, please forgive the inconvenience', are making inter-chronic reference to Subcomandante Marcos's famous response to the complaining tourists during the 1 January 1994 Chiapas uprising: 'Apologies for the inconvenience, but this is revolution'. Other anti-neoliberal slogans read: 'Free market, imprisoned people'; or more humorously: 'Less mortgage, more dance clubs'. Some also created meaningful connections with the events unfolding in Greece, at the same time cultivating a transnational solidarity activism that brings together antifascist and anti-regime communities transnationally. This was the case of a mural in Madrid depicting the Greek rapper 'Killah P' – who was assassinated by a member of the far-right party, Golden Dawn – accompanied by a slogan saying, 'From Egypt to Greece, down with the state system'. Within the visual palimpsest of political graffiti, gender and sexual inequalities were also evident on urban landscapes. Radical feminist and queer collectives visualize gender equality claims and problematize the heteronormative discipline. In doing so, many stencils and murals presented a transgressive feminist iconography, often accompanied by militant slogans such as: 'Neither machism, nor racism'; 'My body – my decision'; and 'Anti-systemic feminism'.

Spanish activists employed spatial tactics by appropriating neighbourhoods with high political symbolism to visualize anti-capitalist imaginary. They created their own performance spaces that challenge the neoliberal politics of enclosure within a striated city. Similar to the Exarchia area in Athens, Madrid's Lavapiés neighbourhood is a stronghold for street artists and counterculture movements who visualize their positions adorning the walls with belligerent graffiti condemning capitalism, racism, gentrification and patriarchy. In this area, a piece by Roc Blackblock[5] on the facade of the squatted social centre, La Quimera, in Mandela Square depicts a gagged worker on the side of an urban street in a 'disturbed city' that reverberates past moments of (civil) war. The slogan at the top of the graffiti saying 'This is not a crisis, this is capitalism' echoes a popular anti-capitalist critique which ascribes the economic boom that accelerated in the 1990s and crashed so spectacularly during the 2008 financial crisis as an inevitable symptom of the uneven capitalist development. Close beside the graffiti is inscribed a manifesto-writing that ends up with the militant motto: 'We came to find partners to conspire against our oppressors'.

In this vein, graffiti unveil existing tensions and ideologies concerning practices of resistance and collective vision towards radical political change, offering a new imagery of what it is possible to think and feel in a given temporality. Drawing upon visual material, including graffiti, and employing a poetic metaphor of opposing views – 'the slaughter of the pigs' versus 'the supermarket of the gods' – Labrador Méntez examines different

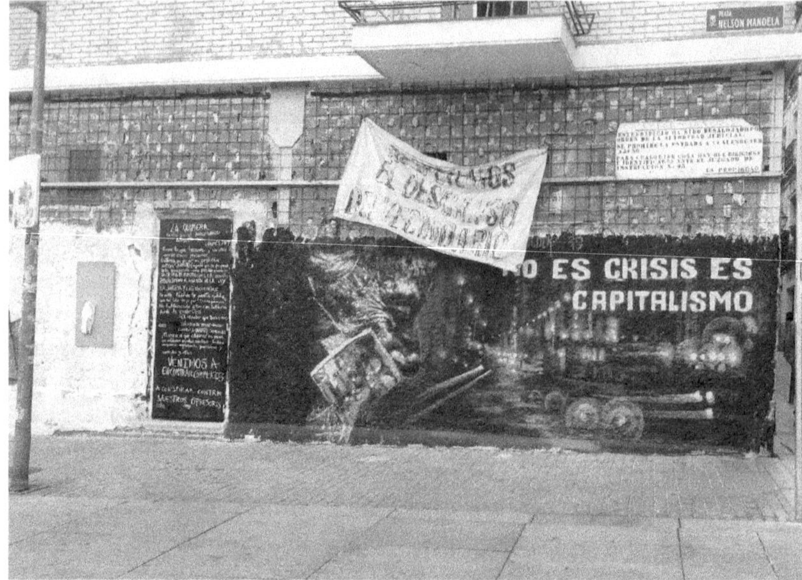

Figure 3.3 Anti-capitalist graffiti on the facade of squat La Quimera, Madrid. © Luisa Martin Rojo.

representations of the crisis to reveal the cultural logic of Spain's temporality of crisis. He shows the divided political economies of Spanish society through the role of the citizens, the state and the corporations in the control and management of the collective access to nutritional goods. Similar to their Greek counterparts, Spanish graffitists criticized mainstream politicians, put the blame on international institutions and used historical symbols such as the guillotine, a metonymy of the pending revolution, to point out the need for more militant reaction (Labrador Méntez 2014).

Political Graffiti in Periods of Political Tension in Latin America

Argentina

Similar to some countries in Southern Europe, Latin America has a rich history of street-level activism in which politicized graffitists have often been at the vanguard of change-oriented political struggles. The cases of Bolivia and Argentina both signify that creative protest flourishes during cycles of protest around democratic struggles (in periods under dictatorship, for example) and 'bread and butter' politics, especially during the 2000–2005 (Bolivia) and 1999–2003 (Argentina) anti-neoliberal cycles. In Argentina, the roots of political graffiti in the form of stencil or paintings with tar are traced back to the early twentieth century. Political street art became an affective tool of the educated and self-affirmed migrants from Western Europe demanding a more inclusive social order and open space for their own representative aesthetic in an expanding multicultural society (Ryan 2018: 168). Street art and graffiti was gradually transformed into a clandestine means of communication for the emerging working-class movement, and served as a catalyst for the development of Peronism as a populist movement (Chaffee 1993).

During the early Peron years, the trade unions (which were brought under the regime's control) and grass-roots communities (such as the Partido Justicialista street brigade) used stencil to materialize claims for social justice and to propagate nationalist ideas. In the post-1955 era after the overthrow of Peronism, midnight-graffiti brigades developed a network of street-level activism circulating Peronist political messages on urban walls (Levitsky 2003: 42). In the late 1960s, political graffiti were employed by the Rosario street artists 'Experimental Art Cycle' to engender a cultural militancy against governmental authoritarianism. Street artists visualized claims of the oppressed in Argentina, and experimented with novel forms of political aesthetic akin to those that had emerged in Europe with Situationists, seeking to blend (revolutionary) politics with street art (Ryan 2013: 187).

In Argentina under the dictatorship (1976–1983), street art became a propaganda tool of state organizations for encouraging people to contribute to governmental planning or to participate in the Malvinas War (Chaffee 1993). In the late dictatorship era, grass-roots groups, inspired by the Peronist movement and Trotskyist or Che Guevara ideals, conveyed political grievance with militant slogans, sometimes adorning them with the iconic figures of Che Guevara and Evita Peron, symbols of resistance to government authoritarianism and memorials of the fallen revolution (Ryan 2013).

An important wave of visual protest occurred in Latin America during the approximate period of the early 1980s to the early 2000s – what is known in Latin American progressive circles as 'the long neoliberal night' (Escobar 2010: 2) It was marked by the dominance of neoliberal austerity policies in almost every country of the region except Cuba. If we exclude the dictatorial regimes of Chile and Argentina, which imposed measures suppressing all democratic state functioning (Klein 2008), the imposition of neoliberal policies in Latin America under democratic regimes started with the Mexican debt crisis of the early 1980s and was fuelled by IMF-led debt diplomacy. Austerity-related grievances triggered a series of popular anti-neoliberal events such as the Caracazo of 1989, the Zapatista uprising in 1994, and Cochabamba's Water War in 2000. Overall, this wave of popular protests led to the toppling of governments and presidents in several countries (Venezuela, Argentina, Ecuador, Bolivia, Nicaragua, Paraguay) and to the election of progressive governments, in a process that is known as the 'pink tide' (Webber and Carr 2013; Webber 2017). Under these circumstances, street art became part and parcel of social movement repertoires to propagate issues around the enclosure of the commons, gender and racial oppression, the dirty politics of corruption and the crimes of dictatorial regimes of previous times that had remained unaccounted for.

Argentina in 1999–2003 is a paradigmatic pink-tide case that breaks with the neoliberal cultural, political and economic domination in Latin America. Since 1999, popular movements (the *piqueteros* for example) and neighbourhood assemblies have challenged the country's political and economic status quo, and toppled five presidents, ultimately electing in 2003 Nestor Kirchner, a 'left of the Peronist Party' president who promised to break with austerity and neoliberalism. In this period, both the legitimization of the political party as an organizational form and an agent of social change (Holloway 2005; Sitrin 2006; Mayorga 2012: 123) and the legitimacy of neoliberal capitalism at the economic level, were seriously challenged.

Schuster notices that during Argentina's financial and political crisis (1999–2003) collectives of independent art went out onto the streets to re-establish their bond with society, socializing the production process and promoting a relational, 'participatory' art. For them, crisis was understood as an opportunity for intensity of artistic and political practices and their dynamic reflections (Schuster 2015: 86). Artist collectives involved with various social struggles associated with the most deprived parts of society, and were at the forefront of popular assembles. At times, spatial strategies, actions and slogans were decided through direct democratic assemblies, while some of the action groups actually formed their political identities through these strategies of visibility. Walls near the centres of power, especially in the Buenos Aires area, were inscribed with political messages and symbols, and became part of the creative protest strategies of social movements fighting for social justice and civil rights.

In this climate, class- and work-related issues returned to the foreground of Argentinean politics. The resurgence of factories recovered by workers provided artists with an opportunity to publicly express denunciation, dissatisfaction or demands. Slogans like 'Work for all' and 'Being poor is not a crime' materialized the discontent of a movement of unemployed youth

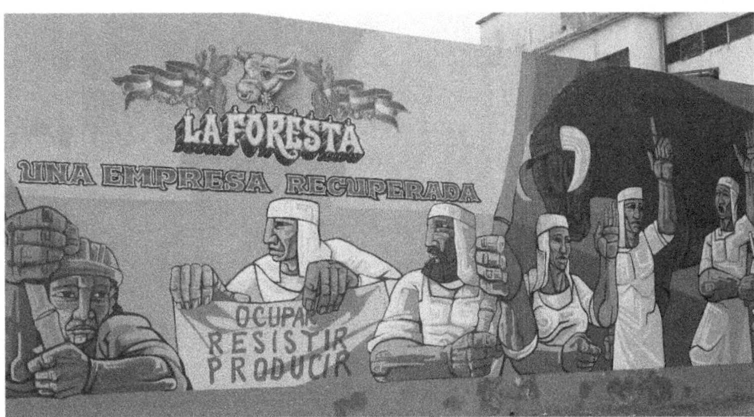

Figure 3.4 Mural in front of recuperated industrial slaughterhouse La Floresta, Buenos Aires. Photo: RECUPERAR blog under Creative Commons Licence.

and 'recuperated'[6] factory workers. Some *piquetero* fractions also made direct references to the Zapatistas' political vocabulary, and borrowed their organizational traits of what Holloway (2005) calls 'Zapatisto urbano' (Zibechi 2004).

The mural adorning Recuperated Slaughterhouse's La Foresta in La Matanza neighbourhood of Buenos Aires was made by Grupo de Arte Paredón y Después on the cooperative's second anniversary (2007), and is a striking example of street-level visual protest. The mural depicts La Foresta's workers, in whose hands the slaughter house has been self-managed since 2005 after it went bankrupt in 1999 leaving 185 of them without a job. After experimenting with different ideas, they eventually decided to occupy and self-manage the factory. The mural's workers have some indigenous characteristics and some European, a reminder of the multicultural character of Argentina as a mestizo (mixed blood) country. Street artists consider themselves *art workers* and not *artists*, underlying not just the aesthetic but also the political and ethical dimensions of street art, and its role in accompanying social movements' struggles (*Cultura y Trabajo* 2008). La Foresta is just one of the numerous social and solidarity economy initiatives that flourished in Argentina from 1999 onwards, and the slogan visible in the mural is that of the movement of recuperated factory workers 'OCCUPY, RESIST, PRODUCE', which was used years later by their counterparts at the recuperated Viome factory in Thessaloniki, Greece as well. Both examples show that in critical moments new forms of a collectively produced counterpublics emerged, dealing with what is possible to think, to feel and to challenge.

The Argentine crisis sparked women's street activism against patriarchy, sexual repression and masculinity, and brought to the foreground novel feminist counterpublics fighting for gender equity, social justice and human rights. Engaging with graffiti writing, feminist collectives subverted everyday gendered practices by displaying humorous, sarcastic and often transgressive slogans such as 'God is a woman, black, Jewish and lesbian', 'Woman building popular power', and 'Revolution in the home, in the plaza, and in the bed' (Borland and Sutton 2007).

According Anne Buckley (2014), graffiti played an important role not only during Argentina's return to democracy but also in the early years of Kirchnerism. The issue of the tortures and mass assassinations committed by the generals during the last military dictatorship was prominent on the Kirchners' political agenda, mainly because it did not affect the economy and was easier to push forward. Slogans like 'Never Again', images of General Videla to remind that the legacy of the dictatorship was still alive, and stencils of the iconic headscarves of Las Madres de la Plaza de Mayo were all over Buenos Aires and other major cities. In this vein, social movements visualized collectively held views and engaged in public political communication. By linking past heroic-tragic struggles with modern ones, these movements managed to represent themselves as the successors of past movements, thus gaining further political legitimacy.

Ryan (2013: 226) points out the affective imperative of graffiti in the context of the Argentinean peso crisis: painting the streets and leaving comments on the collective sufferings enabled politically committed writers to reimagine their responsibilities as creative citizens rather than as passive recipients. At the same time, however, flocks of 'activists-tourists' started arriving in Buenos Aires to get a glimpse of 'resistance', and they did not fail to notice the forms of creative protest that were evolving in the country. In this sense, '*turismo piquetero*' brought back home the images of Argentina's visual protest, rocketing several street artists to global fame and international exhibitions in Europe and the United States; this, however, eventually created tensions within the groups involved with political graffiti culture and other forms of creative protest (Ryan 2013: 219, 223).

Bolivia

In the landlocked Andean country of Bolivia, graffiti have been used as form of political expression in communities that face challenges in having their voices heard during periods of social tensions and civil unrest (Palmer 2017: 3665–66), and acquired an important role in social movements' tactical repertoires during anti-neoliberal protests in the late 1990s and early 2000s.

In the mid-1970s and under a number of dictatorial regimes that succeeded each other, political messages were regularly visible on the walls of La Paz, El Alto, Oruro, Potosì, Santa Cruz, Sucre, and other major urban centres. The slogans were unsigned in order to avoid the harsh punishment of the state, and mirrored the anti-imperialistic revolutionary climate of the era calling for resistance to the dictatorship. 'Freedom for the prisoners', 'Death to dictatorship', 'Death to US imperialism' and 'Viva la democracia' are some of the examples Ryan (2013: 124) cites. In post-dictatorship Bolivia, graffiti was even used as means of advertising by marketing firms, and at the same time anarcho-feminist groups like Mujeres Creando (Women [who are] Creating) sought to reappropriate public space promoting anti-patriarchal and anti-state artistic works. The logic was simple: if political parties and commercial enterprises can instrumentally use graffiti for propaganda or for profit-making purposes and it is socially tolerated, the same can be done by feminist movements struggling for sexual rights and gender self-determination.

Creative protest reappeared with renewed enthusiasm during the anti-neoliberal protests that eventually brought Evo Morales to power in the early 2000s. After the Water War of Cochabamba in April 2000, Bolivia witnessed five years of social and political unrest that toppled two presidents (in 2003 and 2005), which included another Water War and two Gas Wars over the ownership and management of the country's natural resources.[7] Bolivia's 'turbulent years'[8] culminated with the election of Morales to the country's presidential seat, becoming the first indigenous president in its history, even though roughly 60 per cent of its population self-identifies themselves as 'indigenous'. During this era, the country witnessed unprecedented levels of social mobilization that managed to overturn the privatization of public assets and resources such as water and gas. Cochabamba, the country's third biggest city, played a prominent role in these mobilizations, being the venue of the 2000 Water War as well as the closest city to Chapare, the region that gave birth to Evo Morales' Cocalero Movement.[9] The slogan 'Water is ours, damn it' was omnipresent in the streets of Cochabamba during the Water War; the same slogan together with the figure of Oscar Olivera, the spokesperson of the Coordinadora por la Defensa del Agua y la Vida, can still be seen in the streets of the city, keeping the memory of the movement alive.

Another example is the mural below (Figure 3.5) that, at least in 2013 (when this photo was taken), is decorating the streets of La Paz. It depicts La Paz as a big chessboard, with the main forces that were the protagonists of Bolivia's turbulent years moving towards the city: the coca growers under the banner 'La coca es nuestra', the COB (Central Obrera Boliviana – Central Bolivian Workers' Union), the FSTMB (Federaciòn Sindical de Trabajadores

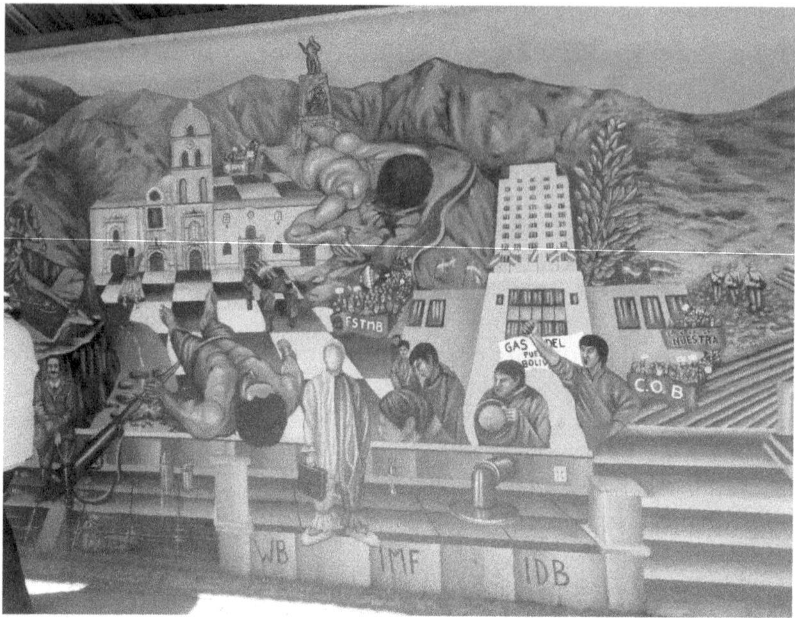

Figure 3.5 Mural commemorating the popular struggles during Bolivia's turbulent years, La Paz. © Leonidas Oikonomakis.

Mineros de Bolivia – Bolivian Miners' Syndical Federation), and of course the army and the state's repression in the image of the dead body and the funeral on the Plaza Mayor de San Francisco. Other issues at stake are also visible: the question of the ownership of natural gas in the banner 'Gas del Pueblo Boliviano' [the gas belongs to the Bolivian people], and of course the organizations that the Bolivians considered responsible for their sufferings at the time: the IMF, the World Bank and the Inter-American Development Bank (IDB). Images of indigenous peoples, coca leaves and gas pipelines are also present, as well as the images of a *payaso* (clown) representing either the political elites or the international organizations' officials, holding a suitcase full of money, undoubtedly a symbol of corruption.

As Lucia Mulherin Palmer (2017) notes, the local graffiti scene has a straightforward alignment with indigenous, feminist and anti-capitalist movements that employ micro-spatial tactics and influential modes of visual protest to affect political change. To this end, the bodies of predominantly indigenous women and children have been stencilled in life-sized portraits on columns in the plazas, displaying their resolute presence and reclaiming for them visibility and inclusion. Protesters created alternative public spaces in which indigenous activists could question liberal ideas of citizenship that do not guarantee liberty or equality, unsettle the idealized exclusionary visions of city planners, and challenge the invisibility of indigenous migrants and their exclusion from public space. In the same vein, feminist groups used familiar iconography to fight the patriarchal status quo and other structures of social exclusion (Palmer 2017: 3665–66). Graffitists materialized their opposition to the process of modernization and neoliberal enclosures of the commons, expressing solidarity with global anti-capitalist subcultures. They borrowed elements from famous artists such as Blek le Rat and Bansky, using words and images that are easily understood transnationally – for example, figures of rats to express metaphorically their protest against environmental and political corruption (ibid.: 3671).

Another prominent theme of creative protest in Bolivian streets is related to LGBTQ rights, evident in the creations of the anarcho-feminist group Mujeres Creando and the transgender group Familia Galán. Mujeres Creando consider themselves more as street agitators than artists, and embrace graffiti as an important part of their political action repertoire. For them, graffiti is an instrument of struggle and a visual sign of their identity (Rushmore 2013). Since these groups are some of the most active in Bolivia nowadays, it is no surprise that slogans like 'My body – my territory', 'Woman, I don't like it when you keep your mouth shut' and 'The street is my colourful home without a husband or bosses', appear more and more in the main cities, especially in La Paz, making the anarcho-feminist movement's struggle for recognition more visible. Although creative protest may have played a vital role in the cycle of protest that brought Morales to state power, it also turned against him in certain cases, such as the struggle against the government-backed TIPNIS highway that would cut through a national park whose indigenous population firmly resisted it. Therefore it is not rare to see graffiti and stencils against Morales nowadays, such as 'TIPNIS resist!' What goes around comes around applies also when it comes to creative protest.

The landscape of La Paz has been widely used as a means of political communication, not only by social movements but also by political parties. Groups like Los Torucos, for example, affiliated with the 'progressive' MAS, today's governing party, have been active in the city since 2004. Slogans like 'I love you MAS' and 'Out with USAID' have often appeared in La Paz or El Alto during this period. When Gustavo Torrico, an ex-MAS deputy who is involved with Los Torucos, was interviewed by Nicola Maksimovic regarding his view on graffiti, he highlighted both their political and aesthetic dimensions: 'What makes us happy is that we have revolutionized, but above all, reclaimed the streets as a political mural ... which can be opposed to or supportive of a political cause' (Maksimovic 2014).

Conclusion

To use Jameson's terms, in times of crisis, when 'the system really seems in the process of losing its legitimacy, when the ruling elite is palpably uncertain of itself and full of divisions and self-doubts, [and] when popular demand grows louder and more confident, then what also happens is that those grievances and demands grow more precise in their insistence and urgency' (Jameson 2004: 46). During highly repressive periods such as dictatorships (in all four of our case studies) and in civil wars (in Spain and Greece) graffiti was used by institutional forces to reinforce state control over public space, and also by grass-roots actors in the framework of anti-establishment protest. It was also used during the return to democracy as part of the politics of emancipation claiming the expansion of human rights and the democratization of important spheres of society. Political graffiti activism resurged again during the cycles of protest against austerity measures imposed, in all four cases, at different time periods.

Attempting to turn financial crisis into opportunity for political action, graffitists enacted their right to the city linking their small-scale tactical intervention in urban landscapes with wider social movement struggles towards a city free of enclosed spaces, where the public realm is freely available for non-commercial public address by any of the city's inhabitants (Iveson 2013: 953). In doing so, they reoccupied urban spaces, revealed the alternative city – that is aesthetically challenging and politically radical – within the existing city, and produced performative spaces of resistance during collectively shared events and through DIY practices in which active participation is exercised, and novel, playful and sometimes carnivalesque forms of protest are formulated.

Various forms of graffiti on the walls, ranging from aggressive and populist slogans to allusive, sarcastic and ironic catchphrases, and intriguing, elaborate and playful murals or stencils, witness the multiplicity of resistance measures and styles in the social movements' spatial strategies. They tend to reappropriate public space offering imaginaries of the elusive temporality of crisis associated 'with political affections, aesthetic energies and lines of desires' (Labrador Méntez 2015: 118). While the crisis facilitated the rise of xenophobic and racist graffiti as a cultural outlet of the emerging extreme-right discourse, especially in Greece and Spain, the vast majority of political graffiti seems to be focused on various anti-capitalist, anti-regime and libertarian discourses in struggles against racial, gender and sexual oppression and more aggressive forms of neoliberal capitalism.

Graffiti reflects the structures of feelings as they are actually experienced in everyday life (Williams 1977) under crisis circumstances. In a changing and uncertain society, voices on the walls reflect a scream of anguish and protest – a deeper existential anxiety of grass-roots actors to let their voices be heard. Performing as free-floating nomads, activists celebrate the subversive aura of ephemerality, illegality, anonymity and sarcasm of political graffiti, and employ everyday practices of commoning to build playful, smooth and 'sonorous' spaces that resist neoliberal acts of enclosure and dispossession, challenge the dominant crisis politics, and sometimes promote social imaginary towards an emancipated post-capitalist society beyond the present.

The study of protest graffiti offers us an anthropological journey in the untold stories, micropolitics and sites of resistance of urban social movements, unveiling affective intensities, existential quests, impulses and politics of utopia that lie behind the experiential worlds of street activism. In this vein, the space of political graffiti can be seen as a visual microhistory, a form of bellow associated with edgy vibes, and an overlooked and sometimes distasteful experience of the oppressed groups, providing us with an underground reading as well as an affective understanding of the circulating counterideologies of movements within cities of crisis (Avramides and Tsimpounidou 2017).

The heterogeneous cityscapes in critical times show the dialectic of compliance and opposition that takes into account the concealed and the visible, the scattered and the organized, and the nomad/smooth space of rhizomatic politics within the striated, fixed and ordered urbanity (Deleuze and Guattari 1988; Marche 2012: 87). Drawing on Deleuze and Guattari's writings, Fieni points out that walls symbolize not only forms of neocolonial exclusion, confinement or immobility generated as a function of race, class or gender, but also the very mobility of capital itself. Graffiti writings often scramble 'the codes used to negotiate the contradictions of capitalist democracies, evoking at once post-civilized wilderness and neo-tribal anarchist', as well as anti-systemic sentiments that challenge space surveillance, formal boundaries and dominant urban aesthetics. They hold up the possibility of breaking through this wall of the signifier, which is also the wall of capital's mobile inner limit (Fieni 2012: 88).

Although political graffiti is embedded in local and national sociopolitical social movements, often graffitists form connections with other graffiti cultures globally, making a 'networked social movement' that links up the cyberspace activism with local acts of creative resistance (Castells 2012; Davies 2017) and allows the circulation of creative visual protest worldwide. Specific examples of graffiti in this study reveal the nexus between the visual modalities of visual protest scenes in Latin America and Southern Europe. Within this distinctive global network of political graffiti, creative protest may, ironically enough, have opposite results to those intended. As Ryan

(2013, 2018) notes, the Argentinean cycle of protest created what is called 'turismo piquetero', whose cameras did not miss the new visual landscape that street art had created, catapulting certain artistic collectives to *Biennales* and other art festivals all over the Western world. The same is observed in the case of Bolivia, Greece and Spain: Athens has repeatedly been portrayed as 'the world graffiti capital' by various international media (and so has Madrid). 'Graffitourists' regularly visit the city not only to photograph but also to produce their own – usually crisis related – graffiti, unintentionally contributing in this way to the gentrification and touristification of certain cityscapes.

Despite these indirect effects though, what is certain is that visual protest poetically provides activists with an affective and effective means to creatively express sociopolitical content, reminding us that ideologies and politics reflect sentimental emotional investment. Since the role of visual protest in contentious politics has received little attention in social movement scholarship, further research on the across-time-and-space language of political graffiti may open up paths for a better understanding of the structures of feeling at the micro-level of experience in which the effects of power are felt (Foucault 1986).

Yiannis Zaimakis is Professor of Sociology of Culture and Local Societies, and Director of the Social Analysis and Applied Social Research Laboratory at the University of Crete. He publishes in the areas of sociology of popular music and rebetika, street activism and political graffiti, sport cultures and fandom identities, social and solidarity economy, and the politics of the commons. He coordinated the research programme 'Political and existential graffiti and voices of protest on urban landscapes in times of crises – Greece' and currently coordinates two research projects ('The many faces of "Trouba": A socio-cultural study of prostitution in Piraeus' red-light district in the Post-War years-Greece' and 'Need assessment and local value-system in Lasithi highland plateau – Crete').

Leonidas Oikonomakis holds a PhD in political and social sciences from the European University Institute. He is also affiliated with the Centre on Social Movement Studies (COSMOS) at the Scuola Normale Superiore. His research and teaching focuses on Latin American politics, social movements, autonomy, revolutions, electoral politics, development, and the commons. He is the author of the monograph *Political Strategies and Social Movements in Latin America: The Zapatistas and Bolivian Cocaleros* (Palgrave, 2019) and has published articles in international journals, as well as chapters in edited volumes on social movements in Latin America and Southern Europe.

Notes

1. See, for example, Chaffee 1993; Marche 2012; Ryan 2013, 2018; Waldner and Dobratz 2013; Campos 2016; Rolston and Berastegi 2016; Zaimakis 2016; and Palmer 2017.
2. Many political graffiti photos are found in the C. Papoutsakis and A. Baharian's collection 'Art in Resistance', available in the Contemporary Social History Archives (ASKI) in Athens.
3. WD (Wild Drawings) is a politicized street artist from Indonesia who has lived in Athens during the austerity period.
4. The song was set in music by the famous militant composer Mikis Theodorakis in 1961.
5. He is a street artist who has been involved with spatial tactics of anti-racist, antifascist and counter-globalization movements.
6. In Latin America, the phrase recuperated factories/companies (*fábricas/empresas recuperadas*) refers to the occupied-by-their-workers factories/companies – normally after their bankruptcy – in order to keep producing under communal worker ownership (Ruggeri 2014).
7. The two Water Wars, in Cochabamba (2000) and El Alto (2005), refer to the privatizations of the two municipality water companies, and the counter-movements that emerged and managed eventually to overturn them. The two Gas Wars refer to the effort by the Bolivian state to build a pipeline through Chile for the exportation of Bolivian gas to the United States, which was heavily protested against (2003) and evolved into a demand for gas nationalization (2005).
8. For a more detailed analysis, see Oikonomakis and Espinoza 2014.
9. The social movement of coca leaf growers that demanded the legalization of coca leaf production, the end of repression against the producers, and the leaf's disassociation from cocaine in government policy. The Six Federations of the Tropics of Cochabamba is the cocalero organization that Evo Morales led and is still leading, which eventually brought him to the presidential seat of Bolivia.

References

Avramides, K., and M. Tsilimpounidi. 2017. 'Graffiti and Street Art: Reading, Writing and Representing the City', in K. Avramides and M. Tsilimpounidi (eds), *Graffiti and Street Art: Reading, Writing and Representing the City*. New York: Routledge, pp. 1–24.

Bassets, L. 2008. 'Clandestine Communication: Notes on the Press and Propaganda of the Anti-Franco Resistance, 1939–1975'. *Studies in Language & Capitalism* 3(4): 21–39.

Blitzer, J. 2012. 'The Writing on the Walls'. *Latitude* (blog). 19 June 2012. Retrieved 3 December 2018 from https://latitude.blogs.nytimes.com/2012/06/19/reading-spains-economic-woes-in-graffiti/.

Borland, E., and B. Sutton. 2007. 'Quotidian Disruption and Women's Activism in Times of Crisis, Argentina 2002–03'. *Gender and Society* 21(5): 700–22.

Buckley, A. 2014. 'Self-Expression in Spray Paint: Graffiti as a Popular Tool for Democratization in Argentina'. Unpublished thesis. Boulder: University of Colorado.

Campos, R. 2016. 'From Marx to Merkel: Political Muralism and Street Art in Lisbon', in J. Ross (ed.), *Routledge Handbook of Graffiti and Street Art*. London: Routledge, pp. 301–17.

Carrington, V. 2009. '"I Write, Therefore I Am": Texts in the City'. *Visual Communication* 8(4): 409–25.

Castells, M. 2012. *Networks of Outrage and Hope: Social Movements in the Internet Age*. Cambridge: Polity Press.

Chaffee, L.G. 1988. 'Social Conflict and Alternative Mass Communications: Public Art and Politics in the Service of Spanish-Basque Nationalism'. *European Journal of Political Research* 16: 545–72.

———. 1993. *Political Protest and Street Art: Popular Tools for Democratization in Hispanic Countries*. Westport, CT: Greenwood Press.

Cultura y Trabajo. 2008. 'Trabajadores del arte, primera entrega: "Paredón y después"'. *Cultura y Trabajo* (blog), 11 August 2008. Retrieved 9 March 2019 from http://culturaytrabajo.blogspot.com/2008/08/trabajadores-del-arte-primera-entrega.html.

Davies, D. 2017. '"Walls of Freedom": Street Art and Structural Violence in the Global City'. *Rupkatha Journal of Intersciplinary Studies in Humanities* IX(2): 6–18.

Deleuze, G., and F. Guattari. 1988. *A Thousand Plateaus: Capitalism and Schizophrenia II*. London: Athlone.

Della Porta, D. 2015. *Social Movements in Times of Austerity: Bringing Capitalism Back into Protest Analysis*. Malden, MA: Polity Press.

Diani, M., and M. Kousis. 2012. 'The Duality of Claims and Events: The Greek Campaign against the Troika Memoranda and Austerity, 2010–2012'. *Mobilization: An International Quarterly* 19(4): 387–404.

Escobar, A. 2010. 'Latin America at a Crossroads: Alternative Modernizations, Post-Liberalism, or Post-Development?' *Cultural Studies* 24(1): 1–65.

Fieni, D. 2016. 'Tagging the Spectral Mobility of the Stateless Body: Deleuze, Stasis, and Graffiti'. *Journal for Cultural Research* 20(4): 350–65.

Fieni, D. 2012. 'What a Wall Wants, or How Graffiti Thinks: Nomad Grammatology in the Frence Banlieue', *Diacritics* 40(2): 72–93.

Flemming, J. 2001. *Graffiti and the Writings Arts of Early Modern England*. Philadelphia: University of Pennsylvania Press.

Foucault, M. 1986. 'Polemics, Politics and Problematizations: An Interview', in P. Rabinow (ed.), *The Foucault Reader*. London: Penguin, pp. 381–90.

Gerbaudo, P. (ed.). 2012. *Tweets and the Streets: Social Media and Contemporary Activism*. New York: Pluto Press.

———. 2017. 'The Indignant Citizen: Anti-Austerity Movements in Southern Europe and the Anti-oligarchic Reclaiming of Citizenship'. *Social Movements Studies* 16(1): 36–50.

Halvorsen K. 2016. 'Economic, Financial, and Political Crisis and Well-Being in the PIGS-Countries', *SAGE Open* 6(4): 1–13.

Harvey, D. 2013. *Rebel Cities: From the Right to the City to the Urban Revolution*. London: Verso.

Holloway, J. 2005. 'Zapatismo Urbano'. *Humboldt Journal of Social Relations* 29(1): 168–78.

Iveson, K. 2013. 'Cities within the City: Do-It-Yourself Urbanism and the Right to City'. *City* 37(3): 941–56.

Jameson, F. 2004. 'The Politics of Utopia'. *New Left Review* 25: 35–73.

Johnson, P. 2006. 'Unravelling Foucault's "Different Spaces"'. *History of the Human Sciences* 19(4): 75–90.

Klein, N. 2008. *The Shock Doctrine: The Rise of Disaster Capitalism*. New York: Picador.

Knight, D., and C. Stewart. 2016. 'Ethnographies of Austerity: Temporality, Crisis and Affect in Southern Europe'. *History and Anthropology* 27(1): 1–18.

Labrador Méntez, G.L. 2014. 'The Cannibal Wave: The Cultural Logic of Spain's Temporality of Crisis (Revolution, Biopolitics, Hunger and Memory)'. *Journal of Spanish Cultural Studies* 15(1–2): 241–71.

———. 2015. 'They Call It Democracy? The Aesthetic Politics of the Spanish Transition to Democracy and Some Collective Hijackings of History after the 15M Movements'. *Historein* 15(1): 117–54.

Lefebvre, H. 2003. *The Urban Revolution*. Minneapolis: University of Minessota Press.

Levitas, R. 2003. 'Introduction: The Elusive Idea of Utopia'. *History of the Human Sciences* 16: 1–10.

Levitsky, S. 2003. *Transforming Labor-Based Parties in Latin America: Argentine Peronism in Comparative Perspective*. Cambridge: Cambridge University Press.

Maksimovic, N. 2014. 'The Street Art of La Paz'. *Bolivian Express*, 26 September 2014. Retrieved 30 August 2018 from http://www.bolivianexpress.org/blog/posts/the-street-art-of-la-paz.

Marche, G. 2012. 'Expressivism and Resistance: Graffiti as an Infrapolitical Form of Protest against the War on Terror'. *Revue Française d'Etudes Américaines* 131: 78–97.

Martin García, O.J. 2014. 'Soft Repression and the Current Wave of Social Mobilization in Spain'. *Social Movements Studies* 13(2): 303–8.

Mayorga, F. 2012. *Estado, Ampliacion de La Democracia y Disputa Politica: Bolivia 2000–2010*. Cochabamba: CESU-UMSS.

Novy, J., and C. Colomb. 2013. 'Struggling for the Right to the (Creative) City in Berlin and Hamburg: New Urban Social Movements, New "Spaces of Hope"?' *International Journal of Urban and Regional Research* 37(5): 1816–38.

Oikonomakis, L., and F. Espinoza. 2014. 'Bolivia: MAS and the Movements That Brought It to State Power', in R. Stahler-Sholk, H.E. Vanden and M. Becker (eds), *Rethinking Latin American Social Movements: Radical Action from Below*. London: Rowman & Littlefield, pp. 285–307.

Paento, P. 1997. 'Political Mobilisation and Place-Specificity: Radical Nationalist Street Campaigning in the Spanish Basque Country'. *Space & Polity* 1(2): 191–204.

Palmer, L.M. 2017. 'Rhizomatic Writings on the Wall: Graffiti and Street Art in Cochabamba, Bolivia, as Nomadic Visual Politics'. *International Journal of Communication* 11: 3655–84.

Payne, S. 1987. *El Regime de Frunco, 1936–1975*. Madrid: Alianza Editorial.

Rolston, B., and A.A. Berastegi. 2016. 'Taking Murals Seriously: Basque Murals and Mobilisation'. *International Journal of Politics, Culture and Society* 29: 33–56.

Romanos, E. 2016. 'No es una crisis, es que ya no te quiero': Humor y protesta en el movimiento 15M'. *Revista Internacional de Sociología* 74(3): 1–13.

Roos, J., and L. Oikonomakis. 2014. 'They Don't Represent Us! The Global Resonance of the Real Democracy Movement from the Indignados to Occupy', in D. della

Porta and A. Mattoni (eds), *Spreading Protest Social Movements in Times of Crisis*. Colchester: ECPR Press, pp. 117–36.

Ruggeri, A. 2014. 'Infome del IV relevamiento de Empresas Recuperadas en la Argentina: Las empresas recuperadas en el período 2010–2013'. Open Faculty Programme, SEUBE Faculty of Philosophy and Letters, University of Buenos Aires.

Ruiz, P. 2013. 'Revealing Power: Masked Protest and the Blank Figure'. *Cultural Politics* 9(3): 263–79.

Rushmore, R.J. 2013. '*Mujeres Creando*'s Feminist Graffiti in Bolivia' – Vandalog: A Street Art Blog. Retrieved 10 October 2018 from https://blog.vandalog.com/2013/12/28/mujeres-creandos-feminist-graffiti-in-bolivia/.

Ryan, H. 2013. 'Bringing the Visual into Focus: Street Art and Contentious Politics in Brazil, Bolivia and Argentina'. Unpublished doctoral thesis. City University, London.

———. 2018. *Political Street Art: Communication, Culture and Resistance in Latin America*. London: Routledge.

Schuster, G. 2015. 'The Concept of the Visible between Art and Politics'. *Latin American Perspectives* 42(1): 84–94.

Sitrin, M. 2006. *Horizontalism: Voices of Popular Power in Argentina*. Edinburgh: AK Press.

Sitrin, M., and D. Azzelini. 2014. *They Can't Represent Us!: Reinventing Democracy from Greece to Occupy*. London: Verso.

Sotirakopoulos, N., and G. Sotiropoulos. 2013. 'Direct Democracy Now: The Greek Indignados and the Present Cycle of Struggles'. *Current Sociology* 61: 443–56.

Stavrides, S. 2014. 'Emerging Common Spaces as a Challenge to the City of Crisis'. *City* 18(4–5): 546–50.

Thomas, R., and A. Davies. 2005. 'Theorizing the Micro-politics of Resistance: New Public Management and Managerial Identities in the UK Public Services'. *Organization Studies* 26(5): 683–706.

Tolonen, J. 2017. 'Power of Paint: Political Street Art Confronts the Authorities'. *Street Art & Urban Creativity Scientific Journal* 3(2): 20–30.

Waldner, L., and B. Dobratz. 2013. 'Graffiti as a Form of Contentious Political Participation'. *Sociology Compass* 7(5): 377–89.

Webber, J.R. 2013. 'From Left-Indigenous Insurrection to Reconstituted Neoliberalism in Bolivia: Political Economy, Indigenous Liberation, and Class Struggle, 2000–2011', in J.R. Webber and B. Carr (eds), *The New Latin American Left: Cracks in the Empire*. Lanham, MD: Rowman & Littlefield, pp. 149–89.

Webber, J.R., and B. Carr (eds). 2013. *The New Latin American Left: Cracks in the Empire*. Lanham, MD: Rowman & Littlefield.

Webber, J.R. 2017. *The Last Day of Oppression, and the First Day of the Same: The Politics and Economics of the New Latin American Left*. Chicago: Haymarket Books.

Williams, R. 1977. *Marxism and Literature*. Oxford: Oxford University Press.

Zaimakis, Y. 2015. 'Welcome to the Civilization of Fear': On Political Graffiti Heterotopias in Greece in Times of Crisis'. *Visual Communication* 14(4): 373–96.

———. 2016. 'Youth Precariat Worlds and Protest Graffiti in the Dystopia of the Greek Economic Crisis: A Cross-Disciplinary Perspective'. *Punctum* 2(2): 66–84.

———. 2018. 'Football Fan Culture and Politics in Modern Greece: The Process of Fandom Radicalization during the Austerity Era'. *Soccer & Society* 19(2): 252–70.

Zamora-Kapoor, A., and X. Coller. 2014. 'The Effects of the Crisis: Why Southern Europe?' *American Behaviour Studies* 58(12): 1511–16.

Zibechi, R. 2004. 'Que hay en comun entre piqueteros y zapatistas?' *Rebeldia* 24: 54–61.

Chapter 4

Between the Workshop and the Streets

Graphic Activism and the Student Movement in Chile (2008–2018)

*Javiera Manzi, Matías Marambio,
Isidro Parraguez and María Yaksic*

Introduction

The most recent cycle of social revolt in Chile has once again brought to the foreground the silent but productive relation between graphics and social mobilization (Sontag 1970).[1] Alongside a diverse repertoire of collective actions (strikes, occupation of schools and public spaces, marches, *funas,*[2] etc.), graphic production during this period has permeated the cities of our country with posters whose continuities and breaks allow us to offer a reading of this cycle of protest, which identifies social imaginaries and modes of production that resonate with a long history of social struggle in Chile.

The purpose of this chapter is to present some of the discussions of the Núcleo Gráfica y Movilización Estudiantil (Graphics and Student Movement Research Group, NGME), a space for activist and interdisciplinary research harboured in the University of Chile, and with a very close connection to the archive of the university's student union. The chapter presents some elaborations on a selection of posters produced in the decade 2008–2018, focusing on the link between graphics and politics manifest in their visuality, forms of organization, and uses of public space. We are not only interested in the images, languages and materiality of these posters, but are also drawn to the complex fabric of social relations that enable their production, reproduction and circulation in urban public spaces.

The graphic production we have decided to interrogate constitutes an interesting expression of contemporary visual political imagination. It tries out new social and productive relations in a local and global context characterized by crisis. The link between political graphic languages and the occupations (or reappropriations) of the public in the city situates the urban as a space of struggle for the different meanings of the common and the collective. This articulation between urban activism and counter-hegemonic agendas (against neoliberalism, imperialism, patriarchy, neocolonialism, etc.) can be framed within a global circuit of crisis and discontent, as suggested by Iveson (2013: 946). However, our reading does not suggest that the student movement is an immediate consequence of the global crisis. We argue that it answers to a specific history (almost forty years in the making) of resistance to and contestation of neoliberalism in Chile, and as such it helps us to understand the resurgence of visual activism.

The reflections we present here deal with the graphic production of some of the collectives and propaganda brigades founded during this recent cycle, which, in their way, return to and reposition the place of manual, collective and collaborative production that has historically been characteristic of Chilean political graphics. In this sense, we expect to point out some of the characteristics that distinguish graphic production in its relation to public space, as well as the different forms of appropriation of the city in the framework of recent protests.

The political poster coexists with a heterogeneous variety of visual objects, each with their own patterns of production and circulation. With different formal properties, they make up a constellation of outlines and images on the city walls; older forms, such as the mural, share their place with newer ones, like stencils and stickers. As a long-established technique in Latin America, including Chile, mural painting has its own forms of expression and ways of organizing. It combines the work of brigades and collectives with murals authored by recognizable artists (like Mono González and Inti), combining street art and politics. This prominent place at the intersection of culture and politics has made mural painting a more widely studied practice than serigraphy, both as a technique and in its connection to political interventions in the city.

We first offer a historical background of dictatorship and post-dictatorship Chile, linked to two problems: the political system and urban politics. Then we characterize the Chilean student movement as a contestation of neoliberalism and post-dictatorship politics. In the next section, we reconstitute the trajectory of the intersection between graphics and politics, and then move to the more recent history of graphic collectives linked to the student movement. We first discuss their forms of organization and production, then we analyse the visual and material dimensions of their posters, and finally we concentrate on the circulation of images in urban public space. Graphic brigades and collectives have, in their way, reinstated forms of production that, located in this new cycle of struggle, reoccupy the streets and the city, interrupting traditional forms of control of urban space that hail back to the dictatorship and the neoliberal transition.

More specifically, we propose to interrogate the centrality held by screen printing in the student movement. This printing technique is not a novelty, but rather connects with a graphic tradition of social movements in Chile, which makes it a manual trade practised collectively. The serigraphic production of the collectives we will engage with (Taller de Serigrafía Instantánea, Estudiantes por Chile, Taller Mano Alzada, the Brigada de Propaganda Feminista, and Ser & Gráfica) delineates the visual grammars of social movements in Chile. Serigraphy, therefore, works as both a technique of production and as a way in which the politics of graphic communication uphold the artisanal, the collective and the collaborative. This leads us to think that we are dealing with the formation of a graphic field, whose community of agents start to acquire a relative autonomy from other intersections between arts and politics during this period.

Our reflections emerge from a space of articulation and research that is an active part of these protests and of graphic communication itself. We are part of this organized world that for a decade now has created new forms of action and mobilization. Far from being problematic, this proximity integrates us in an activist research exercise involved with social protest, where both they and the graphic production we are interested in are in no way foreign objects, but are part of our everyday landscape of debates – a landscape we have taken part in and whose history, knowledge and archive we are enthused by in so far as it activates itself as a graphic memory of the present. We, like this graphic production, also locate ourselves in this interstitial place: between the archive and the streets.

Historical Background:
Student Protests in the Neoliberal City

Transition and Post-dictatorship Politics

The graphic production we are interested in inscribes itself in a wider socio-political process that explains the character of the demands pushed by social movements in recent Chilean history, especially the student movement and the struggles for the recovery of social rights. The Chilean transition to democracy was characterized by a transaction between the expectations of governance of the centre-left Concertación coalition, and the veto power exercised by the political right. This resulted in four consecutive Concertación governments, and then an alternation in government with the parties on the right. The continuity of the political system and the deepening or 'correction' of the neoliberal economic model were decisive during this period (Garretón 2012). Here we see the development of an economy based on outsourcing, the expansion of the extractive sector based on the export of commodities, and a growing privatization of social reproduction (education, health care, pensions, housing) that generated strong setbacks in basic social rights (Ruiz and Boccardo 2014). This came with a political model that survives to this day, characterized by a limited participation of civil society and a privileged position for right and centre-left political elites. This model has been designated 'the politics of compromise' (*la política de los acuerdos*) – in other words, a model that tends to minimize or exclude social conflict as a part of political life, and to favour a pretended stability and governance (Moulian 1997; Portales 2000; Garretón 2012).

Under these conditions, the student movement had moments of rapprochement and distance with the ruling coalition, and tried different alternatives to organize the mobilization of university and secondary school students (Boccardo 2016). According to Thielemann (2016), to achieve such goals, the rearticulation of student unions and federations was decisive. Political organization materialized a wide process of politicization that ran contrary to the political imaginaries and repertoires of action of the ruling sectors of society. This process generated zones of friction and ideological conflict between student organizations and the hegemonic political system. Although clearly located on the left, these organizations represented a coalition of heterogeneous political traditions, including anti-authoritarian groups, the Communist Party Youth, democratic socialists, libertarian communists, remnants of radical anti-dictatorship organizations, anti-globalization movements, intersectional collectives, and other groupings of the left that did not participate widely in parliamentary politics.

During the first two decades of this century, students have channelled an ever-growing critical discourse on the effects of neoliberalism in education. One can observe this in the arguments that challenge the post-dictatorship order. If early on the aims of the student movement were related to concrete demands such as an increase in funding for scholarships and loans, or a differentiated fare for public transport, we now observe the appearance of more structural critiques: the rejection of market education, of profit-making as the education system's premise, the demand for universal free education, and the defence of quality state-run education (Boccardo 2016). This increase in critical potential is not the result of a linear and inevitable trajectory, but rather points to the fact that, despite reforms led by the

Concertación governments, the infrastructure of neoliberal education was not altered, but deepened. Some landmarks show the student movement's potential to broaden its critical horizons and to move the limits of the possible to the point of modifying the terms of political discussion in the country.

Even though 2011 was the year in which the student movement escalated towards a political crisis that was unprecedented during the post-dictatorship period (and therefore is better known internationally), what challenged the education system and the political horizon of the transition to democracy was a politicization cycle almost a decade in the making. Its first moment happened in 2001. That year the protests known as the *mochilazo* took place – a movement around the value and functioning of the national student card (Tarjeta Nacional Estudiantil, TNE). These protests constitute a landmark because they expressed the broader social reach of the conflict when compared to previous occasions. They also transformed the organizations and institutions of secondary students, favouring more horizontal coordinating mechanisms and a political autonomy from traditional parties (Boccardo 2016: 90). On this basis, in 2006 and 2011 heavy protests by secondary and university students took place, channelling with more strength and direction the accumulated frustrations caused by the transition to democracy and the consolidation of the economic model (Boccardo 2016). The demands not only focused on specific objectives (like the TNE), but also on the strengthening of public education and statutory reform, and even a demand for the renationalization of natural resources to finance such a platform. These protests rose to prominence due to their massive scale and the multiple uses of public space, which, in a certain way, suspended the reigning atmosphere of a demobilized civil society. The occupation of institutions (government buildings, schools and universities) and demonstrations through the main streets of Santiago and other cities in the country inaugurated a new scene for conflict and a novel political imagination.

The occupation of educational establishments as a pressure strategy posited by the student movement entailed micro- and macro-political challenges: the *toma* (occupation) is a space where new social relations, new activisms, new identities, and a new political imaginary are tried out, often involving the politicization of everyday life by turning these spaces into laboratories for new experiences in the use of the city. In this sense, the experiences of 2006 and 2011 demonstrate that the occupied institution serves, firstly, as a site for the organization of protest and as a rearguard when facing police violence. Occupied territories become political schools that assemble discourses on territorial autonomy and the construction of community power that echo other national[3] and Latin American critiques of neoliberalism that have placed territory and space as their gravitational centres (Svampa 2008, 2015).

Transition and Post-dictatorship: The City

Indeed, the city in which this graphic production is displayed bears the marks of a complex history that is embodied both in its urban landscape and in its uses in a city ruled by the logic of social atomization and by real-estate market values instead of the commons and the public. We locate our research in Santiago, the capital of Chile, a city that, on the one hand, like many of its Latin American counterparts, is constituted by a 'neoliberal urbanism' (Pintos qtd. in Svampa and Viale 2014: 257), and on the other, is the contemporary heir of the post-dictatorship political model. Therefore, we observe a clear tendency towards the deregulation of real-estate markets, the weakening of state-led social housing policies, and the proliferation of spaces for consumption that perform the function of social reproduction, led by profit making rather than the safekeeping of public goods – that is, a city that does not embody the expectations of a desirable everyday life, but the exclusion of social relations based on collective principles (Harvey 2005: 20). Urban policies developed since the 1980s, amid the dictatorship, consolidated a fragmented city, with forced displacements of the urban poor and high levels of segregation between affluent zones and working-class neighbourhoods that reinforce centre–periphery relations (Márquez 2017).

Another 'dictatorial inheritance' is the enclosure of public spaces owing to the suspicions raised by the presence of civil society, as well as a continuity in the policies of repression regarding political appropriations of the urban surroundings (Delamaza 2011). Thus, the singularity of the Chilean way towards democracy is expressed in a city that mistrusts protests and that keeps a strong shutdown of 'unauthorized' uses of public space to this day. Many regulations still exist that back the repression of protest, and there is also an unusual caution by politicians in the exercise of civil control over police authority. Under such circumstances, it is not possible to speak of an effective right to protest because of statutes that obstruct public demonstrations or facilitate their repression (cf. INDH 2015).

Therefore, the discussion regarding a right to the city (Harvey 2012) must bear in mind this complex articulation of urban public space. The use of the streets constitutes the most palpable expression of the recovery of social rights lost during the dictatorship, but also a demand for a right to the occupation of public space that works as a strategic link in the critique of the neoliberalization of urban and everyday life. In those places where the city is managed by real-estate speculation and the restriction of collective rights during the dictatorship, the city obtains a density as a stage for the struggle around the commons and the recovery of spaces for social protest. In this sense, even when we are dealing with artistic and cultural forms of protest, the political coordinates of the post-dictatorship are at stake (Pinochet Cobos 2016).

Social Movements and the Student Movement

The attempts by social and political organizations to occupy the city come into conflict with its neoliberal geography and the subjects produced by it. However, the student movement is not the only example in Chile of critiques of neoliberalism that involve a spatial turn. We are thinking of the inhabitants of the poorest neighbourhoods of the city, known as *pobladores* (Pérez 2017), environmental movements from regions outside the capital, and movements with a national scope, such as national workers movements against labour precariousness, and fronts for pension reform (cf. UNDP 2015). In this scenario, since the 1990s the *mapuche* organizations have played a special role against extractive capitalism (Pairicán 2014). More recently, the later stages of this protest cycle have been defined by the work of feminist movements and their vindication of a politics that foregrounds the links between the patriarchal order and post-dictatorship politics. Here a convergence with the student movement has been a key element that has forced student organizations to elaborate an agenda that deals specifically with issues related to gender and sexuality (Follegatti 2018). This has been a characteristic note since 2011, with a recent feminist revolt in 2018 against sexual harassment and the reproduction of gender hierarchies in educational spaces.

This climate of protests has its own symbolic languages and mechanisms in various fields. We believe that graphic production constitutes a node for several facets of this political configuration. In a city where the public landscape is besieged by the images of advertising, to the detriment of other forms of public visuality, graphic forms of communication set up on the streets participate in a struggle entailing both the concept of the public and the legitimate languages and discourses that circulate in urban space. Hence, the place of graphics and images in this context is of special relevance: we observe a graphic production in action that produces its own visual languages and grammars against the grain of actually existing neoliberal visuality, recognizing the different levels at stake in this struggle.

Graphics and Social Protest in Chile

Historical Trajectories

Since the late nineteenth century, print propaganda has been a 'medium of political expression' (Rivera-Scott 2010: 11) by subaltern groups that have constructed popular imaginaries that refer to different moments in national history (Castillo 2010). Multiple means of graphic communication emanate from processes of protest – posters, pamphlets, periodicals and magazines – and they generate a visual trail that participates in social struggles from below. Within this repertoire, posters have been one of the mediums with more continuity and visual power in the spreading of slogans and the circulation of contested images.

In the 1960s and 1970s, graphics had a central role in election propaganda and the promotion of left-wing political formations, as well as in the communication of projects of democratization at the time. The agrarian reform, the university reform and the 'Chilean road to socialism'[4] deployed their own 'graphic utopia' (Cristi and Manzi 2016: 32) under the wing of design practices and university workshops that hailed to the communicational needs of the Unidad Popular government. In this context, more than a means for the reproduction of images, graphics constituted a model of 'visual pedagogy' (ibid.) conceived to strengthen the identification of the people with ideas of transformation. Despite its early interruption due to the military coup in 1973, the massiveness of poster making – as well as the broad unfolding of images in the editorial and discographic industries and the work of muralist brigades – constructed a visual stage for the masses that impacted the forms and uses of public space. Screen printing, and especially photo serigraphy, directly affected local poster making, with a widespread use of high contrast photographs and CMYK printing. The main sources of inspiration for this production were the visuality promoted by mural-painting brigades, the tradition of social engraving, as well as Cuban posters and North American pop (Vico and Osses 2009). They allowed for the creation of a 'closed form, high contrast, flat inks, irregular shapes, and the manual outline of characters' (Castillo 2010: 113). The most influential and prolific work of the period's print visual culture was carried out by design practices such as those of Vicente and Antonio Larrea, Mario Quiroz and Waldo González, as well the Graphics Workshop of the Universidad Técnica del Estado.

With the coup, the military junta presided by Augusto Pinochet interrupted civil life by silencing any trace of the previous regime that seemed to pose a symbolic threat. Cleansing campaigns were put into place in many cities (Errázuriz 2009), aimed at purging political signs and blocking uses of public space (e.g. raids of cultural institutions, book burnings on the streets, wiping out of murals made by left-wing brigades). Print propaganda was persecuted early on: military decrees threatened trial in military courts for those who were 'caught printing or distributing subversive propaganda'.[5] In this context, graphic production became a practice of resistance. Many popular organizations and artists' collectives took up graphic design and printing with the aim of building clandestine means of communication and agitation to denounce the regime's violence, and to promote the artistic networks and cultural spaces that were run to counter the so-called 'cultural blackout' (Cristi and Manzi 2016). Amongst these, the work of the Agrupación de Plásticos Jóvenes (Young Visual Artists Group) and the graphics workshop at the Centro Cultural Tallersol (Tallersol Cultural Centre) turned graphics into a collective activity in collaboration with unions, leftist parties, human rights groups, student groups, city-dweller organizations, and cultural centres.

Political graphic communication combined underground circulation with minimal printing resources, and was distributed by those who integrated the networks of resistance. Posters tended to be produced monochromatically and ventured into experimentation with scarce resources in the context of open workshops intended to divulge the trade of graphic production. We observe the recovery of artisanal printing technologies like home-made mimeographs and the insistence in serigraphy as a tool that allowed printing at differently scaled workshops. In some cases, the alliances with certain printing presses made offset printing possible, as well as paper matrixes introduced by these groups as an innovation of their own. Photocopying was heavily used owing to its low cost and the multiplication of copying centres during the 1980s, with xerography as an experimental turn of this technique (Cristi and Manzi 2016).

Graphics and the Student Movement

In the early 2000s, the student movement in Chile resumed a public and massive use of political graphics. Inside its technical, visual and ideological heterogeneity we distinguish two main modulations between graphics and politics: first, a push in communication coming from student unions and political organizations that pressed for a significant development of printings (usually in offset) and virtual images as tools for agitation and propaganda; and secondly, a politicization of graphic production in the practices of students in the fields of art and design, as well as self-taught creators. The second case comprised workshops, collectives and brigades whose mode of insertion into the student movement came from their aesthetic and political work, mainly in serigraphy and woodcuts (Manzi, Olmedo and Yaksic 2016).

As a communication tool for students, graphics appear in the early 2000s, when autonomous student groups emerged and transformed it into one their main means for the communication of demands and struggles in the face of a heavy blockade by the traditional news media. Mainstream newspapers and television networks echoed hegemonic political interpretations of student protest, and tended to frame them as violent, disorganized or illegitimate, especially when forms of direct democracy or assembly-based organization were involved. Digital social networks (like Fotolog, Blogspot, Facebook, Instagram and Twitter, depending on the generation) were the most visible ways of communicating demands. They mixed pop culture and politics, virtual communities and lived experience, and had the possibility of going viral because of their circulation in certain political contexts.

Put into perspective, one of the characteristics that distinguished the student movement was its nationwide articulation through federations that linked student unions at university and secondary education level. Federations agreed on the dates for national protests, the strategies of action, and the distribution of thousands of posters. The massive scale of poster production coming from federations and unions allowed for the appearance of nationally shared visual languages and imaginaries. The complexity of this task was taken up by specialized groups within federations, who reached some level of professionalism. In the case of the University of Chile, this phenomenon emerged with the formation of the Secretaría Abierta de Comunicaciones (Open Secretariat for Communications), later renamed the Comisión de Comunicaciones (Communications Committee), with membership comprising students of design and other fields. In the case of the secondary student federation, the organization chose an activist designer who produced its official posters for several years, and whose signature was La Éspora Creatividad.

Parallel to these processes of articulation, we observe the configuration of a practice that constituted a form of 'graphic activism' (Siganevich and Nieto 2017: 10–12), coming not from already-constituted political organizations, but from groups that decided to gear their graphic practice towards social movements. This collective practice recovered the tactics of 'graphic resistance' (Cristi and Manzi 2016) of the dictatorship, not only because of the posters' political contents, but also due to the collaborative and collective forms of organizing visual production in a dialogue with social and political movements. Following Ana Longoni, we conceive of these experiences as 'productions and actions, often collective ones, that tap into artistic resources with the intent of positioning themselves in and influencing the terrain of the political' (Longoni 2009: 18).[6] They are collectives integrated by arts and design students, gathered around a defence of manual gestures, as opposed to industrial production, and workshop methodologies that activate the memory of printing trades from earlier decades that we described above. It is interesting to highlight the way in which serigraphy is one of the most used techniques, with widespread use during the last fifteen years of student protests, to the point that it has become a fundamental part of the movement's visual identity.

Amongst these collectives, several stand out: Taller de Serigrafía Instantánea (Instantaneous Serigraphy Workshop, TSI, 2010), initially composed of design students from the Metropolitan Technological University; Estudiantes por Chile (Students for Chile, 2008); Taller Mano Alzada (Freehand Workshop, 2011), integrated by design students at the University of Chile; Brigada de Propaganda Feminista (Feminist Propaganda Brigade, BPF, 2016), with women members who come from various organizations and institutions; Ser & Gráfica (Being and Graphics, 2017), a collective by two school teachers of arts and biology; and Seri-Insurgentes (Seri-Insurgents, 2015–17), comprising secondary students. We propose to read this field of image-production along the lines of Deborah Poole's study of visual economies (Poole 1997: 9–11). Interlocking levels of production, circulation and exchange are involved in the activity of graphic collectives, giving birth to an 'image world' constituted by 'a combination of … relationships of referral and exchange among images themselves, and the social and discursive relations connecting image-makers and consumers' (ibid.: 7).

Political conflict both mediates and is modified by the visual economy in which graphic collectives participate – here, the field of student graphic production becomes an experience of political subject-formation. While the context of protests allows for the appearance of workshops and the creation of a link to the agendas of social struggle, it also originates concrete spaces for alternative social relations and modes of production through collective work. The workshop turns into a wide space for politicization and production, a new space for the common. This explains the relevance of a micropolitics that involves social bonds, forms of poster creation and reproduction, as well as their very economics, characterized by self-management. Both in their financing and their political and aesthetic definitions, these groups exert a full autonomy from other party-political structures, even if they do not exclude the political as such. This dimension takes shape in their forms of organization, which privilege assemblies and horizontal methods both for decision making and for the circulation of technical and political knowledge.

For example, groups like TSI and BPF have regular assemblies where all members gather to plan actions, projects, and joint interventions.

The option for mutual work is a vindication of the collective as a political and creative entity. Far from being a procedural option, this form of articulation is the result of a localized reflection that aspires to counter the hegemonic fragmentation of the social fabric and the pre-eminence of individualism as a source of action and identity. Each of the groups we have researched has developed a trajectory that, even in its breaks and discontinuities, does not shy away from the idea of a 'we'. On the contrary, all of them, even in times of low participation (between two and fifteen members), position themselves from a plural subjectivity.

This collectiveness is also expressed in the creative dimension of graphic design; that is, in its slogans and visual languages. It is characteristic of this graphic production to condensate discourses and the common sense of protest that circulate widely in the key nodes of political action and debate. In a way, the collective discourse of the mobilized street jumps to the poster, it is then collectively processed in workshops through visual language and the materiality of the poster, and, ultimately, it is returned to public space. We hold that this strategy is crucial to understand the passage from production to circulation, since 'the exchange value of any particular image or image-object is, of course, intimately related to its representational content' (Poole 1997: 11).

Collective means of production acquire a radicalness when we notice that there is a generalized blurring of traditional authorship. In general, the identification of authorship resides in the identification of common outlines and designs, not in a signature. The only case of a collective signing their posters is Estudiantes por Chile, whose emblem/signature appears on all their creations. Although we might posit that this generalized absence of a signature comes from a crisis or lack of sense of authorship, we would like to propose that this is a sign of the constitution of a subject that identifies with graphic production: the *propagandista* and the *brigadista*. Graphic collectives have reappropriated these concepts, related to traditional forms of activism on the left: fronts or sections linked to party structures that seek to express an ideologically distinct message in an idiosyncratic aesthetic (cf. Richard 2017). Although keeping the concept, contemporary *brigadistas* and *propagandistas* uphold their autonomy from leftist parties, and understand their work as an expression of commitment to the processes of transformation of public space borne out of student protests. *Brigadistas* and *propagandistas* have become the subjects of a collective mediation that goes from the streets to the workshop and then back to the streets – the agents of the intersection between visual production, political organization and urban struggle.

Graphic Images: The Poster and Its Visual Languages

In this section we would like to reflect on graphic production as a part of a wider circuit of political visuality inscribed in a field of struggle. One of the inescapable aspects of this landscape is the recognition of the formal and medial properties in the images that have constituted the corpus of Chilean student graphics in recent years. This production generates links between their creators and the public they seek to represent. To this end, we discuss three visual characteristics: (a) the valuation of manual gestures; (b) the maximal use of minimal resources; and (c) the relation between images and slogans.

A broad analysis of the posters created by the collectives we have mentioned shows the predominance of manual serigraphy as the preferred technique. We know that formats like woodcut printing have a close and material relation to manual skills, to the point where they have originated a particular aesthetics in Latin America, linked to popular prints and string literature (see Musacchio 2007; Malachini Soto 2015). Serigraphy, in its turn, is a technique that allows for a greater flexibility regarding the composition of images, since it does not require heavy manual intervention on the printing matrix (designs can be created with photo-montage or in digital composition). However, we observe a constant presence of manual outlines, to the point that many collectives seem to operate solely with this technique.

We suggest that this shows a valuation of the artisanal in poster production. The persistence of this 'traditional' dimension speaks of the counter-hegemonic value of cultural practices that use technical means of production apparently relegated to the sphere of the residual (Williams 1977: 121–27). The organizational form of the workshop reinforces this affinity with craft techniques. However, the predominance of manual outlines does not mean that these posters follow the norms of 'proper draughtsmanship'. On the contrary, the valuation of drawing implies the appearance of various formal solutions. Some of them show a domain of composition techniques and a better-trained outline, while others testify to self-taught experiences that value political effects over formal perfection. At the same time, manual composition establishes a dialogue with previous graphic languages, like Estudiantes por Chile (with a clear orientation towards Unidad Popular posters and the aesthetics of muralist brigades from the 1960s – Figure 4.1) and Taller Mano Alzada (who re-elaborate references from the May 68 Atelier Populaire.)

This calling from the manual gesture coexists with a rather minimal or basic range of resources for printing. On a material level, posters use low-cost paper and are printed using one colour – or, occasionally, two colours that distinguish slogan and image. Although posters in full colour exist, they are

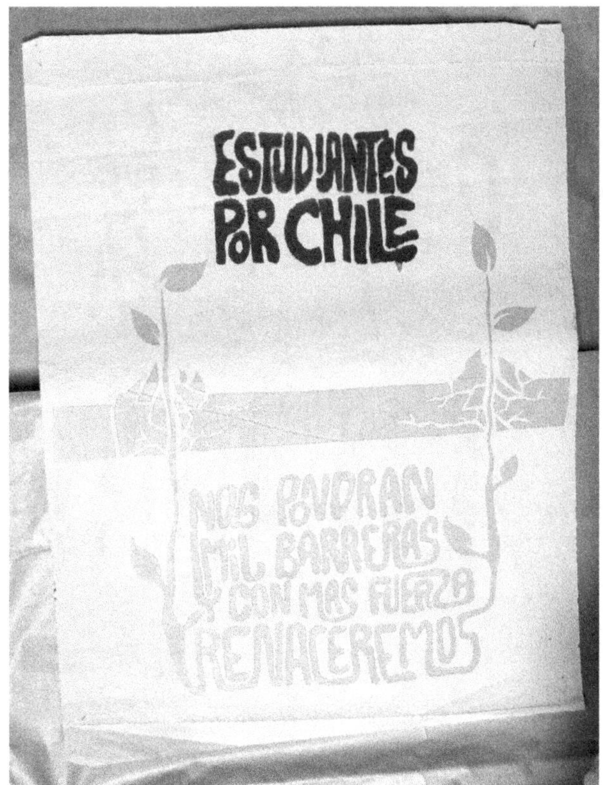

Figure 4.1 *Nos pondrán mil barreras y con más fuerza renaceremos* [They will put up a thousand barriers and with more strength we will be reborn]. Estudiantes por Chile, 2008. Silk screen print (27.9 x 21.7 cm).

less frequent and do not represent this trend towards flat surfaces of ink that establish a stark contrast between figure and background. If we follow Wölfflin's 'fundamental concepts' (Wölfflin 2015: 96–97), monochrome images help to create a closed form that is clearly recognizable on the surface on which it has been printed. We observe many variations within a palette of basic colours (black, green, red, blue) that sometimes relate to certain political imaginaries: violet in feminist posters or cobalt blue in those linked to the *mapuche* movement.[7] This option for a limited range of inks seems to resume the visual economy of resistance graphics during the dictatorship. In our view, this seems to be a choice that has both economic (cost reduction, and maximizing the number of pieces produced) and political motives. Printing on textiles in the context of demonstrations forces the collectives to think of

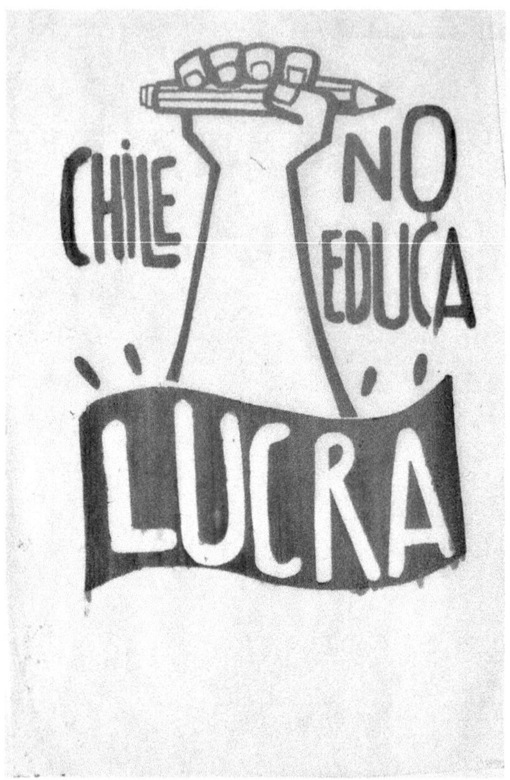

Figure 4.2 *Chile no educa, lucra* [Chile does not educate, it profits]. Taller Mano Alzada, 2008. Silk screen print (38.5 x 54.7 cm).

graphic solutions that are transferrable across different media. This results in an amplification of results with the least possible amount of resources. Variations in serigraphic images are achieved by changing inks and surfaces, which allows for a recontextualization of design and an increased circulation.

Lastly, we would like to comment on the iconic value acquired by texts. The links between word and image constitute a complex theoretical field (see Puppo and Queirolo 2017), from which we gain some intuitions to analyse our corpus. We notice moments in which printed text functions as a support to the image, performing a paratextual function by commenting on the image or giving keys for its interpretation on political terms. Posters by Estudiantes por Chile use phrases like 'The struggle belongs to everyone', 'Wake up, dawn shall come', and 'Let us give hope to our children', coupled with drawings that do not refer to a specific political event. These slogans

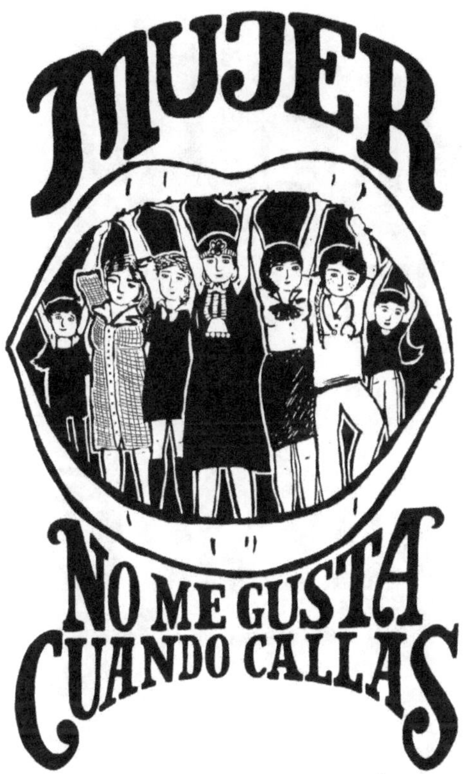

Figure 4.3 *Mujer no me gusta cuando callas* [Woman, I don't like it when you're quiet]. Brigada de Propaganda Feminista and Colectivo Serigrafía Instantánea, 2015. Silk screen print (110 x 77 cm).

inscribe posters in a circuit of political interpretation through discursive reference or interpellation, since the image itself does not carry an immediately political reading. Other cases, like Taller Mano Alzada, evidence a more tightly knit interaction of text and image by tapping into an iconography that locates itself in the visual repertoire of the left, like raised fists joined by the phrase 'Chile doesn't educate, it profits' (Figure 4.2), or the criticism of police violence through a police hat with the slogan 'Too much policing, too little education'.

Also, one of the most emblematic posters of feminist serigraphy – linked to BPF and TSI – provides an example of the interactions between text and imagen. 'Woman, I don't like it when you're quiet' (Figure 4.3) is an ironic rewriting and criticism of Pablo Neruda's famous verse 'I like it when you're

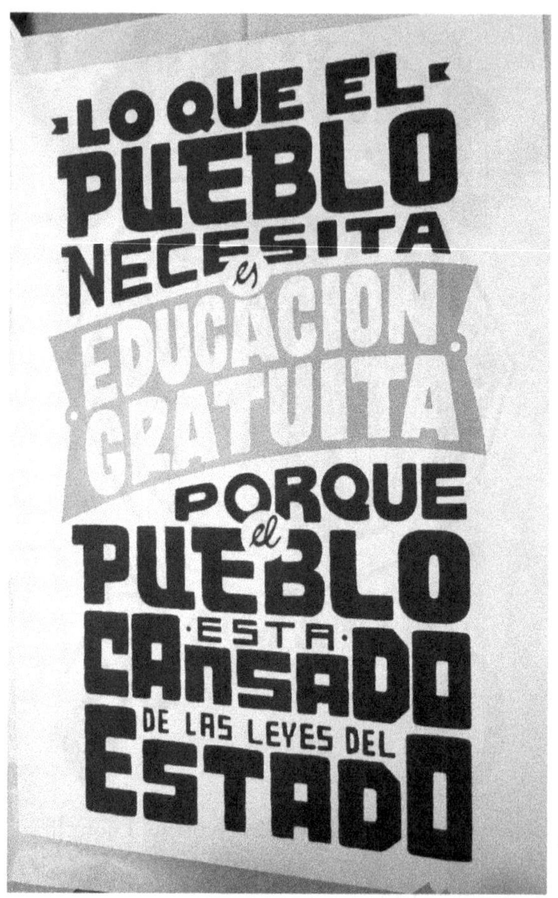

Figure 4.4 *Lo que el pueblo necesita es educación gratuita* [What the people need is free education]. Colectivo Serigrafía Instantánea, 2013. Silk screen print (100 x 70 cm).

quiet: it's as though you were absent'. It shows a group of women opening a mouth, inviting the spectator to identify herself with the collective gesture of speaking up and inverting the historical meaning of silent female subjection. At the same time, the poster functions as an assemblage of its verbal and visual elements that cannot be divorced from each other, since the text is key for 'meaning production' and for the political effects of the piece.

These last two cases bring us to a set produced by TSI. Some of these posters are made up only of slogans, manually designed with a lettering that echoes the signs of popular trading spots in Santiago. Slogans like 'The only lost struggle is the one we abandon' and 'What the people need is free education. For the people are tired of the state's laws' (Figure 4.4) are set on a printed surface and become images in themselves. They do not seem to require any iconography to join them. This is because, in the case of the second phrase, they are the chants of the mobilized student masses. Posters become 'a scream on the wall', although not in the figure of speech by Josep Renau, but rather literally. Slogans from the streets enter the poster and remain in the city as a persistent echo of the student struggle.

In summary, we see that formal and material properties from serigraphic posters converge in the pretended maximization of the political effects of images. With their austere approach they make us think of a 'communication guerrilla' that rescues manual aesthetics and gives a decisive weight to text as part of the design. It may be that manual design is a way to humanize this centrality of callings and interpellations in posters, a way of politicizing iconography at a human scale, shared by both graphic collectives and student organizations.

Graphics in Motion: Visual Circulations in the City

Graphic activism in the student movement chooses the streets as its preferred stage. It coexists with traditional demonstrations and adds its own detours. Unlike previous moments, these protests are rich in creative strategies and spatial practices (Taylor 2003; Banda and Navea 2013). The carnivalization of protest included marching bands and dance troupes, performances that highlighted the political connotations of the body and flashmobs[8] that interrupted the everyday pace of the city. They integrated pop culture codes with student demands, and reconstituted the political experience of the streets while 'removing the solemnity in the uses of public space' (Marambio 2016: 105.)

As proposed by Iveson (2013) and Hou (2010), contemporary contestations of the city involve various creative strategies, such as the ones described above. However, we do not read them as expressions of DIY urbanism (Finn 2014; Talen 2015), as they do not *directly* address the concerns of city dwellers. Rather, they modify urban public space as a means to an end, which is a contribution to the political struggle. We see a closer connection here with the work of BUGA UP described by Iveson (2013: 948–50), though we argue that the experience of radicalization *within* the student movement is key to understand the work of graphic collectives.

In this context, graphic production is not only a medium but also a visual practice for the student movement – images 'accrue value through the social processes of accumulation, possession, circulation and exchange'

(Poole 1997: 11). In 2008, Estudiantes por Chile began a series of artistic interventions on bus stops and the surroundings of the Faculty of Architecture and Urban Planning of the University of Chile. It is interesting to note that, before the 2011 mass demonstrations, the only safe time to use the streets was at night, as the police would close off any unauthorized political use of them (Delamaza 2011). In 2011 Taller Mano Alzada took to the streets to hand out posters marked with a sticker. This gift-giving on the streets sought to promote the logic of free education and circulate decorative graphic pieces that bore the demands and slogans of the student movement. Posters such as 'This is a family matter', 'Down with market education', and 'A better education, a better Chile' are some of the pieces that circulated in this student exchange mechanism. The idea of gift-giving aspired to enter people's homes and bring the discussion of student debt to the intimacy of domestic conversation. The struggle against the privatization of education and the criminalization of protests had to take place at universities, on the streets and inside homes, instituting a sphere of circulation where the public and the private intermingled against the grain of the hegemonic neoliberal mechanisms.

If the free distribution of posters to passers-by was a strategy to bring visual production into the everyday, participating in demonstrations was a way of showing the workshop in its emergence. TSI were one of the first collectives to set up shop in the middle of the Alameda (Santiago's main avenue) to print designs with slogans made by themselves or picked up from the streets. In the middle of the crowd, TSI invited people to print a poster or their own clothing in order to continue the demonstration's route as human propagators of student demands. The collective integrated students into the printing process by having a member set the ink on the frame with the demonstrator holding the frame, while the TSI member used the blade to transfer the ink. This gesture, lasting only a couple of seconds, required bodily collaboration to produce a collective piece. As well as sharing the printing process, the exercise of taking the workshop to the streets made it possible to socialize screen printing. This has become a central part of their work as graphic communicators, in so far as it allows more organizations to gain the autonomy to produce their own propaganda. It is interesting to note how this process brings to the fore the emergence of self-education initiatives in the student movement – or, as one poster by TSI states: 'Educate yourself' (Figure 4.5).

A third way of using the city is through groups or 'brigades' that paper the walls along the demonstration's route. Dressed in overalls and using carts prepared for the task, they cover walls, shopfronts, traffic signs and

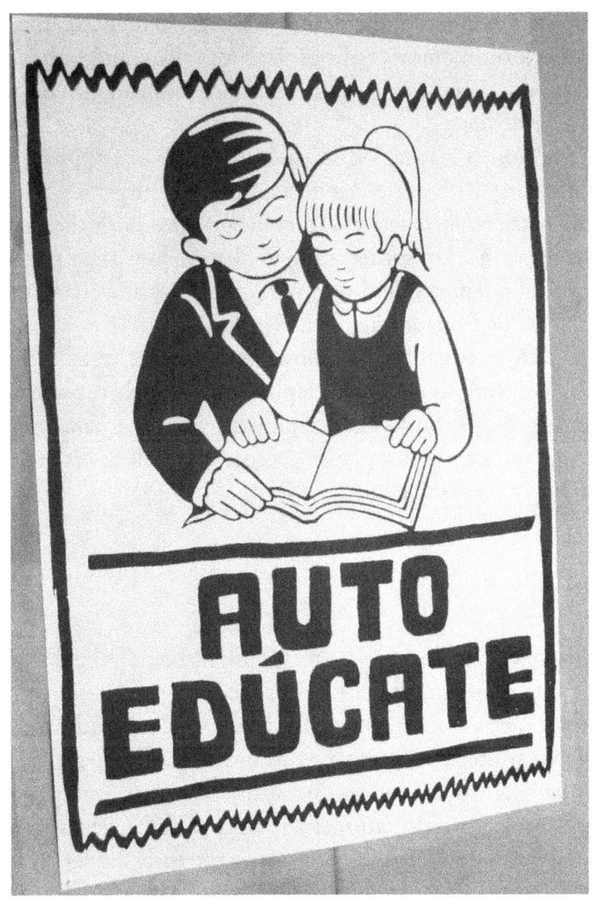

Figure 4.5 *Autoedúcate* [Educate yourself]. Colectivo Serigrafía Instantánea, 2011. Silk screen print (70 x 49.5 cm).

bus stops. On their way they build up ephemeral human structures to reach the higher parts of billboards and commercial buildings. These collective bodies move forward with the tide of demonstrators, and reterritorialize the city, hacking into everyday urban space and establishing new chains of value for the images they carry. Temporary occupation of the streets produces a liberation from police control, and poster-sticking ceases to be a clandestine and nocturnal activity, becoming a form of protest in plain sight, protected by the demonstration. Graphics constitute an assemblage that visually prolongs the contestation of the post-dictatorship sociopolitical order, for it temporally extends the trail of the social movement in the neoliberal city. It calls back on memories of political muralism and political graphics interrupted by the dictatorship, and then relegated to a distant past by the transition to democracy.

This disruption is intensified in the experience of feminist graphic collectives, particularly BPF, Ser & Gráfica and Seri-insurgentes, which operate from an anti-patriarchal practice and conceptualize both the body and the streets as battlegrounds. It is interesting to observe how their public presence takes the form of a feminist and non-party political subversion of the figure of the 1960s/1970s brigade member. Feminist collectives echo a criticism of neoliberal urban visuality that shows the complicity of capitalism and patriarchy by pointing to the iconographic sites of male supremacy. In these cases, posters on public buildings are joined by an interpellation to institutions and companies with misogynistic records, as well as a rejection of sexist and objectifying advertisements.

Conclusion

In our analysis we have been able to highlight some salient points in the relation between graphics, the city, and social movements in contemporary Chile. Graphic activism by the collectives we have studied shows some of the available strategies to recover the urban public space that has been transformed and privatized by neoliberalism. The visual imagery created by such activism projects itself nationally thanks to the articulations that have been activated by student organizations since the early 2000s. In this graphic activism we observe a craftsman-like, collective and collaborative production that is integrated with political struggles that foster the emergence of a graphic field. Its community of agents and producers, as we stated above, is a novelty that begins to show some signs of relative autonomy.

We have surveyed different modes of poster production that emphasize collective aspects within graphic workshops. A social experience is thus constituted that goes against the grain of neoliberal subjectivity and its forms of organization of the everyday. This form of urban activism can also be recognized in other political struggles: on the one hand, the historical link with periods that preceded the dictatorship manifested in images that activate a graphic memory and relate to a visual tradition of the Chilean left; on the other, the presence and multiple uses of these posters in a heretofore enclosed public space is characteristic of the student movement as a political subject. The reoccupation of urban public space is carried out by graphic collectives through their own creative practice. *Brigadistas* and *propagandistas* amplify demonstrations in the city by leaving visual traces of the protests.

What these experiences demonstrate is the centrality of protest as a political school in the formation of a graphic field. The routes of social movements have changed their coordinates, and graphics answer to these transformations. The life experience of struggles has transformed the streets of neoliberal Santiago into a heterogeneous machine: a production site, a contested object, a visual reference, a means of communication, and a surface for posters.

Javiera Manzi is a sociologist from the Universidad de Chile, researcher and independent archivist, as well as co-author of the book *Resistencia gráfica a la dictadura en Chile: APJ y Tallersol* (LOM, 2016) and coordinator of the Red de Conceptualismos del Sur and researcher for the exhibition *¡A la Calle Nuevamente! Gráfica y Movilización Estudiantil en Chile* (Casa de las Américas, Havana, 2016).

Matías Marambio is a BA in History, MA in Latin American studies and PhD in Latin American Studies, Universidad de Chile. He is Adjunct Lecturer in the Department of Anthropology at Universidad Alberto Hurtado. His research interests are intellectual and cultural history, history of political thought, visual studies and the study of cultural activism in Latin America. He also is a researcher for the exhibition *¡A la Calle Nuevamente! Gráfica y Movilización Estudiantil en Chile* (Casa de las Américas, Havana, Cuba, 2016).

Isidro Parraguez is a sociologist and MA in Latin American studies, Universidad de Chile and Adjunct Lecturer of Latin American Sociology at Sociology Department, Universidad de Chile. He is an editorial assistant of *Meridional: Revista Chilena de Estudios Latinoamericanos*, Centro de Estudios Culturales Latinoamericanos, Universidad de Chile, and member of Núcleo Gráfica y Movilización Estudiantil (Graphics and Student Movement Research Group).

María Yaksic is a BA in literature, MA in Latin American studies, Universidad de Chile and currently a PhD student at the Centro de Estudios Culturales Latinoamericanos, Universidad de Chile (CONICYT PhD Scholar, 2020). She is project coordinator of *¡A la Calle Nuevamente! Gráfica y Movilización Estudiantil en Chile* (Casa de Las Américas, Havana, Cuba, 2016) and Editorial Director at Banda Propia Editoras.

Notes

1. This chapter was concluded before the social protests that occurred in Chile from October 2019.
2. The term designates the practice of publicly calling out and shaming public figures. It is an equivalent of the Argentine *escrache*, and both originate in human rights organizations. Their tactics are aimed at publicly identifying perpetrators of human rights violations. Today the *funa* has extended beyond its original political terrain.
3. For example, territorial autonomy that issues from the occupation of rural or urban land, or the reclaiming of ancestral land, as in the demands of the *mapuche* people.
4. The concept of 'Chilean road to socialism' was used in the manifesto of the Unidad Popular (1970–73) to express its proposal to construct a socialist society with clear differences from 'actually existing socialism'. The main one was the persecution of socialist-oriented transformation through democratic and institutional means.
5. Decree N°32, published by the military junta on 15 September 1973.
6. All translations from Spanish by the authors.
7. The link with this colour is a reference to *mapuche* struggles against Spanish conquest, and has been associated with *mapuche* society for a long time.
8. During 2011, several choreographies of pop songs were performed in public spaces, like Michael Jackson's 'Thriller' and Lady Gaga's 'Judas'. Other interventions included an 1,800-hour run around the presidential palace, which was meant to symbolize the 1,800 million dollars that was estimated as the figure needed to cover free education for all.

References

Banda, C., and V. Navea. 2013. *En marcha: Ensayos sobre arte, violencia y cuerpo en la movilización social.* Santiago: Adrede Editora.

Boccardo, G. 2016. 'Crisis política y movimiento estudiantil chileno', in A.N. Albo and C. Valdés (eds), *Juventud y espacio público en las Américas: I Taller Casa Tomada.* La Habana: Casa de las Américas.

Castillo, E. 2010. *Artesanos, artistas, artífices: La Escuela de Artes Aplicadas de la Universidad de Chile, 1928–1968.* Santiago: Ocho Libros y Pie de texto editores.

Cristi, N., and J. Manzi. 2016. *Resistencia Gráfica: Dictadura en Chile: APJ–Tallersol.* Santiago: LOM.

Delamaza, G. 2011. 'Espacio público y participación ciudadana en la gestión pública en Chile: límites y posibilidades'. *Polis, Revista de la Universidad Bolivariana* 10(30): 45–75.

Errázuriz, L.H. 'Dictadura Militar en Chile: Antecedentes del golpe estético-cultural'. *Latin American Research Review* 44(2): 136–57.

Finn, D. 2014. 'DIY Urbanism: Implications for Cities'. *Journal of Urbanism: International Research on Placemaking and Urban Sustainability* 7(4): 381–98.

Follegatti, L. 2018. 'El feminismo se ha vuelto una necesidad: movimiento estudiantil y organización feminista (2000–2017)'. *Mujeres insurrectas. Anales de la Universidad de Chile* 14(7): 261–91.

Garretón, M.A. 2012. *Neoliberalismo corregido y progresismo limitado: Los gobiernos de la Concertación en Chile (1990–2010)*. Santiago: ARCIS-CLACSO.

Harvey, D. 2005. *A Brief History of Neoliberalism*. New York: Oxford University Press.

———. 2012. *Rebel Cities: From the Right to the City to the Urban Revolution*. London: Verso.

Hou, D. (ed.). 2010. *Insurgent Public Space: Guerrilla Urbanism and the Remaking of the Contemporary Cities*. London: Routledge.

INDH. 2015. *Informe Programa de Derechos Humanos, Función Policial y Orden Público 2014*. INDH Digital Library. Retrieved 16 February 2020 from https://biblioteca digital.indh.cl/handle/123456789/844.

Iveson, K. 2013. 'Cities within the City: Do-It-Yourself Urbanism and the Right to the City'. *International Journal of Urban and Regional Research* 37(3): 941–56.

Longoni, A. 2009. 'Activismo artístico en la última década en Argentina: algunas acciones en torno a la segunda desaparición de Jorge Julio López'. *Revista Errata No.* 0: 16–35.

Malacchini Soto, S. 2015. *Lira Popular: Identidad gráfica de un medio impreso chileno*. Santiago: Ocho Libros.

Manzi, J., C. Olmedo and M.J. Yaksic. 2016. 'A la calle nuevamente: Gráfica y movimiento estudiantil en Chile', in A.N. Albo and C. Valdés (eds), *Juventud y espacio público en las Américas: I Taller Casa Tomada*. La Habana: Casa de las Américas.

Marambio, M. 2016. 'Movimiento estudiantil: jóvenes y espacio público', in A.N. Albo and C. Valdés (eds), *Juventud y espacio público en las Américas: I Taller Casa Tomada*. La Habana: Casa de las Américas.

Márquez, F. 2017. *Relatos de una ciudad trizada: Santiago de Chile*. Santiago: Ocho Libros.

Moulian, T. 1997. *Chile actual: anatomía de un mito*. Santiago: LOM-ARCIS.

Musacchio, H. 2007. *El Taller de Gráfica Popular*. Mexico: Fondo de Cultura Económica.

Pairicán, F. 2014. *Malón: La rebelión del movimiento mapuche, 1990–2013*. Santiago: Pehuén Editores.

Pérez, M. 2017. 'Reframing Housing Struggles: Right to the City and Urban Citizenship in Santiago, Chile'. *City* 21(5): 530–49.

Pinochet Cobos, C. 2016. 'Abrir las grandes alamedas: Festivales culturales y espacio público en la construcción de un imaginario de la democracia'. *Revista Estudios Avanzados* 26: 1–18.

Poole, D. 1997. *Vision, Race and Modernity: A Visual Economy of the Andean Image World*. Princeton, NJ: Princeton University Press.

Portales, F. 2000. *Chile: una democracia tutelada*. Santiago: Sudamericana.

Puppo, M., and G. Queirolo. 2017. 'Correspondencias y tensiones de la relación palabra/imagen en la cultura latinoamericana'. *Meridional: Revista Chilena de Estudios Latino-americanos* 9: 7–26.

Richard, N. (ed.). 2017. *Arte y política en Chile*. Santiago: Metales Pesados.

Rivera-Scott, H. 2010. 'Arte y modernidad en torno a la Escuela de Artes Aplicadas', in E. Castillo, *Artesanos, artistas, artífices: La Escuela de Artes Aplicadas de la Universidad de Chile, 1928–1968*. Santiago: Ocho Libros y Pie de texto editores.

Ruiz, C., and G. Boccardo. 2014. *Los chilenos bajo el neoliberalismo: Clases y conflicto social*. Santiago: El Desconcierto.

Siganevich, P., and M.L. Nieto. 2017. *Activismo gráfico: Conversaciones sobre diseño, arte y política*. Florida: Wolkowicz editores.

Sontag, S. 1970. 'Posters: Advertisement, Art, Political Artifact, Commodity', in Michael Bierut (ed.), *Looking Closer 3*. New York: Allworth Press (1999), pp. 196–218.

Svampa, M. 2008. *Cambio de época: Movimientos sociales y poder político*. Buenos Aires: CLACSO-Siglo XXI.

———. 2015. 'Commodities Consensus: Neoextractivism and Enclosure of the Commons in Latin America'. *South Atlantic Quarterly* 114(1): 65–82.

Svampa, M., and E. Viale. 2014. *Maldesarrollo: La Argentina del extractivismo y el despojo*. Buenos Aires: Katz editores.

Talen, E. 2015. 'Do-It-Yourself Urbanism: A History'. *Journal of Planning History* 14(2) 135–48.

Taylor, D. 2003. *The Archive and the Repertoire: Performing Cultural Memory in the Americas*. Durham, NC: Duke University Press.

Thielemann, L. 2016. *La anomalía social de la transición: Movimiento estudiantil e izquierda universitaria en el Chile de los noventa (1987–2000)*. Santiago: Tiempo Robado.

United Nations Development Programme (UNDP). 2015. 'Desarrollo humano en Chile. Los tiempos de la politización'. Santiago.

Vico, M., and M. Osses. 2009. *Un grito en la pared, psicodelia, compromiso, político y exilio en el cartel chileno*. Santiago: Ocholibros editores.

Williams, R. 1977. *Marxism and Literature*. London: Oxford University Press.

Wölfflin, H. 2015. *Principles of Art History: The Problem of the Development of Style in Early Modern Art*, trans. Jonathan Blower. Los Angeles: Getty Publications.

Chapter 5

Anti-Trump Graffiti and Street Art

A Case Study of Washington, DC

Jeffrey Ian Ross

Introduction

When contentious individuals get elected to political office, and/or unpopular policies, practices and laws are discussed or passed, we frequently witness all kinds of visual indicators of protest and resistance. Posters, bumper stickers, T-shirts and hats with messages printed on them, protest signs, and signs that people place in their windows and on their lawns proliferate when the public wish to express their discontent. Also present in some communities is graffiti and street art.

Graffiti and street art[1] can be interpreted a number of ways including, but not limited to: a type of vandalism, a weapon of the weak (Scott 1990), a type of resistance against powerful political forces (Ferrell 1996, 1997), an activity that increases camaraderie among a subculture (Macdonald 2001; Snyder 2009), and a method of communication (Phillips 1999). Although this kind of activity has existed for centuries, there has been an increased frequency of graffiti and street art, and awareness of it, since the 1970s.

Since then, numerous images and subjects have been depicted, surfaces suitable for its application have been exploited, and many people have engaged in and responded to this activity (Ross 2016c). Since 2016, in addition to an upsurge in racist and antisemitic graffiti and street art, one of the dominant contemporary subjects of graffiti and street art has focused on Donald J. Trump, the current president of the United States, his family, White House personnel, his closest associates, senior members of his administration, and unpopular policies and practices that are associated with this new regime.[2]

Although graffiti and street art critical of and mocking Trump has appeared within the United States (Tanner 2016) and throughout the world (Moran 2017; Schwartz 2017), in order to best understand anti-Trump graffiti and street art it may be helpful to examine an important location where it has appeared.[3] In many respects there is no better place to review this kind of activity than in the nation's capital. Having lived there for over twenty-six years, the author is very familiar with the city, and is very knowledgeable about the diversity of its neighborhoods, the shifting demographics, and the people who live and work there. Even though Washington, DC has, for the past four decades, experienced its fair share of graffiti and street art (e.g. Gastman 2001; Yoseph 2012; iwillnot 2018),[4] and was the home of numerous well known and prolific East Coast graffiti artists like Cool 'Disco' Dan, the city has never been regarded as an epicentre for this kind of work. But given that DC is the centre of US federal politics and where Trump currently primarily lives and works, it represents a unique location for this type of analysis.

Thus this chapter describes the results of a data collection effort to document a significant amount of anti-Trump graffiti and street art in the District of Columbia over a reasonable period, paying attention to its content and its placement, both in terms of the neighbourhoods where it is found and the types of surface on which it is located. It concludes by interpreting why, despite other forms of anti-Trump protest in DC, the amount of anti-Trump graffiti and street art seems to be relatively low.

To date, most of the coverage of anti-Trump graffiti and street art has been done through the popular/mainstream news media. On a periodic basis there are news reports of anti-Trump graffiti or street art appearing on bypasses, sidewalks, curbs, and other structures. Alternatively, some websites have posted photos of this kind of imagery. Tulke (2018), for example, has created an archive of anti-Trump graffiti throughout the world. This freely available website contains images posted on the file-sharing website Flicker. At the time of writing, the portal includes 1,441 images of graffiti and street art that are anti-Trump. In her summary post, she divides twenty-one images into different categories focusing on messages that criticize and/or mock Trump's racism or misogyny, or plays on slogans that the Trump campaign used during his election campaign (e.g. 'drain the swamp'). Despite these efforts, no scholarly studies have looked at this emerging phenomenon.

It is important to keep in mind that graffiti and street art are not the only kind of protest that take place against Trump in Washington DC (e.g. Boone, Secci and Gallant 2018; Myer and Tarrow 2018). The nation's capital has always been an epicentre for public demonstrations. From the March on Washington by veterans who ended up camping out on the Mall (1932), to the Civil Rights March (1963), the Million-Man March (1995), and the Women's March in January 2017, shortly after Trump's inauguration, the District of Columbia has experienced a considerable amount of public protest. The district has had numerous disputes with the federal government, which has led to the long-standing phrase 'No Taxation without representation', a reflection that DC residents do not have the right to elect their own members to the House of Representatives or the Senate. This slogan can be found on DC license plates, bumper stickers, and other District of Columbia government literature. This kind of messaging has the potential to affect residents and visitors on a deep psychological level.

Nevertheless, with respect to DC, there is a significant number of 'Fuck Trump' tags throughout the city (Muller 2017). Waldron (2018), in particular, traces the escapades of 'Dirty Knucklez', a self-described homeless DC rapper who spends his days putting up 'Fuck Trump' graffiti throughout the city. But this is just the tip of the iceberg. One of the favorite locations not only for anti-Trump public protests, but for graffiti, has been the Trump International Hotel, located in the Old Post Office, not far from the White House, the official residence of the president. Not only has this hotel been subjected to graffiti, but it has also been the target of frequent provocative light projections saying, 'Pay Trump Bribes Here', and 'Shithole' (Arnold and Uliano 2016; Chavez and Smith 2017).[5]

Literature Review

There are all sorts of graffiti and street art, and many contexts where one can find this kind of activity (Ross et al. 2017). It has been the subject of numerous articles and books, aimed at both popular and academic audiences (Ross 2016a; Avramidis and Tsilimpounidi 2017). A full review of this work is neither necessary nor relevant here. Suffice to say, at the core of a significant amount of graffiti and street art is a political message supporting or protesting against a candidate, politician, party, policy, practice or law. Thus, among its numerous attributes, graffiti and street art is often a method of non-violent political participation, and is sometimes seen as a non-violent weapon of the weak (Scott 1985, 1990).

To elaborate, according to Waldner and Dobratz, 'graffiti is not only another form of political participation, but also contentious politics. What is usually defined as contentious is also non-institutional or considered outside the "normal" bounds of political discourse' (Waldner and Dobratz 2013: 283). These scholars 'define political graffiti as containing ideas or values designed to influence public opinion, policy, or governmental decision-making' (ibid.:

378). Unlike tags, political graffiti carries specific oppositional messages, in that it 'presents opinions against governments, institutions, authorities, politicians' majorities, etc.' (Jørgensen 2008: 242). Anti-Trump graffiti and street art would clearly fit this description, and also be considered part of conflict and political graffiti. Having abandoned the words 'graffiti' and 'street art', David (2007) settles on the term 'visual resistance' to describe the contentious images, words and expressions that were placed on multiple surfaces in New Orleans. Although one could quibble with his need to develop an alternative term, and with the motivations David ascribes to the so-called 'artist activists' (the people he suggests are engaging in this work), his interpretations regarding the power of graffiti and street art in the context of New Orleans are consistent with the notions of political and conflict graffiti.

It must also be recognized that not all neighbourhoods in Washington, DC are the same (according to a recent unofficial count, there are roughly 130 of them). For instance, some have back alleys, while others do not. Some are disproportionately commercial, while others are mainly residential. This has an effect on numerous dynamics, including the placement of graffiti and street art (Ross 2013). That being said, as a bulwark against the graffiti and street art that is placed on different surfaces (not to mention streets and sidewalks that are filled with trash and litter) very active Business Improvement Districts (BIDs) operate in many of the neighbourhoods, and their clean-up crew employees patrol the streets in search of litter, trash, graffiti and street art, and attempt to remove it as soon as possible (Wolf 2006; Lewis 2010).[6]

According to a conversation I had with a BID cleaner, individuals primarily create graffiti and street art on the weekends, and cleaners try to remove it as soon as they see it. They suspect that it is the same people who are engaging in this activity week after week. The BID activities are mainly concentrated on the main streets rather than the back alleys. This makes sense as there is considerably more motorized and pedestrian traffic on the main streets, thus giving a higher visibility for the graffiti and street art. The BID cleaners say they will go in 50 feet from the main streets to clean up. Often 'ghost buffers' – citizens who either try to remove or deface graffiti or street art – scratch over stickers or damage them in different ways, again pointing to the possibility that there is probably more graffiti and street art, regardless of the content, than I was able to find.

Method

No single book or article outlines how to conduct research on graffiti and street art. From intense ethnographies to participant observation, most researchers who conduct scholarship on graffiti and street art appear to adopt an eclectic method (Ferrell 1996; Macdonald 2001; David 2007: 228–32; Snyder 2009). In order to understand the production and placement of anti-Trump graffiti and street art, I spent a significant amount of time (on a sporadic basis between 2017 and the early months of 2019) scanning appropriate surfaces in selected neighbourhoods in the nation's capital looking for evidence of this kind of activity.[7]

I made sure to walk not only the main streets, but also, where appropriate, to explore the back alleys in search of relevant graffiti and street art. In many respects, I encountered a snapshot in time, as what I discovered in the designated locations was that the graffiti and street art, through the combined processes of eradication/abatement, climatic conditions and the work of other practitioners, would most likely be different the next time.

Once located, I attempted to determine the content (including images and symbols), and the kinds of surfaces this activity was placed on. I took photos of relevant graffiti and street art, and documented the exact location. Sometimes I also took notes on my iPhone and later transcribed them into a primary document. At other times, after walking through a neighbourhood, I would sit somewhere and transcribe what I had observed.

In addition to scanning, I also talked to people I encountered on the street, like cleaning crews, and police officers who appeared to work in the areas I was observing.[8] I was also engaged in different levels of communication with individuals who appeared to be closely connected to the DC graffiti and street art scene. These included people who provided instruction in graffiti and street art, and were listed through the Airbnb 'top-rated experiences' section of the website. At one point, I reached Dirty Knucklez via Instagram direct message (DM). He was the subject of a couple of news media articles (Muller 2017; Waldron 2017), and was predictably cautious at first; despite a lengthy exchange, he was not willing to be interviewed face to face. Based on my DMs with Dirtzy Knucklez, his posts on Instagram (including his frequent requests for donations via PayPal to finance his 'outlaw' activist lifestyle), and conversations I had with others in the DC graffiti/street art world, he appeared to have some significant challenges.

Results

The process of analysing what I saw required minimal risk, considerable patience, and the process of categorization and reflection. The balance of this discussion is broken down into two parts. The first is a description of what I encountered in each of the neighbourhoods, and the second is a basic data analysis. To begin with there is a lot of diversity among DC's neighbourhoods, and not all places are equally appropriate for graffiti and street art, so I concentrated my efforts in locations where I thought there would be a higher likelihood of it, having also asked informants for recommendations about such places.

All in all, I visited fifteen key neighbourhoods. These included, but were not limited to: Adams Morgan, Dupont Circle, 14th Street, Georgetown, Glover Park, H Street Corridor, Shaw, the White House, Union Market, and the U Street Corridor.[9] With the exception of H Street and Union Market, these locations are in the north-west part of DC.[10] The following is a brief review of what I encountered in most of the neighbourhoods I toured. They are reviewed sequentially, from east to west, to capture moving easily from one neighbourhood to the next.[11]

Georgetown

Once a very hip area, Georgetown is now the setting for major internationally well-known brand clothing and furniture stores (not to mention an Apple store), and restaurants and bars that seem to cater primarily to college students (from nearby Georgetown University and George Washington University) and tourists. The majority of permanent residents of this area tend to be wealthy and politically conservative. Dominant throughout the Georgetown area were yellow stickers with anti-Trump statements, written in capital letters, placed at eye level, and affixed to lampposts and garbage cans. Surprisingly no stickers were found on dumpsters, green supercans, or blue recycling bins in back alleys. The majority of graffiti was located in the same spots I had visited a couple of years previously, such as along the C & O Canal, and underneath the on–off ramps of the Key Bridge, connecting DC with Rosslyn, Virginia. There was a plywood structure underneath the bridge that would be a logical place for placing this kind of activity, but although there was tagging on it, none of it contained anti-Trump material.

Glover Park

This neighbourhood, north of Georgetown, was once a prominent working-class area, and the formerly thriving commercial strip then became home to a number of retail businesses such as Whole Foods and Starbucks that are now closed. Residents are typically students from Georgetown University and American University, and young professionals with budding families.

Here we find a handful of anti-Trump stickers, but little other graffiti or street art.

Adams Morgan

Once one of the city's hippest areas, this location has little graffiti or street art. Although there are prominent murals around two of the back alleys near the intersection of Columbia Road and 18th Street NW, graffiti and street art is mostly absent, not only on the main streets, but in the back alleys too. Most of the anti-Trump graffiti/street art in this neighbourhood just consisted of stickers; there seemed to be some clustering of this work in a back alley adjacent to Smash Records, a used record store on 18th Street NW.

DuPont Circle

Like Adams Morgan, DuPont Circle used to be a major centre of young adult activity, but is now more subdued. The main streets feature restaurants and upscale clothing stores that cater to wealthier residents, tourists who stay at the hotels located here, and to the daytime workers. Also present are homeless people camped out on sidewalks. DuPont Circle does not have the edge that more hip neighbourhoods in Washington have. That being said, there is some anti-Trump sticker activity on signs and poles.

White House/Lafayette Park

I started at the White House, a location that I assumed would be the epi-centre of anti-Trump graffiti and street art, and walked in concentric circles around the building looking for evidence of it. To the south of the White House is the mall, and as it is heavily policed, I imagined there would be a reluctance to commit vandalism of any sort here. In front of the White House is Lafayette Park. This area is also heavily policed, with Secret Service officers guarding all entrances to the White House – some patrol the area on bicycles, and a handful of law enforcement officers sit in strategically placed police cars. Meanwhile there is a constant movement of tourists on foot who walk past or around the White House and the two federal buildings on either side. In other words, one could understand if there was a reluctance for individuals to do graffiti or street art there, especially as there would also be an emphasis by the authorities to remove it as quickly as possible. Needless to say, I did find some anti-Trump stickers and a poster located on an adjoining street.

14th Street/Logan Circle

Over the past decade, 14th Street has rapidly gentrified (Hyra 2018). On both sides of the street, from Scott Circle and north past U Street, a number of condominiums have been built, and two upscale supermarkets – a Whole Foods on P Street, and Trader Joes on 14th Street – have opened. This has had an influence on the types of people who have moved into this neighbourhood and the ones who visit, and on the amount of pedestrian traffic. Contrary to years past, not much graffiti or street art is visible. As you move closer to 14th and U Street there is more graffiti and street art, but it is located in the back alleys. Just east of this intersection is the famous Ben's Chili Bowl and the Lincoln Theatre, two iconic DC institutions. On both the north and south side of the street there are alleyways, and commissioned murals and graffiti featuring DC themes exist there.

Shaw/U Street Corridor

The majority of businesses located on the north and south side of U Street are restaurants and drinking establishments. There is also a lot of gentrification in this area (Hyra 2018). Some of the businesses have commissioned murals on their exterior walls, which I suspect was done as way to reduce the amount of tagging on their buildings. Comparatively speaking there is a lot of graffiti and street art in Shaw, especially in the back alleys, but it is more hip hop in nature, and consists of tagging and throwies; a percentage of this work is anti-Trump. Most of the tagging is the pervasive 'Fuck Trump' of Dirty Knucklez, and has most likely been undercounted in the quantitative part of this study. There is a house on 9th Street with a very large and visible '#resist' painted on it. This hash tag has been associated with numerous activists against Trump, and the Republican Party and its policies. I suspect that the tag was authorized by the owner of the house.

Capitol Hill/Eastern Market/Barracks Row

Capitol Hill refers to the area to the north, south and east of the Capital Buildings. It is mostly residential, with businesses located on the major streets off Pennsylvania Avenue. Eastern Market refers not only to the structure, built in 1871 on 7th Street SE, but to the surrounding neighbourhood. A number of restaurants, a couple of coffee shops, and a used book store are located there. On the weekends, in addition to the food purveyors inside, other produce and craft merchants sell their goods from stalls outside

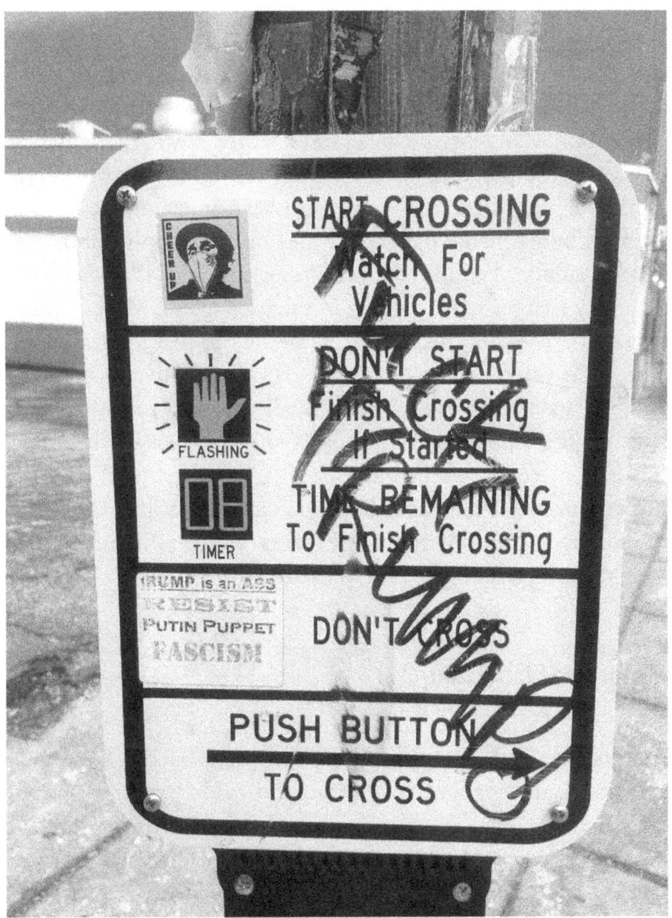

Figure 5.1 'Fuck Trump' by Dirty Knucklez. © Jeffrey Ian Ross.

the building. Despite the expectation of seeing graffiti or street art in this neighbourhood, I could not locate any. As I moved south of the Eastern Market, crossing Pennsylvania Avenue SE, and shifting to the commercial strip of 8th Street SE, I encountered Barracks Row. Although a handful of fast food chains are located here, this street now boasts a considerable number of restaurants. Walking the back alleys produced little graffiti or street art, however there was a significant amount in an alley beside the Fridge art gallery, but no anti-Trump graffiti was visible.

H Street

Located in the north-eastern part of Washington DC is H Street. During the 1968 riots, there was overwhelming damage done to commercial buildings in this location. Many of the businesses either never reopened or never recovered. Over the past decade there has been rapid gentrification in this neighbourhood (Summers 2015). Hipster bars, pubs and restaurants have opened up, in between the old barber and beauty supply shops. There are still a number of boarded up retail businesses, and lots of new construction.

Predictably there is more tagging in the back alleys. Most of it looks like it was placed there a long time ago. Some of the graffiti is around empty lots facing H Street. The person tagging 'Fuck Trump' (most likely Dirty Knucklez, but maybe others too) occasionally shows a considerable amount of diversity in the choice of colours, and an awareness of the background on which it is placed. This includes double letters painted on brick, particleboard and glass. In the back alleys you can see not just tagging but also some hip-hop-style graffiti with bubble letters, which sometimes are filled in. Otherwise, nothing as complicated as a throw-up[12] exists.

Union Market/Gallaudet

Just north of the H Street Corridor is Union Market, where a disproportionate number of jobbers and wholesaler businesses are located. Over the past five years this area has undergone a major transformation, and the central market is now a hipster haven. Some developers have torn down the structures surrounding the market, and have built condominiums and apartments. A variety of new restaurants, clothing stores and a bookstore are now occupying renovated spaces. This neighbourhood is also very accessible to the Metro station that was constructed in 2004. There is considerable tagging on the metal roll-down shutters of shops. Just south of the market is a parking lot, and some Robbie Conal-type posters parodying the president and his closest associates are visible, affixed to two sides of an abandoned parking attendant's booth. Some of the posters are political, with anti-capitalist messages, but not necessarily anti-Trump. Across the street from the market, in the back alleys behind the businesses located there, is a considerable amount of tagging and other graffiti, in particular bubble and hip-hop pieces, either using one colour or two. Also located a block away from the market are numerous white Isuzu cube vans that are parked in front of businesses. Almost all of them have been tagged with black spray paint, but none have anti-Trump messages on them. I saw a couple of 'Fuck Trump' tags spray painted on curbs, but that was all.

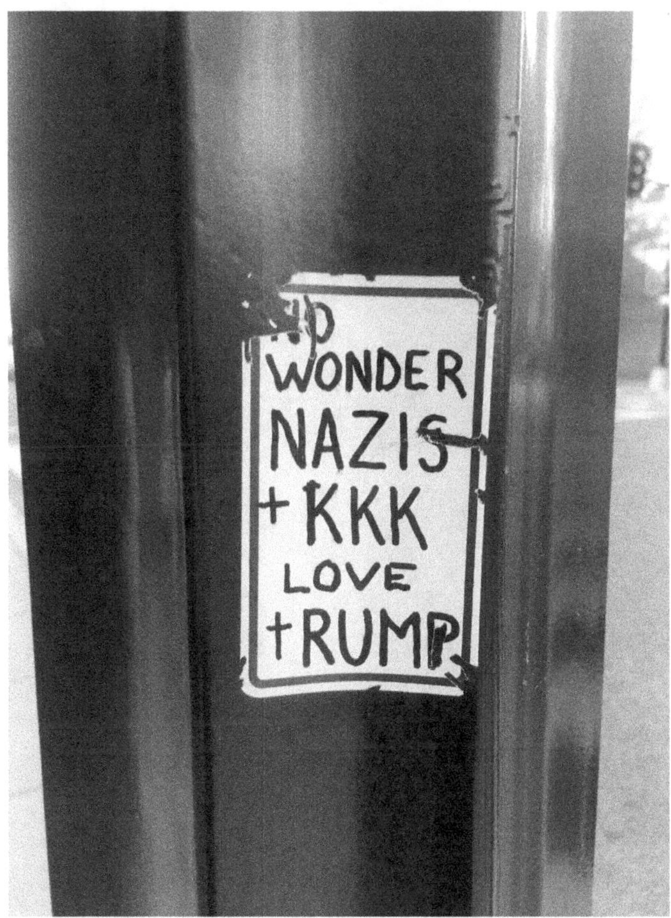

Figure 5.2 'NO WONDER NAZIS + KKK LOVE tRUMP'. © Jeffrey Ian Ross.

Brookland/Rhode Island Metro/Edgewood

There are lots of mixed-use structures in this neighbourhood, with residential and commercial buildings and empty lots. A large commercial district exists on Benning Road, with a retail plaza that includes a Home Depot and a Giant store. There are also numerous back alleys, and the infamous Edgewood wall where there is a significant amount of graffiti and street art (Shuler 2019). Some 'Fuck Trump' tags are placed on the stairs to the subway, but nothing anti-Trump besides this message.

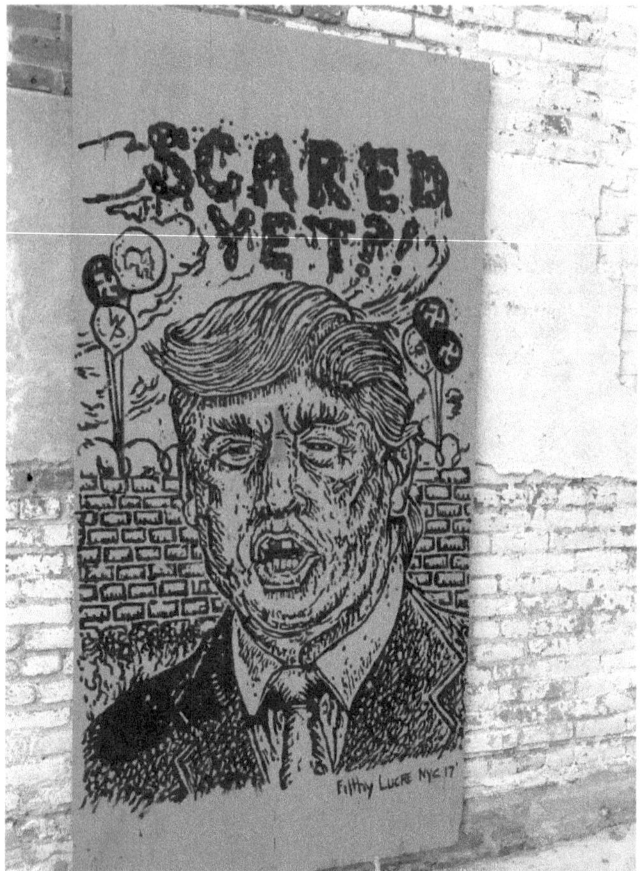

Figure 5.3 'Scared Yet'. © Jeffrey Ian Ross.

Summary

Regardless of the neighbourhood, although graffiti and street art are part of the DC visual landscape, little of it is anti-Trump in nature. In order to further contextualize my observations from the neighbourhoods I explored, I will now provide a basic statistical analysis of the work I encountered.

Graffiti

The majority of graffiti in any large city is undoubtedly tags (i.e. markings often containing a graffitists unique street name and signature). This is as

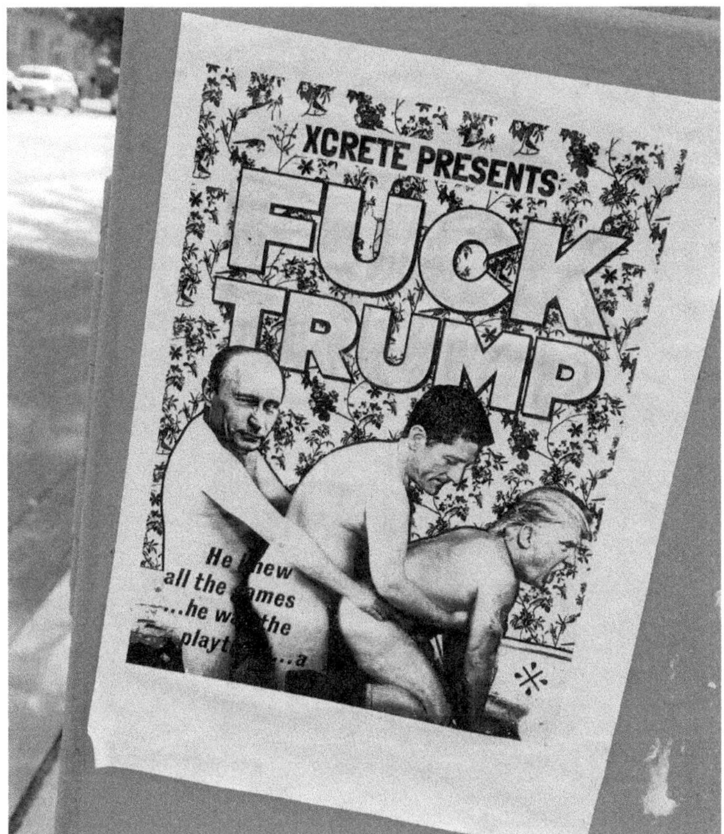

Figure 5.4 XCRETE Presents. © Jeffrey Ian Ross.

true in Washington DC as it is in other urban locations. Despite Washington boasting a relatively large activist community, and being the setting for frequent anti-Trump protests, very little of the graffiti or street art is anti-Trump. The majority of the anti-Trump graffiti are the 'Fuck Trump' tags, some of which is signed by Dirty Knucklez.

Street Art

Most of street art that was critical of Trump was in the form of stickers, with statements written in capital letters, posted to traffic signs. Many were quite simple, like 'NO WONDER NAZIS + KKK LOVE tRUMP'. Many made sexual references. Others included posters of Trump and/or Jared Kushner,

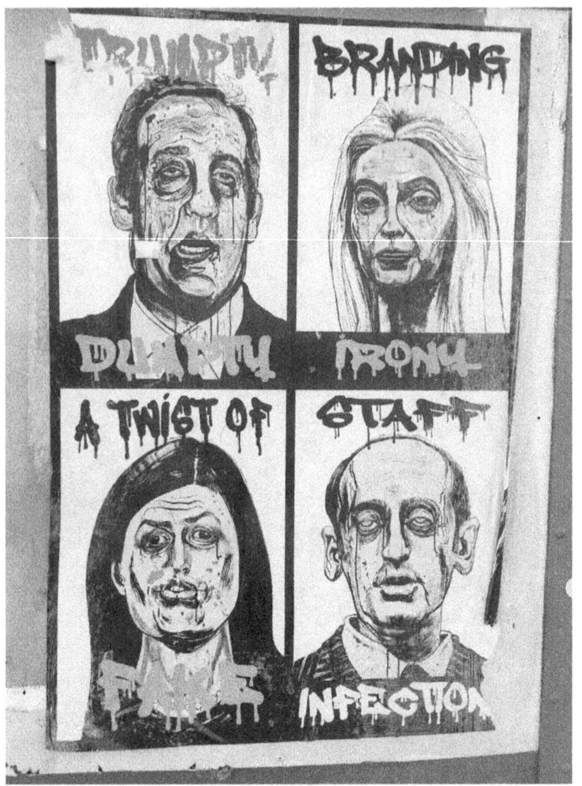

Figure 5.5 Robbie Conal posters. © Jeffrey Ian Ross.

Trump's son-in-law.[13] As one got closer to the downtown office complexes, less graffiti and street art was found. The majority of all graffiti and street art is at eye level, and little of it is to be found in inaccessible places.

Data Analysis

Type of Graffiti and Street Art

Among the fifty-five separate observations, the majority of work was stickers and then posters (see Table 5.1). Few of the neighbourhoods had the same stickers. The most dominant stickers were the previously mentioned yellow ones, with what appeared to be handwritten statements covering many different expressions. Other than those previously mentioned, and the pervasive 'Fuck Trump' graffiti presented as tags, there was very little tagging.

Table 5.1 Type of graffiti and street art.

Type	No.	Percentage
Stickers	38	69.09
Posters	10	18.18
Tags	7	12.73
Total	**55**	**100**

Placement of Graffiti and Street Art

Anti-Trump graffiti and street art was placed on a variety of surfaces. Four locations seemed to be most dominant: traffic signs, walls, garbage cans and poles (see Table 5.2). This makes sense because the majority of those pieces were stickers. They could be affixed quickly so the perpetrator could leave the scene quickly. Almost all of the graffiti and street art was at eye level, and thus readily accessible to pedestrians and motorists alike. None of this work was on the subways, and even though there was graffiti/street art on the walls of open stretches of the subway line, none of it was anti-Trump related.

Table 5.2 Placement of graffiti and street art.

Placement	No.	Percentage
Traffic sign	12	21.82
Wall	11	20.00
Garbage can	9	16.36
Pole	7	12.72
Newspaper box	3	5.46
Parking meter	3	5.46
Electrical box	2	3.64
Parking lot attendant booth	2	3.64
Abandoned fire and police call box	2	3.64
Silver metal panel	1	1.82
Curb	1	1.82
Planter	1	1.82
Cigarette disposal bin	1	1.82
Total	**55**	**100**

Location/Neighbourhood of Graffiti and Street Art

All neighbourhoods visited had at least one piece of graffiti or street art, but three locations stood out: Capitol Hill/Barracks Row/Eastern Market, Shaw, and DuPont Circle (see Table 5.3). As this was not a citywide study, but highly selective in terms of the neighbourhoods visited, it is difficult to comment with any degree of certainty about why there may be more graffiti and street art in some neighbourhoods than others. Again, this may come down more to anti-graffiti and street art abatement patterns than to actual attempts by perpetrators/practitioners to engage in this activity.

Summary

Each place and neighbourhood attracts different taggers, graffiti and street artists/writers, and audiences, and this work is done in a context in which BIDs and the DC Department of Public Works remove and/or abate graffiti and street art. Although not my intent, I did not find any pro-Trump graffiti or street art, or any work that was against any oppositional politicians (e.g. elected members of the Democratic Party). This might be different in those parts of the country where there is a high level of support for Trump, and where there has been an upsurge in racist and antisemitic graffiti and/or street art.

Conclusion

For a city that is so intimately connected to the federal government of the United States and the presidency, I was a little perplexed that there was so little anti-Trump graffiti and street art in Washington DC. In general, this contrasts with my perceptions of graffiti/street art in other major capital cities I have visited like Berlin, Buenos Aries, London, Madrid, Ottawa, Paris, Rome and Santiago.

What might explain this low level of graffiti and street art? One reason may be the fact that Washington, DC is one of the most heavily policed cities in the world. There are close to twenty-three different municipal and federal departments that operate in this city (Ross 2013), and the latter patrol federal buildings, monuments and land, thus these surfaces would be difficult for graffiti and street artists to reach. It is noted, however, that in some jurisdictions in the United States police officers may be reluctant to ticket or arrest individuals who engage in graffiti and street art (Ross and Wright 2014).

Table 5.3 Location/neighbourhood of graffiti and street art.

Location	No.	Percentage
Capitol Hill/Barracks Row/Eastern Market	11	20.00
Shaw	10	18.18
DuPont Circle	6	10.91
Adams Morgan	4	7.27
Union Market/Gallaudet	4	7.27
Brookland/Rhode Island Metro	3	5.45
Glover Park	3	5.45
Georgetown	3	5.45
White House/Lafayette Park	3	5.45
14th Street/Logan Circle	2	3.64
Friendship Heights	1	1.82
Kalorama	1	1.82
H Street	1	1.82
Bryce Park	1	1.82
Blagden Alley	1	1.82
Miscellaneous	1	1.82
Total	**55**	**100**

Similarly, the BIDs and the Department of Public Works may be more efficient at graffiti and street art abatement in DC than in other cities. They may do a better job of removing both regular graffiti and street art, and that which refers to Trump, than in places like New York City. Although I somehow doubt this, it is a hypothesis worthy of consideration.

It could also be that there are already enough different types of protest in Washington DC that have a sufficient visual impact. We can see anti-Trump bumper stickers, and signs and posters placed in shop windows and residences, and messages placed on clothing. Some of the materials appeared to be the same ones used in the Women's March (2017), and seemed to include some of the numerous signs that people brought to anti-Trump rallies. In other words, the city may have reached a normative level of saturation, and those inclined to engage in graffiti or street art have determined that any more anti-Trump visual communication was unnecessary.

Engaging in anti-Trump graffiti and street art requires a different level of commitment. Putting a sticker on your car is one step up from 'liking' a post on Facebook. But putting words and images in the form of graffiti and street art in the streets is typically illegal, and certainly another step. It may also be that while graffiti and street art is more normative in cities like New York and London, in Washington it may be a less acceptable means of protest amongst those who are against the Trump presidency.

Most importantly, the low level of anti-Trump graffiti and street art may be a reflection of the overall conservative nature of Washington DC. This is reflected in a variety of cultural processes, such as consumer choices (fashions, food choices, music preferences, etc.), individual aspirations, and selection of educational institutions. Also, like most big cities, a great number of people work in DC, but many of them commute in from the more tranquil Virginia and Maryland suburbs. The practice of graffiti and street art may thus be perceived by this demographic to be outside the realm of conventional political activity that they would engage in. These individuals, instead, may confine themselves to the simple act of voting during election cycles. Thus, in analysing any location for the presence of visual resistance, it is important to take into consideration the prevailing political culture of that city.

Where do we go from here? Clearly there are multiple avenues for further research connected to anti-Trump graffiti/street art in Washington DC and elsewhere that I could explore. I might expand the number of neighbourhoods in DC where one might find graffiti or street art, and scour them for evidence of anti-Trump pieces. That said, the places that were visited have historically been known to contain a considerable amount of graffiti and street art, and I believe that I am now entering a situation of diminishing returns. I could also expend more effort to connect with DC-based graffiti writers and street artists, and see what their understanding of the anti-Trump aspect is, and learn if there are additional untapped areas where I might find this work.

I could also attempt to interview progressive (including anarchist) activist groups and see if they use graffiti and street art in their political protest practices. This strategy could include asking questions about why they engage in this activity, including issues concerning placement and types of surfaces. In addition, a systematic comparison between DC and other large urban centres, both in the United States and elsewhere, could be conducted. This would help us to better contextualize what is happening in the US capital. I could also increase the length of the observational period. In other words, I could continue to look for graffiti and street art in DC and see what else I find.

In order to better understand graffiti and street art, it will be necessary to develop and encourage a literacy amongst people about graffiti and street art, including its types, its practitioners, its viewers, and the effects it may and may not have (Ross and Lennon 2018).

There is another element to understand. The internet, in particular social media, has become a major platform for the dissemination, consumption and appreciation of graffiti and street art. Anti-Trump graffiti and street art does not need to be confined to the surfaces of one's own city. Regardless where it is placed, one cannot dismiss the importance of social media sites like Facebook, Twitter, YouTube, and especially Instagram to magnify the effect of anti-Trump messages. More people can see the effects of this kind of protest. The images and slogans can be painted over and are thus transient. But their shelf life is extended on the web, they can be viewed by many more people, and thus they will have a greater visual impact (MacDowell 2017; MacDowell and de Souza 2017).

Regardless of the amount, type or location of graffiti and street art critical of Trump, it is clear that many citizens of the District of Columbia are not happy about him, and they have chosen a variety of modalities to express this sentiment.

Acknowledgements

An earlier version of this chapter was presented at Erasmus Law School, Rotterdam, on 5 September 2019. Special thanks to Jai Pandit for coding data and its analysis, to John F. Lennon and Dakota Ross-Cabrera for their comments, and to Chris Chappell and the editors of this book for their feedback.

Jeffrey Ian Ross, PhD, is a professor at the University of Baltimore. He specializes in corrections, policing, crimes of the powerful, and street culture. Ross's books include the *Routledge Handbook of Graffiti and Street Art* (2016). He is the co-editor of a special issue of *Visual Inquiry* on 'Interrogating the Co-optation and Commodification of modern Graffiti and Street Art'. In 2018, he was given the Hans W. Mattick Award, 'for an individual who has made a distinguished contribution to the field of Criminology and Criminal Justice practice', from the University of Illinois at Chicago. In 2020, Ross received the John Howard Award from the Academy of Criminal Justice Sciences' Division of Corrections.

Notes

1. For a review of the multiple definitions of graffiti and street art, see, for example, Ross 2016b.
2. All future references to anti-Trump graffiti and street art should be assumed to be work directed towards his family, his administration, or unpopular policies and practices associated with his regime.
3. The intense analysis of graffiti and/or street art in a particular city is not without its precedents. See, for example, Ferrell 1996, Macdonald 2001, Ross 2016c.
4. These three books should not be interpreted as the only discussions of graffiti and street art in the district, as short (typically 2–3 page) chapters featuring DC-based graffiti writers have appeared in other books.
5. The first expression refers to the fact that the hotel is viewed by many as a way that Trump has helped to funnel money to his business from foreign dignitaries who may be staying there, and the 'Shithole' comment refers to Trump's negative statement about lesser-developed countries.
6. Although there are private individuals who engage in buffing graffiti and street art, and the Department of Public Works is responsible for removing this material from public buildings, there is not so much of this activity in DC. For a review on how major cities respond to graffiti and street art, see, for example, Ross 2016d.
7. Indeed, over these years new political issues developed as the Trump administration kept on implementing controversial policies, practices and laws. This time frame also ignores the considerable amount of graffiti and street art that appeared in Washington, DC during the spring of 2020, in the context of the protests in connection with the death of George Floyd, an African-American man, at the hands of a Minneapolis police officer.
8. Not everyone I encountered working for a BID was friendly or approachable – in fact, some were very dismissive.
9. This survey of the neighborhoods was not meant to be comprehensive, but believe that it is representative of the kinds of work that was available on the surfaces of DC.
10. There are significant differences among the four divisions of DC. For a review of the crime patterns based on these divisions see, for example, Ross (2013).
11. With hindsight, the majority of areas of the city that I scanned were disproportionately white, in terms of residents, and were mainly either wealthy or currently being gentrified. If I had spent more time in those parts of the city that were mainly poor or predominantly black then there may have been a possibility to see more anti-Trump graffiti and street art.
12. Produced with spray paint, and spell out the writer's name in bubble-style letters that are typically filled in with a single colour (Ross 2016a: 478).
13. Some of these stickers had websites connected to them.

References

Arnold, T., and D. Uliano. 2016. 'Police: Trump's New DC Hotel Vandalized with "Black Lives Matter" Graffiti', WTOP, 2 October. Retrieved 2 May 2019 from https://wtop.com/dc/2016/10/police-trumps-new-dc-hotel-vandalized-black-lives-matter-graffiti/.

Avramidis, K., and M. Tsilimpounidi (eds). 2017. *Graffiti and Street Art: Reading, Writing and Representing the City*. New York: Routledge.

Boone, G.M., J. Secci and L.M. Gallant. 2018. 'Resistance: Active and Creative Political Protest Strategies'. *American Behavioral Scientist* 62(3): 353–74.

Chavez, N., and E. Smith. 2017. '"Pay Trump Bribes Here" Sign Projected onto Trump's DC Hotel', *CNN*, 16 May. Retrieved 17 September 2020 from https://www.cnn.com/2017/05/16/politics/trump-hotel-projection/index.html.

David, E. 2007. 'Signs of Resistance: Marking Public Space through a Renewed Cultural Activism', in G.C. Starczak (ed.), *Visual Research Methods*. Thousand Oaks, CA: Sage Publications, pp. 225–54

Ferrell, J. 1996. *Crimes of Style: Urban Graffiti and the Politics of Criminality*. Boston, MA: Northeastern University Press.

Gastman, R. 2001. *Free Agents: A History of Washington, DC Graffiti*. New York: Soft Sckull Press.

Hyra, D.S. 2018. *Race, Class, and Politics in the Cappuccino City*. Chicago, IL: University of Chicago Press.

iwillnot. 2018. *Smashed: The Art of the Sticker Combo: Featuring the Art of the DC Street Sticker Expo*. Pennsauken, NJ: BookBaby.

Jørgensen, N. 2008. 'Urban Wall Languaging'. *International Journal of Multilingualism* 5: 237–52.

Lewis, N.M. 2010. 'Grappling with Governance: The Emergence of Business Improvement Districts in a National Capital'. *Urban Affairs Review* 46(2): 180–217.

Macdonald, N. 2001. *The Graffiti Subculture: Youth, Masculinity and Identity in London and New York*. New York: Palgrave Macmillan.

MacDowall, L.J. 2017. '#Instafame Aesthetics, Audiences, Data', in K. Avramidis and M. Tsilimpounidi (eds), *Graffiti and Street Art: Reading, Writing, and Representing the City*. New York: Routledge, pp. 231–49.

MacDowall, L.J., and P. de Souza. 2017. '"I'd Double Tap That!!": Street Art, Graffiti, and Instagram Research'. *Media, Culture and Society* 40(1): 3–22.

Moran, L. 2017. 'A Tremendous Roundup of Street Art Ridiculing Donald Trump: From England and Austria to New York and Los Angeles, the Writing Is on the Wall'. Huffington Post, 2 February. Retrieved 10 January 2019 from https://www.huffingtonpost.com/entry/anti-trump-street-art_us_58820c24e4b070d8cad1ead2.

Muller, J. 2017. '"Fuck Trump" is DC's Street Art Anthem: And It Won't Be Going Away Anytime Soon'. *Washington City Paper*, 28 April. Retrieved 10 January 2019 from https://www.washingtoncitypaper.com/news/city-desk/article/20859779/fuck-trump-is-dcs-street-art-anthem.

Myer, D.S., and S. Tarrow (eds). 2018. *The Resistance: The Dawn of the Anti-Trump Opposition Movement*. New York: Oxford University Press.

Phillips, S.A. 1999. *Wallbanging: Graffiti and Gangs in L.A.* Chicago, IL: University of Chicago Press.

Ross, J.I. 2013. 'Washington, DC', in J.I. Ross (ed.), *Encyclopedia of Street Crime in America*. Thousand Oaks, CA: Sage Publications, pp. 447–49.

——— (ed.). 2016a. *Routledge Handbook on Graffiti and Street Art*. New York: Routledge.

———. 2016b. 'Introduction: Sorting It All Out', in J.I. Ross (ed.), *Routledge Handbook on Graffiti and Street Art*. New York: Routledge, pp. 1–10

———. 2016c. 'Effects of Graffiti and Street Art', in J.I. Ross (ed.), *Routledge Handbook on Graffiti and Street Art*. New York: Routledge, pp. 389–92.

———. 2016d. 'How Major Urban Centers in the United States Respond to Graffiti/Street Art', in J.I. Ross (ed.), *Routledge Handbook on Graffiti and Street Art*. New York: Routledge, pp. 393–403.

Ross, J.I., et al. 2017. 'In Search of Academic Legitimacy: The Current State of Scholarship on Graffiti and Street Art'. *The Social Science Journal* 54(4): 411–19.

Ross, J.I., and J.F. Lennon. 2018. 'Teaching about Graffiti and Street Art to Undergraduate Students at U.S. Universities: Confronting Challenges and Seizing Opportunities'. *Journal of Interdisciplinary Studies in Education* 6(2): 1–19.

Ross, J.I., and B. Wright. 2014. '"I've Got Better Things to Worry About": Police Perceptions of Graffiti and Street Art in a Large Mid-Atlantic City'. *Police Quarterly* 17(2): 176–200.

Schwartz, H. 2017. 'Political Street Art Sightings from across the Country and around the World'. *CNN*, 3 November. Retrieved 17 September 2020 from https://www.cnn.com/2017/11/03/politics/cover-line-street-art/index.html.

Scott, J.C. 1985. *Weapons of the Weak*. New Haven, CT: Yale University Press.

———. 1990. *Domination and the Art of Resistance*. New Haven, CT: Yale University Press.

Shuler, M. 2019. '"The Art of Vandalism": A Built Environment Analysis of Edgewood Washington, DC'. Retrieved 2 May 2019 from https://edspace.american.edu/ms4241a/about-me/.

Snyder, G.J. 2009. *Graffiti Lives: Beyond the Tag in New York's Urban Underground*. New York: New York University Press.

Summers, B. 2015. 'H Street, Main Street and the Neoliberal Aesthetics of Cool', in D. Hyra and S. Prince (eds), *Capital Dilemma: Growth and Inequality in Washington, DC*. New York: Routledge, pp. 299–314.

Tanner, J. 2016. 'Donald Trump Inspires US Street Artists to Reach for the Spray Paint'. *Independent*, 2 November. Retrieved 28 January 2019 from https://www.independent.co.uk/news/world/americas/donald-trump-us-presidential-election-graffiti-street-art-murals-a7393626.html.

Tulke, J. 2018. 'Not My President, Ever! One Year of Anti-Trump Street Art and Graffiti'. *Aesthetics of Crisis*, 20 January. Retrieved 10 January 2019 from http://aestheticsofcrisis.org/2018/not-my-president-ever-one-year-of-anti-trump-street-art-and-graffiti/.

Waldner, L.K., and B.A. Dobratz. 2013. 'Graffiti as a Form of Contentious Political Participation'. *Sociology Compass* 7(5): 377–89.

Waldron, T. 2018. 'This Guy's Got 2 Words for the President, and He's Putting Them All Over DC'. *Huffington Post*, 22 January. Retrieved 17 September 2020 from https://www.huffpost.com/entry/fuck-trump-graffiti-washington_n_5a660f7be4b0e563007201fd.

Wolf, J.F. 2006. 'Urban Governance and Business Improvement Districts: The Washington, DC BIDs'. *International Journal of Public Administration* 29(1–3): 53–75.

Yoseph, S. 2012. 'Red, Read, Remix: A Documentary and Cultural Exploration of Metro Graffiti'. Master's thesis, Georgetown University.

Chapter 6

Vandalizing the Commons

Andrea Pavoni

Erasure

On the morning of 12 March 2016, in the streets of Bologna, people woke to find that several famous street artworks had suddenly disappeared overnight, covered by generous coats of grey paint. A few people were still working on it, using paint-rollers with long extension poles, thoroughly applying layer after layer of paint over one of Bologna's most famous murals, *Occupy Mordor*, which had been made by the Italian street artist Blu. The atmosphere was convivial, a musical band playing, while a small crowd of journalists and passers-by gazed with curiosity. The sight of people erasing graffiti from Bologna's walls, as in any city, was certainly not unusual, especially at a time in which the whole country was obsessed with the aesthetic-moral category of urban *decorum* (Tulumello and Bertoni 2019). Removing 'signs' of degradation from the streets had become a moral duty of the responsible citizen. In Milan the year before, more than a thousand volunteers had cleaned the streets of graffiti as part of the *Beautiful Milan* initiative, but also erasing, while carried away with cleaning zeal, a mural by street artists Pau and Linda that had been authorized by the municipality itself (Liso 2015). Likewise in Bologna, the 'NO TAG project' has involved since 2013 a team of volunteers with the purpose of removing 'tags, graffiti and other acts of graphic vandalism' from the city's walls.[1] The previous December, the mayor Virgilio Merola had enthusiastically endorsed the NO TAG project, coherent with the long-standing battle that the city is waging against graffiti, with the consequent criminalization of many writers, whose arrests are usually trumpeted on the front pages of the local conservative newspaper.[2] And yet something in this scene was out of place. These people were clearly not working for the municipality. Their look, their movements and attires were much closer to those who usually *write* on walls than to those who *clean* them. In fact, these people were for the most part activists belonging to two local social centres, Crash and XM24.

At the time of its appearance in 2013, *Occupy Mordor* was acclaimed as a street art masterpiece. Truly beautiful, and powerful, it depicted in the style of a Tolkien's epic a fateful battle between the forces of urban speculation – the political and economic powers running the city – and a variegated population of activists, farmers, cyclists: city-dwellers. The mural perfectly captured the gentrifying zeitgeist, and was positioned in the most appropriate site to do so: a wall of XM24, a social centre constantly under threat of eviction and demolition. *Occupy Mordor* 'is an "artistic barricade" in the defence of a social space threatened by the *gentrification* of the surrounding Bolognina district. [In this place] the City Council intends to build a roundabout, flattening the social centre' (wu ming 2013, my translation). Thus wrote the *wu ming* collective at the time. Six years on, the situation has not changed much. XM24, which has occupied the space of a former food market since 2002, still remains on the brink of eviction – at the time of writing, all the more so.[3]

There were also municipal police officers looking at the scene, puzzled. Usually they are the ones ordering people to erase writings from the walls. What should they do? They asked some questions. They left. They came back: 'This wall is Council property, and they want to know what is going on', they uttered. 'We're eliminating urban decay', one of the painters rebutted. 'Did you ask the permission to the artist?', the agents continued, making a half-hearted attempt to stop the action, only to refrain,[4] as there were too many people around. 'What should I fine them for? I don't even know what kind of crime this is…', one agent is said to have exclaimed. They had no clue.[5]

Destruction

A notorious photographic sequence from 1995 shows Ai Weiwei impassively letting a Han dynasty urn fall from his hands and smash on the ground.[6] Weiwei had regularly bought the urn, together with others that he then painted in different colours and with advertising slogans. One of them would become the protagonist of another photographic triptych, realized in 2012 by Swiss artist Manuel Salvisberg, and performed by his fellow countryman, art collector and former ambassador in China, Uli Sigg, who is shown dropping and smashing on the ground the Weiwei's *Coca-Cola Urn*, in Weiwei-esque pose. Could he do it? In the byzantine world of copyright, the notion of 'moral right' is a particularly idiosyncratic one. It inserts an animistic dimension in the juridical jargon, in so far as it is supposed to embody 'a belief that an artist in the process of creation injects his spirit into the work, and that the artist's personality as well as the integrity of the work should therefore be protected and preserved'.[7] Although it had been a regular purchase from the Chinese artist, did Salvisberg respect Weiwei's moral right vis-à-vis the *Coca-Cola Urn*? Asked about this matter, he swiftly responded: 'Did Ai Weiwei ask the masters who created the vessels he uses in his work many years ago?' (in Yap 2012).

Two years later, in 2014, the Dominican artist Maximo Carminero bought a regular ticket for a Weiwei exhibition at the Pérez Art Museum in Miami. Once inside, he took one of the painted ancient urns on display, and calmly smashed it on the ground. Confusingly, he painted this gesture as a political act against the museum for allegedly paying little attention to local artists, and compared it with Weiwei's most famous act: was he not the first to smash urns which were 'patrimony of humanity'? Weiwei did not see much sense in Caminero's gesture (Madigan 2014). The Dominican got an 18-month probation, a fine, and a good deal of notoriety from the event.

'Short of witnessing grievous bodily harm, few things are as astonishing as seeing the casual, physical destruction of what one holds sacred', writes Teju Cole (2012). While all three gestures ended up with a similar outcome, the striking effect they produce on the viewer is unavoidably filtered by the context in which they occur, and the normative framework through which they are seen. Searching among the dusty debris of the three urns one may find that some relations are more resilient than others: some have been shattered, while some are still perfectly in place even after the physical destruction. Property is made of a more resistant material than terracotta. This is why Caminero's gesture appears so shocking: what is held sacred here is not an ancient urn but the right to property, both in its private and collective sense (as cultural heritage). This is the sacredness these gestures differently affect. This is the magical operator able to turn vandalism into art, and vice versa. The crux of the matter was expressed clearly in the words of curator Kerry Brougher: 'Ai Weiwei, I believe, has owned in one way or other the things that he has destroyed [in his art]. [Caminero] was destroying someone else's property. That strikes me as a form of vandalism and not a form of art' (in Steinhauer 2014)

Preservation

According to the theory of loss aversion coined by Nobel laureate Daniel Kahneman, averting a loss is always a strong preference for individuals vis-à-vis acquiring gains of the same value. Loss aversion, as Cornelius

Holtorf (2015) suggests, appears to indeed be the case in current attitudes to heritage, where 'the remains of the past seems to exist only to be preserved' (Fairclough 2009: 158). This 'obsession with physical conservation' (ibid.) is perfectly consistent with the words of Abbé Henri Grégoire ([1794] 1977), to whom we owe the modern notion of vandalism, coined in 1794 to criticize the destruction of cultural patrimony that followed the French Revolution: 'Barbarians and slaves hate science and destroy monuments of art. Free men love and conserve them'.

In his classic 1933 report, Raphael Lemkin proposed to outlaw 'acts of vandalism', namely those acts that have to do with the destruction of 'works of cultural or artistic heritage'. These acts, akin to those of 'barbarity' (acts of extermination, for which he would later coin the notion of *genocide*), express 'the *asocial* and *destructive* spirit of the author' (Lemkin 1933). In the 1956 Hague Convention for the Protection of Cultural Property in the Event of Armed Conflict, the concept was updated to refer to 'any act of vandalism directed against cultural property'. Subsequently, the definition would gradually widen from the question of heritage to encompass that of criminal activity *tout court*, eventually coming to signify 'an intentional or malicious act to destroy, damage or deface the property of another, whether cultural or not' (Merrill 2011: 62). Today, vandalism defines an act that targets the physical materialization of the (private or collective) right to property, and more generally, any act that may be said to threaten a normative constellation formed by culture, property, physical integrity, or preservation.

However, asks Holtorf, 'is the value of cultural heritage really inherent in a given object so that it might be damaged with the object'? (Holtorf 2015: 4). In a brilliant short text, Tim Ingold (2010) takes aim at this preservationist tendency by challenging its underlying ontological assumption about the hylomorphic origin of beings: what if, by shifting paradigm, we understand ontology as a continuum in which formations, beings, emerge and persist as crystallizations that do not originate at a precise moment in time, but rather contribute, by happening, to constitute time itself? Following this position may imply shifting away from 'the current emphasis on the material fossilisation of heritage as "product", towards a focus on heritage as "process"' (Jones 2006: 120–21), and a necessary recalibration of the contemporary tendency to musealize everything existing. After all, how do we define the essential properties of a given site, if not by singling out, arbitrarily, a given point in time (Morris 1877)? We also find the same oscillation between product – or, more precisely, 'resource' – and process in the current debate over a fundamental concept in which the notion of heritage is included – namely, the commons.

Commons

Since the seminal work of Garrett Hardin (1968), and through influential theorizations such as that by Nobel laureate Elinor Ostrom (1990), the notion of commons has often been framed as a static and depletable resource that is to be protected, enclosed and safeguarded so as to be *preserved* against its unilateral appropriation, abuse and destruction. This interpretation has been applied not only to so-called 'subtractive' resources (that is, resources reduced by use, e.g. water), but also, implicitly, to 'nonsubtractive' ones (not reduced by use, e.g. knowledge). In both cases, in fact, the commons has been still understood 'substantially' – that is, as a given 'product' that to some extent remains external to those who produced it, use it and enjoy it – and thus from the panoply of interactions and practices that emerge around it (cf. Hess and Ostrom 2007). The question is further complicated moving to the urban context. As Christian Borch and Martin Kornberger ask, can we really assume, as this reasoning implies, that an urban street be a subtractive resource – in other words, something that is affected negatively by use? Are not urban streets 'reduced' when suffering an absence of interaction and relations – that is, when not 'used' and lived? In this case, evidently 'the act of consuming does not detract but rather increases value' (Borch and Kornberger 2015: 6).

A wave of radical thinking around the commons has convincingly integrated its sedentary picture as an external 'resource' with a more complex, dynamic and processual one. In their well-known study, Michael Hardt and Toni Negri define the commons as 'not only the earth we share but also the languages we create, the social practices we establish, the modes of sociality that define our relationships, and so forth' (Hardt and Negri 2009: 139). The urban commons (from now UC), in this sense, would be the coming together of human and non-human bodies, ideas, knowledge, images and practices, that constitute a city. An immanent, socio-material and transformative relation that cannot be reduced to a given object, space or domain (for example, knowledge), and cannot be clearly distinguished between material and immaterial. Albeit David Harvey somewhat struggles to accept the latter point,[8] he is spot on when defining the commons as not 'something that existed once upon a time that has since been lost, but something that is, like the urban commons, continuously being produced': a *commoning*, that is (Harvey 2012: 77; Linebaugh 2008). Not simply 'something' that is shared, the UC would be an emergent process through which 'sharing' itself assumes an ontological quality, to the extent that 'the commons is not just something that is shared by pre-existing commoners; rather the commoners may be constituted in the creation of production of a commons' (Borch and Kornberger 2015: 8–9; Stavrides 2016: 7).

Providing an 'urban' dimension to the commons is not only convenient to the present text; it also emphasizes its relational, spatial and affective dimension, as a sort of urban atmosphere, as again Borch and Kornberger (2015) propose. This notion is particularly valuable, well beyond its metaphoric sense. Take the specific vibe of a neighbourhood, and frame it as an atmosphere emerging out of the relationality and density of its built environment, sociocultural histories, legal rules, daily interactions, aesthetic designs, and local and global imaginaries. Its atmosphere is this 'coming together of people, buildings, technologies and various forms of non-human life in particular geographical settings' (Conradson and Latham 2007: 238). This concept makes explicit how UC is a 'common space' that is co-produced at the intersection between structures, representations and experience (cf. Sloterdijk 2004). In this way, it avoids the immateriality of certain theorizations of cultural commons, emphasizing instead both the ontological materiality of tangible and intangible bodies, relations and practices that produce a city, as well as the phenomenological and thus aesthetic (e.g. sensorial) immersion in and through which its inhabitants experience and live the urban every day. While there is no room here to explore the promising ways in which this notion has been dealt with in the last decade (see Adey et al. 2013; Bille, Bjerregaard and Flohr Sørensen 2015; see Pavoni 2018: ch. 2), suffice to highlight its value in focusing on the emergent (contingent) and stratified (historical) configurations of affects, senses, bodies and spaces that constitute the UC and, at the same time, to the way they are acted upon, reproduced and retuned for political, economic or securitarian purposes (e.g. Anderson 2009; Thibaud 2011; Philippopoulos-Mihalopoulos 2016). One may indeed argue that the key aesthetic-political urban question is that of how to organize –materially, emotionally and symbolically – our common (physical, affective, cultural) spaces of co-existence, and thus, our UC (cf. Sloterdijk 2013).

This is particularly evident vis-à-vis the contemporary rise of 'creative city' policies, today grown into a hegemonic 'meta-policy' shaping urbanization dynamics worldwide (Peck 2012), as urban branding has become an all-encompassing urban development strategy in which discourses and policies of planning, security, marketing and law converge, producing safe, commodified and entertaining urban atmospheres (Pavoni 2018). In this context, the UC may be decomposed into creativity index parameters (Florida 2002) that fuel unequal processes of financial valorization, commodification, gentrification and so on (Smith 1996). While exploring these processes is not the task of the present text, it is important to stress that any such explorations should not assume the UC as a somewhat pristine, homogeneous and pacific set of relations, which would only be subsequently acted upon by the forces of market, security and control. The urban being-together is always normatively tuned in one way or another (cf. Pavoni 2011), and there is no pure, ideal, or intrinsically 'just' UC waiting to be 'liberated' from the manipulation of power. Paraphrasing Andreas Philippopoulos-Mihalopoulos (2015: 3), the UC is not a 'culturally-relative flat ontology but a tilted, power-structured surface', always asymmetric, conflictual and political.

Against the tendency to idealize it as such, therefore, we should stress that the UC is 'not just about *opposing* power and capitalism' since 'all sorts of power and politics go into how commons are produced' (Borch and Kornberger 2015: 16). We should be wary, for instance, of the implicit depoliticization of the commons, which subtends the call for increasing participation, sharing and collectivization. Not only because this is the very language on which neoliberalism thrives, but also because, as Jodi Dean remarks, the commons are internally antagonistic, divisive, heterogeneous and conflictual (Dean 2012). Taking aim at one of the main representatives of this tendency, i.e. the free culture movement championed by the likes of Lawrence Lessig and Yochai Benkler, Matteo Pasquinelli (2014: 171) explains that 'the commons of culture are not an independent domain of pure freedom, cooperation and autonomy, but they are constantly subjected to the force field of capitalism'. This is strategically significant: if the UC is always a conflictual, asymmetrical and power-structured surface, with no pre-existing 'pure' commons to be somehow recovered, then the political question will not be that of 'liberating' a given and static resource from the grasp of power, but rather that of reorienting an always power-structured process into more desirable configurations – the difference, that is, between a passive and reactive politics of preservation, protection and enclosure, and an active politics of reconfiguration, production and becoming.

It may be useful, in this sense, to mention Jacques Rancière and his understanding of politics as having to do with the 'distribution of the sensible'; that is, 'the system of self-evident facts of sense perception that simultaneously discloses the existence of something in common and the delimitations that define the respective parts and positions within it' (Rancière 2004: 12). Politics, in other words, has to do with the normative organization of a common: the way in which it is experienced, sensed and reproduced according to a spatially and historically situated aesthetic regime, given a consensually accepted 'common sense'. In a radically opposite sense to that of Jurgen Habermas, therefore, *political* would be the act of rupturing this common sense, reverting the existent distribution of the sensible by letting appear something, someone, some instance, that cannot be contained within the existent configuration. What Rancière (cf. 2010) refers to as *dissensus*, in our terms, would be an aesthetic praxis that, by challenging the given configuration of power relations, asymmetries and structures that normatively *tunes* the UC, will make it visible and thus amenable to action, reconfiguration and transformation. Not a reduction or destruction, this vandalization of the UC would entail the reframing of coordinates of perception, experience and engagement, and would thus, in this way, be an active and productive *re-commoning*.

Vandalism

According to Godofredo Nobre, vandalism removes the profane patina of banality (its apparent 'inconspicuousness', as Robert Musil once wrote) from a monument or a building by showing its deep sacredness, 'the *real* power of the building and the truth of architecture. One vandalizes because it's worth it, because the building represents something' (Nobre 2010). As he continues: 'Vandalism is an attack against the profane (against the building that pretends to be profane) showing that it is deeply sacred, bringing to the fore the totemic monument that lurks behind the mundane routine of everyday life' (ibid.).

This is, to be sure, not in the sense of unfolding some kind of hidden reality that lies beyond the building, but rather in order to break the spell that the building – or a given heritage site for that matter – with its sheer materiality, embodies. One is reminded of George Bataille's words: 'Actually, it is evident that monuments inspire social wisdom and arouse a veritable awe. The storming of the Bastille is symbolic of this state of affairs: it is difficult to explain such a crowd movement, except by taking into account the animosity of a people against those monuments, who are their real masters' (Bataille 1929).

Vandalism makes explicit the sacredness of property (either individual or common, as in the 'patrimony of humanity' definition) by challenging both its *immunity* and (physical) *integrity*, as well as, as we saw, by embodying its original, anarchic and 'dirty' act of appropriation. In their seminal article introducing the Broken Windows theory, James Wilson and George Kelling wrote that 'vandalism can occur anywhere, once communal barriers – the sense of mutual regard and the obligations of civility – are lowered by actions that seem to signal that "no one cares"' (Wilson and Kelling 1982). 'Caring for the common', they seem to imply, requires maintaining protective barriers so as to keep the vandals outside. Graffiti, they famously observed, is understood as a vandalistic practice that, by lowering such barriers, exposes the common to the risk of depletion.

Surfacing in the dilapidated landscape of the late 1970s US East Coast, modern graffiti did indeed incarnate a transgression vis-à-vis the quintessential moral and aesthetic barriers of 'civilization': order, beauty and cleanliness (Freud [1930] 2002).[9] From the beginning, their trajectory violently intersected that of social control measures inspired by the Broken Windows theory, most enthusiastically employed to address 'quality of life' crime by New York City police commissioner William Bratton and mayor Rudolph Giuliani in the 1990s. The 'moral panic' narratives of the time defined graffiti as a visual sign of decay and an incentive to criminal activity – a symptom as well as a scapegoat of the ongoing crisis. New York's mayor Ed Koch famously coined the slogan: 'Make your mark in society, not on society' – to which it was all too easy to answer 'no', because as writer Iz the Wiz summarized, 'When you're poor that's all you got' (in Huertas 2015: 10). In fact, it would be more correct to say that graffiti artists were making their mark both *in* and *on* society. Graffiti emerged because of social and environmental decay, plus the lowering of controls released possibilities for this form of visual appropriation. More profoundly, graffiti expressed the systematic crisis of the 'civilized' world.[10] It provided a dissensus to the aesthetic and moral status quo, reframing the existent landscape of physical and social ruination not simply by opposing the given order, but rather by letting the multiple and incompatible realities lying beneath to reveal it 'in crisis' (cf. Austin 2001).[11] Not simply a disruption to the UC, graffiti were a form of commoning in themselves, constitutive of a site of *critique* (in its etymological sense, i.e. as a rupture), aesthetically experienced and expressed against quintessential barriers of the hegemonic aesthetic regime: the physical border (the wall as the fundamental protection), the legal border (private property) and the moral border (decorum).

Arguing for the need to reconcile vandalism with its original link to cultural property, Sam Merrill has proposed to recognize its 'potential cultural significance' by focusing on 'one particular form of vandalism, graffiti' (Merrill 2011: 63). Looking at graffiti through this lens, from the perspective of heritage studies and archaeology, Merrill makes a point for reclaiming a value for them as constitutive of the heritage site itself. In this sense, graffiti at heritage sites may be understood as not simply a vandalistic defacing, damaging or destroying of the site's essence, but as an eventful layer added to its very history – or, as Ingold would have it, to its *pastness*; thus, a recognition that buildings, individuals and sites neither originate from nor finish at a given time in history, but rather carry 'on along temporal trajectories that continue in the present' (Ingold 2010: 164). Graffiti in this sense are 'one of a site's many layers of history', an addition that may 'represent heritage on their artistic merit and also due to the academic and cultural significance they embody as mirrors of contemporary society' (Merrill 2011: 63). These approaches, Merrill eventually suggests, 'may encourage the actual preservation of examples of vandalism', pointing towards a paradoxical notion of 'heritage vandalism' (ibid.).

It is certainly useful to reflect on the cultural value of practices that are too hastily categorized as defacement, soiling or destruction. More recently there have been attempts to specifically refer to graffiti and street art as a form of urban cultural commons which reinforces local knowledge, identity and struggles, and adds to the visual and informational palimpsests of the urban (McCullough 2013; cf. MacInnis 2016). What if, taking this reasoning to its conclusion, we were to recognize vandalism as significant in itself? In so far as inserting an event within the processual flow of a given object, situation, or set of relations – that is, in so far as prompting a potential change of state, and thus a novel crystallization of the given socio-material constellation and distribution of the sensible – vandalism could accordingly be recognized as a process of commoning, but not, however, in the sense of adding another layer to a given site, which would thus require to be passively preserved. More profoundly, because they prompt the reconfiguration of the site itself, translating this observation to the field of graffiti would mean understanding their political value independently from their aesthetic quality or ideological content: not as some form of beautification or context added to a given site, but rather because, by embodying its vandalization, they open the possibility for its re-commoning.

Let us rephrase this point. Graffiti do not add to the commons. More profoundly, graffiti always constitute an act of appropriation and a problematization of the commons, one that is performed by means of soiling. In *Malfeasance: Appropriation through Pollution?* (2010) Michel Serres has suggested that property, before being a precise legal construct, is a natural act, exemplified in the animal act of marking space with bodily fluids. As Danilo Mandic (2017: 515) explains, 'the common become one's own by the act of soiling', a unilateral, abusive and violent act – the dirty birth of law. The essentially vandalistic quality of graffiti may be said to rest on the way they challenge property by means of rehashing property's institutive act: graffiti affirm and embody a unilateral possibility of appropriation, which, although surreptitiously legitimizing the reality of property, at the same time incorporates a constitutive excess to its legal apparatus. The hypothesis here is that their political value lies in their capacity to unpack the complexity of a given site exactly by means of breaking the spell that its physical materiality exerts – a spell that ultimately the conservation paradigm, repurposed in today's heritage graffiti sites, seemingly reproduces. Rather than the adding of a layer of meaningful (or meaningless) decoration to a given heritage or, more generally, to an urban site, this value would rest on graffiti's capacity to problematize the particular socio-material relations that hold that site together, and thus prompting their reconfiguration.[12]

Countless pages have been written on the evolution (or involution) of graffiti, with the surfacing of street art or post-graffiti, and the gradual, remarkable change of their relationship with the social, legal and moral normativity of worldwide cities. There are many accounts that trace this history, more or less polemically, and this is certainly not the place to rehash it one more time (see e.g. Ross 2016). Whatever the position one holds, it is safe to say that the previous oppositional relation with the civilizing pillars of the urban normative landscape has been in many cases (though by no means all) reversed, as graffiti have followed the path of other subcultures by gradually becoming consistent and coherent with the spatial aesthetic of contemporary urban capitalism, while slowly but steadily moving towards mainstream acceptance. This was most crucially an effect of the advent of street art, which, besides the multifaceted and complex stylistic considerations (see, for instance, the Introduction to this volume), brought about a prioritization of the aesthetic (visual) 'look' and the sociopolitical 'message' of the artwork, over the eventful contingency of its gesture and its relational inscription within a given urban site (Kramer 2010; Pavoni 2019). As a consequence, street art has been increasingly accepted and legitimated as far as is compatible with the aesthetic and sociocultural parameters of the contemporary urban visual regime, with the result of making it increasingly indistinguishable from other practices of urban planning and design, in the context of wider cultural and creative strategies of regeneration and city-branding (cf. Schacter 2016). Today, street art is variously recognized as a way to valorize and increase the common good, to the point that we assist to its gradual entrance into the realm of common heritage, and thus to the beginning of practices of musealization, institutionalization, preservation, and legal protection.

While it is all too easy to romanticize their 'illegal' status, or to provide them with a moral superiority to 'legal' forms of street art, it is worth stressing that graffiti's illegality, at least initially, did undeniably play a key role in releasing their 'political' potential. Paraphrasing Andrew Russeth, simply by means of placing 'artists or viewers at risk, opening them both to the possibility of physical or emotional harm, or at the very least, the power of the state,' graffiti 'la[y] bare systems of power in ways that other art cannot, rendering them painfully visible' (Russeth 2016). Yet, to equate graffiti's 'vandalistic' potential with their illegal, unauthorized or informal dimension would be a correlational fallacy. There is something more to graffiti than their (aesthetic) form, (ideological) content, or (legal) status:

something that has to do with the way they intersect and problematize the normative structure of the urban, and thus the composition of the UC itself. Andrea Mubi Brighenti argues that 'the two conventional, opposing views that interpret writing alternatively as art or as deviance fail to identify the real stake in the practice of writing. Such stake is not "art or crime". The stake is, on the contrary, the definition of the nature and the limits of public space qua public' (Brighenti 2010: 328–29). As with any form of urban artistic intervention, what is at stake is the production of the public, the testing of its spatial and aesthetic conditions of possibility, and thus the politics of urban commoning itself. The hypothesis here is that it is the capacity to vandalize the normative integrity of (urban) structures to be the critical core of graffiti, besides, and beyond, their (certainly neither uninfluential nor redundant) *beautifying* capacity to decorate a grey city, their *meaningful* capacity to communicate a given sociopolitical message, or their *transgressing* capacity to shock and awe. There is, in other words, something more at stake with graffiti vis-à-vis their political potential, and this has not to do with their enchanting power (cf. Young 2013), but with their capacity to disenchant urban life by breaking the spell of its invisible normativity, and the socio-material relations, forces and structures that hold it together. It is in this sense that we may locate their political potential. Paraphrasing Rancière, therefore, graffiti is

> not political owing to the messages and feelings that it carries on the state of social and political issues. It is not political owing to the way it represents social structures, conflicts or identities. It is political by virtue of the very distance that it takes with regard to those functions. It is political as it frames a specific space–time sensorium, as it redefines on this stage the power of speech or the coordinates of perception, shifts the places of the actor and the spectator, etc. Because politics is not the exercise of power or the struggle for power. Politics is first of all the configuration of a space as political, the framing of a specific sphere of experience, the setting of objects posed as 'common' and subjects to whom the capacity is recognized to designate these objects and argue about them. (Rancière 2006)

Removal

In the months preceding the scene narrated at the beginning of this text, a few of the graffiti had already disappeared from the walls of Bologna – and not only because of the municipal cleaning zeal. Some of them had surreptitiously been surgically removed for another purpose. They were to populate *Street Art. Banksy & Co. – L'Arte allo Stato Urbano* [the Art at the Urban

State], an exhibition organized by Genus Bononiae, a cultural entity financed by the city's most powerful bank foundation, Carisbo. The exhibition was to open on 18 March 2016. Some of the works removed from the street belonged to Blu himself, who had been contacted by the organizers prior to the removal, to which he did not give his consent – in fact, he had not replied at all. Assuming that a contact, even if unanswered, was sufficient to proceed to the removal, the exhibition organizers duly carried it out. As the curators Luca Ciancabilla, Christian Omodeo and Sean Corcoran explained, the purpose of this removal was to 'salvage the works from demolition and preserve them from the injuries of time' (in wu ming 2016a). 'Preservation' and 'musealization': this is what the exhibition intended to reflect upon, questioning the relation between street art, urban space, and time.[13]

To many, the removal of graffiti from the street and their translation into a museum space where they could be contemplated upon the payment of a rather hefty fee (13 euros) sounded preposterous. Some complained that the exhibition had no right to take these works. This argument's legal basis was shaky, however. Does not doing street art entail that the artist cannot pretend to maintain control over the artwork and its social life? Was not the drawing of (most of) those graffiti illicit in the first place? Can one speak of legal protection for something that has been realized illegally? Surely controversial, the questions posed by the organizers were not easy to challenge from a legal point of view, and showed the contradictions one may encounter when attempting to challenge the removal of graffiti by upholding a proprietary paradigm.[14] If, as suggested above, graffiti's *critical* essence is encapsulated in their aesthetic, moral and legal excessiveness to the urban articulation of property and preservation, then it follows that mobilizing the latter to protect the former is an effort fraught with contradictions – contradictions that were bound to explode, in fact, as the same argument was used against Blu after the artist reacted by erasing all of his works (more than twenty) from the walls of Bologna.[15]

The city's mayor swiftly lamented that, as a result of this gesture, the city would wake up 'poorer, with less art and fewer spaces of liberty' (in *Bologna Today*, 2016, my translation). A rather brave statement, taking into account the criminalizing stance of the city council against writers, and its penchant for evicting 'spaces of liberty' such as social centres and other occupations around town. Political hypocrisy aside, it is worth reflecting on the assumptions that fed this reasoning. As explicitly put in a piece that appeared on *Wired*: 'Who is Blu to decide whether or not other publics deserve to enjoy his works?' (Cosimi 2016, my translation). The art journal *Artribune* echoed the mayor, arguing that Bologna had been culturally impoverished by the gesture, which moreover provided the supporters of street art's musealization with a strong argument in their favour. Blu had committed an 'ideological own goal', the argument went, in failing to understanding the 'public' quality of his artwork: by deciding unilaterally over its fate, he had acted according to the same logic that fed the removals performed by the exhibition organizers (Giacomelli 2016, my translation). One could hear the World Heritage Convention resonating here: the 'deterioration or disappearance of any item of the cultural or natural heritage constitutes a harmful impoverishment of the heritage of all the nations of the world'. The president of the district where the most famous piece, *Occupy Mordor*, appeared, offered the most comprehensive framing of this argument:

> I understand the political intervention against those whose purpose is turning everything into a commodity, but Blu has been completely disinterested as regards the fact that his works have become a collective good. I am astonished; now the usual idiotic writing will appear in place of that artwork … it took years to make people understand that such artworks may valorize a neighbourhood like Bolognina. Today it is the same author who, by turning his back on Roversi Monaco, also turns his back on all those citizens who have learned to love that place. (In Miele 2016, my translation)

One could hardly find a most exemplificative case of the reduction of UC to a physical and depletable resource: objectively and tangibly defined (in this case, a specific artwork); its value supposedly resides on the possibility of its being 'seen' and 'enjoyed'; and consequently, it is to be *physically* preserved, no matter what, against both the 'injuries of time' and possible vandalistic acts that may impoverish the cultural commons of the city. The same argument could be moved against both the exhibition and Blu, both allegedly guilty of having unilaterally appropriated and thus *subtracted* from public enjoyment a common good. The exhibition curators would certainly agree, only contending that their action did increase the longevity of the artwork, albeit in decontextualized form.

Equally unconvincing was the argument of those who noted that graffiti has from its origins been an ephemeral practice, bound to deterioration, erasure and disappearance. This somewhat romantic point overlooks the possibility that art forms evolve and change and, moreover, that the purpose of the exhibition was to reflect and question this very assumption in the first place – what Omodeo himself termed an 'ideology of memory', that is, the 'necessity of ephemerality at all costs' (Viti and Omodeo 2017: 156, my translation). Incidentally, the systematic use of ephemerality as a rhetorical device to justify and support neoliberal policies of regeneration would caution against its uncritical endorsement (e.g. Ferreri 2015). Another argument, with a similarly conservative nuance, stressed the site-specific quality of graffiti, it being a practice that cannot be severed from its own context. Many contemporary instances of street art musealization question this statement, Omodeo argued, adding that the context is not always or necessarily essential to the artwork (Viti and Omodeo 2017: 156). Decades after the advent of Institutional Critique, this argument does not sound as preposterous as many critics claimed.[16] While it is evident that the relation between graffiti and its own site is crucial, the meaning of this affirmation greatly depends on the definition of site on which it rests. The risk, otherwise, is that the debate remains at the superficial level of discussing whether an object–site relation could and should be severed or not, without actually addressing the nature of said relation, and, most importantly, its changing form in the context of contemporary capitalist urbanization.[17]

Ultimately, the debate that accompanied this controversy for the most part took the form of a sterile set of skirmishes among different opinions around temporality, context, preservation and artistic value. Beneath the superficial differences, in fact, there remained a consistent if implicit agreement around a set of taken-for-granted assumptions: that a street artwork coincides with a physical painting on a given surface, the removal of which equals the disappearance of the street artwork itself; that the 'site' of a street artwork is a physical location, be this a street, a square, or a gallery; that the reason a street artwork exists is the aesthetic experience of spectators; and that its aesthetic value is dependent on a consensual aesthetic agreement – which would accordingly differentiate a piece by Blu from worthless 'idiotic writings', for instance. What was taken for granted, in other words, was a constellation of art, experience and preservation, linked to a static and objectified definition of UC. The corollary was that, provided a graffiti is consensually recognized as a street artwork, this becomes part of the UC and it must be physically preserved against deterioration or defacement. As a famous Italian political columnist emphatically stated, while Blu may have been informed by good intentions, his gesture went *against* the people, as the only ones to suffer as a result will be the neighbourhoods affected (Serra 2016). It is exactly this 'being against', I would instead suggest, that is Blu's gesture's most interesting aspect. A 'being against' that should be understood with respect to the just mentioned 'constellation' and, more generally, vis-à-vis the way in which the UC tends to be perverted and parasitically exploited in the context of contemporary creative city politics and aesthetic capitalism. As stated by the wu ming collective (one of the few lucid voices in that debate), perhaps one should consider whether what is at stake in the whole affair – and in the question of UC at large – is the aesthetic beautification of the city, or the political conflict that lies beneath (wu ming 2016b).

Fight-Specific Art

Reflecting on his most (in)famous piece, *The Tilted Arc*, Richard Serra reclaimed the necessity for art 'to work in opposition to the constrains of the context, so that the work cannot be read as an affirmation of questionable ideologies and political power' (Serra 1994: 203). Commenting on this passage, Milton Kwon writes that 'it is only [in] working *against* the given site … that art can resist co-optation' (Kwon 2004: 74). In the case of graffiti, while this *working against* has certainly characterized its early surfacing, as noted above, the subsequent evolution has gradually defused this subversive potential by absorbing it into the all-ingesting realm of urban branding. This, to be sure, occurred as much to legal and authorized as to illegal and unauthorized graffiti. Contrary to those who imply an equivalence between subversive potential and illegal/unauthorized status (e.g. McCormick et al. 2010; Bacharach 2015), it is easy to show the extent to which, for instance, an illegal graffiti may provide a transgressive and edgy vibe to a neighbourhood, which in turn may be recuperated into branding strategies and trigger processes of gentrification. The quest for purity is fraught with contradictions, even more so in the contemporary urban context.

From Henri Lefebvre to David Harvey, and from Ed Soja to Neil Brenner, countless are the urban scholars and critical geographers who have analysed the extent to which, in the contemporary age, urban sites are increasingly stretched, prolonged, multiplied and emptied out, most significantly as a result of the global process of neoliberal urbanization and its related outcomes – gentrification, commodification, touristification, and so on. As argued above, the aesthetics of the urban space have been profoundly reshaped by this process, as cultural industries, creative city politics and urban branding have become central in urban politics. This is all too evident to anyone living in contemporary cities, where urban branding has grown into a key urban development strategy, enrolling discourses and policies of planning, security, marketing and law. In this context then, it is naive at best, and complicit at worst, to understand such a *working against* as a voluntaristic matter of transgressing a given law or moral code. The political potential of aesthetic dissensus will have to be assessed far more carefully, looking at its contingent and contextual outcome vis-à-vis the given, spatially and historically situated distribution of the sensible, in and through which the UC is configured.

Suhail Malik, in an essay provocatively titled 'Reason to Destroy Contemporary Art' (Malik 2015), lamented the priority that contemporary art assigns to the sensorial and phenomenological experience, as if this should be the only condition and horizon of art. Contrary to that, he proposes a *realist* art, from which experience and interpretation would be expunged – in other words, an art that would be indifferent to aesthetic experience: an art of rational knowledge, which would not need to be experienced, but only known. While unpacking this suggestion here would lead us astray, it is worth pondering on the background from which it emerges. If 'half a century of consumer society has produced an insatiable appetite for aestheticisation' (Berry-Slater and Iles 2009), the need for art to extricate itself from the experience economy of aesthetic capitalism (cf. Böhme 2017) appears paramount. For graffiti and street art, or any other form of public art for that matter, to conserve a political potential means to counter their ongoing entanglement within the very aesthetics of contemporary capitalism, and thus their surreptitious co-optation as tools fostering the ongoing commodification of urban space. Doing so, I suggested, may require rescuing its vandalizing quality – not necessarily in the illegal sense but, more profoundly, against the constellation of art, experience and preservation, which remains dominant in the current urban aesthetic regime, and is responsible for the ongoing objectification and exploitation of the UC.

In his speculation on the 'specificity of sitedness', Matthew Poole argues that those artworks that are 'brought in', or 'fabricated for', or 'performed within', or 'enacted upon' already given sites – that is, artworks that are premised on some sort of 'suitability', even in oppositional terms, to a give site – are bound to become 'merely functional … appendages of the already existing ideological vectors' (Poole 2015: 89). Addressing a site, in this sense, means more than engaging with its empirical dimension: it entails dealing with its conditions of possibility, by moving 'away from finished form to the matrix of form, to the conditions that produce it' (Lütticken 2012). Facing an increasingly planetary process of urbanization, having to work 'with measures we can no longer handle' (Nelson Brissac, quoted in Yúdice 2005), it may be time for street art to radically rethink its relation with the complexity of its urban site. As Andrea Phillips suggests more generally vis-à-vis contemporary art, it may be time to focus on 'changing not the form of art, but the structure of its relation to social-political context' (Phillips 2015: 83) – that is, shifting from a concern for a finished form, such as a given mural, and to focus on the *real* conditions of possibility of something like graffiti and, more profoundly, the conditions of possibility for the very surfacing of the UC.

From this perspective, Blu's gesture assumes another quality, one that can hardly be captured by merely focusing on the grey surface it left behind. Instead, it requires turning the attention to the detonating effect it had vis-à-vis the complex web of socio-political and economic relations that is reshaping the city of Bologna, in the age of its massive gentrification, commodification and securitization (see Della Puppa, this volume). Traversing and exceeding the debate over the preservation or musealization of a given street artwork, this collective and participatory artistic performance did plug into the conflict that has fermented in the last decades in the city, *working against* the neutralizing role that street art is all too often made to play in this context. This was no decorative supplement to dramatic processes of urbanization, but rather the 'beauty of a collective action in defence of a common good', as wu ming put it (in wu ming 2016a, my translation), with this 'good' not being understood as a static piece of street art to be preserved, but the collective and *commoning* force of the sociopolitical conflict that revolved around it. The *site* of this erasure was not the wall of a social centre, but rather the fight around its occupation, defence and eviction – and, more generally, the fight around the ongoing commodification of Bologna's UC.

In an insightful reflection on the relation between monumentalization and dissent, Lize Mogel (2002) asks whether it is possible to monumentalize something without rendering it innocuous – that is, how to materialize dissent in a work of public art. This collective erasure provides a possible response, in the form of a piece of veritable fight-specific art (Esche et al. 2013), a piece in which the vandalistic potential of street art is actualized, and legally so, by challenging the dominant parameters of heritage and property, aesthetic and social legitimation, as well as the current failure of street art vis-à-vis its ongoing co-optation within the logic of neoliberal urbanization, therefore gesturing towards a novel, uncertain direction to break out from this contradiction.

Acknowledgements

Andrea Pavoni's research is funded by FCT/MCTES under CEEC Individual contract [CEECINST/00066/2018/CP1496/CT0001].

Andrea Pavoni is Research Fellow at DINAMIA'CET [Centre for Socio-economic and Territorial Studies], ISCTE-IUL – Instituto Universitário de Lisboa, Portugal. Drawing from various areas such as critical geography, urban studies, legal theory, sociology and philosophy, his research explores the relation between materiality, normativity and aesthetics in the urban context. He is Associate Editor at *Lo Squaderno, Explorations in Space and Society,* and co-editor of the Law and the Senses Series [University of Westminster Press]. His book, *Controlling Urban Events: Law, Ethics and the Material,* has been published with Routledge.

Notes

1. https://notagbo.wordpress.com/info/.
2. For instance, the writer AliCé had been fined 800 euros for defacing a wall just a month before this scene took place (Fatto Quotidiano 2016).
3. After months of tension, the XM24 was eventually evicted at the beginning of August 2019.
4. Retrieved 10 August 2019 from https://www.radiocittadelcapo.it/archives/blu-cancella-murales-bologna-171310/ (my translation).
5. Three activists from Crash were subsequently charged with 'defacing and trespassing', an accusation that usually pertains to writers, not to erasers (reported in *Corriere di Bologna*, 13 March 2016).
6. The sequence *Dropping a Han Dynasty Urn* (1995) comprises three gelatine silver prints.
7. *Carter v. Helmsley-Spear*, Inc.., 71 F.3d 77 (2nd Cir. 1995).
8. See, for instance, Hardt, Negri and Harvey 2009.
9. While this is only one of modern graffiti's multiple 'origins', it has surely been the most influential, culturally and stylistically, at the global level.
10. This was similar to what hip hop was doing, at the same time, in the same place. When it appeared, hip hop embodied a critical fracture to the aesthetic and moral common sense. At the same time, however, as put by one of its most prominent early protagonists, RUN-DMC's Darryl McDaniels, while it looked 'different to the civilized world … to everybody uncivilized it was the familiar thing, and that's why it worked', in *Hip Hop Evolution*, HBO (season 1, episode 3), 18 September 2016.
11. I am here paraphrasing a passage by Hal Foster who, reflecting on the relation between art and transgression, argues that this is a matter of 'rethink[ing] transgression not as a rupture produced by a heroic avant-garde posited somehow outside the symbolic order, but as a fracture traced by a strategic avant-garde inside the order', with the goal of not simply breaking with the order 'but to reveal it in crisis' (Foster 2015: 17).
12. This is something Jean Baudrillard ([1976] 2016: 82) brilliantly intuited, when arguing that graffiti 'free them [the walls] from architecture, and turn them once again into living, social matter'.
13. From the exhibition website, at https://genusbononiae.it/mostre/street-art-bansky-co-larte-allo-urbano/
14. For instance, Marcilio Franca (2016) argues that law could provide protection to the integrity of the artwork. This seems to him the most practical solution, since graffiti *deserve* legal protection in so far as they are works of art. While appreciating this effort, one may wonder whether it risks producing undesired effects, such as implying that licit graffiti are only those that have been 'authorized'. More recently, the verdict on the 5Pointz building in New York provides a crucial addition to the debate. 5pointz was a world-famous street art playground for decades. When in 2013 the owner decided to demolish it, erasing the graffiti overnight, protests ensued. In February 2018, twenty-one street artists won a $6.75 million lawsuit against the developer, on account that their work, although painted on a building that did not belong to them, was eligible for protection under VARA, the Visual Art Rights Act (see Meiselman 2018)

15. This is not the first time he did so. In 2014 Blu had already performed a similar gesture, albeit in a smaller scale, erasing a mural from an occupied building in Kreutzberg, Berlin, after the squatters living there had been evicted, and his mural had appeared on the advertising video of a real estate company (see Pavoni 2019).

16. The notion of Institutional Critique refers to an artistic approach or, more precisely, a critical complement to site-specific art, that emerged in the 1960s in opposition to the sacred site of art (i.e. the museum or art gallery) and its assumption as a neutral and innocent – that is, normatively flat and power-free – 'white cube' of artistic and spectatorial freedom (for an anthology of IC, see Alberro and Stimson 2009).

17. Scarce are the reflections on the relation between graffiti and site that take into account the ontological modification that the site undergoes in the current epoch – a subject that instead is variously addressed with reference to contemporary art (e.g. Kwon 2004; Osborne 2013; Mackay 2015).

References

Adey, P., et al. 2013. 'Pour votre tranquillité': Ambiance, Atmosphere, and Surveillance'. *Geoforum* 49: 299–309.

Alberro, A., and B. Stimson (eds). 2009. *Institutional Critique: An Anthology of Artists' Writings*. Cambridge, MA: MIT Press.

Anderson, B. 2009. 'Affective Atmospheres'. *Emotion, Space and Society* 2: 77–81.

Austin, J. 2001. *Taking the Train: How Graffiti Art became an Urban Crisis in New York City*. New York: Columbia University Press.

Bacharach, S. 2015. 'Street Art and Consent'. *British Journal of Aesthetics* 55(4): 481–95.

Bataille, G. 1929. 'Architecture'. Dictionnaire Critique 2. Retrieved 29 July 2019 from https://lepelikan.files.wordpress.com/2014/03/bataille-architecture_ordi.pdf

Baudrillard, J. (1976) 2016. 'Kool Killer, or the Insurrection of Signs', in J. Baudrillard (ed.), *Symbolic Exchange and Death*. Thousand Oaks, CA: Sage, pp. 76–86.

Berry-Slater, J., and A. Iles. 2009. 'No Room to Move: Radical Art and the Regenerate City'. *Mute*, 24 November. Retrieved 16 August 2020 from http://www.metamute.org/editorial/articles/no-room-to-move-radical-art-and-regenerate-city#

Bille, M., P. Bjerregaard and T. Flohr Sørensen. 2015. 'Staging Atmospheres: Materiality, Culture, and the Texture of the In-Between'. *Emotion, Space and Society* 14: 31–38.

Böhme, G. 2017. *Critique of Aesthetic Capitalism*. Milan: Mimesis International.

Bologna Today. 2016. 'Caso Blu, sindaco in difesa della street art e boicottaggio della mostra del Genus', *Bologna Today*, 14 March. Retrieved 29 July 2019 from http://www.bolognatoday.it/cronaca/blu-opere-bologna-polemica-merola-arte-urbana.html.

Borch, C., and M. Kornberger (eds). 2015. *Urban Commons: Rethinking the City*. Abingdon: Routledge.

Brighenti, A.M. 2010. 'At the Wall: Graffiti Writers, Urban Territoriality, and the Public Domain'. *Space and Culture* 13(3): 315–32.

Cole, T. 2012. 'Break It Down'. *The New Inquiry*, 3 July. Retrieved 29 July 2019 from https://thenewinquiry.com/blog/break-it-down/.

Conradson, D., and A. Latham. 2007. 'The Affective Possibilities of London: Antipodean Transnationals and the Overseas Experience'. *Mobilities* 2(2): 231–54.

Cosimi, S. 2016. 'Perché la decisione di Blu a Bologna è più capriccio che protesta', *Wired.it*, 14 March. Retrieved 29 July 2019 from https://www.wired.it/play/cultura/2016/03/14/perche-decisione-blu-bologna-fallimento-totale/?refresh_ce=.

Dean, J. 2012. *The Communist Horizon*. New York: Verso.

Esche, C., I. Lorey, G. Rauning, and B. Theis. 2013. 'Isola Art Center, alcuni concetti', in *Fight-Specific Isola: Art, Architecture, Activism and the Future of the City*. Berlin: Archive Books, pp. 265-80.

Fairclough, G. 2009. 'Conservation and the British', in J. Schofield (ed.), *Defining Moments: Dramatic Archaeologies of the Twentieth-Century*. Oxfort: BAR Publishing, pp. 157–164.

Fatto Quotidiano. 2016. 'Bologna, AliCè condannata: "Imbrattò muro": Multa di 800 euro per la street artist consacrata dal New York Times', *Il Fatto Quotidiano*, 15 February. Retrieved 29 July 2019 from https://www.ilfattoquotidiano.it/2016/02/15/bologna-alice-condannata-imbratto-muro-multa-di-800-euro-per-la-street-artist-consacrata-dal-new-york-times/2468233/.

Ferreri, M. 2015. 'The Seductions of Temporary Urbanism'. *ephemera* 15(1): 181–91.

Florida, R. 2002. *The Rise of the Creative Class: And How It's Transforming Work, Leisure, Community and Everyday Life*. New York: Basic Books.

Foster, H. 2015. *Bad New Days: Art, Criticism, Emergency*. London: Verso Books.

Franca, M.T. 2016. 'O grafite e a preservação de sua integridade: a pele da cidade e o 'droit au respect' no direito brasileiro e comparado'. *Revista de Direito da Cidade* 8(4): 1344–61.

Freud, S. (1930) 2002. *Civilization and Its Discontents*. London: Penguin.

Giacomelli, M.E. 2016. 'Bufera street art a Bologna: Blu cancella le sue opere', *Artribune*, 12 March. Retrieved 29 July 2019 from https://www.artribune.com/attualita/2016/03/bufera-street-art-a-bologna-blu-cancella-le-sue-opere/.

Grégoire, H. (1794) 1977. 'Rapport Publique: Sur les destructions opérées par le Vandalisme, et sur le moyens de le réprimer', in *Oeuvres de l'abbé Grégoire*, vol. 2. Nendeln: KTO Press, pp. 257–78.

Hardin, G. 1968. 'The Tragedy of the Commons'. *Science* 162(3859): 1243–48.

Hardt, M., and A. Negri. 2009. *Commonwealth*. Cambridge, MA: Harvard University Press.

Hardt, M., A. Negri and D. Harvey. 2009. 'Commonwelath: An Exchange'. *Artforum 48(3): 210*–21.

Harvey, D. 2012. *Rebel Cities: From the Right to the City to the Urban Revolution*. London: Verso Books.

Hess, C., and E. Ostrom. 2007. *Understanding Knowledge as a Commons: From Theory to Practice*. Cambridge, MA: MIT Press.

Holtorf, C. 2015. 'Averting Loss Aversion in Cultural Heritage'. *International Journal of Heritage Studies* 21(4): 405–21.

Huertas, J. 2015. '"It's Out of Control and Spreading": Graffiti as the Supposed Cause of Urban Crisis in 1970s–1980s New York City'. *Bowdoin Journal of Art*: 1–26.

Ingold, T. 2010. 'No More Ancient, No More Human: The Future Past of Archaeology and Anthropology', in D. Garrow and T. Yarrow (eds), *Archaeology and Anthropology*. Oxford: Oxbow, pp. 160–70.

Jones, S. 2006. '"They Made It a Living Thing Didn't They": The Growth of Things and the Fossilisation of Heritage', in R. Layton, S. Shennan and P. Stone (eds), *A Future for Archaeology: The Past in the Present*. London: UCL Press, pp. 107–26.

Kramer, R. 2010. 'Painting with Permission: Legal Graffiti in New York City'. *Ethnography* 11(2): 235–53.

Kwon, M. 2004. *One Place After Another: Site-Specific Art and Locational Identity*. Cambridge, MA: MIT Press.

Lemkin, R. 1933. 'Acts Constituting a General (Transnational) Danger Considered as Offences against the Law of Nations'. Retrieved 10 August 2019 from http://www .preventgenocide.org/lemkin/madrid1933-english.htm#Vandalism

Linebaugh, P. 2008. *The Magna Carta Manifesto: Liberties and Commons For All*. Berkeley: University of California Press.

Liso, O. 2015. 'Milano, volontari anti-graffiti cancellano le opere di Pao: il Comune chiede scusa', *La Repubblica*, 16 May. Retrieved 29 July 2019 from https://milano .repubblica.it/cronaca/2015/05/16/news/bella_milano-114487749/.

Lütticken, S. 2012. 'Inside Abstraction'. *e-flux journal* 38. Retrieved 16 August 2020 from http://www.e-flux.com/journal/38/61196/inside-abstraction/.

MacInnis, P.W. 2016. 'On Cultural Commons and Commoning in Aboriginal Street Art Murals'. *The Political Economy of Communication* 4(1): 102–25.

Madigan, N. 2014. 'Man Gets Probation in Attack on Ai Weiwei Vase', *New York Times*, 13 August. Retrieved 10 August 2019 from https://www.nytimes.com/2014/08/14/ arts/design/man-gets-probation-in-attack-on-ai-weiwei-vase.html.

Mackay, R. (ed.). 2015. *When Site Lost the Plot*. Falmouth: Urbanomic.

Malik, S. 2015. 'Reason to Destroy Contemporary Art', in S. Malik, C. Cox and J. Jaskey (eds). *Realism, Materialism, Art*. Berlin: Sternberg Press, pp. 185–91.

Mandic, D. 2017. 'Listening to the World: Sounding Out the Surroundings of Environmental Law with Michel Serres', in V. Brooks and A. Philippopoulos-Mihalopoulos (eds), *Research Methods in Environmental Law*. Cheltenham: Edward Elgar, pp. 509–33.

McCullough, M. 2013. *Ambient Commons: Attention in the Age of Embodied Information*. Cambridge, MA: MIT Press.

McCormick, C., et al. 2010. *Trespass: A History of Uncommissioned Urban Art*. Los Angeles, CA: Taschen.

Meiselman, J. 2018. 'How 5Pointz Artists Won $6.75 Million in Lawsuit against Developer That Destroyed Their Work', *Art Market*, 18 February. Retrieved 10 August 2019 from https://www.artsy.net/article/artsy-editorial-5-pointz-artists-won-675-million-lawsuit-developer-destroyed-work.

Merrill, S. 2011. 'Graffiti at Heritage Places: Vandalism as Cultural Significance or Conservation Sacrilege?'. *Time and Mind* 4(1): 59–75.

Miele, E. 2016. 'Bologna, attivisti denunciati per aver cancellato i murales di Blu: E la città si divide', *La Repubblica*, 12 March. Retrieved 29 July 2019 from https://bologna .repubblica.it/cronaca/2016/03/12/news/bologna_blu_reazioni-135324726/.

Mogel, L. 2002. 'Temporary Monuments'. *The Journal of Aesthetics & Protest* 1(1). Retrieved 10 August 2019 from http://www.joaap.org/1/monuments/

Morris, W. 1877. 'The Society for the Protection of Ancient Buildings Manifesto'. Retrieved 10 August 2020 from https://www.spab.org.uk/about-us/spab-manifesto.

Nobre, G. 2010. 'Profanation and Vandalism: On Chance in the Life of Monuments'. *Revista Pukto* 1. Retrieved 10 August 2019 from https://www.revistapunkto.com/2011/02/profanation-and-vandalism-godofredo.html

Osborne, P. 2013. *Anywhere or Not At All: The Philosophy of Contemporary Art*. London: Verso Books.

Ostrom, E. 1990. *Governing the Commons: The Evolution of Institutions for Collective Action*. Cambridge: Cambridge University Press.

Pasquinelli, M. 2014. 'The Sabotage of Rent'. *Cesura//Acceso* 1: 162–73.

Pavoni, A. 2011. 'Tuning the City: Johannesburg and the 2010 World Cup'. *Urbe* 2(3): 191–209.

———. 2018. *Controlling Urban Events: Law, Ethics and the Material*. Abingdon: Routledge.

———. 2019. 'Speculating on (the) *Urban* (of) Art: (Un)Siting Street Art in the Age of Neoliberal Urbanisation'. *Horizontes Antropologicos* 55: 51–88.

Peck, J. 2012. 'Recreative City: Amsterdam, Vehicular Ideas and the Adaptive Spaces of Creativity Policy'. *IJURR* 36(3): 462–85.

Phillips, A. 2015. 'Making the Public', in R. Mackay (ed.), *When Site Lost the Plot*. Falmouth: Urbanomic, pp. 77–84.

Philippopoulos-Mihalopoulos, A. 2015. *Spatial Justice: Body, Lawscape, Atmosphere*. Abingdon: Routledge.

———. 2016. 'Withdrawing from Atmosphere: An Ontology of Air Partitioning and Affective Engineering'. *Environment and Planning D: Society and Space* 34(1): 150–67.

Poole, M. 2015. 'Specificities of Sitedness: A Speculative Sketch', in R. Mackay (ed.), *When Site Lost the Plot*. Falmouth: Urbanomic, pp. 85–104.

Rancière, J. 2004. *The Politics of Aesthetics: The Distribution of the Sensible*. London: Continuum.

———. 2006. 'Aesthetics and Politics: Rethinking the Link'. Lecture given at the University of California, Berkeley, 6 May. Retrieved 10 August 2019 from http://16beavergroup.org/mondays/2006/05/06/monday-night-05-08-06-discussion-on-rancieres-politics-of-aesthetics/

———. 2010. *Dissensus: On Politics and Aesthetics*. London: Continuum.

Ross, J.I. (ed.). 2016. *Routledge Handbook of Graffiti and Street Art*. Abingdon: Routledge.

Russeth, A. 2016. 'When Felonies Become Form: The Secret History of Artists Who Use Lawbreaking as Their Medium', *ARTnews*, 17 May. Retrieved 29 July 2019 from http://www.artnews.com/2016/05/17/when-felonies-become-form-the-secret-history-of-artists-who-use-lawbreaking-as-their-medium/.

Schacter, R. 2016. 'Street Art is a Period, PERIOD: Or, Classificatory Confusion and Intermural Art', in K. Avramidis and M. Tsilimpounidi (eds), *Graffiti and Street Art: Reading, Writing and Representing the City*. Abingdon: Routledge, pp. 103–18.

Serra, R. 1994. 'Tilted Arc Destroyed', in R. Serra, *Writings/Interviews*. Chicago: University of Chicago Press, pp. 193–213.

Serra, M. 2016. 'L'Amaca', *La Repubblica*, 13 March. Retrieved 29 July 2019 from https://triskel182.wordpress.com/2016/03/14/lamaca-del-13032016-michele-serra/.

Serres, M. 2010. *Malfeasance: Appropriation through Pollution?* Stanford, CA: Stanford University Press.

Sloterdijk, P. 2004. *Sphären III – Schäume, Plurale Sphärologie.* Frankfurt-am-Main: Suhrkamp.

———. 2013. *In the World Interior of Capital.* Malden, MA: Polity Press.

Smith, N. 1996. *The New Urban Frontier: Gentrification and the Revanchist City.* London: Routledge.

Stavrides, S. 2016. *Common Space: The City as Commons.* London: Zed Books.

Steinhauer, J. 2014. 'Ai Weiwei Responds to Vase Dropper', *Hyperallergic*, 19 February. Retrieved 29 July 2019 from https://hyperallergic.com/110081/ai-weiwei-responds-to-vase-dropper/.

Thibaud, J.P. 2011. 'The Sensory Fabric of Urban Ambiances'. *The Senses and Society* 6: 203–15.

Tulumello, S., and F. Bertoni. 2019. '"Nessun decoro sui nostri corpi": sicurezza, produzione di margini e movimenti indecoros*'. *Tracce Urbane: Rivista Italiana Transdisciplinare di Studi Urbani* 3(5): 90–109.

Viti, S., and C. Omodeo. 2017. 'Street art come patrimonio: Quale musealizzazione' (interview). *Ocula* 18: 154–60.

Wilson, J.Q., and G.L. Kelling. 1982. 'Broken Windows: The Police and Neighbourhood Safety'. *Atlantic Monthly* 127: 29–38.

wu ming. 2013. '#OccupyMordor! Video, audio, fotografie e resoconti. #Bologna', *Giap blog*, 16 April. Retrieved 29 July 2019 from https://www.wumingfoundation.com/giap/2013/04/occupymordor-sintesi-video-audio-completo-fotografie-e-resoconti/

———. 2016a. 'Street Artist #Blu Is Erasing All The Murals He Painted in #Bologna', *Giap blog*, 12 March. Retrieved 29 July 2019 from https://www.wumingfoundation.com/giap/2016/03/street-artist-blu-is-erasing-all-the-murals-he-painted-in-bologna/#english.

———. 2016b. 'Blu, i mostrificatori e le sfumature di grigio', *Internazionale*, 18 March. Retrieved 8 July 2016 from https://www.internazionale.it/opinione/wu-ming/2016/03/18/blu-bologna-murales-mostra.

Yap, C. 2012. 'Devastating History'. *Art Asia Pacific* 78. Retrieved 10 August 2019 from http://artasiapacific.com/Magazine/78/DevastatingHistory

Young, A. 2013. 'The Laws of Enchantment: Street Art as Inopinatum in City Spaces', in L. Borriello and C. Ruggiero (eds), *Inopinatum: The Unexpected Impertinence of Urban Creativity*. Naples: Arti Grafiche Boccia.

Yúdice, G. 2005. 'The Heuristics of Contemporary Urban Art Interventions'. *Public* 32: 8–21.

Part II

Socio-cultural Divisions and Anti-gentrification Protests

Chapter 7

Berlin Political Crises, Street Art and Graffiti from 1945 to 2019

Betty A. Dobratz and Lisa K. Waldner

Introduction

In this chapter we explore how political graffiti has played a role in selected political crises and facets of spatial life in Berlin, Germany from 1945 to 2019. We define political graffiti as 'containing ideas or values designed to influence public opinion, policy, or government decision making' (Waldner and Dobratz 2013: 378). We especially analyse how political street art and graffiti intersect with the political crises surrounding the division and reunification of Germany and Berlin, the Cold War conflict over socialism versus capitalism, the ultimate dominance of capitalism especially as seen in gentrification and touristification, and the current growth of anti-immigrant right-wing politics. Political graffiti and street artists in Berlin often, but not always, provided alternative oppositional messages to the public as they struggled with these political crises.

Global attention to graffiti and street art is increasing because the art often enables viewers to understand the subtext of a city without resorting to mainstream accounts or official histories. This can be 'an alternative history; a mapping of social trails or subcultural behaviours – a voyeuristic pleasure at entering the story of the city' (Avramidis and Tsilimpounidi 2017: 4). We specifically focus on graffiti and street art in Berlin, the largest city and the capital. We look at the Reichstag; the Berlin Wall; Prenzlauer Berg, a heavily gentrified and touristic neighbourhood in former East Berlin; and Kreuzberg, in former West Berlin, also struggling with gentrification and touristification. Finally, we turn to the rise of right-wing politics, which seems somewhat more evident in former East Berlin than West Berlin.

Reichstag: Dealing with Negative Images from Nazi Germany

The Reichstag building housed the freely elected German parliament from 1895 to 1932, and again from 1999 to the present. At the end of the Second World War, the Reichstag was initially occupied by the Soviets, who were the only allied military force entering Berlin. Soviet troops wrote graffiti, such as their names, their paths of personal journey, and standard public-toilet fare – including some quite vulgar entries. One nasty one, still existing in the south-west corner of the building, stated 'I fuck Hitler in the arse'. When Berlin was divided, the Reichstag was just inside the British zone, but only a few metres from the Soviet one, and it was not used. After reunification, the German Parliament approved moving the capital from Bonn back to Berlin, where the Reichstag building, once it had been fully restored, would house the German Parliament. In 1995, restoration workers rediscovered the 1945 Soviet graffiti behind the plasterboard panelling that covered it, as well as bullet holes.

Rita Süssmuth, president of the Parliament at the time the graffiti was revealed, reported that the initial consensus was simply to document what was written, but she and others successfully argued to preserve and display the graffiti as part of history. For Süssmuth the decision meant a transformation to 'liberation' in which 'the past and its scars … must instead be acknowledged, preserved and displayed as an implicit reprimand to be moral and responsible in the here and now' (Kluth 2014).

The relevant sections of graffiti were photographed and the Russian Embassy in Berlin translated them and successfully requested that some of the smuttier and more embarrassing graffiti be removed. The German Parliament and the Russian Embassy, organs of two different states, functioned as major players in shaping whether and how the graffiti would be preserved. Putting it on public display helped to affirm the Reichstag as a 'testament to the transparent practice of democracy' (Kluth 2014). The preservation of writing meant to be both ephemeral and an act of vandalism makes sense; but others have questioned the practice of preserving graffiti and street art, because the act of preservation undercuts the protest. In writing about street art, Colombini argues that 'the notion of temporality, by dissociating conservation and transmission must be considered. The growing interest leads to different perceptions probably with greater attention to the act of "heritage" at the expense of the act of protest' (Colombini 2018). This tension between preservation and protest can also be seen with the Berlin Wall murals.

Post-Second World War Cold War, Brain Drain and the Wall

Carpenter (1968) argues that the division of Berlin into separate zones in the aftermath of the war meant that, unlike many other cities, political considerations would dominate the spatial distribution of the population, the economic situation, and the symbolic significance of the city. The building of the Berlin Wall in 1961 would further complicate the relations between politics and space.

Concerns about the brain drain of East Germans migrating to the West resulted in tighter border controls between East and West Germany. The number of people leaving the East was eventually significantly reduced, but it was still relatively easy to go from East Berlin to West Berlin. Pressure continued as the Cold War intensified due to skilled labour shortages in East Germany, which was hindering negotiations between the Western powers and the Soviets. In the first two weeks of July 1961 alone, 12,578 people escaped from East Berlin to West Berlin (Harrison 2003). Soviet leader Khrushchev ultimately agreed to close the border, and East German soldiers started erecting a barbed-wire fence on 13 August 1961. Two parallel walls were then constructed, and the area between became known as the death strip, overlooked by watchtowers and guards. East Berliners were forbidden to call it a wall, and were told to call it the antifascist protection bulwark protecting the socialist East from capitalist infiltration (Leuenberger 2006).

The outflow of East Germans was thereby greatly reduced, leading Langerbein (2009: 23) to conclude that this resulted in the continuing existence of the East German state and East Berlin for an additional twenty-eight years, and furthered long-lasting differences and prejudices between communism and democracy or capitalism. John F. Kennedy went to West Berlin and on 26 June 1963 delivered his famous speech supporting capitalism, including the statement 'All free men, wherever they may live, are citizens of Berlin … Ich bin ein Berliner'. The wall benefited the West, including having a calming effect once the brain drain had been reduced, and it offered 'a simple solution to complex social, political and economic problems' (Ryback quoted in Spitzer 1988: 121).

There were different iterations of the wall, and it was only by the late 1970s with the smooth concrete version that artists and others found it relatively easy to paint or scribble on it. Kuzdas suggests that then squatters, tourists, and others developed a type of artistic expression that reflected the 'Zeitgeist' or spirit and ideas of the time (Kuzdas n.d.: 16), and the western wall was filled with graffiti (Langerbein 2009; Perez 2013a). Most of the early art was done quickly to avoid being caught, and was not particularly professional. Eventually though, in the 1980s, the amateur art became more sophisticated as Thierry Noir (one of the first artists to draw on the wall), Christopher Bouchet, Keith Haring and others became more daring and added more elaborate art. Their art protested and resisted the fact that West Berliners had to encounter the wall in their daily lives. They wanted to send a message to the East German government and Soviets that West Berliners were not ignoring the wall (Noir n.d., 2016; Kuzdas n.d.; Perez 2013a).

Pugh (2015) examined two pieces of graffiti that were placed on the west side in different periods: Gordon Matta-Clark's *Made in America* in 1976, and Keith Haring's 1986 Berlin Wall mural. Matta-Clark's work was designed to illustrate the divisions that existed during the Cold War within the West, while Haring's art criticized the eastern side of the East–West divide. Both artists were invited by highly regarded institutions to paint on the wall, and that site was key to their themes about the urban processes of Berlin in the post-Second World War period.

Pugh further points out that the United States led a significant propaganda campaign to portray the Berlin Wall as a moral and symbolic divide, as well as a spatial one, separating a free democratic West Berlin from an oppressed East Berlin. The actual *Made in America* piece criticized American consumerism by portraying billboard advertisements for various German consumer products. 'Matta-Clark's quick, sloppy application of paint and of some of the advertising emphasized the Wall's ugliness, and the desolate character of the space that abutted it' (Pugh 2015: 425).

Haring's work, on the other hand, fitted the dominant discourse of the free West Berlin and the oppressed East Berlin. Using yellow paint, he painted over a 350-foot section of the wall (covering Noir and Bouchet's Statues of Liberty), and then added a chain of human figures in the German national colours of red, yellow and black, fused through their hands and feet. This image was meant to suggest the future reunification of West and East Germany. Pugh (2015: 429) described Haring's Berlin Wall mural as 'the work's colorful, affirmative image of social harmony visually confirming the existing notion, first articulated by John F. Kennedy in 1963, that West Berlin was an extension of a global community: every "free man" was "ein Berliner"'.

There were no formal rules regarding writing on the wall and/or painting over someone else's work, although excellent work tended to stay up much longer. Bouchet and Noir's 42 separate panels of the US Statue of Liberty being painted over by Haring illustrates how art work on the wall changed over time. Although Noir was upset, he recognized that it was not Haring's fault, and called him 'a great artist' (Noir 2014). Later in 1988 at the same site, Ron English painted a 'gigantic surrealist story in pictures … a number of embryonic half beings united in pairs to form hearts or yin yang, a chained dog whose head is composed of two human faces, the symbolism of duality, a metaphor for a divided Germany' (Kuzdas n.d.: 53).

Kuzdas (n.d.: 22) suggests that although there were diverse artistic techniques used, a high percentage of images were 'depicting the hope of overcoming borders, and wish for the Wall to fall'. Drawings of ladders, stairs, holes, doors and zippers illustrated there was 'a better world on the other side'. Perez (2013a) concluded that although the graffiti was illegal, it provided 'an invaluable form of visual protest … the objective of the graffiti was not to embellish or beautify the border. Instead, graffiti artists maintained that the inexistence of graffiti would lead the GDR to believe that West Berliners accepted the Wall'. This illustrated a type of resistance that otherwise would have been very difficult to consistently express, as no one in West Berlin was able to tear the wall down. Greer (2010) calls the wall's graffiti 'the greatest artwork of the 20th century … 100 miles long and nearly 12ft high', taking thirteen years to complete, using house paint, spray paint and any paint available. The artists worked under stressful conditions, needing to evade guards because defacing the wall was illegal. Noir's less complicated artistic style was developed in the context of painting the wall where work had to be done quickly to avoid arrest by the GDR soldiers (Noir 2016).

In October 1989, Soviet leader Mikhail Gorbachev warned East German leader Erich Honecker, the person mainly responsible for the construction of the wall, that 'Life punishes those who come too late' (Cornwell 2014). Gorbachev refused to send tanks to help to support the socialist government in East Berlin (Harrison 2003: 233). On 9 November 1989, there was confusion about orders pertaining to the Berlin Wall, and the borders were opened and would not be shut again (Cornwell 2014).

With the fall of the Berlin Wall leading to reunification, there was enormous celebration and fanfare. More than a hundred street artists from many countries were invited to place their work on the previously untouched open-air east side of the wall that became known as the East Side Gallery (ESG). In 2009, eighty-five artists from eighteen countries returned to update and reconstruct their work because of outdoor environmental weathering and other factors, and each artist was offered 3,000 euros to do so. If they did not return and update their work, they were told that it would be whitewashed and painted over by someone else. Some believed they deserved more money, and a few refused to redo their work (Pidd 2011; Weber 2016). Harvey has pointed out that such conflictual relationships can result from 'widespread alienation and resentment among the cultural producers who experience

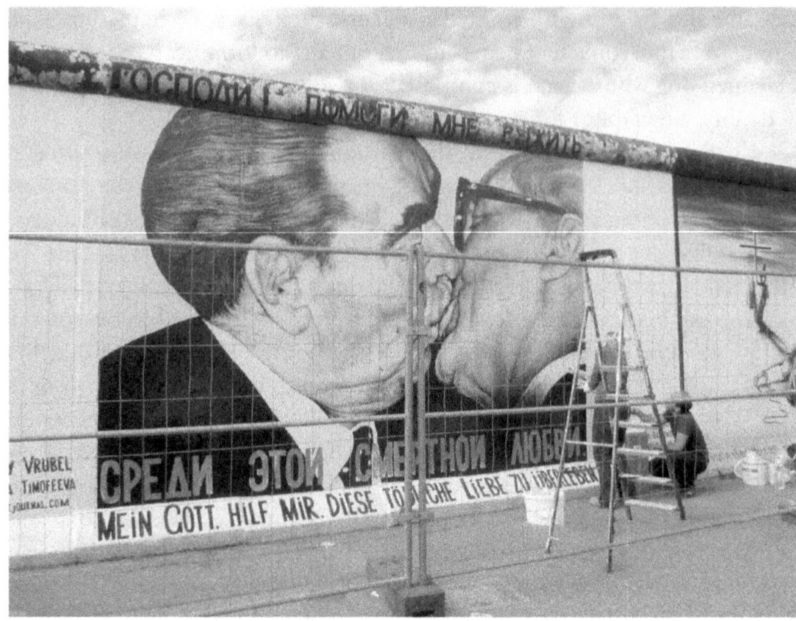

Figure 7.1 The fraternal kiss between Leonid Brezhnev and Erich Honecker, by Dimitri Vrubel, Berlin, 2016. The caption below the picture reads in English 'My God, help me to survive this deadly love.' © Betty A. Dobratz.

first-hand the appropriation and exploitation of their creativity for the economic benefit of others' (Harvey 2002, quoted in Colomb 2012: 143).

The artists produced some extremely creative pieces of political street art, including murals on global politics, peace, friendship and human rights, with little about the historical wall (Young 2013). We include photographs of two murals that dealt specifically with the politics surrounding the Berlin Wall. In Figure 7.1, Soviet leader Leonid Brezhnev is kissing Honecker; this mural is certainly one of the most famous images on the wall, and was painted by Russian artist Dimitri Vrubel. It was based on a photograph taken by Regis Bossu while both men were celebrating the thirtieth anniversary of the GDR. Numerous magazines reprinted the photo, with one publication labelling it 'The Kiss' (Rare Historical Photos 2014). Brezhnev is delivering what seems to be a passionate kiss on the lips of East Germany's President Honecker. Among socialist leaders, fraternal kisses on the cheeks were relatively common but this appeared to be an extremely enthusiastic kiss on the lips. The caption below Vrubel's painting states, 'God help me to survive this deadly love affair'. Vrubel claimed that the piece was not intended to be a

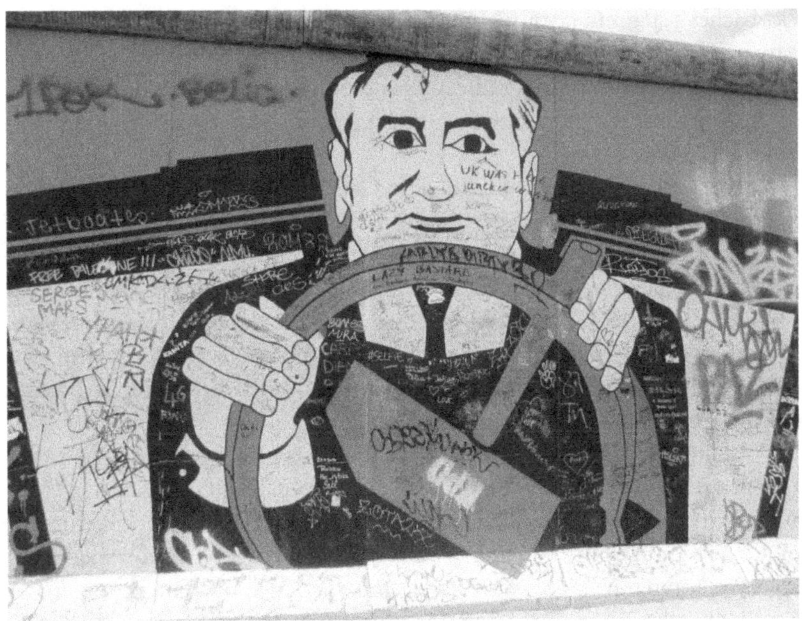

Figure 7.2 Mikhail Gorbachev steering a car through a crack in the Berlin Wall, painted by Georg Lutz Rauschebar and recreated in 2009 by G. Schaefer, Berlin, 2016. Note the upside-down hammer and sickle steering wheel and the political graffiti. © Betty A. Dobratz.

political image, but rather was about love. However, the image of these two men kissing wielded great power, and they were willing to use it to control East German citizens. Vrubel's initial mural was destroyed, but he returned and recreated it in 2009 (Rare Historical Photos 2014; Göbel 2009; Peterson 2012).

The next image, in Figure 7.2, shows Gorbachev steering a small car through a crack in the Berlin Wall. It was painted by German artist Georg Lutz (Rauschebart). Gorbachev appears to be turning the hammer-and-sickle symbol upside down and trying to get through the opening he might have created (Thorson 1990). The piece was recreated in 2009 by G. Schaefer for the twentieth anniversary of the fall of the wall (Katsouras n.d.). According to Judt, 'Gorbachev cannot take direct credit for what happened in 1989 – he did not plan it and only hazily grasped its long-term import. But he was the permissive and precipitating cause' (Judt 2005: 633). By 2016 we see that the mural had been covered with graffiti, including for example the statement 'Lazy Bastard'. This suggests certainly not everyone viewed

Gorbachev's actions favourably, and it illustrates the potential interactive nature of graffiti, where viewers are not passive consumers but can react to the artist and the message, and can create new messages by tagging a mural or dueling graffiti by crossing out or using counter messages (Waldner and Dobratz 2013).

Perez (2013b) views the East Side Gallery as a symbol of overcoming repression and the promise of a better future, while Noir (n.d.) saw it as a symbol of the Cold War, reminding people that although walls do not last forever they should never make the same error again. Most significantly, for Young (2013: 79) the wall affected 'the topography and organization of Berlin's society that helped to produce the prolific, extensive graffiti that covers Berlin's surfaces today, … [and] walls all over Berlin continue to speak of creativity, memorialisation and protest'.

The hundred miles or so of original wall was torn down first due to so-called 'wall-peckers' (Greer 2010), who chipped off small pieces that eventually led to holes large enough to walk through. The East German government took down most of the remaining wall, with much of it reused for road base; however, numerous pieces were saved and auctioned off. For example, at a June 1990 sale in Monaco, 81 pieces – including 33 by Thierry Noir and 12 by Kiddy Citny – were sold for 1.5 million euros. Noir sued for part of the proceeds, and eventually his claim was upheld. Berlin has very little of the original graffiti on display, with many pieces now found elsewhere, including the United States, the Vatican, Poland, Spain and Japan (Greer 2010).

One debate is whether removing a mural or other public art from its original location may limit its impact, as the street provides local context. This debate is also specific to Berlin with the opening of Urban Nation, a museum that displays in its gallery the work of street artists, but done on canvas or sculpture rather than in a public location, raising questions about the institutionalization and commercialization of street art (Ellis-Petersen 2017), including whether the latter speeds up the gentrification process.

As a memorial to the fall of the Berlin Wall, the ESG is now one of the most visited tourist attractions in Berlin. With the construction boom and gentrification, its future has been questioned. In 2013, part of its wall was moved to provide an access road for new luxury apartments. In 2018 the Berlin Wall Foundation was entrusted with the preservation and care of this monument, and it plans to not only preserve the artwork but to run guided tours (Angerer 2018).

Drissel (2011) argues the reunification process in Germany and Berlin was very uneven, with the burden placed on the Easterners who were expected to adjust quickly to the West's political and economic system – indeed, 'West shock' occurred for many who were not prepared for the very competitive capitalist market economy. Many West Germans resisted the financial burden of reunification with the East. Rieber (1997) hypothesized that because of the rapid social changes occurring during Germany's reunification, one could expect an increase in social distress. Economic disparities existed, and East Germans felt 'degraded' (Leuenberger 2006: 29) by job losses and by their lack of relevant knowledge and experience with consumer culture. This served in a sense as a 'mental wall', which also could be associated with 'racist and authoritarian attitudes' (ibid.: 28). Some referenced this as the 'wall in the head' that replaced the geopolitical Berlin Wall (Drissel 2011: 19). The fall of the wall was supposed to help to make Germany part of a safer world, but instead Kimmelman, on the eve of the twenty-fifth anniversary of the fall, characterized Germany as a 'fuzzier, more reticent nation' that is not safer but exists in a 'more violent, tribal, fractured and unpredictable' world (Kimmelman 2014).

Commodification, Urban Renewal, Gentrification and Touristification

While reunification meant increased democracy and often economic growth, many in the East felt that 'the community spirit that had [been] fostered under communism had quickly evaporated under capitalism' (Smith and Eckardt 2018). Giddens points out how Marx identified commodification as fundamental to capitalism: 'The buying and selling of goods, including labour-power, in order to generate profit …We should not be surprised to find, therefore, that commodification extends to the very milieu in which human beings live … *space itself becomes commodified*' (Giddens 1987: 101). We examine urban renewal, gentrification and touristification as phenomena associated with commodification in the urban built environment, including how street art has contributed to that commodification of space.

Gentrification is one of the results of this economic disparity between East and West that disadvantages former East Berliners. Holm defines gentrification as 'a process of structural and economic upgrading, during which households with higher incomes displace inhabitant[s] with lower incomes, and which is accompanied by a substantial change in the character and spirit of a neighborhood' (Holm 2006: 122). Urban renewal and gentrification occurred in various areas of East Berlin after the wall fell because many relatively prosperous West Germans moved to the less expensive traditional working-class areas of former East Berlin, exacerbating socio-spatial tensions.

Prenzlauer Berg is an example of a former East Berlin neighbourhood that experienced rapid gentrification. Its housing stock was built before 1914, and was in an inner-city neighbourhood where employees in lower positions had traditionally dominated its social structure. In the 1970s and 1980s it was a niche for artists, students and squatters seeking an escape from the East Berlin regime (Papen 2015). In the early 1990s, the public agenda for housing renewal began as anti-displacement of individuals and avoidance of rent increases (Bernt and Holm 2009), but by the late 1990s urban renewal was moving towards a neoliberal strategy that renounced the earlier orientation towards welfare: 'East Berlin became a laboratory for the transformation from socialism to capitalism, as well as for new urban policies' (Holm 2006: 114). Private investors and interests in urban development grew, public subsidies declined, weaker legal rent caps were introduced, and people were displaced (Bernt and Holm 2009). After 2000, rental housing changed to single ownership and quick monetary gain. The educational level of occupants rose significantly (Holm 2006; Bernt and Holm 2009). In absolute numbers, Berlin now had the largest shortfall of affordable housing for those households earning below the mean, with more than 310,000 apartments needed, especially in the form of public housing (Dettmer and Knuth 2018).

In the 1980s, before unification, Prenzlauer Berg had had a history of protest that involved using public space to oppose the East Berlin government and its rules (Papen 2012). Certainly, the Berlin Wall murals provided an opportunity to develop a graffiti and street art subculture that expanded to other parts of Berlin. Early gentrification was coupled with political graffiti, slogans and posters reflecting a liberal orientation supporting gay rights, Nazis out, and others. Some resistance was shown in 'anti-yuppie' graffiti (White and Gutting 1998). Grass-roots movements used public spaces to get their message out, including political graffiti and street art that expressed their discontent (Papen 2012).

Young (2016), drawing on discussions with Holm, points out how street art is a key part of Berlin's identity that is being marketed towards tourism, whereas earlier it was associated with resistance to the Berlin Wall. Berlin's graffiti and street art became strongly promoted but in a very commodified and controlled way, especially in places in Prenzlauer Berg and around Checkpoint Charlie. She notes that when Platoon, a huge arts complex, was opened in Prenzlauer Berg in 2012, some hoped that it would support the urban creativity that gentrification seemed to be threatening; however, this did not occur. The very pointed message of the graffiti seen in Figure 7.3 ('diese Stadt ist aufgekauft' meaning 'this city has been bought') was painted by someone using paint rollers while hanging over the top of a building along the Prenzlauer Berg–Mitte border.

While not writing about Berlin, Rafael Schacter discusses the role of commercialized street art (which he distinguishes from graffiti). He writes:

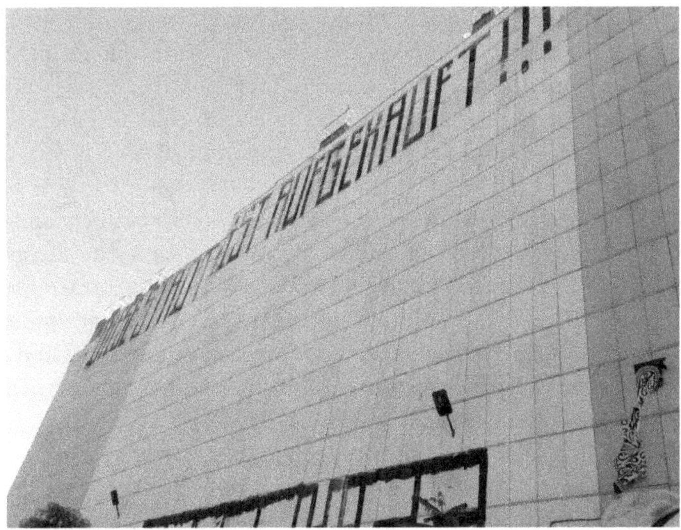

Figure 7.3. The caption '*diese Stadt ist aufgekauft*' [This city has been bought] is painted on a building on the border between Prenzlauer Berg and Mitte, Berlin, 2016. © Lisa K. Waldner.

'Rather than simply seeping into the mainstream art market (as is the case with nearly all once-radical art), street art has been re-purposed to reel the creative class into particular urban spaces. Street art and street artists are today employed (quite literally) to accelerate the process of gentrification, and [to] mainline a sense of "authenticity" into a site' (Schacter 2015).

Schacter used Richard Florida's 'creative city' to discuss what he argues is a recent phenomenon of the corporatization and privatization of public space by using street art to entice the creative class to move to an urban location. He argues that city officials use street art to 'entice the key demographic of well-educated professionals and "bohemians" (the coders, the designers, the "knowledge-based" professionals) who form the basis for a post-industrial economy'. Art is a 'cog in the regenerative wheel, aimed at attracting and retaining these individuals to build wealth and develop cities. The movements and developments of contemporary art practice are here subordinated to the desires and objectives of urban planning policy: the development of the private sector takes priority over the development of the aesthetic or the social'. The message 'this city has been bought' is protesting the use of street art as a means of gentrifying Prenzlauer Berg to bring in the creative class at the expense of the working class and those displaced.

Novy and Colomb (2013), however, found empirical support for Harvey's hypothesis that cultural producers will resist the increasing exploitation and appropriation of local cultures. They looked at two specific case studies in Berlin and Hamburg, and found artists, cultural producers and the 'creative class' successfully engaged in oppositional movements against market-based urban development agendas.

While Holm described the gentrification in Prenzlauer Berg and Mitte as 'super-gentrification through luxury housing projects', he identified a different pattern of 'careful urban renewal' for Kreuzberg formerly located in urban West Berlin. This occurred in part because of militant protests in the 1980s that resulted in the preservation of existing structures and of the social composition of the population. Extensive public funds were initially committed to such development (Holm 2013).

Clarkson describes how various ideologically diverse subcultures were developing in certain parts of West Berlin by the 1950s that were opposed to the cultural mainstream. By the mid-1970s, working-class and lower-middle-class youth without university training were searching for urban social space to avoid both draft/conscription into the military and capitalist socio-economic pressures (Clarkson 2012: 80). Areas in West Berlin such as Kreuzberg that were close to the Berlin Wall experienced major declines in their population and real estate values, making them attractive to squatters' movements, politicized immigrants, radical feminists, and punks, promoting an underground economy and alternative networks of consumption and production (ibid.: 84–85). 'Different elements of the local scene could meet, drink, and occasionally get around to organizing political action' (ibid.: 85).

Drissel researched anarcho-punks, and found that major gentrification battles gradually shifted from Prenzlauer Berg and Mitte to Friedrichshaim and Kreuzberg. Anarcho-punks especially provided the major resistance to commodification. Most of Drissel's interviewees believed there were lingering sociocultural distinctions between East and West, with those from the former East especially feeling they were negatively stereotyped, more likely to be in lower-paid occupations, harassed by police, and displaced from their homes owing to gentrification. Anti-gentrification supporters in Kreuzberg advocated an 'uglification strategy', which recommended that long-time inhabitants refrain from repairing home-related items such as roofs and broken windows to 'keep out unwanted residents' (Drissel 2011: 33). That strategy in conjunction with squatting, protest marches, rioting, boycotts, vandalism, and writing graffiti were used to contest urban space gentrification.

Punk art tends to be 'in your face' to shock or create strong emotional reactions to the artwork. One 25-year-old punk anarchist-graffitist who had moved to Kreuzberg from East Berlin due to gentrification explained: 'Bombing the city with graffiti is my way of having my voice heard ... so people can see that we're fed up with this gentrification shit' (Drissel 2011: 34–35). One of his pieces had the iconic heading 'The Berlin Wall' placed 'directly above a grumpy-looking Karl Marx grasping an aerosol can in one hand, [and] seemingly poised to spray paint into the faces of unsuspecting passers-by' (ibid.: 34).

Drissel found numerous punk graffiti graphics and slogans that strongly opposed or questioned capitalization and gentrification, including a graphic of Mahatma Gandhi spray-painted with 'Truth is God' that seemed to picture him staring at a US dollar sign defaced with a red mark, above the statement 'Don't Believe the Hype'. This likely was intended as a strong critique of Western capitalist values like greed and conspicuous consumption. It was especially young punk anarchists who contested urban space in their art. Although divisions between former East and West Berlin youth existed, they tended to unify around their militant opposition to gentrification, and their desires to reconfigure parts of Berlin (Drissel 2011).

Holm identified a more recent set of gentrification dynamics occurring in places like Kreuzberg, in part because occupancy and price caps for those houses modernized in the 1980s had already expired. Thus, the dwellings are now subject to general rental laws. Poor households faced with possible economic displacement have resorted to sharing apartments. Drawing on the experiences of other European cities, he refers to this phenomenon as 'displacement from the lifestyle' (Holm 2013: 181).

Young (2016: 114) explored parts of Kreuzberg, including a building that appeared warehouse-like with 10-metre-high ceilings, several floors, broken windows, and no running water or electricity. After reunification the building had been abandoned, but in 2012 artists rediscovered it and asked the owner if they could use it for storage. He agreed, and artists moved in creating makeshift studios, exhibition spaces, and group shows. The owner discovered this and kicked the artists out, illustrating an example of dispossession. The neighbouring area around the building included both squats and a luxury condo development.

Graffiti and street art on the Berlin Wall before and after reunification were ways artists contested space and separation. Graffiti in Berlin has played another role that has been more questionable, namely, a signal for and possibly also a conduit to more rapid gentrification. Gentrification is seen as a positive by some because it comes with an upgrade in the neighbourhood with more access to shops and restaurants as well as a more pleasing aesthetic, as blighted properties are removed and replaced with commercial ventures or newer residential properties. For the poor though, gentrification means not only economic hardship but also the disruption of social networks when residents are priced out of neighbourhoods they may have lived in for many years (Bernt and Holm 2009). For housing areas where the majority is not owner-occupied, rentals put an additional strain on poorer residents. Compared to other cities in Europe, and in the United States, Berlin's housing market is dominated by rentals, and Prenzlauer Berg specifically is noted for the high number of residents coming from other places or countries of origin to live in newer luxury apartments, displacing poorer residents (Holm 2013). One study found that only 40 per cent of the original Prenzlauer Berg residents were able to stay in their renovated apartments, and these were mainly from the upper strata (Häußermann, Holm and Zunzer 2002, cited in Bernt and Holm 2009).

Increasing gentrification is associated with graffiti and street art in two ways. First, artists often choose poorer neighbourhoods to practise their art, as abandoned buildings that are in disrepair provide a ready canvas and possibly a place to live. Abandoned buildings may also not be surveilled by the police and property owners to the same level as property under current commercial or residential use. Street art then acts as a signal that an area is ready for urban renewal. Secondly, the appearance of street art may unwittingly cause an increase in property values and real estate prices. While street art often contains messages that oppose gentrification, and sometimes artists have used their art to try and protect those living in illegal squats, the appearance of street art may make an area more trendy and popular, which then increases demand leading to higher rents and real estate prices. This has happened in many cities, including Berlin, London and New York (Arlandis 2013). Rental prices in the eastern section of Berlin rose 90 per cent between 2000 and 2012 according to the German newspaper *Der Spiegel* (ibid.).

Using the platform Flickr, one group of researchers examined London neighbourhoods and found that those with more photographs of art experienced higher gains in property prices (Seresinhe, Preis and Moat 2016). Forte and De Paola (2019) argue that in the case of Naples, Italy, street art is associated with an edgy vibe that not only attracts more people but also businesses such as cafes and restaurants, which certainly is the case with Berlin's Prenzlauer Berg (Martinique 2016). This is consistent with Schacter's critique of the commodification of space in the pursuit of the creative city that serves capitalist interests by drawing in knowledge professionals. Martinique (2016) writes that street art is a new tool used to encourage gentrification where 'public space is monetized and transformed into high-priced trendy areas attractive to the emerging creative class'. Graffiti has historically been associated with crime and vandalism, and is a sign of a distressed neighbourhood. This has taken a 180-degree turn, with street art and stylized graffiti writing now associated with neighbourhoods that are considered creative and edgy but cool with a hipster vibe (Ross 2016). Relatedly, Evans argues that a duality now exists between 'high' street art and '(un)popular' graffiti (Evans 2016: 179), with street art thought to increase the desirability of a neighbourhood, while graffiti is still associated with crime and urban decay.

This transformation has not come without negative consequences for current residents, as increasing commodification and touristification have made these neighbourhoods less affordable, liveable and sustainable for working-class residents. Papen (2015: 3) suggests that street art and other like images 'contribute to how a neighbourhood is commodified and sold to new residents, visitors, tourists and investors'. In her study of Prenzlauer Berg, she argues that while some research documents the anti-consumerism and commercialism of street art, her research found that the street art form 'not only blends in but supports the commercial discourses that dominate the semiotic landscape' (ibid.: 18). She found that business owners in Prenzlauer Berg valued street art because it improved the aesthetic feel of the neighbourhood.

The tourist industry in Berlin certainly benefited from historic events like the rise and fall of the Berlin Wall, the reunification of Berlin and Germany, and the return of the capital to Berlin, but it is also advantaged by its cultural variety and diversity, as well as its relative affordability. Berlin is rich in heritage, arts, recreational facilities and entertainment (Novy and Huning 2009). Harvey (2006: 92) points out how 'the appropriation of cultural histories' in tourism as commodities has become big business' and 'creates a premium on the commodification of phenomena that are in other respects unique, authentic and therefore non-replicable'. Further this 'pillaging of cultural histories', as he labels it, 'has little or nothing to do with creating', and 'carries over into the realms of individual creativity'.

We do note though that at times street artists conduct street art tours in Berlin (King 2017). Also, we have observed such tours in Athens, Greece and Melbourne, Australia. In Melbourne, Blender Studios, composed of twenty-five or so street artists, founded Melborune Street Art Tours conducted only by street artists. A possible research topic could be whether being involved in the ownership of such an organization influences how they feel about conducting such tours.

Touristification alters life for residents, who must tolerate alternative or graffiti tours bringing in more noise and traffic. In discussing one Berlin neighbourhood, Young found residents complained about tourists on political street art tours who photograph the art and blame them for rising rents. Young argues that 'Prenzlauer Berg has become a key component of a corporatized approach to streetness, and a commercialized exploitation of Berlin's

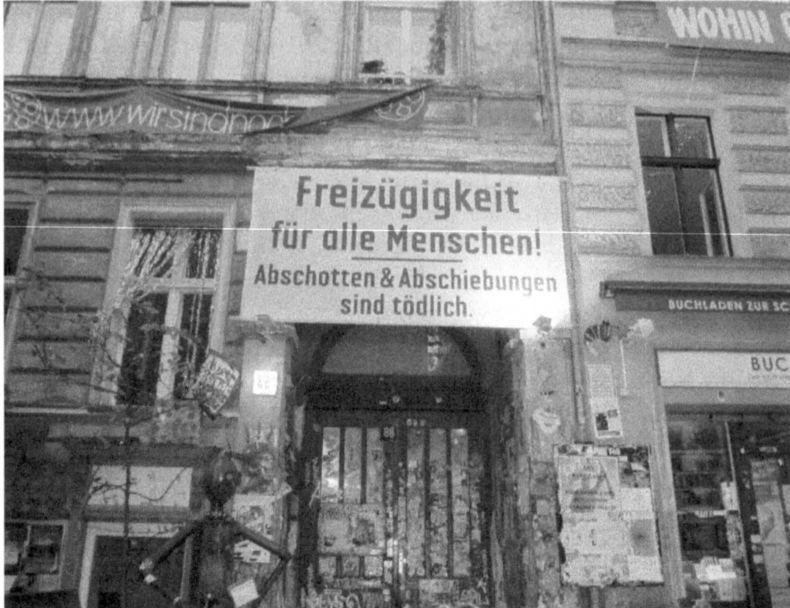

Figure 7.4 Tuntenhaus is an ex-squat in Prenzlauer Berg that is now a queer house project. The banner on the entrance is pro-migration and immigration with the slogan 'Free movement for all people! Deportations are deadly'. Berlin, 2016. More information can be found on their website: https:// tuntenhaus.org/?Tuntenhaus. © Betty A. Dobratz.

history of subversive art' (Young 2016: 113). Schacter (2015) discusses how street art institutions (e.g. festivals) rob locations of their local character and history, and provide a false message that suggests protest and transgression, while in reality the messages are devoid of local character and context.

Colomb examined the commodification, transformation and resistance to temporary uses of space that have been associated with Berlin's economic and urban development policies and city marketing discourse since 2000. City planners search for new marketing images such as underground or subcultural ones suggesting 'hipness' (Colomb 2012: 143) to help to identify Berlin as a creative city. Thus, boundaries of legitimate culture can be extended 'to include new, previously illegitimate art and cultural forms (like street art and graffiti)' (ibid.: 142). Colomb concluded that when this occurs, subculture 'can no longer be understood primarily as a cultural attack against the mainstream' or as resistance to a hegemonic culture. They will then have become 'niche markets'.

Only certain types of subculture 'fit into the image of a young, vibrant creative city' (Colomb 2012: 143). Kreuzberg's alternative living projects of squatters were not included in the city's marketing, as some interim spaces were seen as too radical and politicized, in part because they provided 'alternatives to dominant (capitalist) forms of urban development' (ibid.). Some artistic squats, such as Tacheles in Mitte, were integrated into part of the tourism promotion imagery; however, we note that Tacheles was actually closed by the city in 2012, illustrating just how temporary the touristic uses of such space can be. In 2018, five of the former artists and others started another Tacheles-type project in Lichtenberg Berlin (Lindsay 2018). Like before, they are selling their art, but now they are paying 10,000 euros a month for rent, which dramatically illustrates the commodification process.

Of course, commodification does not go uncontested, and there are still areas in Prenzlauer Berg that look like squatted and contested space. Figure 7.4, for example, is of the entrance of Tuntenhaus, a queer house project and ex-squat. Another way to contest the association between street art and gentrification is to erase the murals. Lutz Henke, co-creator of the famous Kreuzberg murals along with Italian artist Blu, wrote about his deliberate painting over of these iconic murals in an opinion published in the *Guardian*. He writes: 'Berlin's gentrification and zombification is in full swing. We would rather destroy our street art than let it contribute to that process' (Henke 2014).

Turn to More Extreme Right-Wing Attitudes

In Prenzlauer Berg, resistance to gentrification was displayed in 'anti-yuppie' graffiti (White and Gutting 1998), and slogans like 'Schwabe raus' (Swabians out) followed by TSH (likely referring to Total Swabian Hate) (Papen 2012). The Swabians are a group of people from a south-west region of Germany that includes Stuttgart. Some compare Swabians to the Scots of Germany, who were known for their thriftiness and as penny-pinching misers who were overly tidy and uptight (Local Collection 2016). Up to three hundred thousand Swabians could be living in Berlin. Some blame Swabians for the gentrification of certain neighbourhoods and for 'bringing a bourgeois sense of order to the chaotic capital' (ibid.).

In Figure 7.5, 'Ich bin Berliner, du nicht. TSH' ('I am a Berliner. You are not. TSH') identifies who has the right to regard themselves as a Berliner and who does not. The writer is likely challenging gentrification and claiming that only long-time residents have that right. Disgruntled residents or former residents of Prenzlauer Berg seemed to focus on how wealthy south-west

Figure 7.5 Graffiti in Prenzlauer Berg stating 'I am a Berliner. You are not. TSH' (with TSH likely referring to Total Swabian Hate). Berlin, 2012. © Betty A. Dobratz.

Germans were 'driving out residents' who could no longer afford to live there. Other graffiti stated things like 'Shoot Swabians' and 'Swabians Out!' (Tempest 2013). Wilder (2013) reported that some graffiti wordings were similar to the Nazi propaganda used to persecute Jews and other targeted groups. For example, 'Don't buy from the Swabians' echoes the 1930s Nazi propaganda to boycott Jewish businesses.

While the attacks against Swabians seem to have declined, another migration concern has intensified. Noack (2016) claims that 'No issue has caused more tensions than the influx of refugees into Germany'. Since unification, East Germans have felt disadvantaged by many economic and political factors, in addition to gentrification. That feeling could well have been 'simmering' for about twenty-five years, but it 'boiled over' when Merkel's 2015 immigration policy allowed in many refugees. The far-right political party, AfD (Alternative for Germany), which began in 2013 with an anti-EU stance, has since developed a 'contentious anti-Muslim and anti-immigration platform' (Smith and Eckardt 2018).

There were 1,645 incidents involving anti-refugee violence and social unrest in Germany in 2014–15, with 640 of the 11,306 municipalities experiencing at least one. Berlin had 215 events, the highest number of any

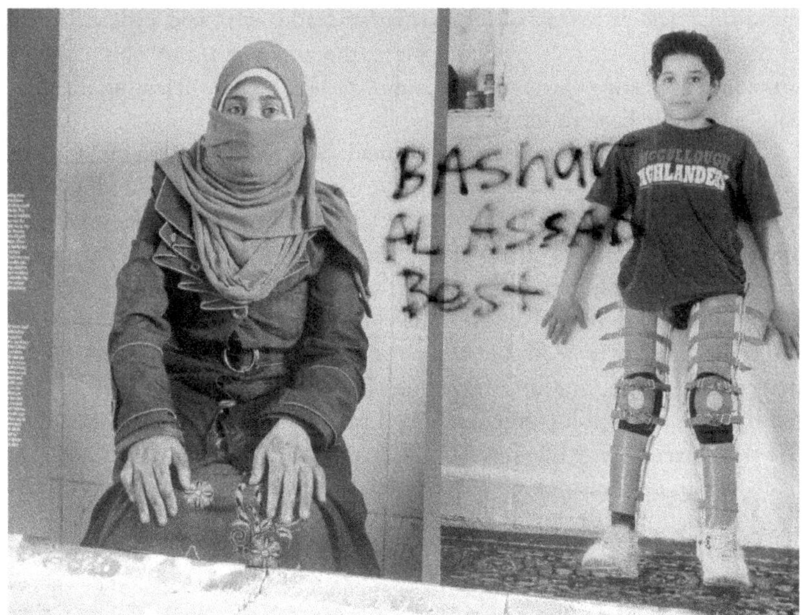

Figure 7.6 Graffiti written on part of the display of Kai Wiedenhofer's WARONWALL. (An exhibition about the war in Syria, which showed how the civilian population was being harmed by the war. The display was shown in Berlin, 23 June–25 September 2016.) Someone has written graffiti praising Bashar al-Assad, the Syrian leader, on this display of a Syrian youth who has lost his legs. Berlin, 2016. © Betty A. Dobratz.

municipality – by region, it had 6.1 incidents per 100,000 inhabitants. This was the third highest German region, with the two highest regions being located in the former East Germany (Bencek and Strasheim 2016; Noack 2016).

An Institute for New Social Answers (INSA) poll found that even twenty-seven years after German reunification, 64.6 per cent of Germans perceived persistent divisions between the former communist East and the capitalist West, and only 22.9 per cent believed that the divisions had been overcome. Of those perceiving divisions, 74 per cent tended to be from the former East Germany (Reuters 2017).

Figure 7.6 shows graffiti defacing part of Kai Wiedenhofer's 2016 exhibit illustrating how the Syrian civilian population were experiencing collateral damage in the Syrian civil war (Wiedenhofer n.d.). The graffiti written on the display showed support for the Syrian leader who had ordered much of the bombing. Like the previous piece, the graffiti was probably done by someone supporting extreme right causes, and in this case opposing the presence of Middle Eastern refugees in Berlin.

This rise in anti-immigrant sentiment as expressed in graffiti mirrors other political behaviour. The refugee crisis as well as long-standing concerns about globalization and the weakening of national identity also affected political views (BBC 2018). AfD obtained 12.6 per cent of the vote in 2017, and ninety-four seats in the federal parliament. It became the largest opposition party because Merkel had formed a coalition with SPD, the centre-left party, to secure her position as chancellor (ibid.). A higher percentage of support for AfD comes from voters living in former East Germany,[1] although a comparable level of support is also found for more left-wing parties (e.g. Die Linke) as well. AfD's major electoral success was likely due to its challenging Merkel's policy of opening the German borders to about a million migrants and refugees, mostly from the Middle East (BBC 2017).

In 2017, the Berlin vote for AfD was generally similar to that of Germany as a whole (12.0 per cent to 12.6 per cent), with certain but not all former areas of East Berlin more likely to support the AfD. In the former East Berlin district Marzahn-Hellersdorf, AfD won 21.6 per cent of the vote, increasing its total by 15.3 per cent (Clarke 2017; Wright 2017). Die Linke received 26.1 per cent of the vote, although its vote declined by 6.8 per cent from 2013. The Greens received 4.1 per cent of the vote, an increase of 0.2 per cent; CDU received 20.9 per cent, a decline of 5.1 per cent; and SPD had 14.5 per cent, down 4.7 per cent (Federal Returning Officer 2017). Wright believed these major changes in the Marzahn-Hellersdorf vote from 2013 were partly because nearly three thousand refugees (6.5 per cent of Berlin asylum seekers) were being housed in the Marzahn-Hellersdorf district in Berlin. His interviews revealed that residents felt other parties, including Die Linke, were not paying attention to their needs.

We acknowledge the 2019 European Parliament elections showed a decline in AfD support (11 per cent), with a stronger showing for the Greens compared to the 2017 German Parliament election. Because the elections are different types, we believe it problematic to compare results between German and European Union parliamentary elections. However, compared to the 2014 European Parliament election, AfD increased its vote by 3.9 per cent in Germany and 2 per cent in Berlin, while the Greens increased their support by 9.8 per cent in Germany and 8.8 per cent in Berlin. The CDU, SPD and Die Linke had lower percentages in both locations (Federal Returning Officer 2019).

Conclusion

The most significant use of street art involved the Berlin Wall before its fall, because there was no better way to convey resistance. The remnants of the wall and the artwork associated with the east wall are major factors in the touristification of Berlin. However, graffiti and street art have been influential and informative in many other circumstances, including advancing both left- and right-wing causes. The display of graffiti in the Reichstag illustrates the willingness of at least some government officials to publicly acknowledge its Nazi history, albeit with modification. The preservation or memorialization of graffiti and street art, including its removal from the original location, raises questions about the efficacy of graffiti as a protest tool, and promotes increasing touristification and commodification of public space displacing locals. The separation of Germany and a divided Berlin during the Cold War still seems to significantly influence people's perceptions and behaviour. After reunification, various issues reflecting the economic and political divides among classes and regions developed, including gentrification, commodification, touristification, and recently the growth of AfD linked to its anti-immigrant policy.

Graffiti and political street art have provided alternative means to inform the public about events and crises, which might not otherwise have been available from 1945 to the present. Ironically, while much street art is critical of gentrification, its presence is also associated with rising property values and the eventual displacement of long-time residents that tends to follow. While street art and graffiti are deployed to protest gentrification and displacement, street art may be the engine responsible for attracting the creative class into former working-class neighbourhoods in the quest to achieve the creative city that further distresses an urban neighbourhood already facing a shortage of affordable housing.

We believe the Berlin Wall murals helped to create a street art culture that translated into protests beyond the wall, and became part of the battle against gentrification, but we are still concerned about how it has been used to facilitate gentrification and touristification. By presenting key examples of the use of political graffiti in Berlin, we argue that social scientists need to study this political phenomenon further in order to understand its impact on the public. We wonder if street art and political graffiti will increasingly become part of the 'niche markets' and less of a resistance to a hegemonic culture that Colomb (2012) alluded to. We find it significant and worthy of social scientific study to analyse political street art as a challenge to mainstream culture and capitalism, but looking at how street art and graffiti are being utilized or co-opted as part of increasing commodification, and the reactions of street artists to this, are important and necessary to consider as well.

Acknowledgements

This chapter is a revised version of a paper presented at the International Political Science Association meeting, Brisbane, Australia, 25 July 2018. We wish to thank Heinz Kuzdas and Thierry Noir for meeting with us and discussing street art and the Berlin Wall. We also thank Julia Tulke for a tour of Prenzlauer Berg, and Caro Eickhoff for a tour of Kreuzberg.

Betty A. Dobratz is professor of sociology at Iowa State University. She has co-authored 'White Power, White Pride!': The White Separatist Movement in the United States with Stephanie Shanks-Meile (Twayne, 2000), and Power, Politics, and Society with Lisa Waldner and Timothy Buzzell (Routledge, 2019); she has also edited and co-edited (with George Kourvetaris) the Journal of Political and Military Sociology, and co-edited (with Lisa Waldner) The Sociological Quarterly. Her research and teaching interests include political sociology and social inequality. She received a NATO postdoctoral fellowship to study Greek politics. Her PhD in sociology is from the University of Wisconsin.

Lisa K. Waldner is professor of sociology and associate dean for the College of Arts and Sciences at the University of St. Thomas in St. Paul, Minnesota (United States) where she teaches undergraduate courses in research methods and statistics. She publishes in the areas of interpersonal relationship violence, sexual coercion, anti-gay hate crimes, political graffiti and right-wing extremism. She is a co-author (with Betty A. Dobratz and Timothy Buzzell) of Power, Politics, and Society (Routledge, 2019). In 2015 she was named a John Ireland Presidential Scholar by the University of St. Thomas. With Betty Dobratz, she co-edited The Sociological Quarterly from 2012 to 2016. She received her PhD in sociology from Iowa State University.

Note

1. The respective percentages of the vote for the political parties AfD, Green and Die Linke (The Left) from the 2017 Federal elections are provided for these former East German states: Brandenberg 20.2, 5.0, 17.2; Mecklenburg-Vorpommern 18.6, 4.3, 17.8; Saxony 27.0, 4.6, 16.1; Saxony-Anhalt 19.6, 3.7, 17.8; and Thuringia 22.7, 4.1, 16.9 (Federal Returning Officer 2017).

References

Angerer, C. 2018. 'Berlin Wall's East Side Gallery Wins Protection from Developers', *NBC News*, 22 November. Retrieved 24 February 2019 from https://www.nbcnews.com/news/world/berlin-wall-s-east-side-gallery-wins-protection-developers-n939311.

Arlandis, F. 2013. 'The Perverse Effect of Street Art on Neighborhood Gentrification', *Le Monde*, 4 March. Retrieved 11 February 2018 from https://www.worldcrunch.com/culture-society/the-perverse-effect-of-street-art-on-neighborhood-gentrification.

Avramidis, K., and M. Tsilimpounidi. 2017. *Graffiti and Street Art: Reading, Writing and Representing the City*. London: Routledge.

Bencek, D., and J. Strasheim. 2016. 'Refugees Welcome? A Dataset on Anti-Refugee Violence in Germany'. *Research and Politics* (October–December): 1–11.

Bernt, M., and A. Holm. 2009. 'Is It, or Is Not? The Conceptualisation of Gentrification and Displacement, and Its Political Implications in the Case of Berlin-Prenzlauer Berg'. *City* 13(2–3): 312–24.

British Broadcasting Corporation (BBC). 2017. 'German Election: How Right-Wing is Nationalist AfD?' *BBC News*, 13 October. Retrieved 10 September 2018 from https://www.bbc.com/news/world-europe-37274201.

———. 2018. 'Europe and Right-Wing Nationalism: A Country-by-Country Guide', *BBC News*, 10 September. Retrieved 31 January 2019 from www.bbc.com/news/world-europe-36130006.

Carpenter, J.O. 1968. 'Berlin'. *Sociological Focus* 1(4): 48–58.

Clarke, S. 2017. 'German Elections 2017: Full Results', *Guardian*, 25 September. Retrieved 1 February 2019 from www.theguardian.com/world/ng-interactive/2017/sep/24/german-elections-2017-latest-results-live-merkel-bundestag-afd.

Clarkson, A. 2012. 'Urban Tribes: Subcultures and Political Conflict in West Berlin 1945–1991'. *Social Justice* 38(4): 71–90.

Colomb, C. 2012. 'Pushing the Urban Frontier: Temporary Uses of Space, City Marketing, and the Creative City Discourse in 2000s Berlin'. *Journal of Urban Affairs* 34(2): 131–52.

Colombini, A. 2018. 'The Duality of Graffiti: Is It Vandalism or Art?' *CeROArt* [Online]. Retrieved 6 July 2019 from http://journals.openedition.org/ceroart/5745.

Cornwell, R. 2014. 'Fall of the Berlin Wall: It Was Thanks to Soviet Leader Mikhail Gorbachev That This Symbol of Division Fell', *Independent*, 30 October. Retrieved 10 June 2018 from https://www.independent.co.uk/news/world/world-history/fall-of-the-berlin-wall-it-was-thanks-to-soviet-leader-mikhail-gorbachev-that-this-symbol-of-9829298.html.

Dettmer, M., and H. Knuth. 2018. 'Rising Rents Are Putting the Squeeze on Germans', *Der Spiegel*, 13 April. Retrieved 20 February 2019 from http://www.spiegel.de/international/germany/germany-rising-rents-are-putting-squeeze-on-germans-a-1202311.html.

Drissel, D. 2011. 'Anarchist Punks Resisting Gentrification: Countercultural Contestations of Space in the New Berlin'. *International Journal of the Humanities* 8(1): 19–44.

Ellis-Petersen, H. 2017. 'Street Art Goes Home: Museum of Graffiti Opens in Berlin', *Guardian*, 20 September. Retrieved 15 March 2019 from https://www.theguardian.com/artanddesign/2017/sep/20/street-art-goes-home-museum-of-graffiti-opens-in-berlin-urban-nation.

Evans, G. 2016. 'Graffiti Art and the City: From Piece-Making to Place-Making', in J.I. Ross (ed.), *Routledge Handbook of Graffiti and Street Art*. London: Routledge, pp. 168–81.

Federal Returning Officer. 2017. 'Bundestag Election 2017'. Retrieved 8 July 2019 from https://www.bundeswahlleiter.de/en/bundestagswahlen/2017/ergebnisse/bund-99.html.

———. 2019. '9th European Parliament Election on 26 May 2019'. Retrieved 15 July 2019 from https://www.bundeswahlleiter.de/en/europawahlen/2019.html.

Forte, F., and P. De Paola. 2019. 'How Can Street Art Have Economic Value?' *Sustainability* 11(3): 580.

Giddens, A. 1987. *Sociology: A Brief but Critical Introduction*. San Diego, CA: Harcourt Brace Jovanovich.

Göbel, M. 2009. 'Officials Erase Historic Berlin Wall Mural'. *Der Spiegel*, 27 March. Retrieved 1 July 2018 from www.spiegel.de/international/germany/kiss-of-death-officials-erase-historic-berlin-wall-mural-a-615900.html.

Greer, G. 2010. 'It Was a Stunning Work of Art – So Why Is the Wall Hanging in a Las Vegas Loo? *Guardian*, 14 February. Retrieved 1 July 2018 from www.theguardian.com/artanddesign/2010/feb/14/germaine-greer-berlin-wall-thierry-noir.

Harrison, H.M. 2003. *Driving the Soviets Up the Wall: Soviet–East German Relations, 1953–1961*. Princeton, NJ: Princeton University Press.

Harvey, D. 2002. 'The Art of Rent: Globalization, Monopoly and the Commodification of Culture', in L. Panitch and C. Leys (eds), *A World of Contradictions: Socialist Register*. New York: Monthly Review Press, pp. 93–110.

———. 2006. *Spaces of Global Capitalism*. London: Verso.

Häußermann, H., A. Holm and D. Zunzer. 2002. *Stadtemeuerung in der Berliner Republik: Modernisierung in Berlin Prenzlauer Berg*. Opladen: Leske + Budrich.

Henke, Lutz. 2014. 'Why We Painted Over Berlin's Most Famous Graffiti', *Guardian*, 19 December. Retrieved 18 March 2019 from https://www.theguardian.com/comment isfree/2014/dec/19/why-we-painted-over-berlin-graffiti-kreuzberg-murals.

Holm, A. 2006. 'Urban Renewal and the End of Social Housing: The Roll Out of Neoliberalism in East Berlin's Prenzlauer Berg'. *Social Justice* 33(3)#105: 114–28.

———. 2013. 'Berlin's Gentrification Mainstream', in B. Greel, M. Bernt and A. Holm (eds), *The Berlin Reader: A Compendium on Urban Change and Activism*. Berlin: Verlag, pp. 173–89.

Judt, T. 2005. *Postwar: A History of Europe Since 1945*. New York: Penguin Press.

Katsouras, I. n.d. 'Mikhail Take the Wheel', *Flickr*. Retrieved 2 July 2018 from www.flickr.com/photos/eliosk/43666891631.

Kimmelman, M. 2014. 'Berlin After the Wall: A Microcosm of the World's Chaotic Change', *New York Times*, 17 November. Retrieved 1 July 2018 from https://www.nytimes.com/2014/11/18/world/europe/berlin-after-the-wall-a-microcosm-of-the-worlds-chaotic-change-.html.

King, M. 2017. 'The Best Street Art Tours in Berlin', *Culture Trip*, 22 February. Retrieved 16 July 2019 from https://theculturetrip.com/europe/germany/articles/the-best-street-art-tours-in-berlin/.

Kluth, Andreas. 2014. 'The Graffiti That Made Germany Better', *The Atlantic*, 3 July. Retrieved 1 July 2018 from www.theatlantic.com/international/archive/2014/07/the-graffiti-that-made-germany-better/373872/.

Kuzdas, H. n.d. *Berlin Wall Art*. Text by Michael Nungesser. Berlin: Elefanten Press.

Langerbein, Helmut. 2009. 'Great Blunders? The Great Wall of China, the Berlin Wall, and the Proposed United States/Mexico Border Fence'. *The History Teacher* 43(1): 9–29.

Leuenberger, C. 2006. 'Constructions of the Berlin Wall'. *Social Problems* 53(1): 18–37.

Lindsay, T. 2018. 'Life After Tacheles: What's Become of the Artist Squatters?' *Exberliner* #171, 27 May. Retrieved 15 July 2019 from http://www.exberliner.com/features/culture/life-after-tacheles/.

Local Collection. 2016. 'Introducing Swabians – "the Scots of Germany"'. Retrieved 23 October 2018 from https://www.thelocal.de/20161027/new-exhibition-tests-swabian-stereotypes.

Martinique, E. 2016. 'What Is the Effect of Street Art on Real Estate Prices?' *Widewalls*, 30 May. Retrieved 11 February 2019 from https://www.widewalls.ch/street-art-real-estate/.

Noack, R. 2016. 'Germany Reunified 26 Years Ago, but Some Divisions Are Still Strong', *Washington Post*, 3 October. Retrieved 1 September 2018 from https://www.washingtonpost.com/news/worldviews/wp/2016/10/03/germany-reunified-26-years-ago-but-some-divisions-are-still-strong/?utm_term=.accd56d9280e.

Noir, T. 2014. 'Graffiti in the Death Strip: The Berlin Wall's First Street Artist Tells His Story', *Guardian*, 3 April. Retrieved 11 June 2018 from https://www.theguardian.com/artanddesign/gallery/2014/apr/03/thierry-noir-graffiti-berlin-wall#img-1.

———. 2016. Interview with Betty Dobratz and Lisa Waldner, 19 July 2016.

———. n.d. 'Frequently Asked Questions to Thierry Noir about the East Side Gallery'. Retrieved 12 February 2019 from http://www.galerie-noir.de/ArchivesEnglish/FAQ-NoirESG.html.

Novy, J., and C. Colomb. 2013. 'Struggling for the Right to the (Creative) City in Berlin and Hamburg'. *International Journal of Urban and Regional Research* 37(5): 1816–38.

Novy, J., and S. Huning. 2009. 'New Tourism (Areas) in the "New Berlin"', in R. Maitland and P. Newman (eds), *Pin World Tourism Cities: Developing Tourism off the Beaten Track*. London: Routledge, pp. 87–108.

Papen, U. 2012. 'Commercial Discourses, Gentrification and Citizens' Protest: The Linguistic Landscape of Prenzlauer Berg, Berlin'. *Journal of Sociolinguistics* 16: 56–80.

———. 2015. 'Signs in Cities: The Discursive Production and Commodification of Urban Spaces'. *Sociolinguistic Studies* 9(1): 1–26.

Perez, Y.B. 2013a. 'The Berlin Canvas (Part I)', *Fair Observer*, 4 February. Retrieved 12 June 2018 from https://www.fairobserver.com/region/europe/berlin-canvas-part-i/.

———. 2013b. 'The Berlin Canvas (Part III)', *Fair Observer*, 6 February. Retrieved 12 June 2018 from https://www.fairobserver.com/region/europe/berlin-canvas-part-iii/.

Peterson, D. 2012. 'The Kiss', *Disappearing Man*, 18 April. Retrieved 1 July 2018 from http://www.disappearingman.com/berlin-wall/the-kiss/.

Pidd, H. 2011. 'Berlin Wall Artists Sue City in Copyright Controversy', *Guardian*, 3 May. Retrieved 1 September 2018 from https://www.theguardian.com/world/2011/may/03/berlin-wall-artists-sue-city.

Pugh, E. 2015. 'Graffiti and the Critical Power of Urban Space: Gordon Matta-Clark's Made in America and Keith Haring's Berlin Wall Mural'. *Space and Culture* 18(4): 421–35.

Rare Historical Photos. 2014. 'The Socialist Fraternal Kiss between Leonid Brezhnev and Erich Honecker, 1979', 25 March. Retrieved 20 September 2018 from rarehistorical photos.com/socialist-fraternal-kiss-leonid-brezhnev-erich-honecker-1979/

Reuters. 2017. 'Two-Thirds of Germans See Persistent East–West Divisions: Poll', *World News*, 2 October. Retrieved 10 September 2018 from https://www.reuters .com/article/us-germany-politics-reunification/two-thirds-of-germans-see-pers istent-east-west-divisions-poll-idUSKCN1C71CY.

Rieber, R.W. 1997. 'Social Distress, through Perceptions of the Berlin Wall before and after the Fall: A Preliminary Report'. *Psychology and Developing Societies* 9(2): 263–73.

Ross, J.I. 2016. 'Effects of Graffiti and Street Art', in J.I. Ross (ed.), *Routledge Handbook of Graffiti and Street Art*. London: Routledge, pp. 389–403.

Schacter, R. 2015. 'From Dissident to Decorative: Why Street Art Sold Out and Gentrified Our Cities', *The Conversation*, 9 November. Retrieved 6 July 2019 from https://theconversation.com/from-dissident-to-decorative-why-street-art-sold-out-and-gentrified-our-cities-46030.

Seresinhe, C.I., T. Preis and H.S. Moat. 2016. 'Quantifying the Link between Art and Property Prices in Urban Neighbourhoods', *Royal Society Open Science*, 1 April. Retrieved 12 June 2018 from http://dx.doi.org/10.1098/rsos.160146.

Smith, A., and A. Eckardt. 2018. 'How Fall of the Berlin Wall Paved Way for Germany's Populists', *NBCNews*, 2 May. Retrieved 10 September 2018 from https://www.euronews .com/2018/02/05/how-fall-of-the-berlin-wall-paved-way-for-germany-s-populists.

Spitzer, N. 1988. 'Dividing a City'. *The Wilson Quarterly* 12(3): 100–122.

Tempest, M. 2013. 'Scorn for Eastern Berlin's Well-Heeled Newcomers', *Der Spiegel*, 3 January. Retrieved 26 June 2018 from https://www.spiegel.de/international/ germany/gentrification-row-in-berlin-reveals-tensions-over-disparities-between-states-a-875528.html.

Thorson, L. 1990. 'Wall Art Lasts in Berlin, May Travel the World', APNews, 8 November. Retrieved 2 September 2018 from www.apnews.com/7c18e712f6520758d476ef3c 126761ba._

Waldner, L.K., and B. Dobratz. 2013. 'Graffiti as a Form of Contentious Political Participation'. *Sociology Compass* 7(5): 377–89.

Weber, J. 2016. *A Walk Along the East Side Gallery*. Berlin: Berlin Story Verlag GmbH.

White, P., and D. Gutting. 1998. 'Berlin: Social Convergences and Contrasts in the Reunited City'. *Geography* 83(July): 214–26.

Wiedenhofer, K. n.d. *War on Wall*. Retrieved 1 February 2019 from http://www.waron wall.org/.

Wilder, C. 2013. 'Nazi Slogans: Has Berlin's Gentrification Feud Gone Too Far?' *Der Speigel*, 16 May. Retrieved 12 June 2017 from http://www.spiegel.de/international/ germany/nazi-references-used-in-anti-swabian-berlin-gentrification-feud-a-900078. html.

Wright, L. 2017. 'How the Far-Right AfD Crept into Berlin's Left-Wing Strongholds', *Deutsche Welle*, 30 September. Retrieved 1 February 2019 from https://www.dw.com/ en/how-the-far-right-afd-crept-into-berlins-left-wing-strongholds/a-40743484.

Young, A. 2013. *Street Art, Public City*. London: Routledge.

———. 2016. *Street Art World*. London: Reaktion Books.

Chapter 8

Writing in a City in Crisis

Stencil Graffiti in the Old Town of Nicosia

Pafsanias Karathanasis

The Cypriot 'Crisis'

In March of 2013, the Republic of Cyprus, the divided eastern Mediterranean country, experienced its own version of the global 'economic crisis', and of the 'crisis of the eurozone'. The events of the Cypriot 'financial crisis' unfolded during the last two weeks of March, and they were unique in many ways. They included a twelve-day bank closure, a rejection by the Republic of Cyprus parliament of the first agreement with the lending institutions of Troika,[1] and a 'haircut' of the people's bank deposits. These took place in a climate of demonstrations, and under intense global media interest in this small island country. The final agreement between the government of the Republic of Cyprus and the Troika marked the end of an era; it marked the end of the economic prosperity that had been a characteristic of Cyprus from the late 1980s and throughout the 1990s, a period that has been referred to as the 'Cypriot economic miracle' (Theophanous 1995; Ioannides and Apostolopoulos 1999).

As Olga Demetriou argues, the events of the Cypriot financial crisis were shocking and surprising for the Greek-Cypriot community (Demetriou 2013). In the official discourses promoted by the media on a future under austerity, the crisis was presented as a collective challenge, 'where "all of us" will work hard, rebuild the economy, rise up again as "the Cypriot people" have done before' (ibid.). This statement, for Cyprus, was a clear reference to the events of 1974, when more than a hundred thousand Greek-Cypriots were displaced from the northern part of the island by the actions of Turkish armed forces.[2] The Turkish military invasion of the summer of 1974 was prompted by a coup d'état orchestrated by the Greek junta to try to achieve the island's union (*enosis*) with 'motherland' Greece. The coup itself came after a decade of instability in the newly formed Republic of Cyprus,[3] during which Turkish-Cypriots were pushed into enclaves and barred from asserting their constitutional rights, while the Greek-Cypriot political sphere was dominated by a left–right split, which was fought out by paramilitary forces. In the Cypriot sociopolitical context, I would suggest, 'financial crisis' is not a 'separate' event, as it is for example in the Greek context, as it cannot be understood outside Cyprus's political reality of prolonged territorial and sociocultural division, or the trauma this has entailed. In other words, the social meanings that 'crisis' acquires in Cyprus's sociopolitical reality, and more specifically in its divided capital, are officially and unofficially linked with the events of 1974, which remain *the* initial 'crisis'.

This chapter is based upon extended ethnographic fieldwork in Nicosia, conducted between 2009 and 2011, as well as during research visits to the island at different times during the years 2013–2015. In my fieldwork I worked mainly with Greek- and Turkish-Cypriot activists, who were involved in cultural and political activities organized from below on both sides of the divided capital, Nicosia. I will engage in a discussion of some examples of self-authorized *stencil graffiti* pieces, found between 2011 and 2013 on the walls of the Old Town of Nicosia, in the centre of the divided capital. Here I should underline that I choose the term 'self-authorized' interventions following Ulrich Blanche, who argues that although in the West graffiti is considered vandalism from a legal point of view, given that surfaces in public space are either private or public property, he prefers the term 'self-authorized'. This is because it does not have the legal or even moral connotations of terms like 'illegal' and 'illicit' (Blanche 2015: 34). Thus, focusing on the images that these stencil graffiti pieces present, and on the analysis of the meanings they communicate to their viewers, I describe a city that has been 'in crisis' for most of its recent history. In order to do so, I will begin with a short description of sociopolitical reality(s) in Cyprus, as well as of the urban development of the Old Town of Nicosia. What will follow will be an ethnographically informed semiotic and spatial analysis of political street art pieces – in other words, a cultural reading of self-authorized political stencils collected from the walls of the Old Town of Nicosia during the 2011–2013 period, before and during the Cypriot 'financial crisis'.

'Post-1974 (Everyday) Crisis'

The initial crisis event for Cyprus as a whole, and especially for the Greek Cypriot community, was the division of the island that followed the events of 1974. Life during the 'post-1974 crisis' has been hard for both Greek- and Turkish-Cypriot communities, but for different reasons. In the northern part, the division led to economic demise and dependence on Turkey. At the same time, official discourse was permeated with the narrative of freedom and safety under 'mother's protection'. However, after some years under Turkey's political and economic control,[4] some Turkish-Cypriots – citizens of the self-declared (1983) and unrecognized 'Turkish Republic of Northern Cyprus' (hereafter TRNC) – began considering dependence on Turkey as a constraint on their development and the main reason for international boycotts and isolation.[5]

On the other part of the island, the effects of war, occupation, and mass and violent displacement created a widespread feeling of insecurity and fear amongst the Greek-Cypriot community. Yet the fact that the Republic of Cyprus kept its international recognition offered the opportunity for economic recovery, mainly based on tourism, and this helped that community to prosper. Therefore, the Greek-Cypriot political elite presented economic recovery as a success of the republic's political and economic system. However, this same system was unable to foster an environment conducive to sociopolitical recovery. This was largely because of its inability to acknowledge the Greek-Cypriot community's part in the 1974 crisis and to attend to the trauma experienced by that community. It was also due to its inability to recognize the Turkish-Cypriot community as equals, and to work towards a peaceful coexistence with them.

After more than forty years of negotiations, no progress has been made towards a solution to the 'Cypriot Issue'. For that reason, despite the fact that the Republic of Cyprus managed to recover economically, one can argue that the 1974 crisis never actually ended. On both sides of the island, the 1974 crisis-event gradually gave way to an everyday sociopolitical crisis. Thus, it turned into a normalized crisis that was embedded within the fabric of daily life. Following the above, I would like to argue that in a divided country like Cyprus the term 'crisis' should not be understood only in relation to the contemporary 'crisis of the eurozone'. After a relatively recent war that created thousands of refugees, followed by decades of ethno-national and territorial division that established extensive military zones, and with a still unresolved political dispute, in the Cypriot context the term 'crisis' clearly acquires very varied meanings. In Cyprus, the 'financial crisis' of 2013 emerged in a sociopolitical context dominated by an already existing crisis. In other words, even if within official discourse the 'financial crisis' is not directly connected with the events of 1974, socially it seems that it is inseparable from the wider sociopolitical 'post-1974 crisis'.[6]

Divided Nicosia within the Walls

My research field-site in Cyprus is the Old Town of Nicosia, the historic centre of the city. It is surrounded by circular sixteenth-century Venetian walls, which separate it from the rest of the city. Nicosia within the walls presents an urban landscape that is marked by the material remains of division; a landscape in prolonged crisis. The Cypriot Green Line, the United Nations controlled Buffer Zone[7] that divides the island, passes right through the middle of the Old Town, and serves as a constant reminder of war and partition. Along its way through the medieval town, the Buffer Zone creates an urban landscape characterized by army posts, abandoned buildings or buildings seized by the army, barricades, roadblocks and walls. Most of the inhabitants of the southern part of the Old Town, the Greek-Cypriot Lefkosia,[8] moved away after the events of 1974. Over the past forty years, different groups of inhabitants, among them many migrants and Greek-Cypriot refugees, as well as new industries and businesses, have moved into the area and altered the former residential and commercial character. Today, diverse migrant and local groups are gathered in this border area, and together they constitute a heterogeneous and complex sociocultural landscape that combines the militarized zone of the Green Line with crowded shopping streets, as well as poor migrant neighbourhoods and newly renovated areas for the upper-class residents. Additionally, in recent years the area has been going through an intense process of gentrification, which is related to the 'financial crisis' of 2013 that brought the rapid development of leisure and nightlife businesses into this run-down area.

In Turkish-Cypriot Lefkoşa, on the other side of the Green Line, the Old Town presents similar architectural and historical characteristics. The former Turkish-Cypriot inhabitants have also moved out of the area, to newer areas outside the walls. The newcomers here, however, are not migrants from faraway countries, but Turkish settler families[9] and young working-class men. Moreover, the area is more militarized than its Greek-Cypriot counterpart. This is because the Turkish military has built more permanent structures along the Green Line, following the official position of the Turkish-Cypriot authorities that posits a separate state, with the dividing line as its border. Lastly, even if there has been some development during the past years, gentrification has not yet been as intense as in the other part of the city.

Nicosia is the only inhabited urban area in Cyprus in which material reminders of the 1974 crisis are so strikingly present. In addition, regardless of which side of the Buffer Zone one is in, one encounters analogous characteristics in terms of the development of the area within the walls. Since 1974, the whole of the Old Town of Nicosia has been through a process of borderization, marginalization and, recently, gentrification: borderization, because the Old Town stands on a territory that used to be at the centre of the wider city, but now stands at the militarized borders of two rivaling entities; marginalization, because what used to be at the social, economic and historical centre of the city became a walled area at the city's margins; and lastly, gentrification, because it was an urban area in decline. As is always the case in a gentrification process, artists and activists came first to live and work in the area in the mid-2000s, finding appropriate spaces for the development of alternative cultural and political practices. However, since the early 2010s, there has been a development of leisure, nightlife and tourist businesses, which take advantage of the low property prices, while feeding on the area's promoted alternative character.

Nevertheless, regardless of the recent gentrification, what remains as the main characteristic of the Old Town is its proximity to the militarized Buffer Zone that symbolizes the prolonged, unresolved Cypriot Issue and its divisions. As such, it is a liminal area, and this is what makes this divided Old Town a city 'in crisis', and therefore a very interesting field-site for the study of the everyday sociopolitical crisis on both sides of the island. Although all border areas can be considered liminal areas, the notion of 'liminality', as introduced by the anthropologist Arnold van Gennep (as early as 1909), presents a very useful theoretical tool for approaching the unresolved division of Nicosia. The anthropological idea of liminality was introduced through the study of rituals of transition (rites of passage) in African communities. It refers to the 'in-between' space or position that people find themselves in when they are going through a transition. The idea of 'passage' is central to the notion of liminality. This can be either a spatial or a spiritual passage (van Gennep 1960: 22, in Thomassen 2014: 91), but it has to be a passage through the in-between, to some kind of end point. Liminality, the in-between position, is understood as only a temporary position; it is the second of the three stages of a ritual (separation, liminality, reaggregation) through which, after separation from a previous social condition (identity or stage in life), the subject arrives at a new social condition or status and is reintroduced into the society. What happens, however, if the liminal condition is prolonged indefinitely, like in the case of Cyprus, where the political issue and the division have yet to be resolved?

Sociologist Arpad Szakolczai (2000, 2009) has written on liminality in contemporary societies, describing a condition that can be understood as a 'permanent liminality'. As he argues, 'liminality becomes a permanent condition when any of the phases in this (van Gennep's) sequence becomes frozen, as if a film stopped at a particular frame' (Szakolczai 2000: 212). What is interesting in this idea, in the case of Nicosia's Old Town, is that someone could argue that until the opening of the Green Line crossings in 2003, the area was frozen in the first phase of the sequence, the phase of separation. However, since the re-establishment of contact between the two sides, the area is frozen in the in-between or liminal state, the second phase of the sequence. Although actually the same urban area, it is stuck in between two separate state formations (the one recognized and the other not), in between two economic, cultural and sociopolitical worlds, and in between two differently developed cities, Lefkosia and Lefkoşa. However, in-between or liminal spaces are transitory spaces; they act as thresholds where there is the possibility of encounter with the 'other', and where identities and subjectivities can be opened up for negotiation.

Nicosia has indeed become a place where someone could encounter the 'other', bringing together the two communities through the negotiation of established national identities. This is especially true after the 2008 opening of the Buffer Zone crossing in the Ledra Street–Lokmaci area[10] at the heart of the Old Town, which changed the whole area within the walls, reinforcing its in-betweenness, and transforming it into a transitory and liminal zone. Antreas, a Greek-Cypriot reunification activist in his late thirties, told me in a 2011 interview about the opening of the crossing:

> After Ledras Street opened, even if you do not cross to the other side, but you just walk on the street or sit for a coffee in this part of Old Lefkosia, you can come in contact with Turkish-Cypriots. You can at least hear someone talking in Turkish! This was not the case for the area before the opening. There was a difference, of course, after the first opening of a crossing in 2003, but it was nothing like that!

The above discussion on the liminality of the Old Town provides the background for understanding the fact that, since the opening of the crossings on the Green Line, for the first time after the 1974 division, the area within the walls has been the place where graffiti, street art and other political and activist interventions have proliferated. This is related with our argument that after the opening of the Green Line crossings, Nicosia's Old Town became an in-between area where people and groups from both sides of the city could meet up, exchange ideas and act together. This change resulted in the development, for the first time in the Cypriot capital, of a grass-roots political movement, which is closely related with the appearance and establishment of political and activist interventions, but also with the fact that during my research period (2009–2013) the vast majority of political and activist interventions were found in the area within the walls.

In a very early analysis of public inscriptions in urban spaces in Hawaii, the anthropologist F.C. Blake, following Victor Turner's analysis of liminality and performance (Turner [1969] 1995), argues that graffiti tends to be a product of liminal spaces, 'where social boundaries are blurred and normal rules of conduct and role expectations are held in abeyance or even in opposition' (Blake 1981: 95). However, in a liminal space like the Old Town of Nicosia, it is not only social but also political, religious and ethnic boundaries that become blurred, and in becoming blurred, they also come to be contested. In such an area, the relation between the material characteristics of the liminal space, and the political and activist interventions within it, reveals alternative views to official narratives of both the border and the everyday sociopolitical crisis of Cypriot society. In other words, I argue that it is precisely the in-betweenness of the area that provided the necessary space for the development of a grass-roots political movement, which was territorialized almost explicitly in the Old Town, where it was expressed politically and culturally in collected practices, like the squatting of buildings, demonstrations and other political events, but also visually through numerous political interventions on the walls and other public surfaces.

However, political slogans, as well as graffiti and street art pieces, act not only as visual but also as spatial interventions in public space. This means that they should always be understood as being in a dialogue with the spatiality of the area, the specificity of public space, and the other visual and material elements of the built environment. As Hagi Kenaan puts it,

> street art belongs to the street. It is not merely located in the street, but is also shaped by its reciprocal relations with the physical infrastructure of the urban sphere and with street life. Just as the appearance of the city is transformed by the inscriptions and images created on its streets, so the significance of these images or inscriptions is shaped by their location within a specific urban context'. (Kenaan 2011: 101)

Following Kenaan, I argue that in the case of the specific urban context of the liminal Old Town of Nicosia, the public political interventions transform the appearance of the area, producing a place connected with the practices of a radical grass-roots political movement, while, at the same time, the inscriptions themselves become significant in the Cypriot political context, exactly because they are located in this liminal area.

Street Art and the Cities-in-Crisis

The last decade has seen the eruption of multiple forms of sociopolitical unrest and mass public protest in cities across the globe, which have been a result of the Western 'economic crisis'; but they were also connected with the wider process of the 'sociopolitical crisis' in or at the periphery of the Western world. In most of these events, the majority of which have taken place in cities, graffiti and street art were central features of the demonstrations and protests, becoming part of the changing urban landscapes of these cities-in-crisis.[11] In the case of divided Nicosia, the pieces found on its walls do not necessarily address the recent 'economic crisis'. In contrast to other cities-in-crisis like Athens, where the proliferation of political graffiti has been a response of artists, graffiti writers and activists to the Greek 'economic crisis',[12] Nicosia' s political graffiti does not present such a direct connection with the recent financial 'crisis'. For at least the past ten to fifteen years (the period of the appearance and growth of the aforementioned grassroots political movement), the issues that arise from the liminality of the area, a result of the unresolved Cypriot division, have been central themes of political interventions in the Old Town. However, despite their ongoing presence and significance, Nicosia's cultural practices of self-authorized political intervention, on both sides of the division, remain understudied. In contrast with other European capital cities, very few research papers have been published on the subject, and fewer still focus on political graffiti and other self-authorized interventions.[13]

Stencil Graffiti across the Lefkosia–Lefkoşa Division

In this section, I consider five examples of self-authorized stencils, which are a specific iconic style of street art. In my discussion, I address the ways in which these pieces represent and visualize ideas and attitudes towards Cyprus's sociopolitical reality, in relation to the spatiality and the locality of the Old Town, where they are placed. To do so, I built on ethnographic fieldwork, interviews and participant observation between 2009 and 2013. In most cases, these stencil graffiti pieces contest the dominant narratives (of the division, of 'crisis' and of urban development) put forward by the political elites.

At this point, I would like to briefly present the geography of the self-authorized interventions in Nicosia during the period of study, in order to explain why I focused on certain specific stencil graffiti examples. To a great extent, the geography of such interventions depends on the spatiality of the different areas of the wider city. This means that there are major differences not only between the two sides of the Green Line, but also between those areas within the Venetian walls and those outside it. In the Greek-Cypriot Lefkosia, on the south side, there are numerous and different kinds of interventions, including personal name writing, football fans' writing, hip-hop graffiti and tagging, street art, and political slogans. In the areas outside the walls, one can find mostly hip-hop graffiti and tagging, political slogans, and football fan's writing, which, in Lefkosia, often includes popular political symbols.[14] However, within the walls of the city, while there are some hip-hop graffiti pieces and tags, as well as some football fans' writing, the area is characterized more by the wide presence of political slogans, often aiming explicitly to gain the support of the grass-roots political movements of the area, and by street art pieces, which are often oriented towards sociopolitical criticism.

In Lefkoşa, on the north side, however, there are far fewer interventions in general, but most of them are personal name writing, and some political slogans. However, what is particularly interesting is that there is a noticeable absence of hip-hop graffiti or tagging, while, at the same time, there is a growing street art scene, mainly expressed with stencils and found mainly in the area within the walls. This is connected with the fact that the north part of Cyprus was internationally isolated throughout the 1980s and 1990s, when hip-hop graffiti was spreading across Europe, but also with the fact that, according to my informants, the regime in north Cyprus was much more repressive during this period. Only after 2003, and the opening of the Green Line crossings, was there the opportunity for the development of self-authorized intervention in Lefkoşa. This was because people were allowed to cross to the other side, where there was already a graffiti and street art scene that they could follow, and because after the so-called Jasmine Revolution[15], there was a regime change. However, the area where these stencil graffiti interventions mostly appeared was in the liminal Old Town.

Stencil graffiti is a form of public visual intervention, which became popular at a worldwide level during the 2000s. Although they are considered part of the wider street art movement, stencils have their own tradition, which relates to their use within political movements in Europe and the Americas (Karathanasis 2008, 2011). Additionally, stencil graffiti is based on a technique that has been used in decoration and in applied arts for more than a century. Because the technique allows for the copying of an image and its re-creation on a surface, stencils have a specific iconic visuality that enables the creator to express ideas through images. Moreover, the iconicity of stencils offers their creators the opportunity to use and alter popular images from local and global imagery. In this way, creators can relate their stencils with specific social or political issues, and through popular imagery they manage to communicate ideas to their viewers in a direct and comprehensive way. At the same time, stencils, like any other form of street art or graffiti, act and produce meaning in relation with their urban context. Thus, the meanings produced by this form of public expression are always related with public space and the specific characteristics of each area, adding to their

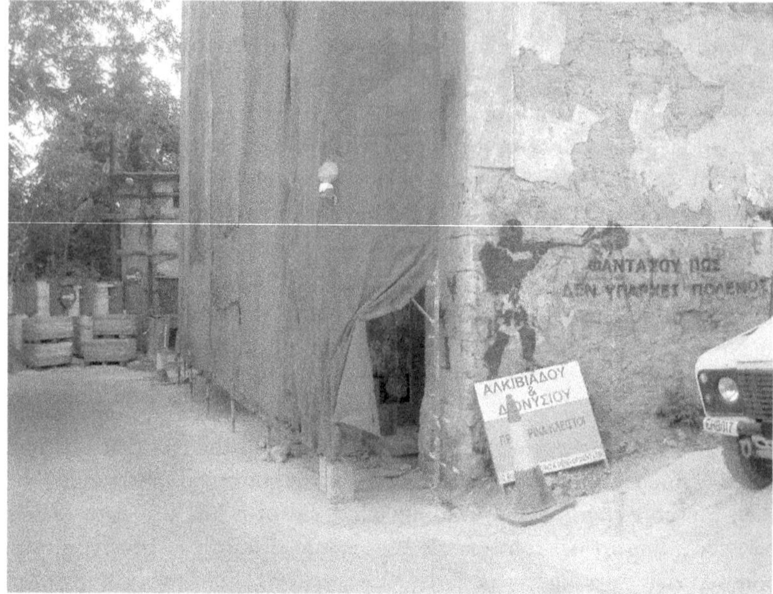

Figure 8.1 'Imagine there is no war'. On the wall of a confiscated and abandoned building in Old Town Lefkosia. © Pafsanias Karathanasis.

meaning as they socially and culturally produce public space. Focusing on these particular stencil graffiti pieces does not mean that other kinds of graffiti and street art found in the Cypriot capital are any less significant. Making this choice, I wish firstly to draw attention towards the political significance of self-authorized intervention in the liminal Old Town, and secondly, to address the ways in which specifically stencil graffiti pieces produce meaning through using popular imagery, which they emplace in the specific urban context of division.

On the left side of the above photograph, we can see a barricade installed by the Greek-Cypriot army, made with barrels painted in the blue and white colours of the Greek flag. The stencil is placed on one of the buildings that was confiscated by the Greek-Cypriot army, right after the events of 1974, to form a militarized zone along the south side of the Green Line. The stencil depicts a man taking aim with a rifle. However, instead of a bullet, we see a red flower coming out of the rifle barrel. In this way, the stencil refers to the popular anti-war image of a carnation in an army rifle, originating from the historic photograph 'Flower Power' taken in 1967 during the march on the Pentagon by the National Mobilization Committee to End the War in Vietnam.[16] In addition, 'Flower Power' was a slogan used during the 1960s and early 1970s as a symbol of the principles of passive resistance and non-violence.[17]

Even if in this stencil there is no clear reference to any particular war, specific meanings are suggested by its relation with its location. Thus, one could argue that beyond the anti-war meaning produced by this popular image, the message '*Imagine there is no war*' written next to it must surely refer to the militarized landscape of the Green Line, which has been normalized in everyday life in Cyprus. Moreover, by being painted on one of the buildings confiscated by the army, and which now stands empty, the stencil presents itself as a direct criticism of the militarization of the Old Town. In this way, it acts against official discourses that promote the idea that the economic development of the past decades has somehow enabled the overcoming of the crisis caused by the Turkish military action in 1974. Criticizing the dominant discourse, the stencil calls its viewers to imagine a reality lived without the apparent material consequences of military strife. It also appears to call for viewers to actively claim that reality by recognizing the oddity of the ongoing sociopolitical crisis, and not avoiding it by hiding its effects in economic prosperity or in the recent development of the area around the militarized zone of the Old Town.

The second stencil I discuss was found on a coffee-shop wall in the south side of the Old Town. It shows an outline of the island with an explosion marked on its south coast. This stencil refers to the massive explosion in the summer of 2011, caused by a large amount of ammunition that had been confiscated by the authorities of the Republic of Cyprus from a ship that was allegedly going to Syria from Iran, and had then been stored at a naval base located on the south coast of the island. The explosion served as a crisis-event that shocked Greek-Cypriot society and triggered mass protests outside the Presidential House, as it had resulted in the deaths of thirteen people and the injuring of a further sixty-two. The organizers of the protests attempted to link them with the mass movement of occupying public squares that was taking place at the same time in Greece. They did so by calling the protesters 'indignants', the name that was used by the Spanish protesters who started the European public squares' occupation movement in 2011. However, the attempt by the Cypriot 'indignants' to be linked with the Greek 'indignants' (*aganaktismenoi*) did not bear fruit. The main characteristic of the European movement was the call for the practice of direct democracy and the abolition of traditional political parties and divisions. However, in the midst of the European economic 'crisis', the Cypriot protests were monopolized by right-wing forces, who, with explicit anti-communist rhetoric, channelled them directly against the left-wing president, Christofias.

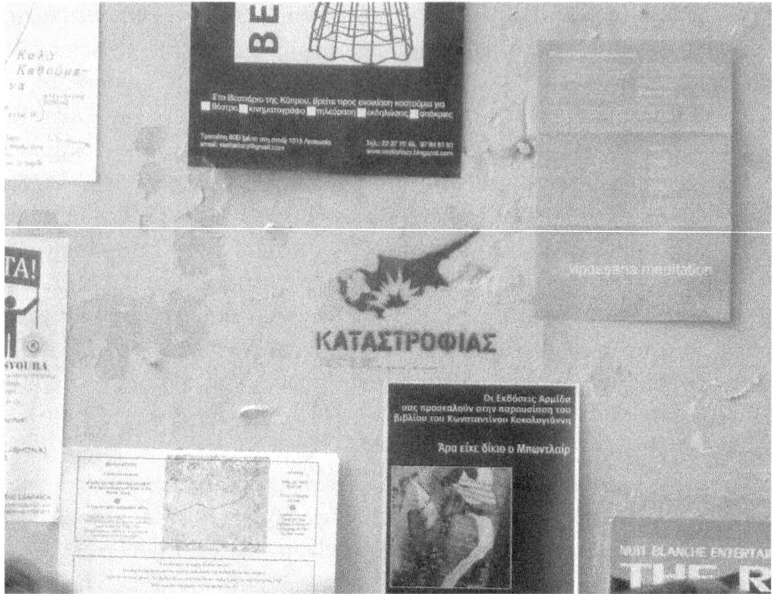

Figure 8.2 'Katastrofias': a word made from the words 'catastrophe' and 'Christofias' (the former president of the Republic of Cyprus). © Pafsanias Karathanasis.

The made-up word 'Katastrofias' is composed from the name of President Christofias and the word 'catastrophe' or disaster. The stencil seems to blame President Christofias for the explosion, and the disaster that it brought to the island. However, if we take into consideration the location in which it was found, different and more complicated interpretations are suggested. The stencil is located on the wall of a coffee shop in the centre of the Old Town. This venue is connected with alternative sociopolitical groups from both communities that have worked together for the reunification of the island, within and beyond the framework of the Cypriot bi-communal movement. In the photograph, we see the stencil surrounded by posters for various events, including activist events promoting rapprochement between the two communities. In this specific context, the stencil acquires additional meanings. Christofias was the first left-wing president of the Republic of Cyprus, who came to power in 2008. Popular aspirations for a fair solution to the Cyprus problem cohered around both him and Mehmet Ali Talat, the first left-wing Turkish-Cypriot president of the unrecognized TRNC. However, during their presidencies, they disappointed those who believed that the left could generate the political momentum for a solution to the long-standing Cypriot Issue. Thus, even if the stencil refers to the disaster of the ammunitions explosion of 2011, through its relation with the Old Town, and the locality of the specific coffee shop, it suggests meanings associated with the inability of the Cypriot left to put an end to the everyday sociopolitical 'crisis' of the post-1974 period. The fact that a stencil, which is clearly critical of a left-wing president, was allowed to remain on the walls of a place with a strong association with left-wing ideas and the bi-communal movement, reveals a significant change in Cypriot politics – a change that was made possible after the opening of the Green Line checkpoints in 2003.

Bi-communalism is a term that refers to the movement that developed in Cyprus during the period of the absolute separation of the two communities. Under the protection of the United Nations, groups of mainly left-wing Greek- and Turkish-Cypriots managed to sustain a space for dialogue and communication that kept the idea of a federal and bi-communal solution to the Cypriot Issue alive. They did so in the face of the nationalistic ideas that dominated political discourse on both sides of the division. However, after the failure of the 2004 referendum to sanction the United Nations plan for a solution, and after the opening of checkpoints on the Green Line in 2003, a different politics emerged, especially in the Old Town of Nicosia. The grass-roots activism and radical politics that developed after 2003[18] expressed strong dissatisfaction towards both the institutionalized bi-communalism of the previous period, and towards the left, which presented itself as the main pro-solution political power on the island. The specific coffee shop where the stencil is located was a central place for both the post-2003 bi-communal movement and for grass-roots activism in general. Thus, the appearance of this anti-Christofias stencil on its walls suggests activists' disenchantment with existing institutionalized activism and with the left, which were no longer seen as forces able to bring the prolonged division and sociopolitical Cypriot 'crisis' to an end.

The next stencil was found in Old Town Lefkoşa. It is a remake of a globally popular stencil by the street artist Banksy that depicts a little girl losing her heart-shaped balloon. This stencil is one of the oldest and best-known pieces by the famous and controversial artist, which visualizes in a simple but powerful way the idea of a young child's disappointment at losing something precious. Moreover, by presenting the red balloon in the shape of a heart, the artist suggests that the piece may also refer to the feeling or the fear of losing love.[19] It is not my intention here to discuss Bansky's work, his criticism of the contemporary art world or the appropriation of street art. What it is interesting here is the way in which this piece has been appropriated in Lefkoşa, and has taken on specific meanings in relation to

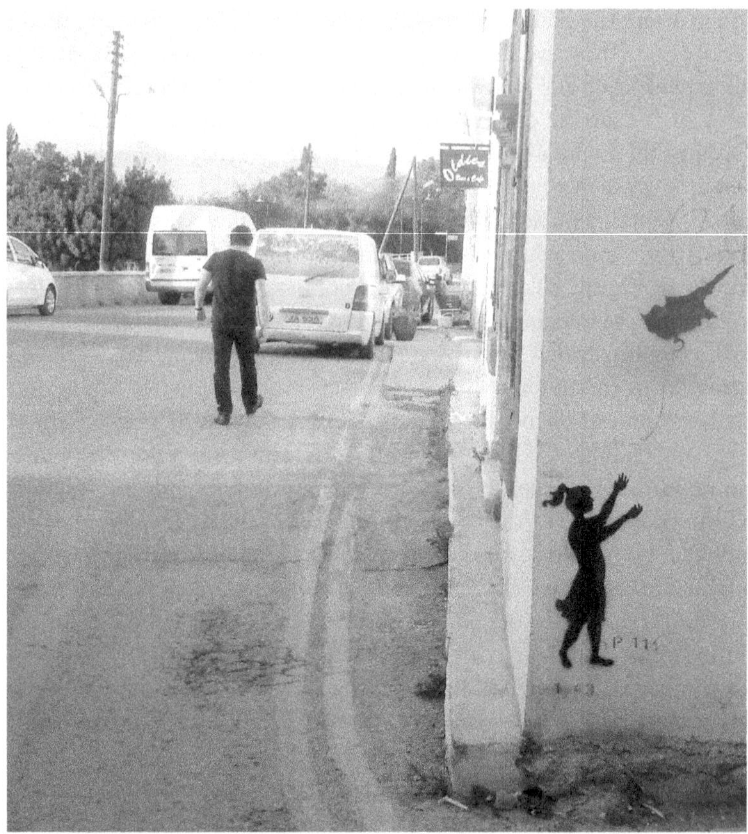

Figure 8.3 Girl with the red balloon (in the shape of Cyprus), at a building right on top of the city walls of Lefkoşa, 2013. © Pafsanias Karathanasis.

Cyprus's sociopolitical context. By presenting the whole island of Cyprus as a red balloon that flies out of a girl's hands, the stencil suggests there is a feeling or fear of losing Cyprus. But in which way might Cypriots (or some of them) have felt that there was a fear of losing Cyprus? Answering this question, one has firstly to take into consideration the fact that the stencil was found in the north (i.e. Turkish-Cypriot) part of the Old Town. One of the most important issues for Turkish-Cypriots has been their feeling of being isolated by the international community because of their position as citizens of an unrecognized state. This feeling is closely related with the Turkish-Cypriot left's view that Cyprus's reunification within the framework of the European Union constituted their best chance of escaping dependence on Turkey for their economic and political survival. This has also been one of the main reasons why the majority of the Turkish-Cypriots, and especially those on the left, voted 'Yes' to the 2004 referendum on the United Nations plan for a solution of the Cypriot Issue, and the reunification of the island. However, as mentioned above, this plan was rejected by the Greek-Cypriots. As has been argued,[20] one of the reasons for this was that the Greek-Cypriots in the south did not want to lose their economic superiority by sharing their wealth with the underdeveloped north, as part of a unified federal state. In this political context, the Cyprus balloon that flies away from the little girl's hands could represent lost opportunities for the reunification of the island, as well as lost opportunities for the Turkish-Cypriot community to move away from their repressing dependence on Turkey.

In addition, this stencil is located in the Arabahmet area in the north part of the Old Town, an area renovated with UN funds,[21] which is also frequented by sociopolitically alternative Turkish-Cypriots. This is an area that has come to symbolize a nostalgic view of the traditional and historic Old Town, which is today inhabited mainly by religious Turkish settler families and young working-class Turkish men – people who are not culturally connected with the more European-oriented and secular Turkish-Cypriots. Additionally, from the perspective of alternative Turkish-Cypriot youth, this appropriation of the globally popular Banksy piece could also express a need to connect and communicate with the rest of the world, from which they have been separated. Whether it expresses lost opportunities for the reunification of the island and a subsequent European future, or a claim to areas from which certain people feel excluded, the Cyprus balloon flying away serves as yet another reminder that the island's post-1974 sociopolitical crisis has yet to end.

'These stencils are designs with antennas and long tails that remind you of insects', Berat told me, while showing me the tests he had done on the upper walls of a shop in the main shopping street of Old Town Lefkoşa. At first sight, the insects do not seem to be implicated in any sociopolitical issue. However, these seemingly innocent insects do have a political significance for the young Turkish-Cypriots who spray them on the streets of the area. According to Berat, who I interviewed during my fieldwork in early 2011:

> 'The "bits" are political stencils as well, because they represent the people from Turkey who populate the Old Town. They mean that in every corner of the city, everywhere, there are Turkish people. Thus, day by day, these "bits" multiply, like the people from Turkey… We also think that we should make nests!'

The 'bits' is the second street art project of a mixed group of activists and artists in Lefkoşa. Their first was a political stencil that was negotiating the

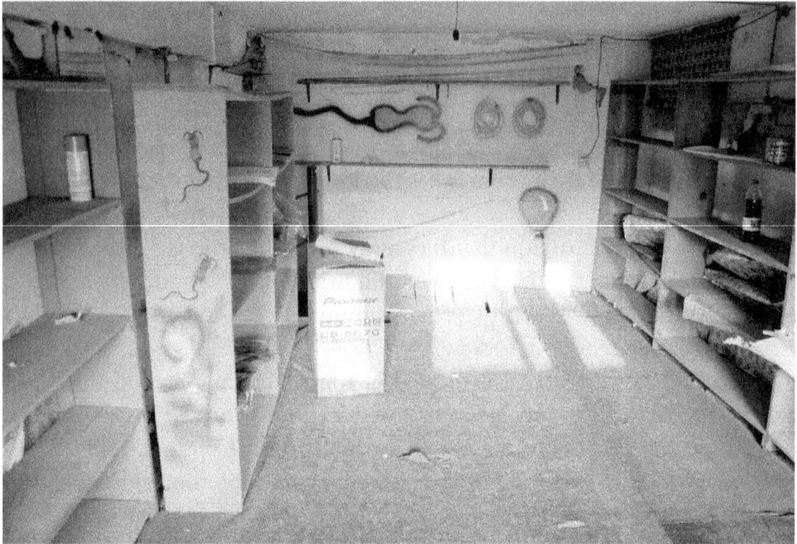

Figure 8.4 The 'bits' sprayed on an inside wall (on the left-hand side of the image) of the upper part of a shop in the main shopping district of Old Town Lefkoşa, 2011. © Pafsanias Karathanasis.

effects of the opening of the Green Line crossings in 2003.[22] In their second project, they touch upon another important issue, the claiming of the north part of the Old Town from the Turkish settlers and migrant workers who have been moving to the area since the 1980s and the 1990s. The populating of the Old Town by culturally different Turkish-Anatolian[23] and religious settler families has been an important issue for many of the young left-wing or non-religious Turkish-Cypriots with whom I talked. This is because they believe that what they consider to be the historic centre of their Cypriot capital has become dominated by conservative and religious people, who enforce their own cultural norms and rules. Thus, contrary to the south, where nightlife businesses are on the rise, in the north of the Old Town people cannot consume alcohol in public spaces, and bars are closed early, because of the influence of conservative Turkish people over the Turkish-Cypriot authorities.

Representing culturally different people as insects might be considered harsh or even racist – and this would be a fair criticism, because it entails a certain dehumanizing view. However, my primary concern here is that this stencil reflects the cultural negotiation of the north part of the Old Town, and the way in which Turkey's role in Cyprus is considered, at least by a part of the Turkish-Cypriot community, as a threat to their cultural particularity, their 'Cypriotness'. In this stencil, conservative Turkish people in Cyprus are being portrayed as mere tools through which Turkey – because of the unresolved 'crisis' – is attempting a 'Turkeyfication' of the north part of the island. Even if, as Mette Hatay and Rebecca Bryant (2008) argue, some Turkish-Cypriots hold a nostalgic view of the Old Town of Lefkoşa, Turkish people are nonetheless viewed as undesirable by those Turkish-Cypriot youths who reject what they view as their conservative and religious influence in the Old Town.

The last stencil I discuss was found on the wall of another coffee shop in Old Town Lefkosia. It presents a popular revolutionary image: the raised fist. The bold Greek letters next to it read: 'The people of Cyprus make revolution with a frappé in (their) hand'. 'Frappé' is an iced instant coffee that many Greek-Cypriots drink while they sit at one of the many new coffee shops that opened in the area during the years of the Cypriot 'financial crisis'. Originating in Greece, frappé is also a drink associated with Greeks in general. It is often regarded as a symbol of Greece's laid-back coffee culture with its leisurely sipping of different kinds of iced coffee.

This stencil serves, firstly, as a comment on the gentrification process in the Old Town, which has manifested itself in the rapid expansion of coffee shops and other leisure and nightlife businesses in the area. This is a localized form of gentrification which is common across Greece and Cyprus. A central feature of it are the numerous small coffee shops and other food and drink establishments, which have tables out in public space, in the open and under the sun. Lefkosia's municipal authorities present this development of the Old Town as a big success. In a statement by the mayor in a Greek-Cypriot

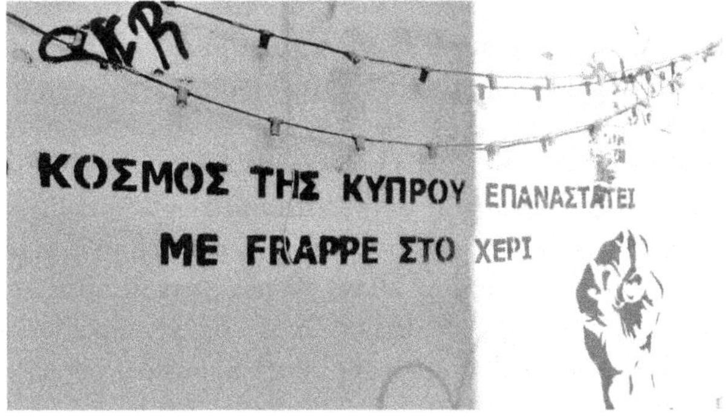

Figure 8.5 'The people of Cyprus make revolution with a frappé in (their) hand'. On the wall of a coffee shop in the commercial district of Old Town Lefkosia, 2013. © Pafsanias Karathanasis.

newspaper in 2013, we read: 'If there is something we feel proud about in the Municipality of Lefkosia, it is the development we have achieved in the historic centre of the capital, which had been run down for years, indeed in the midst of the worst economic crisis of our contemporary history'.[24] However, for the people active in the grass-roots social movements in Lefkosia, who had been living in and using the area during the years when it was run down, the gentrification of the Old Town was not seen as a success. On the contrary, the occupation of the little available public space in the medieval Old Town for consumption, and the problems caused by the increased traffic and the hundreds of visitors, were issues that were shortly picked up by the local grass-roots movement in a negotiation and a claiming of an open and available public space for the different social and economic groups.

Moreover, this stencil also comments, in an ironic way, on the period during which this development of Lefkosia's Old Town took place. At the time of the Cypriot 'financial crisis', when political activists were expecting a surge in social movements, the people of Lefkosia 'made their revolution' by sitting and drinking expensive coffee right next to the Green Line, enjoying the gentrified, but still divided, historic centre. In this way, the stencil makes reference to the (non-)reaction of the Greek-Cypriot public to the 'crisis', which in other European countries such as Greece was a triggering event for mass protests and for the expression of dissatisfaction and dissent through social movements.

What is it that made Cyprus different from Greece and the other countries of Southern Europe that were most affected by the 'crisis'? As I have suggested, Cyprus presents a unique case in Europe, and specifically in the European Union. It is simultaneously a postcolonial country and a post-conflict area in which the notion of 'crisis' does not simply refer to economic crisis, but often, in fact, refers back to the initial '1974 crisis'. This connects the idea of crisis to Cyprus's postcolonial condition, and to the discourse of overcoming the '1974 crisis' through an 'economic miracle'. As Demetriou argues, 'the political subject of the Cypriot crisis is a postcolonial citizen thoroughly embedded in liberal capitalism who will resist the 'haircut' of hard-earned deposits but will also persevere through austere welfare cuts' (Demetriou 2013). What Demetriou describes is a resilient subject – a subject that in addition to being embedded in liberal capitalism is also embedded in crisis, a prolonged crisis, whether economic or sociopolitical.

One could argue that in the case of Cyprus this prolonged crisis has now been normalized in the everydayness. This is most apparent today in the Old Town, where the material evidences of the initial crisis are still present in the urban landscape. However, the ongoing processes of gentrification can be seen as normalizing forces that aim to make these evidences invisible. As I have argued in this chapter, the opening of the Green Line crossings signalled a new era for Nicosia. By entering the second phase of the sequence, the Old Town transformed into an in-between or liminal area, which provided a place for the development of a grass-roots movement that contests dominant narratives, and questions established identities and separations. In this way, the prolonged Cypriot crisis relates to the idea of a 'permanent liminality'. Returning to Szakolczai's idea of 'permanent liminality', which is related to the idea of 'crisis', he points out that it is an inherently paradoxical concept (Szakolczai 2000: 211), because the in-between stage in the ritual passages is understood as only a temporary phase. However, it is a concept that can be used in the understanding of liminal situations in modern societies. As Thomassen puts it, 'the institutions that make up a [modern] society have been created to deal with an extraordinary situation only in order to become permanent. While this in a way is "normal", the experience of being "stuck in liminality" is also highly critical' (Thomassen 2009: 22).

In the case of Nicosia, where the 'prolonged crisis' has produced resilient political subjects who persevere in austerity, the liminality of the Old Town has provided the possibility of transgression – the possibility for the forming of different political identities that through contestation attempt to go beyond established norms. The stencils discussed in this chapter, which are understood as visualized and spatialized results of this sociopolitical change, present attempts to bring forth issues that are being made invisible by the normalization of liminality and crisis. In this way, they could also be seen as attempts to break through the restrictions of the normalized, but still critical, 'prolonged crisis' or 'permanent liminality'.

Dr Pafsanias Karathanasis is a social anthropologist and a post-doc researcher at Panteio University in Greece. He has a BA in social anthropology from Panteio University, an MA in material and visual culture from University College London) and a PhD in historical and social anthropology from University of the Aegean in Greece. His main research interests include anthropology of space and place, visual culture, migration and refugee studies, and political anthropology. He is specifically interested in urban cultures, in political and cultural grass-roots initiatives in urban settings, solidarity movements and in contested landscapes in cities and beyond. He has done fieldwork in Athens, Lesvos and Nicosia.

Notes

1. In the framework of the European financial crisis, the term Troika has been widely used (especially in the media) in Greece, Cyprus, Ireland, Portugal and Spain to refer to a decision group, comprising the European Commission (EC), the European Central Bank (ECB) and the International Monetary Fund (IMF), that had been present in these countries since 2010.
2. The United Nations Peacekeeping Force in Cyprus (UNFICYP), estimates that 160,000 Greek-Cypriots and 40,000 Turkish-Cypriots were displaced during the summer of 1974.
3. The Republic of Cyprus was formed in 1960, when Cyprus finally achieved independence from the United Kingdom. Cyprus had become a protectorate of the UK in 1878; it was under British military occupation from 1914 to 1925, and was a 'Crown colony' until its independence.
4. Turkey's occupying forces never left the island. Today, there are between thirty and forty thousand Turkish Army troops in north Cyprus. Moreover, nearly half of the annual budget of the unrecognized state of TRNC had been guaranteed by Turkey (Osiewicz 2013: 120).
5. For an account of the Turkish position on the Cypriot Issue since 1974, see Osiewicz 2013. For an account on the nostalgia expressed by Turkish-Cypriots of Nicosia for the city's past (before the events of 1974), and the perceived colonization of the island by Turkey, see Hatay and Bryant 2008.
6. The Cypriot 'financial crisis' has been well documented in the international media. However, little is known about the downfall of the economy of TRNC, which started as early as 2007 and before the impact of the global financial crisis. As Umut Bozkurt argues, Turkey, and the ruling AKP (Justice and Development Party), imposed austerity measures and the privatization of state-owned enterprises, becoming a 'disciplining external force with aims to effect a deeper transformation in the economy and politics of the Turkish-Cypriot community' (Bozkurt 2014: 84).
7. 'The Buffer Zone extends approximately 180 km across the island. In some parts of old Nicosia it is only a few metres wide, while in other areas it is a few kilometres wide. Its northern and southern limits are the lines where the belligerents stood following the ceasefire of 16 August 1974, as recorded by UNFICYP'. Retrieved 3 November 2018 from https://unficyp.unmissions.org/about-buffer-zone.
8. While Nicosia is the commonly used name of the Cypriot capital in English, this was the Latin name of the city, used when the city was under the rule of the French and the Venetians. In Greek, the city is called Lefkosia, and in Turkish Lefkoşa.
9. Following the events of 1974, and the occupation of 38 per cent of the island's territory, Turkey implemented a policy of inviting people from Turkey to Cyprus to inhabit the villages that had been left behind by Greek-Cypriot refugees. Niyazi Kizilyürek has argued that the contact between Turkish-Cypriots and the people from Turkey who settled in Cyprus after 1974 was one of the main reasons why Turkish-Cypriots started identifying themselves more with Cyprus than with Turkey, their 'motherland' (Kizilyürek 2001: 202–3). For an ethnography of a former Greek-Cypriot village that is now inhabited by people from Turkey, see Dikomitis 2012. For an ethnography of the 'make-believe' state of TRNC, the management of the Greek-Cypriot properties left behind in 1974, and the relations between the people

from Turkey and the Turkish-Cypriots, with the objects and the houses left behind by the 'enemy', see Navaro-Yashin 2009, 2012.

10. See the survey on the impact of the opening of the Ledra Street–Lokmaci crossing, by PRIO Cyprus, conducted in 2009. According to the survey, 699,673 people had crossed the Ledra Street–Lokmaci in 2008 alone (see https://cyprus.prio.org/Publications/Publication/?x=1177, retrieved 30 November 2018). On the impact on the north side of the area, specifically the Lokmaci area, see Yorucu et al. 2010.

11. See, for example, Hardesty 2012; Abaza 2013; and Taş 2017.

12. During the period of the Greek 'economic crisis', there has been a proliferation of graffiti and street art pieces in Athens. By becoming central features of the cityscape, but also central visualizations of the 'crisis', these pieces on the walls of changing Athens have attracted the attention of many researchers. For this reason, many papers have been published in recent years. They present a very interesting collection of works that relate the practice of self-authorized urban intervention with the changing cityscape of Athens, as well as with different interpretations and experiences of the 'crisis'. For graffiti and street art in Athens in the context of 'crisis', see Avramides 2012, 2014; Tsilimpounidi 2013, 2015; Leventis 2013; Karathanasis 2014; Zaimakis 2015; Stampoulidis 2016; and Tulke 2016, 2017.

13. One of the first to write on the subject in Nicosia is Elizabeth Hoak-Doering (2009, 2010), who, among other interventions, discusses political graffiti on both sides of the city (in Lefkosia and Lefkoşa), through an informed view in relation to gender. Panos Leventis (2017) has also recently published a chapter on graffiti and street art in Lefkosia, in a collected volume by Avramides and Tsilimpounidi (2017). However, Leventis's chapter focuses only on Lefkosia, barely considering the growing practice of street art in Lefkoşa. Lastly, I have also published a piece, which provides an account of graffiti and street art on both sides of the Green Line, in an attempt to discuss their relation with wider political events and dominant narratives (Karathanasis 2010).

14. The use of political symbols in football fans' writing and slogans in Lefkosia is related to the fact that such writing is mainly done by the members of the radical fan clubs of the two rival football teams of the city (APOEL and Omonoia, which have close relations with right and left political ideologies respectively). This has resulted in the explicit use of nationalistic, racist and far-right-wing symbolism by the radical fans of APOEL (Athletic Football Union [of the] Greeks [of] Lefkosia), and anti-nationalistic, anti-racist and anarchist symbolism by the radical fans of Omonoia (i.e. Concord).

15. The mass demonstrations in Lefkoşa, between 2001-2003, that resulted in the fall of the nationalist Rauf Denktaş (that had been the leader of the Turkish-Cypriots since the division of the island in 1974), and brought political change in TRNC has been called the 'Jasmine Revolution'. For more on the 'jasmine revolution' see Hatay and Bryant (2008).

16. For more on the 'Flower Power' photograph, taken by the American photographer Bernie Boston for the now-defunct *The Washington Star* newspaper, see the article 'Be the Flower in the Gun: The Story Behind the Historic Photograph "Flower Power" in 1967' (2017). Retrieved 20 November 2018 from https://www.vintag.es/2017/09/be-flower-in-gun-story-behind-historic.html.

17. The expression was coined by Allen Ginsberg, who was frequently depicted as a leader of the 'Flower Power' anti-war movement (Houen 2008: 363).

18. For more on this development, see Iliopoulou and Karathanasis 2014; Karathanasis 2017.

19. Recently, this stencil acquired even more notoriety when a framed version of it from 2002 appeared in the international media. At the very moment it was being sold for over one million pounds in a London auction, it shred itself to pieces. For more on this staged event, see the Reuters article: '"We just got Banksy-ed": Balloon girl painting self-destructs at sale' (Oct. 2018). Retrieved 30 November 2018 from https://www.reuters.com/article/us-art-banksy/we-just-got-banksy-ed-balloon-girl-painting-self-destructs-at-sale-idUSKCN1MG0B4.

20. This has been argued widely in the analysis of the reasons for the rejection of the UN Anan-Plan by the Greek-Cypriots. For an example of such analysis, see Moulakis 2007: 536.

21. The United Nations has funded renovations in the Old Town under the successful bi-communal project 'Nicosia Masterplan'. For more on the project see: https://www.unece.org/fileadmin/DAM/thepep/en/workplan/urban/documents/petridouNycosiamasterplan.pdf (last accessed 30 November 2018).

22. For more on the 'Drilling the border' stencil in the north Old Town, which criticized controls of the Green Line crossings by Turkish-Cypriots on people who had purchased goods in supermarkets and shopping malls in the south, and for a comparative analysis of the different dominant and alternative views of the Green Line in the two parts of Cyprus, see Karathanasis 2010.

23. After 1974 and the occupation of northern Cyprus by the Turkish Army, Turkey pursued a policy of populating the occupied territories (and especially those villages that had been left empty by Greek-Cypriots who had been displaced to the south) with Turkish citizens, mainly from the Anatolia region in south-east Turkey.

24. Statement of the mayor, Mr Giorkatzis, published in the article 'Zontanepse I PaliaLefkosia' [Old Lefkosia came to life], by Stella Stilianou, on 9 September 2013. Retrieved 5 December 2018 from http://www.sigmalive.com/archive/simerini/news/local/574324.

References

Abaza, M. 2013. 'Walls, Segregating Downtown Cairo and the Mohammed Mahmud Street Graffiti'. *Theory, Culture & Society* 30(1): 122–39.

Avramides, K. 2012. '"Live your Greece in Myths": Reading the Crisis on Athens' Walls'. *Professional Dreamers*, working paper no. 8, pp. 1–17.

———. 2014. 'Mapping the Geographical and Spatial Characteristics of Politicized Urban Art in the Athens of Crisis', in M. Tsilimpounidi and A. Walsh (eds), *Remapping 'Crisis': A Guide to Athens*. London: Zero Books, pp. 183–203.

Avramides, K., and M. Tsilimpounidi (eds). 2017. *Graffiti and Street Art: Reading, Writing and Representing the City*. London: Routledge.

Blake, F.C. 1981. 'Graffiti and Racial Insults: The Archaeology of Ethnic Relations', in R. Gould and M. Schiffer (eds), *Modern Material Culture: The Archaeology of Us*. New York: Academic Press, pp. 87–100.

Blanche, U. 2015. 'Street Art and Related Terms: Discussion and Working Definition'. *Street Art and Urban Creativity Journal* 1(1): 32–39.

Bozkurt, U. 2014. 'Turkey: From the "Motherland" to the "IMF of Northern Cyprus"?' *The Cyprus Review* 26(1): 83–105.

Demetriou, O. 2013. 'A Cultural Reading of the Cyprus Crisis'. *Open Democracy*, 15 April. Retrieved 3 November 2018 from http://www.opendemocracy.net/olga-demetriou/cultural-reading-of-cyprus-crisis.

Dikomitis, L. 2012. *Cyprus and its Places of Desire: Cultures of Displacement among Greek and Turkish Cypriot Refugees*. London: I.B. Tauris.

Hardesty, M. 2012. 'Signs and Banners of Occupy Wall Street'. *Critical Quarterly* 54(2): 23–27.

Hatay, M., and R. Bryant. 2008. 'The Jasmine Scent of Nicosia'. *Journal of Modern Greek Studies* 26: 423–49.

Hoak-Doering, E. 2009. 'With a Spray Can in Lefkosia/Lefkosha: Murals, Graffiti and Identity'. *The Cyprus Review* 29(1): 145–72.

———. 2010. 'Howl(ing) Without Raising Their Voices'. *International Feminist Journal of Politics* 12(1): 91–104.

Houen, A. 2008. '"Back! Back! Back! Central Mind-Machine Pentagon...": Allen Ginsberg and the Vietnam War'. *Cultural Politics* 4(3): 351–74.

Iliopoulou, E., and P. Karathanasis. 2014. 'Towards a Radical Politics: Grassroots Urban Activism in the Walled City of Nicosia'. *Cyprus Review* 26(1): 169–92.

Ioannides, D., and Y. Apostopoloupos. 1999. 'Political Instability, War and Tourism in Cyprus: Effects, Management and Prospects for Recovery'. *Journal of Travel Research* 38: 51–56.

Karathanasis, P. 2008. *Stencil in Athens*. Athens: Oxy publications.

———. 2010. 'Official Memory and Graffiti: The Meanings of the Green Line of Cyprus as Field for Negotiation of Collective Memory', in Special Issue: *Memory, Theory and Art: Utopia Journal* 89 (March–April): 103–25 (in Greek).

———. 2011. 'The City Walls as Contested Spaces: Aesthetics and Urban Landscape in Athens', in C. Giannakopoulos and G. Giannitsiotis (eds), *Contested Spaces in Cities: Spatial Approaches of Culture*. Athens: Alexandreia Publications, pp. 315–48 (in Greek).

———. 2014. 'Re-Image-ing and Re-Imagining the City: Overpainted Landscapes of Central Athens', in M. Tsilimpounidi and A. Walsh (eds), *Remapping 'Crisis': A Guide to Athens*. London: Zero Books, pp. 177–82.

———. 2017. 'Action from Below and Exit from Liminality: Public Events and Activities in the Walled City of Nicosia'. Unpublished PhD thesis, University of the Aegean (in Greek). Available at https://www.didaktorika.gr/eadd/handle/10442/40823.

Kenaan, H. 2011. 'Street Art and the Sovereign's Imagination', in *Street Art in Israel*, Tel Aviv Museum of Art. Retrieved 5 November 2018 from https://www.academia.edu/6265107/Street_Art_and_the_Sovereign_s_Imagination.

Kizilyürek, N. 2001. 'The Politics of Identity in the Turkish Cypriot Community: A Response to the Politics of Denial?', in *Méditerranée: Ruptures et Continuités*. Proceedings of the Symposium held in Nicosia, 20–22 October 2001, Université Lumière Lyon 2, University of Cyprus. Lyon: Maison de l'Orient et de la Méditerranée Jean Pouilloux, 2003, pp. 197–204.

Leventis, P. 2013. 'Walls of Crisis: Street Art and Utopian Fabric in Central Athens 2000–2012'. *Architectural Histories* 1(1): 1–10.

———. 2017. 'Dead Ends and Urban Insignias: Writing Graffiti and Street Art (Hi) Stories along the UN Buffer Zone in Nicosia, 2010–2014', in K. Avramides and M. Tsilimpounidi (eds), *Graffiti and Street Art: Reading, Writing and Representing the City*. London: Routledge, pp. 135–63.

Moulakis, A. 2007. 'Power-Sharing and Its Discontents: Dysfunctional Constitutional Arrangements and the Failure of the Annan Plan for a Reunified Cyprus'. *Middle Eastern Studies* 43(4): 531–56.

Navaro-Yashin, Y. 2009. 'Affective Spaces, Melancholic Objects: Ruination and the Production of Anthropological Knowledge'. *Journal of the Royal Anthropological Institute* 15(1): 1–18.

———. 2012. *The Make-Believe Space: Affective Geography in a Postwar Polity*. Durham, NC: Duke University Press.

Osiewicz, P. 2013. 'Turkey and Its Position on the Cyprus Question Since 1974'. *Rocznik Integracji Europejskiej* 7: 117–28.

Stampoulidis, G. 2016. 'Rethinking Athens as Text: The Linguistic Context of Athenian Graffiti during the Crisis'. *Journal of Language Works* 1(1): 10–23.

Szakolczai, A. 2000. *Reflexive Historical Sociology*. London: Routledge.

———. 2009. 'Liminality and Experience: Structuring Transitory Situations and Transformative Events'. *International Political Anthropology* 2(1): 141–72.

Taş, H. 2017. 'Street Arts of Resistance in Tahrir and Gezi'. *Middle Eastern Studies* 53(5): 802–19.

Theophanous, A. 1995. 'Anatomy of the Economic Miracle 1974–1994', in N. Peristianis and G. Tsagaras (eds), *Anatomy of a Transformation: Cyprus after 1974*. Nicosia: Intercollege Publications, pp. 13–33 (in Greek).

Thomassen, B. 2009. 'The Uses and Meanings of Liminality'. *International Political Anthropology* 2(1): 5–27.

———. 2014. *Liminality and the Modern: Living through the In-Between*. Farnham, Surrey: Ashgate.

Tsilimpounidi, M. 2013. 'See the Writing on the Wall: Street Art and Urban Poetics in Athens', in L. Borriello and C. Ruggiero (eds), *Inopinatum: Urban Creativity*. Rome: Artigrafichebocchia, pp. 215–27.

———. 2015. '"If these Walls Could Talk": Street Art and Urban Belonging in the Athens of Crisis'. *Laboratorium* 7(2): 71–91.

Tulke, J. 2016. 'Tales of Crisis from the Walls of Athens: An Exploration of Urban Austerity through the Cultural Practice of Street Art', in B. Schönig and S. Schipper (eds), *Urban Austerity: Impacts of the Global Financial Crisis in Cities in Europe*. Berlin: Theater der Zeit, pp. 257–70.

———. 2017. 'Visual Encounters with Crisis and Austerity: Reflections on the Cultural Politics of Contemporary Street Art in Athens', in D. Tziovas (ed.), *Greece in Crisis: The Cultural Politics of Austerity*. London: I.B. Tauris, pp. 201–19.

Turner, V. (1969) 1995. *The Ritual Process: Structure and Anti-Structure*. Chicago: Aldine.

Van Gennep, A. (1909) 1960. *The Rites of Passage: A Classical Study of Cultural Celebrations*. Chicago, IL: Chicago University Press.

Yorucu, V., et al. 2010. 'Cross-Border Trade Liberalization: The Case of Lokmaci/Ledra Gate in Divided Nicosia, Cyprus'. *European Planning Studies* 18(10): 1749–64.

Zaimakis, Y. 2015. '"Welcome to the Civilization of Fear": On Political Graffiti Heterotopias in Greece in Times of Crisis'. *Visual Communication* 14(4): 373–96.

Chapter 9

Le Charme Discret de L'Anomie

Contested Spaces and Surfaces in Via Zamboni, Bologna

Anna Giulia Della Puppa

Streets are our brushes, squares are our palettes.

—Vladimir Majakovskij

Introduction

'All the happy cities are alike; each unhappy city is unhappy in its own way' – that's what I always thought when passing through the university district of Bologna, where I happily lived and studied for about seven years, before choosing Athens as a foster happy city. 'All the happy cities are alike; each unhappy city is unhappy in its own way' is what I also thought when I came back to Bologna to recover after an extremely difficult separation from my once-better half, in the place where I knew I could feel safe. I chose via Petroni, one of the most controversial streets of the university district in terms of urban decay and criticality, but a benchmark meeting point for the student population of the city as well. From this toehold I have seen many things changing, and most of them conformed to those kinds of processes taking place in most other European and 'Western' cities, now known as 'gentrification' – quite an unknown phenomenon in this district at the time I left it. What I would like to propose here is a personal and first-hand, albeit anthropological, perspective on the urban dynamics of transformation characterizing this part of the city, in the general context of a peculiar kind of 'bolognaise' gentrification. In this chapter I will diffusely use terms such as 'foodification', borrowed from Wolf Bukowski's work *La Ballata delle Mozzarelle* (2015) and articles from the magazine *Internazionale*. I argue that, when it comes to talking about commodification of the city and gentrification, we do not simply have to inflect general concepts to a particular reality, but should also identify the specific 'unhappiness' of the place we are discussing. For what concerns Bologna *unhappiness* is that all the spurs of the process of the so-called gentrification are connected with the mythological machine of being 'the capital of food', which makes this process unique in its own way. Nevertheless, my aim is to evoke all the stages, including practices of police repression, inhabitant relocation and place resignification, along with the commodification of a public space 'in the name of food', or better on the pretext of food. In doing so, I will focus on the aesthetic and semiotic aspects of the conflict taking place in this very part of the city, which is played over the aesthetic concept of *decoro*. From Latin 'decorum', it indicates etymologically 'what is good is to be done', and it has a strong moral meaning translatable as 'decency'. At the same time, it is interesting how *decoro* and the relative verb *decorare* mean also decoration or garnish, stressing their aesthetical tinge. What is decent, in the end, has to be decorated somehow, but how? And who decides which decoration is appropriate?

The Left's Crisis and Technicized Myth

To begin with, it is worth clarifying how the economic crisis has impacted Bologna, the regional county seat of Emilia-Romagna, and which strategies the public administration is employing in order to deal with it.

Bologna is a relatively small city, located in the Padan Plain, one of the most agriculturally and industrially productive districts in Italy. Having always been considered a 'red' region, it has enjoyed the fruits of a strong cohesiveness between a traditionally left-wing public administration and a cooperative system (Lega Coop) which encourages participatory politics among enterprises and citizens – at least it does so on paper: 'In order to attain results, Lega Coop develops services and projects for cooperative enterprises and promotes cooperative culture, stating its values and supporting with representative action its economic, social and civic role, and offering the ability to provide answers to people's needs' (Lega Coop 2019).

Bologna is indisputably the core of the third sector in the region, and the cooperative system covers all service and production areas, from supermarket security to childcare, through invitations and tenders, making it the true organizational backbone of the city. Moreover, it hosts the oldest university in Europe, and with its vivacity it has been a hotbed of cultural and political ferment for more than a century. The intersection of these layers, namely the cooperative organization, the cultural and student legacy, and the strong political consciousness, constitutes Bologna's main identity.

When, more than twelve years ago, I chose to go and study in Bologna, its 'technicized myth' (Jesi 2011) of an 'open city', one conquered through years of social struggle, was a strong incentive for myself, as it is for the majority of the university students (about 85,000 every year): a young, fresh city, with a strong political consciousness and a long tradition of political battles.

The technicized myth is a concept developed by the philologist Furio Jesi, and refers to the idea that mythical materials – all the pieces that make up a story (Bologna's in this instance) – are never neutral, but instead are always manipulated to serve purposes existing outside the story itself, and are useful to the particular circumstances of the storyteller. As Enrico Manera writes in *Myth, Violence, Memory*, 'fictions, myths, commonplaces are hard-wired into the imaginary, feeding, in turn, widespread practices and producing concrete consequences in historical contexts full of material and political interest' (Manera 2012). This imaginary is precisely the core of what has to be remembered. But whose memory is this?

During the first years of the economic crisis, thanks to its strong 'red' welfare and a wealth conspicuously connected to collateral activities linked to the university – namely rents, businesses, cultural enterprises, bars and restaurants – Bologna resisted well. Nonetheless, at the same time another kind of crisis, which would prove fatal for the very 'spirit' of Bologna, began to slowly compromise its identity as the 'red core' of Italy.[1] Following a general trend within the European centre-left, the Italian Democratic Party (PD), the main reference for the 'red' cooperative system (as opposed to a 'white' one, connected with Catholic initiatives), did undergo a remarkably neoliberal turn, especially under the guidance of Matteo Renzi, which eventually led to an electoral collapse (Momigliano 2018). Bologna's public administration took part in this trend, increasingly opening the city to private initiatives and actively promoting this model (Monti 2017).

After years of political negotiations and struggles, relations today between the left-wing public administration and the social movements of the city are far from peaceful. Bologna is known for its tradition of political occupations, and as being a hotbed of political and underground cultural experimentation, even before the 'Panther movement' of the early 1990s, when this practice reached an acme. In 1990, when student mobilization against the Ruberti university reform was spreading from Palermo in Sicily to the whole country, on the night of 27 December a panther was spotted in Nomentana Street in Rome. After an unsuccessful hunt that lasted for weeks (Casalini 1990), Roman students coined the slogan 'We are the panther' – a reference to them being uncatchable and 'outside the box', like a loose panther in a city – and the slogan was soon adopted all around the country.

The Panther Movement is known for its political practice of squatting, and is often connected with punk, hip hop, and underground counterculture more generally (Delisa 2012).

A crystal-clear example of the tension between these expressions and Bologna public administration is given by the 2014 eviction of Atlantide squat, located in one of the city's ancient gate towers. Since 1999, Atlantide was a landmark and reference point for underground and LGBTQ cultures. After long negotiations between the two sides to find an alternative location (legally assigned), the public administration surrendered under the pressure of a right-wing 'indignant citizens' committee. To date, Atlantide remains an empty and unused building, whose doors and windows have been sealed closed.

One of the neighbourhoods shaping this 'red city' myth is the Bolognina district. It flourished as a working-class neighbourhood at the end of nineteenth century, and today it remains one of the most multicultural areas adjacent to the city centre. It is a vivid and densely populated space, counterbalancing the commercial and consumerist idea of the city that is materialized in most of the rest of the city centre. Bologna urban policy massively involves participatory politics dynamics (with the involvement of citizens' associations and cooperatives) that are attuned to a consumerist agenda. This is nothing new. In *La Revolution Urbaine* (Lefebvre 1970), Henri Lefebvre had already suggested that a city always rises from conflict; it is a preordained space with specific functions (a punitive space, a commercial one, disciplinary, etc.), and is an 'unpredictable' space of social relations, human histories, and specific situations.

Such an unpredictable space, in Lefebvre terms, where spontaneous aggregations and initiatives 'from below' mix with (and are often co-opted by) institutional systems – within a narrative that is often framed by an 'emergency paradigm' allegedly aimed at dealing with social and physical 'decay' – perfectly suits those dynamics of urban regeneration often invoked to cover up an extensively common process of gentrification. Consequences of such a dynamic are not just the conversion of freely available spaces – squares, parks, unbuilt interstices – into spaces for profit (which often become inaccessible for some members of society), but also the 'regeneration' of the social strata traditionally residing in those parts of the city where prices and living costs still have room to increase, forcing previous dwellers to migrate elsewhere. This process very often involves the disintegration of consolidated social networks and communities. Evictions have been taking places for years now. In 2014, one of the largest housing project squats in Italy – located in the Bolognina district, and lodging 280 people – was evicted, to make space for a luxury student hotel. By 2015, no fewer than 1,081 evictions could be counted all across Bologna. This is the very part of the city where perhaps the most important self-managed social centre of Bologna is located: XM24, which has existed for the last seventeen years. Located in what was once the central marketplace, XM24 hosts the weekly farmers' market 'Campi Aperti', an Italian language school for migrants, a rehearsal studio, two stages, a social kitchen, a vegetable garden, an aerial dance school, a boxing gym, a do-it-yourself bike repair space and a hacking lab. With its wide covered square, it is the actual core of the city's social and political countercultures and, predictably, it is constantly under threat of eviction. As we will see later, as far as the central university district of Bologna is concerned, the rhetoric used by the public administration to justify the attack on XM24 (and whatever that represents in terms of a political stance regarding its existence) is interesting, precisely because it downplays the level of conflict taking place. By the time this book has been published, XM24 has been evicted.[2] For many years now, the city has been pelted with a constant rhetoric of urban decay, which has constituted the breeding ground for justifying and legitimizing the current discourse of regeneration. As the geographer Paola Bonora states:

> 'Regeneration' represents next year's core business. The enduring good par excellence, … 'real estate' enters the game of consumptive waste and becomes transient, perishable, reproducible … It is a linear dynamic: central areas are converted, plus new buildings arise on the periphery under the aegis of the public good … Introducing the idea of precariousness, I guarantee myself an everlasting market. A perfect system. (Bonora 2017: 45)

Touristification of the City Centre: 'Bologna, City of Food'

Along with the myth of being a 'red' and 'erudite' city, thanks to the oldest university in Europe, another important 'technicized myth' of the city of Bologna is that it is the capital of good food ('Bologna, the fat'). In fact, its Bolognese sauce (*ragù*), tortellini and mortadella are famous worldwide.

The small crossroads around the central Two Towers area have always attracted gastrotourists, but they were also the place where city residents used to go to shop for local goods. An incredible variety of foods would spread their scent across the area. As the blogger Wolf Bukowski mentions in an article published in *Internazionale* magazine in July 2016 (Bukowski 2016), since the opening of the first food megastore (by Lega Coop) in 1989 in the peripheral area of Borgo Panigale, the citizens' shopping habits have radically changed. A constantly prolific Mass Market Retail (MMR) industry, partnering with the public administration in 2013 in an 'urban food regeneration plan', gradually crippled small food shops in the city centre. The constant opening of new MMR food stores all around the centre led small shops to close or to rebrand and upgrade themselves into 'luxury food retailer' status in order to survive. While this phenomenon has followed a similar path to that in other Italian cities in the last decades, in Bologna this transformation of the city centre's commercial assets has been particularly inscribed within an explicit strategy of 'foodification' that has accompanied and complemented the touristification, as well as the more general gentrification, of the city.

The Eat the Rich collective is mostly concerned with the process of food commodification in Bologna, and with looking for ways to counterbalance it, mainly by organizing social kitchens in public and occupied spaces, and by using grocery leftovers and the direct producers' network Campi Aperti. I asked them to tell me more about the process of foodification:

> In October 2017, it was calculated that one restaurant is registered for every thirty-seven inhabitants; every year there is an average of thirty-four new openings, with an increase of 47 per cent since 2009 [data from the Chamber of Commerce, 2017]. This contributes to the territorial marketing of 'Bologna, city of food' as promoted by the public administration and supported by associations and cooperatives. (Interview with a member of Eat the Rich collective)

A more recent and crucial stage in this process has been the creation of F.I.Co. (a term that in Italian means at the same time 'fig' as well as 'cool', and is an acronym for Agricultural Italian Factory): an aggregator of luxury food retailers and a self-designated 'Food Disneyland'. F.I.Co was strongly backed by the city administration and Lega Coop in collaboration with the food market retail company Eataly. It is located in a peripheral area of the city where the wholesale food market used to be, and where, as a result of its presence, real estate prices have already started to increase.

What seems interesting in this transformation is the shift in food values it has triggered: from a collector of discourses about healthy practices and *commensality* (Levi Strauss 1964) to a *technicized myth* that, by the use of the very health and conviviality rhetorics, brings about a commodification of food and its inherent values. Food is thus reconfigured as a 'cool experience', more a springboard for innovative enterprises than an everyday need, let alone a pleasurable and social one. In this way the 'food experience' tends to be deprived by one of its constitutive anthropological elements: that of sharing. The words *compagno* in Italian and 'companion' in English mean

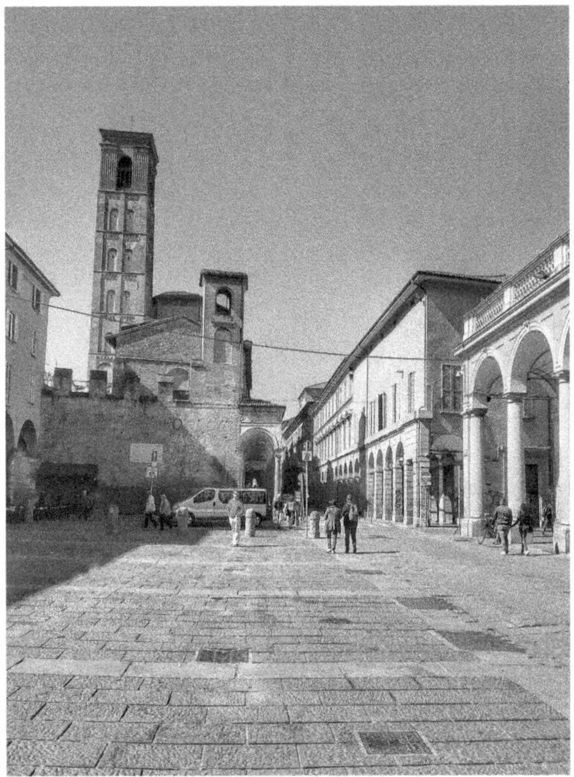

Figure 9.1 Verdi Square. Photo by Maretta Angelini, 7 April 2018. Wikimedia Commons, CC BY-SA 4.0.

'the one I share bread with'. In Greek, *syndrofos* means 'the one with whom I eat', and in both Italian and in Greek this concept stands for someone with whom, symbolically and through the act of sharing food, a strong bond is produced: a partner in life, a political comrade. Now, the 'food experience' has become a symbol of exhibited wealth, a sort of exhibitionist 'potlatch' of the consumer good par excellence. Something that could recall Solange Blonde's exclamation in Marco Ferreri's *La Grande Bouffe*: 'You are grotesque! Grotesque and disgusting! Why do you go on eating, if you are not hungry?!'

I considered Bologna as my city for more than a decade. I have passed through alternating periods of love and distress, of both permanent residency and coming-and-going from other places. And yet, for more than ten years, Verdi Square and Petroni Street have been my home. These two places constitute the very heart of the Bologna University district, located at the core of the city and pivotal to all matters of discourse regarding the city centre's urban transformation. The most characteristic feature of Verdi Square is that, precisely because of the many students and youths crossing it daily, this wide-open space is used as a meeting point all day long. The square's urban ecology is characterized by a mostly free and non-commercial use of space: its rhythm is punctuated by the habit of buying a sandwich and a beer from one of the many small and cheap food stores lining the square, and siting on a bench or directly on the ground to chat with people, listen to music or study. The public administration has tried to repress this kind of sociality for years, accusing it of a lack of 'urban decency' (*decoro*) and branding it a source of decay, particularly unacceptable in such a central and strategic area. Graffiti, tags, political slogans and spontaneous street art, together with the rubbish littering the place, are considered to be a conspicuous part of the problem, along with the noise caused by the crowds of people.

During premières at Bologna Opera House, which is in fact located here, one may find the square closed off by the police (they are always present anyway, 'patrolling' the boundaries of the area and feeding its imaginary as an unruly space) in order to allow taxis and chauffeur-driven cars to pass through and park without mixing with the regular mass of the square's seemingly 'unwealthy' habitués. Over the years, many city ordinances have been passed in an attempt to normalize this locale, which is exemplary to understanding the ongoing process of gentrification operating in the city. In 2008, an ordinance prevented people from sitting on the ground in the square. It never really managed to become effective and the ordinance was soon withdrawn, as the habit of sitting on the ground was too widespread. As I recall, back in the spring of 2009, hundreds of people present in the square during the *aperitivo* reacted by throwing bottles at police, who wanted to detain a person for not giving the authorities his ID when refusing to stand up. Various other ordinances were passed and later abandoned, while the normalization of Verdi Square was being attempted in other ways, such as protracting some repaving works over months, setting a massive stage (covering well over half the square) in collaboration with a residents' committee and the Opera House, and positioning a huge brown shipping container in the middle of the square, supposedly serving as 'tourist info point' (Figure 9.2). Today, there is an active city ordinance in place preventing alcohol consumption and the sale of drinks in glass bottles, 'with the aim of reducing the abuse of alcohol and the waste of glass' (Bologna Today 2014).

In an article by Wolf Bukowski, we read the intervention of Deputy Mayor Matteo Lepore, who was in charge of tourism and city promotion, during a city council meeting on 11 April 2016:

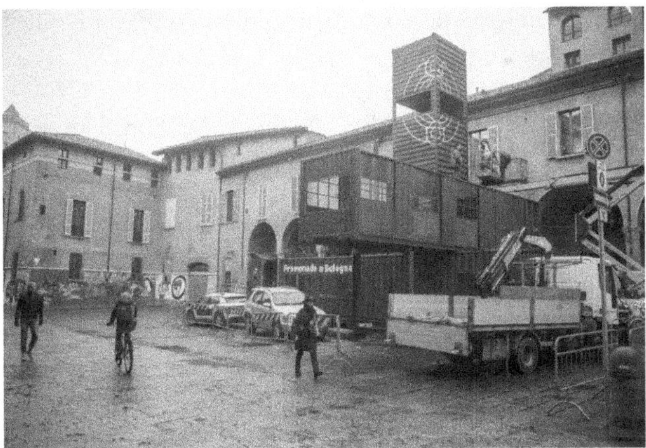

Figure 9.2 Tourist info point container in Verdi Square, winter 2017.
© infoaut.org.

In our squares, we too often see street vendors and shops that, even though unauthorized, sell [alcohol in] glass bottles and other products at low prices. Although not necessarily at lower prices, they are often accessible (too much even) to youngsters, maybe even underage people too; sometimes it happens. In some areas there is a high concentration of so-called 'food shops', which in reality have windows and counters full of alcohol. So, unless one feeds oneself exclusively with rum, I would say it is hard to demonstrate that these are in fact 'food shops'. (Bukowski 2016)

Aside for the fact that selling alcohol is not illegal in either supermarkets or food shops, it is interesting to note that there is often a switch between what is *illegal* and what is legal but considered somehow *immoral* or *not decent*. Here we clearly see the tendency towards the identification of a spatial 'anomy' that is in need of being repressed, rather than a prescription of something actually dangerous, thus leading to the construction of a spatial 'state of exception' (Agamben 2005).

It is enlightening to look at this dynamic of social control, keeping in mind Agamben's conviction that:

The state in which we live now is no more a disciplinary state. Gilles Deleuze suggested to call it the *État de contrôle*, or control state, because what it wants is not to order [or] impose discipline, but rather to manage and to control. Deleuze's definition is correct, because management and control do not necessarily coincide with order and discipline. (Agamben 2013)

Indeed, in this sense, the conflict between the student population on the one side, who enliven the area day by day, and the public administration on the other, who would like to regenerate it, as well as the residents' committee, who fight against noise and decay, takes our discourse back to Verdi Square's very spatial qualities, creating a discourse around the city and its transformative dynamics. In fact, in my multiple conversations with exponents of the residents' committee, it emerges clearly how the public administration goals cannot be univocally overlapped with those of the local residents. While the latter agree with actions against graffiti and dirt – which they consider aesthetically indecent – and proudly organize self-funded volunteering campaigns of wall cleaning, they seem to be much more sceptical about the ongoing process of commodification (read: foodification) in the area. As we will see further on, the local residents' attempt to create a network between them and the existing business owners in the area to organize cultural and civic initiatives in Verdi Square has not been accepted by the public administration, which instead entrusted an external association to plan the nightlife and food promotion in the area. Even the Verdi Square committee, notwithstanding its strenuous voluntary first-hand work against urban decay, and its relations with both municipality and student groups, ultimately seems to be a marginal actor in the urban politics in the area, one that is involved in participatory discussions and initiatives only as far as its aspirations meet those of the public administration. 'The city builds, identifies and refers to the essence of social relations: the mutual existence and manifestation of differences arising from, or resulting in, conflict' (Lefebvre 1970) – not just food, thus, but also conflict.

Bologna, City of Turnstiles

On 9 February 2016, an anti-riot police unit entered the Faculty of Humanities library at 36 Zamboni Street (often referred to as '36'), and evicted some students. In the autumn of 2015, the academic administration had decided to install turnstiles and an electronic identification (eID) device. The justification was that, in order to allow the comfortable use of the library until midnight by those enrolled at the university (i.e. those paying for it), a proper control apparatus was needed, to prevent 'unpleasant subjects' from entering. This was part of an extensive regeneration project involving all the city's libraries and study halls, with the ultimate aim of creating a 'bubble' in the central University District, that by means of security technology would disconnect the paying students from the 'undesirables' frequenting the area.

I met some members of the Marxist-Autonomist Student Collective (CUA, Collettivo Universitario Autonomo), active since 2005, to discuss about the 36:

> The 36 is a fundamental space for certain kinds of social bonds within the University District. First of all, it is the largest library in this area. It overlooks Via Zamboni and almost faces Verdi Square, so the human flux is suitable for the creation of such space-crossing dynamics, and for the construction of social relations that are the basis for certain types of collective behaviours. It has always been a free-access library with a particular history: during the 1990s, it was the 'occupied 36' of the Panther Movement; an incredible social, cultural and political catalyst. ... Its huge historic value is well-known throughout the student community, albeit roughly. (Interview with a member of CUA collective)

Aside from the many study halls, the internal space of the building houses the book-borrowing service, two computer rooms and a small yard with a vending machine for coffee and snacks. Since the 1990s, this space has literally and broadly speaking nurtured many generations of students, who would gather not only to prepare for exams but also to discuss opinions and political stances, building significant social bonds in the process (Figure 9.3).

This space has helped to nurture many loves, friendships, personal aversions, political diatribes and ideological affinities. Its tagged and written walls and surfaces are the witnesses over many years of this expansive social and intellectual network, having made this library a living organism and, in today's context, an obvious symptom of this place's *indecency* for the university administration.

> In its own small way, the '36', without anything particularly significant happening, has always been a gravitational pole, in part thanks to its easy access: after class, one can drop in for a cup of coffee and chat with others, as it's a proper meeting point and not just a study room. It has always been a place for all tastes, where characters and behaviours mingle, and new ones spill over. (Interview with a member of CUA collective)

We can easily see here how the moral and the aesthetic meaning of 'decency' come to play a key role. After a long period of work in progress, the library reopened to the public, the entrance equipped with big glass doors for the turnstile installation. Every morning for more than a week,

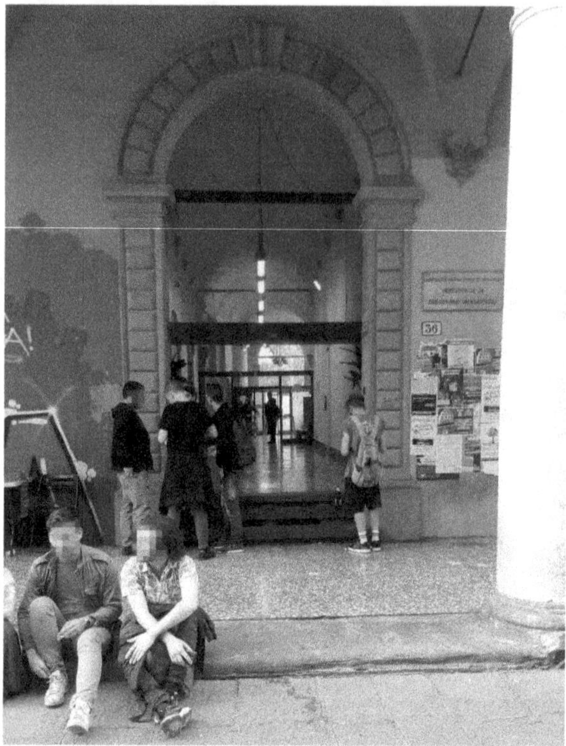

Figure 9.3 Zamboni 36 library entrance. © Morgan Vallari.

students from political collectives took on the task of opening them, so the library could be fully accessible. Furthermore, in an act of symbolism, they carefully removed the glass doors and placed them outside the dean's office. The academic administration reacted to this by closing the library to the public. Consequently, collectives called for an assembly outside the library that saw a large participation from the whole student community, regularly gathering at '36' and eventually forming a block and forcing the library to reopen normally. In response, the dean called for the anti-riot police, who violently entered the public space of the library, causing severe moral and physical injuries, and material damage. In an attempt to defend themselves, the students built barricades with chairs and tables, while a lot of their possessions were destroyed by the police intervention. The following few hours saw confrontations in the streets, ending with armoured vehicles attacking students.

It has also always been a political space; this has contributed to keeping the space a certain way. It is a very conscious community self-managing itself. When the drug dealing issue occurred, for example, it was the whole community that took care of pushing out both dealers and consumers, explaining that such behaviours would not be tolerated. The same happened when a girl faced harassment: the students took care of her and kicked the molester outside … So, there is this community of people who feel the need to belong to something that's not channelled through a predetermined projection about the use of space. … There are also ghosts from the past all around here: 1977 barricades in Zamboni Street and all the things handed down by mass culture, but mostly – and thanks to political collectives for giving continuity to this idea – the notion that universities and university districts are domains to be defended against those who want them 'normalized'. (Interview with a member of CUA collective)

As we will see, an aesthetic/semantic diatribe also configures the spatialization of this conflict, and involves opposite semantics. In some cases, such as the one described, the clash is frontal and polarized. Conversely, in some other spaces, the metamorphosis is so effective it manipulates social behaviours much better than any radical, coercive action.

A 'Cool' Lab of Gentrification

One of the first things one notices upon entering the Nuove Scuderie – the renewed space of the university cafeteria, located in Verdi Square's ancient stable – is the construction of wide common spaces: large wooden steps, long modular tables, everything equipped with electric sockets and bright and comfortable lighting, where people can consume their food and drink, purchased from a bar that provides a wide selection, and sit down to study and prepare exams at the same time. Entirely renovated in 2017, this space has always been designated to food and coffee services: it had a university canteen during the 1970s and 1980s, and in 1993 it was occupied by the Panther Movement and became a cafeteria/luncheonette, with special prices for students. Its wide spaces had no clear 'stylistic' normativity, and allowed large crowds of various people to congregate, mostly for a short time: a sort of covert attachment to the square. It is therefore of some interest that, out of the blue, we witness the construction of a normative private space, attuned to 'cool' consumerist logics while simultaneously equipped to serve the same purposes of a public library. Significantly, this process seemingly occurs in parallel with that of limiting and controlling the use of an already existing free and public space, fully integrated in its historic flux and so potentially 'anomic'.

> The old cafeteria used to be a crossing point for many students, who were quite shocked by this renovation. Also, consider its new function in urban ecology: its collaboration with F.I.Co., first of all, is a matter of political geography of the urban texture. Their aim is to present the city as it has never been before, this myth of 'the city of food.' You can easily see it at the entrance: there is a big map with the whole consumerist network depicted: F.I.Co. there, Scuderie here, the airport down there, the University, LegaCoop… All symbols of the economic power of the city. It is evident that the referents have changed: students are still the economic skeleton supporting the city, but now tourism seems the new target. So there is this on-going transformation; from a city for youngsters to a city exclusively for tourists. (Interview with a member of CUA collective)

This transformation is noteworthy on both the visual and rhetorical level. For what concerns the first, the charming hipster aesthetic, so common worldwide in every gentrified neighbourhood, is dominating the space with its white colour and jubilant indoor greenery, consistent with the pervasive agribusiness hype, and contrasting with the previous minimalistic approach to space that left the medieval architecture in plain view. The rhetorical aspect is hard for non-Italian speakers to understand, as it is characterized by an over abuse of Anglicisms, to begin with the new motto: 'Future Food Urban Cool Lab', where 'cool' is used as both a description for the consumptive experience and the translation of 'F.I.Co'.

It is not just a change in referents, as CUA militants correctly suggest, but also a change in who is investing in the space, now linked to agribusiness start-ups and 'food education'. As the project's founder said in an interview:

> Students, who are regular clients, young workers, but also citizens and tourists: the new Scuderia addresses a large bracket of the population, by organizing its more than 800 square metres around three areas: food, innovation [in English in the text], fluidly animated by coming and going start-ups, and an event space where creative labs and recreational or special initiatives will take place. (Bertossi 2017)

Moreover, if we can consider Nuove Scuderie as the enemy outpost in the anomic territory of Verdi Square, then Guasto Village (the urban regeneration project of the city administration, specifically created for the University District in order to contrast the 'urban decay' symbolized by the homonymous street) implies a shiftier range of values and a more controversial aesthetic. In fact, the location includes several containers, refurbished to become pricey bars and canteens that most of the habitués of the area simply cannot afford, in a very particular and central area of the University District, namely Guasto Street.

This street owes its name to the ruins (*guasto* means wasted, ruined) of Bentivoglio Palace, which it runs by, creating a hill with a small park since the eighteenth century. A very narrow street, this has always been a headache for the authorities, infamous for being a place of drug dealing and use, as well as an open-air *pissoir*. Many initiatives have been taken to solve this place's criticalities. During my university years, it used to host the harm-reduction street unit supporting drug users – an extremely important social function, but hardly one that may be seen as aligned with the urban regeneration policies informing the University District nowadays. In this regard, it has to be pointed out that none of these regeneration initiatives have shown intentions or implemented initiatives to properly dealt with the drug issue, which instead has been for the most part dealt with implicitly, via direct or indirect displacement, as a result of regulations, security measures and price rises. The public urination problem was solved by means of 'porta-potties', wanted by residents' committees, and by the presence of private guards.

The Guasto Village summer project turned into the 'Winter Village', and then back to Guasto Village the following summer. As members of the residents' committee told me, Peacock Lab, the association awarded the €180,000 'Rock project' prize, defeated in the competition the project proposed by the residents' committee, which also involved the traditional shopkeepers of the area. First of all, the Guasto Village draws from the aesthetic imaginary of container urbanism, globally widespread precisely in relation to urban regeneration projects of 'degraded' neighbourhoods all around the world. It consists of cheap prefabricated modules, with an underground aesthetic that can easily blend with a 'decayed' environment, while at the same time being functional to the quintessential aim of gentrifying it. In his article about the emergence of container urbanism in America, architecture historian Mitchell Schwarzer wrote:

Today what dominates more is a photogenic attitude, the possibility of actual (or surrogate) containers to evoke an individual's existence as a global *flaneur*, with lifestyle recast from being embedded within a given place to a restless rhythm of departures and arrivals. (Schwarzer 2013)

This seems to be precisely what does *not* convince the Verdi Square residents' committee:

It created two problems: firstly, all the traditional businesses of the area were affected, and secondly, these containers do not fit into the aesthetic environment of the medieval city. I can possibly understand them in big cities and large peripherals, but they have nothing to do here. Students and CUA militants have something to say in this regard too, I guess. (Interview with Otello Civatti, from Verdi Square residents' committee)

Indeed, CUA militants do not like Guasto Village, but the reasons for this are quite different. It has to do with the idea of global *flaneur* – that is, a consumer of urban space, a space that is filled with depoliticized 'cool' and 'underground' signs that systematically avoid or erase a place's unique, and in this case remarkably political, memory. A discreet and charming anomie. Secondly, we must keep in mind the role of rhetoric on space and dwelling. An article from *Vice* magazine dated 6 September 2018 explicitly endorses Guasto Village as a brilliant example of regeneration and not gentrification. In support of this thesis, a quote by Carlo, a member of Peacock Lab is underlined: 'Gentrification is moving existing communities away. Here there were no communities' (Cannarella 2018). The supposedly 'pioneering' action of Guasto Village is also pervasively remarked upon during a speech that I attended in Verdi Square on 25 September 2018, promoted by Peacock Lab, in which the chief of culture, tourism and urban promotion, Matteo Lepore, stated:

> This is not just a University District, but a neighbourhood where thousands of people live and many professors work. Unfortunately, it is also an area of the city that has been abandoned for too long now, maybe because conflicts here were thought of as a health and safety issue, part of the history, that could be contained here. There may be certain drug issues, and a number of demonstrations occur here, but in the end, it cannot be considered part of the city centre. (From my recordings)

This is a problematic statement for at least two reasons. To begin with, perfectly aligned with Carlo's thesis, it does not (or it refuses to) acknowledge the community network that exists within the University District, and the consequent, common 'taskscapes' of urban practices that sedimented through the years (Ingold 1993). These practices, although anomic and a-normalized, constitute the very outline of what Henri Lefebvre called *droit a la ville*, the performative right of acting on urban space and to build a creative and authentic bond with it (Lefebvre 1967). Moreover, this statement uncovers the real conflict plateaux: the striated space of public order and normalized consumption versus the smooth space of unpredictable anomy – a conflict that is already taking place, constantly configuring and reconfiguring this piece of city via the common rhetoric of 'the sick city generating violence'. In an interview for Crisis-scape Project about urban transformation in Athens during the economic crisis, Professor Stavros Stavrides pointed out that this discourse is always accompanied by the acclaimed necessity of managing space, and specifically urban space, in a containing, restrictive and exclusive way, as opposed to an inclusive one (Stavrides 2015). To put it Deleuzianly, it becomes a space of control, since it has failed to be properly disciplined, and where inclusivity is not taken into account.

Visual Conflicts and Contested Semiotics

The poles of this conflict are crystal clear. On 15 January 2018, *Infoaut* staff wrote:

> We have to understand what is going on. Gentrification? Partially. As far as Verdi Square is concerned, it is not just a matter of one population displacing the population previously living there. Touristification? Partially, as it is not just the project of turning the centre of Bologna into one big shopping window. A fight against 'urban decay'? Partially, but it is well known how it is a battlefield of social perceptions, more than a concrete phenomenon. Hence, it is a combination of the above. What is important and should be taken into consideration, however, is the implicit political level. (Infoaut 2018)

Consequently, if this political level is concerned with a clash of opposite ideas over the city space, we should also consider how this is visually constructed; how do city surfaces embed this conflict? In this perspective, the University District walls are an incredibly prolific terrain of observation. Up until recently, before the summer of 2018, as one walked through the covered walkways of Zamboni Street and until the Faculty of Humanities at number 38, it was possible to see a number of murals and street art pieces. An interesting dynamic of unbidden and non-institutionalized 'musealization' took place, with tourists and citizens coming through the University District to admire the murals, without these having been included in tourist guides or tourist attraction lists. Throughout the years, the left side of the street in particular, where the big doors to the Humanities Faculty and Library are, has seen the creation of some large pieces of street art, projected by CUA and executed by the Milanese crew Volks Writerz. Volks Writerz's style is easily recognizable: they mostly use red, black and white colours

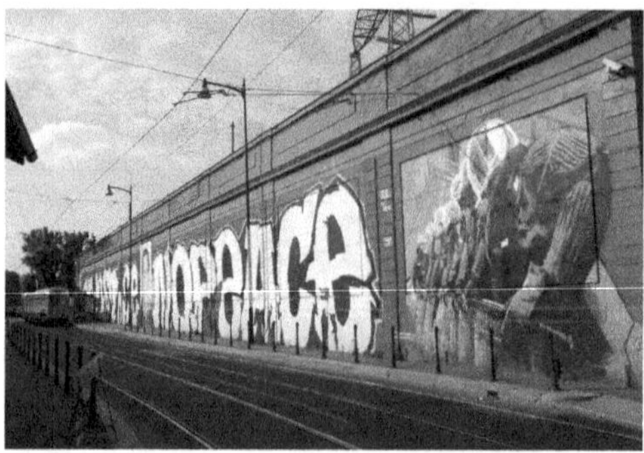

Figure 9.4 Volks Writerz's Carlo Giuliani graffiti in Milan. © Volks Writerz.

to write political content in bold capital letters, with rounded contours. Their pieces are often a combination of political slogans and portraits of Second World War partisans or radical left, anarchist personalities. One of the most famous pieces, many times vandalized, was promoted by the Milan's Bulk squat collective. It consisted in a massive almost 100-metre graffiti dedicated to Carlo Giuliani (killed by police in Genoa, during G8 protests in 2001) in Bramante Street, with his face depicted, an anti-mob police cordon, and an almost 5-metre-high slogan 'No Justice, No Peace' in Volks Writerz typical black, red and white colours (Figure 9.4). Now the mural has been erased and the Bulk has been razed to the ground, but a fancy new cocktail bar called Bulk has just opened next door, in a 5-star hotel building.

M., a member of the crew and a very old friend of mine, told me about how this project was born back in 2001:

We created the first militant writers' crew in Italy. 'Volks writerz' means 'people's writers'. Being firstly comrades and then writers, we decided to give light to this project, actually using written language to convey political context on our city walls. … Being present on the walls in a language comprehensible to other writers also means being intelligible to the young strata of the population, and this gave us the strength to consciously take back the spaces of our city, with something different from a tag or the name of our crew. For more than fifteen years we have spread radical, antifascist, antiracist content and the memory of political Resistance, and this was a small example for many crew members born all around the world, willing to couple written language with a different kind of content. This was our way of being present throughout these difficult years for radical politics, with all the strength and all the visibility mural communication offers, in order to counterbalance a reduction in political feasibility due to repression in our town and elsewhere. (Interview with M.)

While the cancellation of indoor art pieces at the Faculty of Humanities has somehow been negotiated between CUA and the university administration, with big panels placed on the walls so that the graffiti could be done again, Zamboni Street's murals showed a more complicated and conflicting dynamic. This happened precisely because they invested the University District semantics, and visibly rendered this an 'unneutral zone' – in fact, a space where habitués' positionality and political legacy are immediately visible. As CUA members told me: 'It's a fact that surfaces as a space for artistic and political communication have always been a battlefield'.

The many Volks Writerz' murals, succeeding one another along Zamboni Street, are all linked to resistance practices and values that the University District community identifies with. 'We won't pay [for] your crisis' was the slogan in 2008 of a massive wave of student protest, for example. A Gezi Park mural in Verdi Square with a Nâzım Hikmet poem was dedicated to the Taksim Square protests and the worldwide necessity to reclaim free public space. In 2014, a huge mural was done on Zamboni Street dedicated to the Kobane liberation, raising clamour: on the one side, a beautifully depicted woman wrapped in Kurdish flags holding a gun; on the other, a guerrilla woman cutting the head off a Daesh demon; and in the middle, the inscription 'Side by side with rebel people. Kobane resists' (Figure 9.5). As a member of CUA – a promoter of this and all the street art in the area – told me, the immediate reaction of both academic and public administrations was an abrupt condemnation of the mural for being an act of vandalism. Four years later, the mural was erased. It is worth noting that anti-graffiti residents' squads and university and city administrations are not the only enemies of murals in the Zamboni area. They are often vandalized by 'unknown people', but with the CUA suspecting right-wing supporters, clearly showing how much street art embeds political conflict.

In this context, another kind of street art – that designated as 'decorative' by public and university administrations, and therefore as 'decent' – has had a much easier life. Some months before the containers invaded Guasto Street, the press spoke very favourably of a patronized street art project, subsequently integrated into Guasto Village: 'Where there used to be grass and heroine, now there is – also – a city. It happens when dozens of volunteer artists start working on city surfaces' (Papa 2017a).

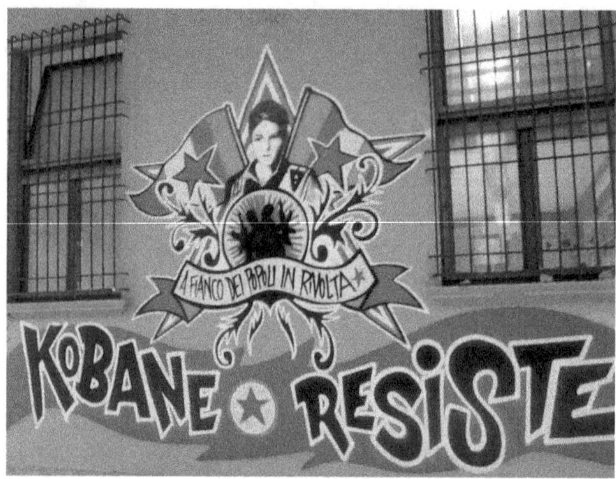

Figure 9.5 Volks Writerz's Kobane resist graffiti in Zamboni Street. © CUA (Collettivo Universitario Autonomo).

Some of these commissioned pieces have political messages too, attracting attention to poverty or migrant issues, even though the impact is quite modest compared to Volks Writerz pieces. Somehow, what makes the difference between the two kinds of street art is the legal framework, intended to establish a 'decent way' for artistic expression, regardless of content. Yet, normative action is in this case specifically aimed at condemning an artistic performativity, namely street art, which is immediately seen as political as it is tied to, and is an expression of, 'the right to the city' (Figure 9.6). 'Writers love the city: they study it, they feel a sense of belonging, even though they compare it to a battlefield. They do so, wearing the city as a dress' (interview with M.).

In this sense, it is not by chance that street art has been involved in this process of urban regeneration, being as it is a visual heritage of this piece of city, but in the needs of being normalized, made 'decent', which merely means made 'decorative'. On the one hand, Guasto Village promoters deny the community nexuses of the University District, concretely creating political and artistic expressivity, and disassociating themselves from its political instances: 'We try as much as possible not to get involved, avoiding taking part in battles and campaigns that don't represent us', says Valentina from Peacock Lab in an interview for the *Zero* online magazine in September 2017 (Papa 2017b). On the other hand, and at the same time, Guasto Village aesthetic winks at an urban imaginary that considers street art as part of its

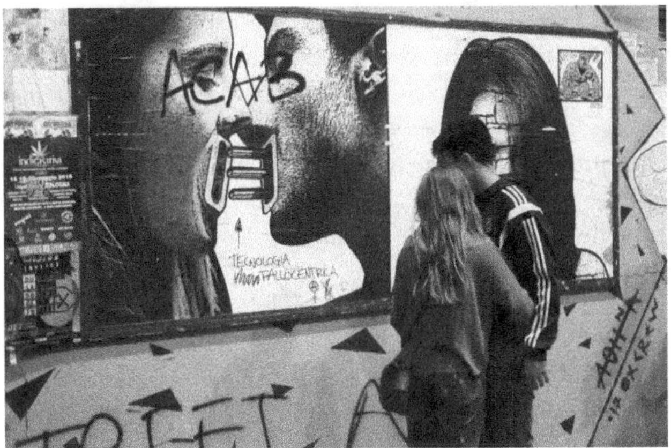

Figure 9.6 Commissioned street art in Guasto Village, vandalized by anarchafeminist activists, spring 2018. © Gianluca Perticoni / Eikon Studio.

cultural code – an urban art expression deprived of its constitutive act of being 'illegal', 'indecent', and sold as an overpriced, watered-down cocktail.

Conclusions

What hits home, and can be taken as visually paradigmatic of the conflict I have tried to delineate here, is the spatial contiguity of these two types of street art, embodying the opposite city models highlighted in this text – a contiguity that can be read as an attempt to harmonize the urban texture, while simultaneously leaving a mark, a semantic laceration.

On 18 April, just a few days before writing these conclusions, one could read on the Guasto Village Facebook page that Peacock Lab did not win the call for bid for the summer activities in the Verdi Square and Guasto Street area. In the comments below the post, supporters' messages of solidarity aside, many users complained about the fact that the district will be at the mercy of drug dealers and heroin users again (Guasto Village 2019). This clearly shows the real criticalities of a space like the one we have analysed in these few pages. These criticalities have never been solved by Guasto Village, as mentioned by members of both the CUA and the residents' committees I interviewed. 'It is clear that those who don't want anything to be changed also like drug dealers and drug addicts at Guasto garden', said Deputy

Mayor Matteo Lepore in response to the criticism raised by the residents' committees about the assignment of the area to Peacock Lab (Ama 2017).

The association 'Macchine Celibi', namely 'Bachelor Machines', which won this year's call for bid, is more open towards local committees and businesses. It promotes a range of initiatives less concerned with 'new types of food and beverage services, as it used to be lately, and implementing the art and culture offer', as the art director Marcello Corvino underlined (Giordano 2019).

It is a partial change of trend for the 'Bologna city of food' politics, which has not stopped spreading undisputedly elsewhere; plus, it is interesting to notice a simultaneous change in Guasto Village semantics, too. In fact, the way it has presented itself since the loss of the call for bid has seen a consistent change: from being a cultural operation acting in a lack of community – as told by Carlo of Peacock Lab – it slipped into one that stands upon the community that live and cross the area, with an online petition intended to save the Guasto Village project. Guasto Village is now haggling with the city council for an alternative space in which to continue their food and beverage activities. Ironically, it instead shares a common fate with XM24, which is strongly deep-seated within its neighbourhood community.

'You have regenerated Guasto Street, and now it has been taken from you! Will it be given to someone more regenerating than you? Fair enough, that's what happens in regeneration processes: there will always be a more effective regenerator', commented a user under the post of the public petition on the Guasto Village webpage. But it is precisely this flattening of spacial and social thickness, its being reported to a mere aesthetic imaginary, that is one of the most interesting aspects of this urban regeneration movement. An unhappy in-its-own-way gentrification process, recalling the restless colonial machine of cultural appropriation that nurtures itself with a subalternity, in the willingness to become an 'inspiration' in the process of digestion. An urban *viveur* hipsterism. Bon appétit!

Anna Giulia Della Puppa, is a PhD candidate in social anthropology at Vrije Universiteit Amsterdam. Although she grew up in a small city in the north-east of Italy, she lived for many years in Bologna. There, she always dwelled in the very core of the university area. Her main area of research is urban transformation dynamics, and her privileged field is the city of Athens, Greece, from where she currently comes and goes, as she collaborates as a researcher with Centro Studi Movimenti in Parma, Italy. Her actual research is concentrated on Greek nationalism as an urban phenomenon, shaped by education and affecting the process of gender formation within the city context. She studied philology at Bologna University and social anthropology at Ca' Foscari University of Venice.

Notes

1. Bologna is nicknamed 'La Dotta, la Grassa, la Rossa' – that is, 'The Erudite, the Fat, the Red'.
2. XM24 has been evicted during the summer of 2019, after a long and unsuccessful negotiation with Matteo Lepore and local institutions. The expected eviction has been saluted with a big day of creative resistance, starting at the arrival of anti-mob police at dawn with fireworks from the roof of the occupation and continued all day long with many 'disturbance initiatives', such as the queer collective dressed as sirens and not leaving the D.I.Y pool of the squat, people of the aerial fabrics lab, hanging from the roof declaring poems and a huge rave party outside in the garden. Until evening, the entire occupation had been destroyed by a scraper. Ironically, the 'scraper' is precisely the iconic and symbolic image the leader of far-onright party Lega and strong opponent of the 'bolognaise left', Matteo Salvini, always calls upon against whatever he dislikes, such as migrants and the radical left.

References

Agamben, G. 2005. *Stato d'Eccezione*. Turin: Bollati Borighieri.

———. 2013. *For a Theory of Destituent Power*. Athens: Χρόνος.

Ama, M. 2017. 'Guasto Village: Merola contro i critici: l'alternativa sono spaccio e caos', *Corri-ere di Bologna*, 4 June.

Bertossi, E. 2017. 'La Scuderia cambia faccia: "Food di qualità, non certo cicchetti a 1 euro"', *Bologna Today*, 12 November. Retrieved 8 January 2019 from http://www.bolognatoday.it/economia/inaugurazione-nuova-scuderia-piazza-verdi.html.

Bologna Today. 2014. 'Lotta all'alcol, nuova ordinanza per i locali del centro: "copri-fuoco" dalle 21', *Bologna Today*, 7 June. Retrieved 8 January 2019 from http://www.bolognatoday.it/cronaca/alcol-chiusura-negozi-centro-bologna-ordinanza-estate.html.

Bonora, P. 2017. 'Rendita e riconversione, la rigenerazione urbana "core business" del nuovo ciclo edilizio', in I. Agostini (ed.), *Consumo di luogo: Neoliberismo nel disegno di legge urban-istica dell'Emilia Romagna*. Bologna: Pendragon, pp. 43–46.

Bukowski, W. 2015. *La ballata delle mozzarella*. Rome: Alegre.

———. 2016. 'Un'estate bolognese di decoro e birre calde', *Internazionale*, 6 July. Retrieved 8 January 2019 from https://www.internazionale.it/opinione/wolf-bukowski/2016/07/22/bologna-ordinanza-alcolici.

Cannarella, G. 2018. 'Il Guasto Village di Bologna è l'esempio perfetto della differenza fra riqual-ificazione e gentrificazione', *Munchies*, 6 September. Retrieved 8 January 2019 from https://munchies.vice.com/it/article/wjkvwq/guasto-village-bologna.

Casalini, S. 1990. 'Roma, ovvero la città dei safari', *La Repubblica*, 3 January. Retrieved 8 January 2019 from https://ricerca.repubblica.it/repubblica/archivio/repubblica/1990/01/03/roma-ovvero-la-citta-dei-safari.html.

Deleuze, G., and F. Guattari. 2010. *Mille Piani: Capitalismo e Schizofrenia*. Rome: Castelvecchi.

Delisa, A. 2012. 'Storia dei movimenti studenteschi: "La Pantera siamo noi" (1989–1990)', storiografia.me, 2 December. Retrieved 8 January 2019 from https://storiografia.me/2012/12/02/storia-dei-movimenti-studenteschi-la-pantera-siamo-noi-1990/.

Giordano, M. 2019. 'Estate in piazza Verdi, vincono gli anti container', *Corriere di Bologna*, 19–20 April 2019. Retrieved 8 January 2019 from https://corrieredibo logna.corriere.it/bologna/cronaca/19_aprile_19/estate-piazza-verdi-vincono-anti-container-12977ec0-62ba-11e9-a5e2-aa9d39bf45cd.shtml.

Guasto Village. 2019. https://www.facebook.com/GuastoVillage/. Retrieved 20 April 2019.

Infoaut. 2018. 'Il container urbanism: da dove viene la nuova installazione in Piazza Verdi?', *InfoAut*, 15 January. Retrieved 8 January 2019 from https://www.infoaut.org/notes/il-container-urbanism-da-dove-viene-la-nuova-installazione-in-piazza-verdi.

Ingold, T. 1993. 'The Temporality of the Landscape', in *World Archaeology*, Vol. 25, No. 2, Con-ceptions of Time and Ancient Society. Oxford: Taylor & Francis.

Jesi, F. 2011. *Cultura di destra con tre inediti e un'intervista*. Rome: Nottetempo.

Lefebvre, H. 1967. 'Le droit à la ville'. *L'Homme et la société* 6: 29–35.

———. 1970. *La Revolution Urbaine*. Paris: Gallimard.

Lega Coop. 2019. http://www.legacoop.coop/associazione2/associazione/legacoop-nazion ale/chi-siamo/. Retrieved 8 January 2019.

Levi Strauss, C. 1964. *Le cru et le cuit*. Paris: Plon.

Manera, E. 2012. *Mito, Violenza, Memoria*. Bologna: Carocci (ebook).

Momigliano, A. 2018. 'The Italian Center-Left Didn't Collapse. It Never Existed', *Foreign Policy*, 7 March. Retrieved 8 January 2019 from https://foreignpolicy .com/2018/03/07/the-italian-center-left-didnt-collapse-it-never-existed/.

Monti, M. 2017. 'Dalla banca 44,5 milioni per Fico', *Il Sole 24ore*, 11 November. Retrieved 8 January 2019 from https://st.ilsole24ore.com/art/finanza-e-mercati/2017-11-11/dalla-banca-445-milioni-fico-081308.shtml?uuid=AEVkIB9C.

Papa, S. 2017a. 'Chi sta trasformando i muri e la storia di via del Guasto', *zero.eu*, 9 May. Retrieved 8 January 2019 from https://zero.eu/en/news/chi-sta-trasformando-i-muri-e-la-storia-di-via-del-guasto/.

———. 2017b. 'Peacocklab'. Retrieved 8 January 2019 from https://zero.eu/en/persone/peacocklab-guasto-village/.

Schwarzer, M. 2013. 'The Emergence of Container Urbanism', *Place Journal*. Retrieved 8 January 2019 from https://placesjournal.org/article/the-emergence-of-container-urbanism/#0.

Stavrides, S. 2015. 'Common Space as Threshold Space: Urban Commoning in Struggles to Re-appropriate Public Space', Footprint, [S.l.], pp. 9–19, June.

Part III

Political Turmoil and Regime Transformation

Chapter 10

'25th April Always, Fascism Never Again'

The Post-revolution Murals in Portugal

Cláudia Madeira, Cristina Pratas Cruzeiro and Ricardo Campos

> Writing on the wall is a fact that truly reveals the liberty of a PEOPLE and a collective manifestation of the communicative force of its will.
>
> —E.M. de Melo e Castro, 'Pode-se escrever com isto' (You Can Write with This), 1977

Introduction

The expression '25th April always, fascism never again', used in the chapter title, has been one of the most repeated slogans since the Portuguese Revolution of 25 April 1974 by movements and parties on the left, especially during those troubled political periods that saw a rekindling of the old revolutionary ideals. The expression is used as an element upholding the identity and cohesion of left-leaning thinking, recapturing the core values of the April Revolution. This antifascist slogan is brought back to life during demonstrations and celebrations, either by being voiced by the people, or by appearing on walls, in paint or on posters. As such, it becomes a powerful symbolic evocation, a people's expression resonating meaningfully and widely in the street.

The Portuguese Revolution brought an end to a long-lasting period of dictatorship, thus opening up the way to the democratization of Portuguese society, and contributing to the rise of a number of social, cultural and economic processes, which were to have a profound impact across the nation. While this was a vibrant period from the perspective of the popular mobilization and transformation of society, it was also a time of turbulence and political unrest. The transition to democracy was accompanied by the multiplication of channels for political expression, and by the development of new mechanisms for civil participation. Cityscapes experienced profound changes with the newly acquired freedoms of expression, which assumed several different forms. Among the street manifestations of popular feeling, murals developed during this period into symbols of the revolution, of democratic plurality, and of resistance to fascism. They acquired a privileged status as a means of political communication, much as has happened in many other geographical and historical contexts.

Their relevance involves questions around political and aesthetics issues. From the political angle, walls came to assume a central role as an instrument for the propaganda and diffusion of ideas, retaining the popular stamp of accessibility that was the hallmark of the revolutionary process and the budding process of democratization. The relevance of the political mural dates back to the October Revolution of 1917, while it also played an important role in the context of the Mexican Revolution, the Cuban Revolution and the Chinese Cultural Revolution from 1966 onwards.

There are already a large number of studies delving into the political role of the wall as an ideal surface for a wide array of messages (Greaney 2002; Figueroa Saavera 2006; Waldner and Dobratz 2013; Hawad and Wagoner 2017). It also seems to play a decisive part during turbulent phases of political and social life, in times of crisis, contestation and revolt, as witnessed in different cultures and places throughout history. The Berlin Wall and May 1968 in Paris are well known, to mention but two West European cases; further afield we could also reference the explosion of political graffiti that occurred in the wake of the revolution in Egypt that brought down the Mubarak regime (Abaza 2016), or during the Gezi Park clashes in Istanbul (Yanik 2015). In the context of the military occupation of Palestine, graffiti on walls has also been used as a tool of political resistance, giving voice to the concerns of the underdog (Peteet 2016). There is also evidence regarding the increase of political graffiti and murals following the recent austerity measures hitting several South European countries (Tsilimpoundi 2012; Zaimakis 2015; Campos 2016, 2018).

Historically, the street has always been the space of choice for expressions of resistance, contestation and struggle against political regimes and agents of power. The urban public space is a territory traditionally associated with the political involvement of the less powerful, while it is also a place of visibility and passage, turning it into an essential resource for political expression.

And the political dimension of using walls may be linked to either the act of appropriation of adjacent space, ignoring or perverting institutionalized norms and property legislation, or the content of the messages being produced (Campos 2018). This chapter, contextualized in a collaborative endeavour on the subject of the aesthetic and image production in periods of crisis, is premised on the understanding that revolution always implies a period of crisis, in the sense that it generates uncertainty regarding the possible outcome, turbulence around the antagonisms and ideological clashes taking place, and lastly some form of physical violence. The revolutionary schism forces a readjustment of the institutions, and gives rise to new actors who, in one way or another, seek to acquire new legitimate positions based on the dismantling of the deposed regime. The alteration of social and political structures in society is, inevitably, followed by a number of actions of a symbolic and discursive nature, facilitating the creation of an ideological horizon of justification to change. Rallies, campaigns, mural paintings, political graffiti, distribution of pamphlets, putting up posters, attacks on the symbols of the regime, among other actions, reveal the importance of visuals and images in political and ideological contestation. The arts and pictorial creations play a crucial role in this context.

The political dimension of the murals which we will be looking at in this chapter is indissociably linked to the revolutionary context and to the intense political and party activity that it precipitated. Regarding the events in Portugal, in the context of the Portuguese Revolution, we highlight not only the quality of many of the murals, but also the insertion of this process within a broader context, which incentivized the artistic output in the public space and the democratization of the access to art. Several of these murals were created by unnamed militants, often benefiting from the support of both professional and amateur plastic artists, who generated relatively complex and well-structured works from the perspective of the plastic arts.

The iconography employed alluded to the revolution and the current ideological context inspired by the socialist and communist ideals in vogue. Marx, Lenin, Mao and images symbolic of collective entities, such as the people, the proletariat, the armed forces or the peasantry, found recurrent representation. Some of the murals, particularly those created by far-left organizations, thematically stressed the 'use of brute physical force, whether by human characters – overly muscular men and women – or by the also very frequent representation of arms'; 'the figures [were] imbued with great dynamism, oftentimes even violence, as they advance toward the specta-tor', while others highlighted 'the glorification of the party, with particular emphasis on the flag'; and 'the presence of armed soldiers and sailors in the company of civilians was also quite frequent' (Pedreirinho 1979: 38–50).

Some of these images suggested the intention of immediate and ephemeral action, often giving voice to fleeting but significant moments linked to the objectives of minor parties, referencing important episodes in the national political life, and at other times focusing on and preserving longer-term realities, when the themes were intertwined with the physical production of labour (Madeira 2015).

In this chapter we intend to revisit this period of Portuguese history, stressing the part played by the street and the mural aesthetic expressions in support of a political struggle and the development of freedom of expression following decades of repression and silencing. This text is the result of a review of the bibliography on the subject, and the revisiting of a range of different archives linked to individuals who in some way intervened or enjoyed a privileged position in this process. We argue that the urban public space has developed into a crucial locus for political and creative communication, and that this has occurred on two levels: first, as a space for the official and regular communication of political institutions, but also for the intense participation of an artistic class largely ostracized by the dictatorship; and second, as a space for popular communication and vernacular creativity, open to the intense participation of anonymous citizens. There has clearly been interaction and overlap between these two levels.

The first section of the chapter contains a brief outline of this historical period. The second will focus on political murals, particularly in the process of their legitimization and institutionalization in the context of the opening up of the democratic process, which has led to the multiplication of political actors and to the increasing complexity of the ideological struggle. The final section will focus predominantly on popular initiatives and on the irruption of the people's voice, which has been duly recognized and analysed by the Portuguese visual poet E.M. de Melo e Castro.

The April Revolution and the Democratization of Portuguese Society

It is not possible to consider the Portuguese twentieth century without referencing the fascist dictatorship, which spanned over four decades and was finally crushed by the 1974 Revolution. The seizure of power – a particularly peaceful affair – triggered by the MFA[1] (Armed Forces Movement) on 25 April 1974, and the revolutionary period which it brought to fruition, came as the result of the gradual decay and erosion of the dictatorial regime manifested in an increasing discontent among a population living in extreme poverty, without democratic rights, where political prisons and torture prevailed, and going through a seemingly endless (and lost) colonial war. This conflict, set in the designated 'overseas territories' (Angola, Guinea-Bissau and Mozambique) involved not only a large mobilization of financial resources, but also of youth conscripted into the military service. What is usually labelled the 'Carnation Revolution' ended the war, allowed for the establishment of democracy in the nation, and gave rise to the process on decolonization. What came to be known as the PREC, the 'Ongoing Revolutionary Process'[2] (1974–75), corresponded to a specific period during which the ideals of the revolution – a socialist, classless society – were pursued. But this was also a period when different political actors were vying for power and affirmation in an attempt to exert control over the revolutionary process. This process ended on 25 November 1975.[3] According to several academic studies, the PREC was also marked by an exceptional social mobilization, one of the most remarkable in postwar Europe (Accornero 2014).

The period following 25 April 1974 was also particularly troubled in political and social terms. Several parties achieved mainstream status, and many others appeared, particularly within the left spectrum, igniting a fierce ideological contest. In addition, a number of small radical and armed right-wing groups emerged, resulting in violent action and attacks on labour centres and party headquarters, particularly those of the Portuguese Communist Party (PCP) but also the Socialist Party (PS). The PREC was marked by the agrarian reform, the nationalization of businesses (banking, insurance, transport, communications, steel, etc.) and the dismantling of large economic organizations. Another important aspect was the attainment of independence by colonialized countries and the ensuing populational flow towards continental Portugal, which welcomed about one million people from the ex-colonies during this period.

We do not see this period as one of crisis in the classical sense, but as one of rupture and split from a political, economic and social order that had been sustained by the Portuguese dictatorial regime. We speak of the defeat of a political and social order defined by the repression and persecution of political opposition, by nationalist rhetoric, and the promotion and defence of the 'colonial empire' and the 'overseas territory'. For this reason, we speak of a revolutionary process that gave rise to a transition period, the pursuit of power and the fragmentation of society, which reflected an intense social dynamic punctuated by some violent and bloody episodes, notwithstanding the generally peaceful nature of the overall process.

As such, this constituted a learning period in the collective democratic experience in which the institutional foundations of a new regime were established (the legalisation of formerly clandestine parties, the emergence of new political parties, a new constitution, etc.) and the foundations of a democratic public sphere were erected. Life in a democracy with the newly acquired freedom of expression resulted in vividly imaginative times, making this a particularly creative period from the perspective of experimentation, inventiveness and rupture with an order that had been beset by conservativism, narrow-mindedness and ferocious censorship.

In the context of the PREC and the years that followed, the urban public space came to assume a central role at the level of political communication. Streets became a symbol of liberty, witnessing a nascent political vitality, not only on account of political demonstrations carried out by a number of parties, but also on account of the type of propaganda that in the meantime became institutionalized. City walls played an extremely important role, as attested by the small number of studies focusing on this question (Aurélio 1999; Caldeira and Marques 2009; Carmo 2011; Madeira 2012, 2015; Campos 2016, 2018).

Art, Politics and the Street

The 1960s and 1970s, particularly in France, saw the development of a solid philosophical and sociological thinking which framed the myriad debates around the role of art in society. The 'space', as a concept, was at the time an object of reflection, particularly when it came to its relevance to a reconceptualized take on society.

During the 1967 conference 'Des espaces autres' at the *Cercle d'études architecturales*, Michel Foucault sought to distance himself from the old conception of space,[4] which had dominated most of philosophical thinking until then. The author defended an understanding of space based on the dimensions that conferred it heterogeneity. This was also a geographical space, but one whose significance was premised on the living that was made in it, with the approach to the concept highlighting a conception of space that was mutable, active and relational, and ultimately social. Michel Foucault's proposed conceptualization was transversal to several authors – among them Henri Lefebvre and Michel de Certeau – and it expressed the conviction that our involvement with the world in great measure hinges on our spatial experience.

In the artistic context, the bridge between the work of art and space was consolidated in this same period from 'two different axes: one oriented by approaches to Space and the other oriented by approaches to Place' (Traquino 2010: 33). If, on the one hand, it is possible to conceptualize space as matter and as an individual location strategy, as proclaimed, for example, by the site-specific proposals at the time, on the other hand, it is possible to consider it as a strategy of experiential location, as put forward by other artistic conceptualizations of the same period, particularly those occurring in the urban space. In these, to the physical dimension of space was added a social dimension, which resulted in their transmutation into approaches to place (Cruzeiro 2014).

In 'The Practice of Everyday Life', Michel de Certeau (1988: 95) argued that the city was 'a place of transformations and appropriations, the object of various kinds of interference but also a subject that is constantly enriched by new attributes; it is simultaneously the machinery and the hero of modernity'. Henri Lefebvre's pioneering studies during the 1960s and 1970s focusing on the quotidian, cities and space, also had a major influence on several intellectuals, movements and artistic groups, including the CoBrA and the Situationist International.

In 'The Production of Space' – an essay in large measure inspired by the controversial urban restructuring of Paris and surrounding areas, published in 1974 – Henri Lefebvre considers the question of space from a conceptual triad, which he believes to be essential to any critical analysis of this theme. The first concept to be considered is 'spatial practice' which, as a concept, corresponds to the perception of space. The second concept is the 'representations of space', referring to a conceptualized space associated 'to knowledge, to signs, to codes, and to "frontal relations"' (Lefebvre 1991: 33). The last in the triad refers to 'representational spaces', which incorporate 'complex symbolisms' linked to 'the clandestine or underground side of social life, as also to art'. It is here that we must insert 'space as directly *lived* through its associated images and symbols' and also 'the space of "inhabitants" and "users", but also of some artists and perhaps of those, such as a few writers and philosophers, who *describe* and aspire to do no more than describe' (ibid.: 39, italics in original). The representational spaces thus reveal a space 'which the imagination seeks to change and appropriate. It overlays physical space, making symbolic use of its objects' (ibid.).

Each of the concepts that make up the triad established by Henri Lefebvre – spatial practice, representation of space and representational space – 'contributes in different ways to the production of space according to their qualities and attributes, according to the society or mode of production in question, and according to the historical period' (Lefebvre 1991: 46).

It is possible to argue that, in several European countries, the 1960s and 1970s were decades that saw an extensive proliferation of the arts in the public space and in the public sphere, as shown by the different processual artistic practices developed outside institutional art spaces. The theoretical development around notions of space and place, and also about artistic activism, allows for a philosophical framing of these artistic practices, giving them a consolidated reflexive foundation. Nevertheless, in Portugal, the main factor framing this issue is the political context. It is this that, before the revolution, characterized the artistic interventions in the public space, and it is also this that would roughly define it in the years following the 25th April. In practical terms, between 1974 and the end of the decade, the Portuguese context was driven above everything else by the political and artistic desire to narrow the distance between the people and the ongoing revolutionary process (PREC).

Political Murals and the Revolution

Throughout the twentieth century, the relationship between art and politics was a controversial, albeit recurrent issue. The politicization of art has often been expressed in disruptive forms of action – that is, in proposals whose aim is to challenge the ruling political and ideological powers (Sholette 2011; De Cauter et al. 2011). Even so, there are exceptions to this compromise – and these exceptions, at the level of participation, are in most cases rooted in revolutionary processes. And then, together with the political rupture the revolution represents – a disruptive process in and of itself – we often witness an active artistic participation and collaboration with the political powers. Examples of this include, among others, the October Revolution, the Cuban Revolution and the Portuguese Revolution. All these cases share a number of similarities in their process: an active participation in the emerging political system; direct intervention in society, ditching traditional forms of mediation and the traditional formats of exposition; and the recourse to collaborative methods of production, thereby extending the creative experience to non-artists.

In Portugal, the art critic Rui Mário Gonçalves, who actively experienced the entire Portuguese revolutionary process, stresses that 'it is within the institutional organizational domain, in teaching, in the creation of new dissemination models, in the demand for improved work conditions, in the search for influence over the means of decision, in the collaboration offered to new governments, etc., that artists and critics develop their generous activity' (Mascarenhas 2004: 6). But the activity linked to the institutional exercise of politics – through the inclusion of artists in government bodies and activities, or their inclusion in activities developed by political parties – does not exclude the existence of other levels of participation. In Portugal this was accompanied by a prolific and anonymous activity carried out by citizens, leading to a highly intense dynamic and intervention in the public space, which may be understood as being rooted in a tradition of activist art intimately linked to the history of social movements. As for intervention via murals, which achieved prominence during this period, both models are clearly represented.

Regarding government cultural politics, the Democratic Movement of Plastic Artists (MDAP), quickly established in May 1974 (Gonçalves 2004: 104), played an important role by maintaining a steady dialogue with the first democratic governments and by launching a series of artistic interventions in the public space. Apart from the performative initiatives they carried out,[5] the Journey of Solidarity with the Armed Forces Movement (MFA) that took place on 10 June 1974 at the Mercado da Primavera in Lisbon[6] was particularly important, and included different interventions in the fields of music, plastic arts and theatre. With regard to plastic arts, a collective painting titled '48 Artists, 48 Years of Fascism'[7] was executed by several plastic artists whose 'contagious power of creativity' (Gonçalves 2004: 110) prompted the attending public to contribute with some murals of their own.

On 6 November 1974, immediately after the official launch of the Campaigns for Cultural Dynamization and Civic Action of the MFA,[8] the MDAP confirmed 'their position of unity, understanding and active participation with the MFA in the process of cultural democratization of the country' (Correia and Gomes 1984: 145).[9] A month afterwards, the National Encounter of Plastic Artists took place at Palácio Foz in Lisbon. It is from this moment on that the revolution began to benefit from the official collaboration of several plastic artists and the Campaigns for Cultural Dynamization and Civic Action with the Plastic Arts section of the Central Steering Commission. Posters, calendars, CTT stamps, stickers, cartoons and brochures, flags, the exhibition 'Portugal – A Year of Revolution'[10] and, of course, murals, all purposefully aimed at kindling popular participation by means of pertinent collaborative methods during the course of these initiatives.

These Campaigns resulted in the creation of four murals in different cities – Viseu, Lisbon, Évora and Figueira da Foz[11] – where we saw 'a new conception of the work of art taking shape, now, as a collective act shared by the general public' (Almeida 2009: 115), whose goal was 'bringing people together' and where 'the end result, in artistic terms, takes second place' (Mascarenhas 2004: 7). In this respect, the most successful mural was created in Viseu as part of the campaign 'Revolution in March' (see Figures 10.1 and 10.2). This consisted of a mural of about 120 m² painted on the facade of a bank by artists from Lisbon and Porto (Correia and Gomes 1984: 147) complemented by a performance by the Army Band, and street clowns from the streets of Viseu. Hanging from scaffolding, the participating artists began painting the exterior facade of the building before the inquisitive eyes

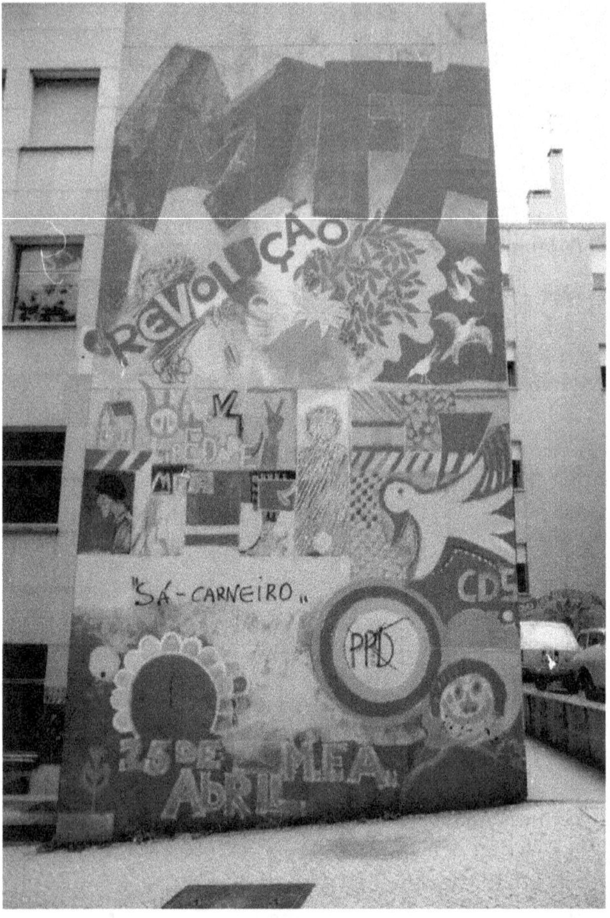

Figure 10.1 MFA's artistic mural (I), Viseu. © António da Paixão Esteves.

of the people; but, as the work progressed, there were many children and adults who gradually joined the artists, and added their own brushstrokes to the image on the wall. At the end, what came out of this mural was the collective experience, the integrating capacity of art, and the creative and imaginative will of the people.

The process of collaboration between plastic artists and the cultural dynamization initiatives of the MFA, premised on 'proposals working towards the replacement of aggressivity by creativity, engendering collective public activities with the participation of the people' (Gonçalves 2004: 38), was interrupted on 25 November 1975 by the counter-revolutionary

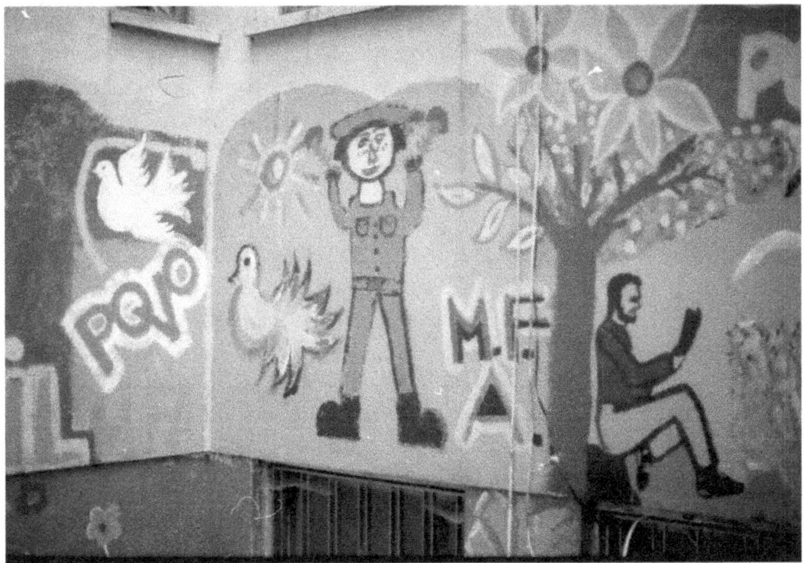

Figure 10.2 MFA's artistic mural (II), Viseu. © António da Paixão Esteves.

military coup that brought the Campaigns for Cultural Dynamization and Civic Action to an end.

The effortlessness of the implementation of collaborative methodologies and principles of popular participation led to the establishment of murals as a privileged means in other, non-governmental, fields of political and social action implemented both through party initiatives and popular motivation. Since April 1974, political parties, cultural associations, committees of residents, and so on have made use of this means on a variety of different initiatives. And here, too, art crossed paths with politics, albeit with a much wider variation of context regarding objectives and promoters.

Proliferating in public spaces, murals gradually developed from the revolution onwards without any expressive opposition to their existence, neither for being on the main road nor on account of its poor aesthetic quality.[12] When opposition occurred, it was triggered by ideological differences – reason enough for these paintings to develop into instances of social compromise and arenas of political expression. In order to avoid conflict, parties began occupying specific zones, particularly in the cities of Lisbon and Porto, thus avoiding the intermingling of paintings; this led to the emergence of 'own territories' occupied by the PCP,[13] the PCTP/MRPP,[14] the PS,[15] the UDP[16] and others. On the other hand, the mural movement easily developed into a collaborative enterprise. While, in some cases, these initiatives were planned from beginning to end, on other occasions they appeared as the result of spontaneous collaboration by the people, particularly when this involved party members or sympathizers with the party organization responsible for painting.

It is possible to say that the imaginary linked to murals followed the general trend of the country, giving voice to the revolution and current political events. So, to symbols alluding to the 25th April – the red carnations, the Chaimites, the painted battle cries such as '25 April Always, Fascism Never Again', 'The People are with the MFA', and 'The People United Shall Never Be Defeated', was added iconography alluding to the current Portuguese political period – the doves, the party iconography, the representations of human figures and popular masses, the symbolic representation of the proletariat and the capitalists (characterized by boiler suits and top hats respectively), and industrial symbols or slogans like 'Be Strong, Be Strong Companion Vasco, We Shall Be a Wall of Steel',[17] 'The Agrarian Reform Will Triumph', and 'Unity'.

Murals of a propagandist typology, linked to political initiatives, demonstrated a higher degree of planning and organization. When speaking of their propagandistic intent, we are aware that, often, the propaganda did not need to be inscribed into the composition of the mural through 'Vote' or other such indicators directly related to electoral activity. It is for this reason that one can say that 'painting more walls does not translate into more votes' (Vieira 2000: 124). The propagandist intention went way beyond the exclusive intent of gathering votes. The emphasis was much more on the clarification and dissemination of political ideas.

Although planning and composition might be contextualized in a broad spectrum of possibilities – where you may observe different methodologies and styles of work – when it comes to programming, murals are integrated into a wider propaganda strategy adopted as the tools and material of propaganda, comparable to the poster, the banner and the sticker. With the added advantage of being comparably low cost in terms of materials, and also being a very resilient medium, plus one that allows for a more localized intervention aimed at different populational strata, there are certainly enough reasons for its rapid proliferation in this context.

In more propagandistic paintings one can find particular identity features. These features, observable mostly due to their political messages, symbolism and visual language, represent the ideological stamp of each party, 'giving birth to what is known as mural schools, deriving from political movements' (Elias and Valente 2018: 92). But while it is possible to attribute aesthetic 'styles' to each party naturally seeking 'to affirm a political presence, from an aesthetic perspective' (ibid.), it seems more relevant to focus on the different methods and procedures, as these have also occasioned distinctive imagery.

Looking at the murals executed in Lisbon, you can see that those signed by the PCP, MRPP, PCTP (as well as the PCTP/MRPP), Aliança Povo Unido (PCP-MDP/CDE-PEV) and by the UJC are predominantly marked by drawing and creative painting, while the mural compositions made by the PS and PSD are not only less frequent, but mostly limited to the depiction of the party symbol.

On the other hand, the more creative or 'artistic' murals, while integrated within regular party activity, end up revealing distinct procedures, particularly when it comes to the contribution of plastic artists and anonymous militants toward their conception and execution. The MRPP, to give an example, was intensely concerned with the question of technical drawing, and following the political decision regarding the mural and theme, it was the graphics committee who developed the proposal. As to the execution, the project was transposed onto the wall through three methodologies: the stencil, the grid, and the direct intervention in plain sight. As such, mural paintings were considered a 'specialized' activity, and the responsibility of plastic and graphic artists.

By contrast, the PCP did not see murals as a specialized activity, even though they had several graphic and plastic artists as collaborators, thus opting for a collaborative model of production whereby militant artists and non-artists participated in a horizontal and decentralized fashion towards the conception and execution of the murals. As consequence, the technical or artistic design component was subordinated to the principle that 'muralism constitutes an opportunity' and a 'tool to give voice to the voiceless', and for that reason, the message should be subjacent to a collective creation paradigm in the production of the mural, which is open to any willing participant[18] (Elias and Valente 2018: 93).

The different ways in which murals were conceptualized by these parties resulted in distinct mediums and imagery. The replacement of an authorial production model for a horizontal collaborative one conferred a social stamp to the murals by the PCP which appeared reflected in its plasticity, creativity and aesthetic identity. Such an example is the mural created in Lisbon near the Torre de Belém. Conceptually simple, based on the partition of the support into two contrasting colours (a cold one – blue, and a warm one – red), the graphic elements and the text are harmoniously distributed, denoting the existence of notions of organization of imagery and expressivity.

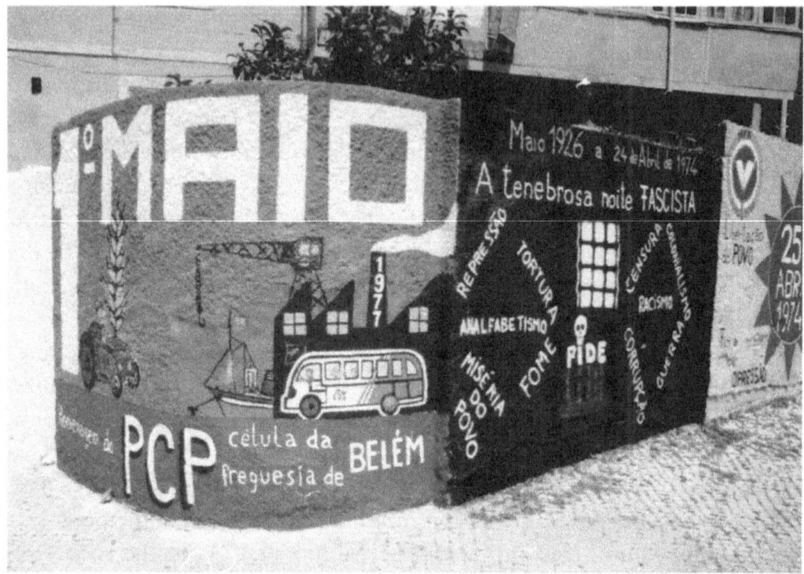

Figure 10.3 PCP's (Borough of Belém) artistic mural, Lisbon. © António da Paixão Esteves

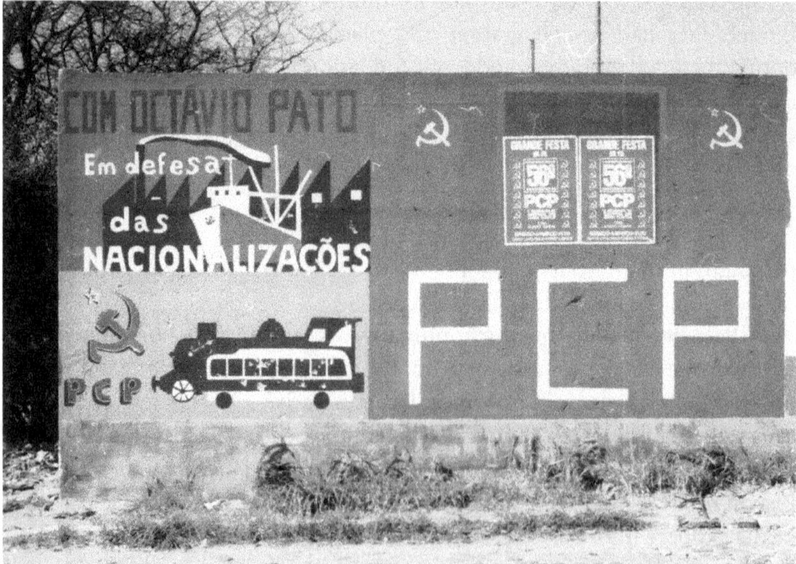

Figure 10.4 PCP's artistic mural with the slogan 'In defence of nationalizations', Lisbon. © António da Paixão Esteves.

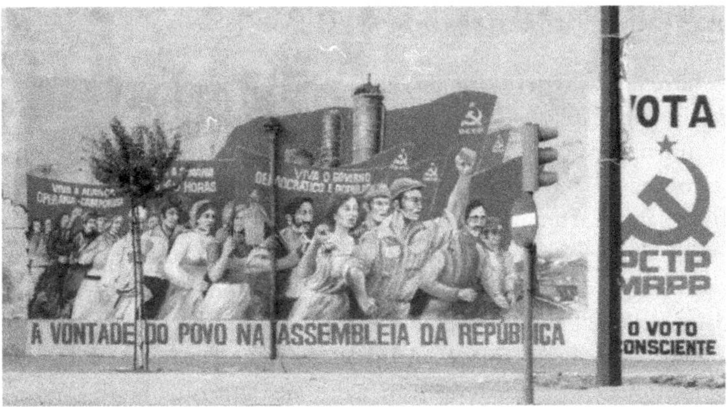

Figure 10.5 PCTP's artistic mural with the slogan: 'The will of the people in the Assembly of the Republic. Vote PCTP / MRPP, the conscious vote', Lisbon. © António da Paixão Esteves.

Even so, it becomes plainly obvious that the execution and the project were not carried out, at least not exclusively, by plastic or graphic artists – something made more explicit by the signature, with the creation of the painting being attributed to the PCP's 'Borough of Belém Wing' (see Figure 10.3). The same graphic elements – a factory, a ship and a bus – appear in another mural, also located in Belém, but this time near the CP station (see Figure 10.4). They are depicted in a very similar fashion, although the theme is different: the first one celebrating the 1st of May, and the second in support of the nationalizations, linking these to the candidate Octávio Pato.

The plastic solutions represented in these two murals, which in a more conservative approach might be considered 'naive', are in stark contrast with the mural created in Alcântara by the PCTP/MRPP (see Figure 10.5), where the involvement of plastic artists with experience in the representation of the elements depicted, and in the composition itself, is clearly noticeable.

We then reach the conclusion that, in this respect, the murals by the PCP mentioned in this text come closer to the paintings created in the context of the Campaigns for Cultural Dynamization and Civic Action. And if this approximation happens at the level of composition and aesthetic identity (see the example of Viseu, mentioned above), it also occurs at the procedural level. As these are murals resulting from a collective discussion, conception and execution, involving questions around message and visuals, the stamp they leave goes beyond the limits of painting, introducing a collaborative methodology that democratizes the creative and imaginary experience by extending it to a populational strata who usually lack easy access to it.

'Uncertain Concepts' and 'Wall Poetry'

As we have seen, the revolutionary period in Portugal was marked by political, social and also artistic manifestations lived out on the streets. Such an environment led to 25 April 1974 being described as the first example of 'anti-monument public art' in Portugal, meaning a period of collective creativity and participation that resulted in the progressive destruction and replacement of the symbols of the regime (including public sculptures) during the dictatorial period (1926–74) and in the emergence of a provisional iconography (Pinharanda 2005: 41). The streets of the main Portuguese cities and villages turned into living canvases in perpetual change. Together with the posters, paintings and murals, the walls gave voice to an anonymous 'writing' by the people, which extended to urban signage and traffic signs. Although closely related to the emerging social and artistic movements of the 1960s, in which the street became the site for new practices of political and artistic intervention, from Debordian Situationism in Paris, to New York graffiti and the mural culture in Mexico, this ephemeral iconography, which included a mixture of performance and visuals, developed in Portugal into a symbol of liberty of expression, communication and reflexivity hitherto banned. Where previously there existed blank walls and traffic signs of univocal meaning, now everywhere sprang up political messages – expressive actions by the political citizen, the ordinary citizen and the artistic class.

With regards to paintings of popular initiative, it is possible to identify, in a similar fashion to what occurred with institutional expressions, some particular features. As their main drive was generally linked to an individual desire to participate in the public debate of political ideas, these were, in most cases, interventions of a spontaneous, hasty and often impulsive character. In addition to that, in the context of this individual will, some murals expressed a propagandistic or even advertising intent, thus complicating the spectrum of intentions.

But if we observe the murals exclusively outside of these particular interests, which in fact constitute the majority, we immediately notice that the presence of the 'word' was more predominant than that of the 'picture'. That is, the people, not very familiarized with representation through drawings, in most cases made use of textual communication to pass their messages.

These are typical forms of protest in revolutionary periods in which the participation of citizens occurs also in an atomized, sporadic and ephemeral fashion, often without a direct link to the emerging political groups. These are technically undemanding, economical and rudimentary ways of demonstrating in the public space. This creative and communicative effervescing by common citizens also had an impact at the level of artists who, as we have seen, sought to actively participate and establish collaborative processes of artistic creation. What is more curious is that these anonymous endeavours and popular expressions served, also, as inspiration to artistic practices. It is, precisely, on the inspiration that the revolution brought to the arts that we will focus in the final section of this chapter, from the perspective of the visual poet, sometimes labelled 'experimental', E. de Melo e Castro.

This process of collective and anonymous street writing was analysed (and artistically reinterpreted) by Melo e Castro. His interest in this 'explosion of street visuals' developed from the close kinship he identified between these manifestations and actions inscribed in the public space, which altered the quotidian environment, with the artistic concepts that experimental and visual poets had been developing in Portugal since the 1960s. This relationship between art and the quotidian is articulated by the artist himself in a cultural television programme titled 'In Conversation with E. de Melo e Castro', which was dedicated to his work and was aired soon after the revolution, on 15 January 1975. The format of this programme involved a dialogue with the critic (and also artist) José Ernesto de Sousa, one of the main promoters of experimental art in the country at the time. The conversation took place on the streets of Lisbon and at the Buchholz Gallery, which had been hosting Melo e Castro's exhibition 'Uncertain Concept' since December 1974.

Using a wall covered in graffiti as a background, the artist presented himself as developing a poetic investigation, of lab scope, where he argued that following the 25th April, this 'lab' had expanded onto the street:

> I have been dedicating myself to visual investigations carried out in a lab. And following the 25th April this lab has opened up its doors and jumped into the street! It has jumped into the street in the violated traffic signs now displaying political messages. It has jumped into the street in the explosion of visuals that we encounter on the walls of Portuguese cities and along Portuguese roads; and as I often drive my car through these roads, I have had the opportunity to confirm the huge importance of many of the hypotheses and many of the investigations that my colleagues and I put forward in the sixties in the field of visuals. I could even say that the explosion of visuals post-25th April gives reasoning and joy … to all the experimentations that appeared somewhat disconnected from this context. The fact is that it was the context prior to 25th April that was disconnected from the true creativity of man. I believe this to be an extremely powerful message, which can be read on the streets, on the roads and on the Portuguese trails.[19]

Walking through the Portuguese streets, Melo e Castro was showing us how the revolution had opened up the doors to the creative expression of the *people*, leading to the development of a dialogue on the walls and traffic signs between revolutionary and reactionary political (over)positions regarding the revolution:

> We have here a very interesting example of two overlapping messages. On this wall in Lisbon, for example, we find a message from the Portuguese Communist Party, PCP, in red, and next to it the hammer and sickle, but anxious to distort this message, and wishing to make it non-communicative as well as filling it with noise, the reaction turned it into a jester and even drew a figure there. What happened here? It distorted absolutely nothing, it only served to show its true colours, as we can all still read PCP underneath and understand the distorting intent of the reaction. Further ahead, we encounter the same intent, the same PCP distorted – albeit not figuratively – with the same intention, in an abstract image, hastily done and in poor calligraphy.[20]

This reading of the signs expressed in graffiti, which he continued to develop in its several variants, not only served as inspiration for his exhibition 'Uncertain Concept', but it also facilitated the development of an analysis of the role of these inscriptions as a 'visual poem by the PEOPLE' (Castro 1977), named a 'visual spectacle' by Ernesto de Sousa, but, as argued in this television programme, also as an important 'signalling of the post-25th April history of Portugal'. He concluded the programme by stating:

> An investigation carried out in a lab is as important in the artistic as in the scientific fields. If many of us, poets from before the 25th April, put our efforts into lab investigations, which are in a certain way closed and hermetic to the general public, which it seems to me is what happened, the fact is that the conditions were not propitious for these investigations to be acknowledged or to acquire meaning in the country's cultural context, regardless of the weight and meaning they experience in all free countries and in all progressive countries.[21]

In a 1977 text written for the magazine *Colóquio Letras* titled 'Pode-se escrever com isto' (You Can Write with This), the artist once again takes stock of this post-25th April period, stating that the visuals that appeared in the streets via several different forms and methods, albeit with less intensity from 25 November 1975 onwards, could be systematized in the following way:

1. Signs, flags, banners and posters used in demonstrations.

2. Collective 'artistic' paintings on the walls and house facades, made by anonymous painters (laypersons) linked to political parties.

3. Posters of political parties, giving shape to massive mural effects.

4. Anarchist, proto-anarchist and surreal messages, usually critical or witty, but without graphic invention.

5. Interventions on traffic signs, taking advantage of, or altering their meaning, as signs of a code well known to all; or using these signs only as support.

6. Corrective or destructive intervention by political groups on inscriptions by opposition political groups.

He reiterates in this text that his analytical interest will centre on points 5 and 6, which are the expression of a popular visual poetry. However, in 1974 there were several art projects that also followed and reinforced this popular street movement, among which, and in direct alignment with this street expression, we would highlight the demonstration by the group ACRE,[22] who in August 1974 painted huge yellow discs on a wide stretch of pavement in one of the busiest streets of Lisbon.

Conclusion

The 25th April 1974 Revolution and the establishment of democracy brought about times of intense political dynamism following forty years of persecution and censorship. The expression 'Poetry is in the street' included in the posters of Maria Helena Vieira da Silva, and in the poem of Sophia de Mello Breyner Andresen, expresses the desire for intervention in the public sphere that emerged with the revolution and, moreover, that went way beyond poetry and art, extending across the whole of society. Apart from the emergence of a profusion of forms of artistic expression, often taking place on the street, the period from the revolution until about the end of the 1970s prompted a range of questions regarding the structure, formats, expositive models and methodologies of artistic production.

During this period, walls became one of the main political communication modalities in line with what had happened in other revolutionary contexts. Murals were used by left- and right-leaning parties, but mostly by the former. The left in Portugal was fragmented into several parties of variable sizes, and most of them used murals as a form of propaganda and politico-ideological dissemination. The approach we took in respect of the post-revolution mural expressions took into consideration, essentially, two frameworks that were common during this period: on the one hand, there were those we identified as actions of a more institutional and legitimized nature; and on the other, expressions by the people of a more spontaneous and non-official nature. The former concerned the models of political propaganda adopted at the time by the different institutional political actors. The latter point us to initiatives by those citizens who took to the streets and vigorously expressed their ideas, consolidating their recently acquired freedom of expression. The years following the revolution were marked by the presence of graffiti with political and ideological slogans, and murals carried out by many different kinds of groups and collectives. The innocent (naive) and vernacular character of many of these works is manifest.

Nonetheless, it could be argued that each of the above corresponded to a differentiated typology with regards to the visual and plastic approach and their goals: if the murals developing out of party initiative fulfilled an essentially propagandistic intent, the paintings generated by the people fulfilled the desire for popular expression articulated and recorded through 'words'. In any case, in both instances, what mattered was to have these inscribed onto the public sphere. The 'visualism' coined by the Portuguese poet Melo e Castro revealed the poetic, creative, chaotic, disruptive and unpredictable side of using the street, which became the repository of a multitude of messages in an explosion of 'voices' springing up from the establishment of liberty of expression after forty years of vigilance and censorship. This shows how, in this period of rupture and transition – and, consequently, experimentation – the public square came to assume a privileged role, sometimes for ideological and aesthetic battles, and at other times for poetic, narcissistic or innocuous elocutions, since the limits of these categories are not always well defined. It is for this reason that spontaneous, popular and vernacular expressions make sense not only for what they reveal in terms of their *content*, but also as forms of *action*. In this case, the action is one towards the liberation of the voice that had been silenced by decades of dictatorship, as we have seen happening in other contexts such as the fall of the Mubarak regime in Egypt (Abaza 2016). In these transition periods, the people are exorcizing the deposed regime through an attack on its symbols, while at the same time new communicative strategies to be used in the public space are explored, thus opening up the space for new themes, configurations and content previously banned or marginalized.

Although popular and anonymous expressions are extremely important, those that remained stored in the collective public memory were the murals, because of their impact on the cityscape and the grandeur that some of them displayed. In spite of their acknowledged historical and cultural value, they have gradually been disappearing owing to a manifest lack of interest by the public authorities in preserving them.

Acknowledgements

This chapter is the outcome of several research projects coordinated by the authors and supported by national funds through FCT/MEC (IF/01592/2015, PTDC/SOC-SOC/28655/2017 and SFRH/BPD/116916/2016).

Cláudia Madeira is an assistant professor and researcher at ICNOVA and an IHA collaborator at the Faculty of Social and Human Sciences of the New University of Lisbon, being responsible at both centres for the Performance Art & Performativity in the Arts cluster. She also collaborates at the CET/FLUL as a researcher in the Theatre and Image Research group. She has completed a postdoctoral programme in Social Art, Performative Art (2009–12) and holds a PhD in sociology on performing arts hybridity in Portugal (2007). In addition to several articles on new forms of hybridism and performativity in the arts, she is the author of *Hybrid: From Myth to Invasive Paradigm?* (Mundos Sociais, 2010) and *New Dignataries: The Cultural Programmers* (Celta, 2002). She teaches performance arts at the Department of Communication Sciences at NOVA FCSH.

Cristina Pratas Cruzeiro is currently a postdoctoral researcher at the FCT, the Portuguese national funding agency for science, research and technology, on the project 'Colaboração e Colisão: intervenção pública e política da arte' (Collaboration and Collision: The public and political intervention of art) at IHA-FCSH, Universidade NOVA de Lisboa. She is an integrated researcher at IHA-FCSH and an invited researcher at CIEBA – FBAUL, Lisbon, Portugal. She was an invited professor at the Faculdade de Belas Artes, Universidade de Lisboa, between 2008 and 2018.

Ricardo Campos holds a Graduation and Master's degree in sociology, and a PhD in visual anthropology. He is a researcher at CICS.NOVA – Interdisciplinary Centre of Social Sciences, Portugal. He currently coordinates two research projects: 'Artcitizenship – Young people and the arts of citizenship: activism, participatory culture and creative practices' (2019–2021), and 'TransUrbArts – Emergent Urban Arts in Lisbon and São Paulo' (2016–2020), both financed by FCT/MCTES. He is also co-coordinator of the Visual

Culture Group of the Portuguese Association of Communication Studies, and co-coordinator of the Luso-Brasilian Network for the Study of Urban Arts and Interventions (RAIU).

Notes

1. MFA – Movimento das Forças Armadas [Armed Forces Movement].
2. PREC – Processo Revolucionário em Curso [Ongoing Revolutionary Process].
3. When two rival factions clashed, resulting in the victory of the designated 'moderates', the 'Movement of Nine', led by army major Melo Antunes, considered an ideologue of 25 April, with all the right-leaning parties, PSD, CDS and the support of the Socialist Party, who put an end to the PREC.
4. Identified by Henri Lefebvre (1991) as a mathematical concept, this was exclusively based in a geographical understanding.
5. Such as the happening of 28 May 1974 at the Palácio Foz, which involved covering with black cloth and tying with ropes the statue of Salazar created by Francisco Franco, and the bust of António Ferro, affixing an inscription of the MDAP and distributing a communique explaining that the initiative represented 'both a symbolic destruction and an act of artistic creation in a gesture of revolutionary freedom. Fascist art is an eyesore' (Almeida 2009: 111).
6. The idea for this initiative, according to António Mendes, an artist mentioned in an article by Ernesto de Sousa, came up 'on the 1st of May, in the street, when a group of painters, recalling the experience that some of them had had recently in Cuba, suggested they should paint the walls of the Técnico' … From an informal initiative, the idea soon achieved a new structure, since, according to the same artist, 'After that, came the organizing phase … and we found ourselves (at least, I found myself) dealing with something very different from the initial idea. And I, who had joined a pure celebration, a party, found myself involved in a very serious "homage"' (de Sousa 1974: 45).
7. In the original, '48 Artistas, 48 Anos de Fascismo'.
8. The campaigns consisted of initiatives including sessions, projects and events organized throughout the country, with the aim of clarifying the revolutionary process and the responsibility of the population in the active participation of social and political change.
9. The collaboration between the MDAP and the MFA through the Central Steering Commission, '48 Artists, 48 Years of Fascism' (destroyed in the fire of August 1981), began on 10 June 1974 at the Galeria de Belém on the occasion of the painting of the great screen (Correia and Gomes 1984: 145).
10. In the original, 'Portugal – Um Ano de Revolução'.
11. According to Correia and Gomes (1984).
12. In this respect, Joaquim Vieira notes: 'No one dared to oppose the painting of an outside wall, because the very fact of it happening in the street granted an automatic right of use to the first group of political artists who decided to use it' (Vieira 2000: 124) .
13. PCP – Partido Comunista Português [Portuguese Communist Party].

14. PCTP – Partido Comunista dos Trabalhadores Portugueses [Portuguese Workers' Communist Party] / MRPP – Movimento Reorganizativo do Partido do Proletariado [Re-Organized Movement of the Party of the Proletariat].
15. PS – Partido Socialista [Socialist Party].
16. UDP – União Democrática Popular [Popular Democratic Union].
17. Vasco Gonçalves was the Portuguese prime minister in the II, III, IV and V provisional governments during the PREC.
18. Interview with Bruno Carvalho, 2017.
19. Statement by Ernesto de Melo e Castro on the TV programme 'In Conversation with E.M. de Melo e Castro', RTP, 15 January 1975. Retrieved 2 September 2020 from on https://arquivos.rtp.pt/conteudos/e-m-de-melo-e-castro/.
20. Ibid.
21. Ibid.
22. Group immediately formed in April 1974 by the artists Alfredo Queiróz Ribeiro, Clara Menéres and Joaquim Carvalho Lima.

References

Abaza, M. 2016. 'The Field of Graffiti and Street-Art in Post-January 2011 Egypt', in J.I. Ross (ed.), *Routledge Handbook of Graffiti and Street Art*. London: Routledge, pp. 318–33.

Accornero, G. 2014. 'O "25 de Abril": uma revolução nas ciências sociais'. *Ler História* 67: 171–77.

Almeida, S.V. 2009. *Camponeses, Cultural e Revolução: Campanhas de Dinamização Cultural e Acção Cívica do M.F.A. (1974–1975)*. Lisbon: Edições Colibri.

Aurélio, D. 1999. 'Mitos, murais e muros'. *Camões – Revista de Letras e Culturas Lusófonas* 5: 83–89.

Caldeira, A., and C. Marques. 2009. *Os murais de Abril*. Lisbon: CML.

Campos, R. 2016. 'From Marx to Merkel: Political Muralism and Graffiti in Lisbon', in J.I. Ross (ed.), *Routledge Handbook of Graffiti and Street Art*. London: Routledge, pp. 301–17.

———. 2018. 'The Crisis on the Wall: Political Muralism and Street Art in Lisbon', in I. David (ed.), *Crisis, Austerity and Transformation: How Disciplining Neoliberalism is Changing Portugal*. Lanham, MD: Lexington Books, pp. 109–30.

Carmo, A. 2011. 'Revolutionary Landscapes: The PCTP/MRPP Mural Paintings in the Lisbon Metropolitan Area'. *Finisterra* XLVI(92): 25–41.

Certeau, M. de. 1988. *The Practice of Everyday Life*. Berkeley: University of California Press.

Correia, R., and V. Gomes. 1984. *Livro Branco da 5ª Divisão 1974–75*. Lisbon: Livraria Ler Editora.

Cruzeiro, C.P. 2014. 'Arte e Realidade: Aproximação, diluição e simbiose no século XX'. PhD thesis. Universidade de Lisboa. Retrieved 20 March 2019 from https://reposi torio.ul.pt/handle/10451/15799.

De Cauter, L., et al. 2011. *Art and Activism in the Age of Globalization*. Rotterdam: Nai Publishers.

de Melo e Castro, E. 1977. 'Pode-se escrever com isto', *Colóquio Letras*, 32: 48-61.

Elias, H., and C. Valente. 2018. 'Da utopia à distopia: O mural como ferramenta participativa nos espaços públicos da cidade'. *Convocarte – Dossier Arte e Activismo Político* 4/5: 81–98.

Figueroa Saavedra, F. 2006. *Graphitfragen: Una mirada reflexiva sobre el graffiti*. Madrid: Ediciones Minotauro Digital.

Gonçalves, R.M. 2004. *Vontade de Mudança: Cinco décadas de artes plásticas*. Lisbon: Caminho.

Greaney, M. E. 2002. 'The Power of the Urban Canvas: Paint, Politics, and Mural Art Policy'. *New England Journal of Public Policy* 18(1). Retrieved 2 August 2020 from https://journals.library.cornell.edu/tmpfiles/CIAR_8_1_2.pdf.

Hawad, S., and B. Wagoner (eds). 2017. *Street Art of Resistance*. Basingstoke, UK: Palgrave Macmillan.

Lefebvre, H. 1991. *The Production of Space*. Oxford: Blackwell Publishing.

Madeira, C. 2012. 'The "Return" of Performance Art from a Glocal Perspective'. *Cadernos de Arte e Antropologia* 1(2): 87–102.

———. 2015. '"O que eu quero é uma revolução!": a performatividade de uma palavra de ordem'. *Cadernos de Arte e Antropologia* 4(2): 29–52.

Mascarenhas, J.M. 2004. *A cor de Abril*. Lisbon: Câmara Municipal de Lisboa.

Pedreirinho, J.M. 1979. 'Gapismo e política em Portugal: propaganda mural de 1974 a 1976'. *História* 13: 38–50.

Peteet, J. 2016. 'Wall Talk: Palestinian Graffiti', in J.I. Ross (ed.), *Routledge Handbook of Graffiti and Street Art*. London: Routledge, pp. 334–44.

Pinharanda, J. 2005. 'Monumentos em Lisboa de 1974 aos nossos dias: enquadramento teórico, político urbano', in *ArtePública – Roteiro Estatuária e Escultura de Lisboa*. Lisbon: Câmara Municipal de Lisboa – Pelouro da Cultura, pp. 40–47.

Sholette, Gregory. 2011. *Dark Matter*. London: Pluto Press.

Sousa, E. de. 1974. 'O Mural do 10 de Junho ou a passagem ao acto'. *Colóquio Artes* 19: 44–47.

Traquino, M. 2010. *A construção do Lugar pela arte contemporânea*. Ribeirão: Edições Húmus.

Tsilimpounidi, M. 2012. 'Athens 2012: Performances "in Crisis" or What Happens When a City Goes Soft?'. *City* 16(5): 546–56.

Vieira, J. 2000. *Portugal Século XX: Crónicas e Imagens 1970–1980*. Lisbon: Círculo de Leitores.

Waldner, L., and B. Dobratz. 2013. 'Graffiti as a Form of Contentious Political Participation'. *Sociology Compass* 7(5): 377–89.

Yanik, L. 2015. 'Humor as Resistance? A Very Short Analysis of the Gezi Park Protest Graffiti', in I. David (ed.), *Everywhere Taksim: Sowing the Seeds for a New Turkey at Gezi*. Amsterdam: Amsterdam University Press, pp. 153–84.

Zaimakis, Y. 2015. '"Welcome to the Civilization of Fear": On Political Graffiti Heterotopias in Greece in Times of Crisis'. *Visual Communication* 14(4): 373–96.

Chapter 11

Street Art in East Timor

Creative (Re)Constructions of Identity in Times of Crisis

Catherine E. Arthur

Introduction

East Timor (or Timor-Leste) is a small half-island in South East Asia, home to a population of around 1.5 million and a vibrant street art scene. The history of East Timor is dark, characterized by foreign occupation and conflict. First colonized in the early sixteenth century by the Portuguese, the East Timorese remained under colonial rule until 1974.[1] On 28 November 1975, the first government of the Democratic Republic of Timor-Leste declared independence, but mere days later, Indonesia invaded. The following twenty-four years of military occupation were characterized by violence, repression, mass human rights violations, and genocide. This recent history and the legacies of the conflict continue to haunt the nation today. Nonetheless, since East Timor regained its independence in 2002, the country has seen much brightness and colour in its streets. At a grass-roots level, messages of peace, love, national unity, and hopes for a prosperous future dominate street art, which combines bold images with written text. The visual representations of these concepts are framed within popular imaginings of national identity, and of East Timor as a land of hope and peace.

Yet, as a post-conflict, transitional society, there are prevailing challenges to overcome in the post-independence state. There have been instances of significant civil unrest and violence since 2002, and, notably, it is at times of political instability and crisis that new waves of street art appear. What is unique about street art in East Timor is precisely its apparent connection to times of crisis as an immediate response. Artists typically paint messages of peace, love and unity in reaction to violence, directly engaging with politics in a positive way and demonstrating how East Timorese street art disrupts assumptions of this medium as typically having illicit or negative connotations (see, for example, Gómez 1992; Ferrell 1995). This chapter explores how art has been used as a positive communicative tool in times of uncertainty to project messages of unity and peace. There are two key moments of 'crisis' in the first decade of independence that will be considered: the now infamous '2006 Crisis', and the post-election violence that took place in July 2012. In each of these moments of crisis, a series of murals and graffiti pieces were painted across the capital city, Dili, calling for peace in the midst of the chaos.

Contextualized by a discussion of 2006, the chapter will analyse a selection of pieces from 2012, contributing new case studies to existing scholarship on street art in East Timor (see Parkinson 2010, 2017; Ramos-Gonçalves 2012a, 2012b, 2013; Arthur 2015, 2016, 2019: 203–37). The authors of these pieces are artists from the Centro Arte Moris, which is a non-profit art school in the capital Dili (Arte Moris n.d.). These artists are males, typically aged over twenty but below forty, and they belong to the Geração Foun (the 'new generation'),[2] having grown up under the Indonesian occupation.[3] The cases from 2012 present key examples of cultural symbols that are invoked with the aim of fostering unity and peace through collective identification with a shared national heritage and identity. The symbols painted in 2012 – the *babdok* (traditional drum), the *Uma Lulik* (traditional house), and the crocodile – are all associated with an indigenous, precolonial cultural heritage that is unique to East Timor, and thus constitute markers of a perceived 'true' East Timorese identity.

The traditional, cultural representations of national identity offer an alternative to the official, institutionalized nationalism as promoted by the state, which is founded on the recent struggle for independence from Indonesia (Leach 2002, 2017). Whilst the national liberation struggle is a source of great unity through common identity, the way in which it has been commemorated since 2002 has also caused contention. There is unanimous respect felt for the struggle by all East Timorese; however, the focus in nation-building on valorizing its leadership and honouring veterans has rendered the process very exclusive. Commemorations of the recent past have divided East Timorese society along generational lines, with the contributions to the struggle of older resistance-era leaders celebrated and recognized, but those of the younger East Timorese resistance movements overlooked, resulting in the so-called 'generation gap' (Arthur 2016; Bexley 2007) – and the generational group that has been overlooked the most is the Geração Foun.

This chapter argues that street artists address this gap by invoking cultural icons and (re)presenting a more inclusive, cultural identity that resonates with the whole national community. This particular articulation of identity is powerful because it is seemingly disconnected from state politics, and transcends boundary markers of the generation gap in an attempt to foster national unity and legitimize the young artists' claims to nationhood.

The analysis focuses on the work and expression of a small group of artists from the Geração Foun, and therefore is not representative of the whole generational group. It does, however, offer insight into the shared grievances and hopes of these young people from those members who use urban spaces as their public, political platform and as a tool for agency. As this chapter will discuss, street art has become a creative political act, presented as seemingly apolitical art. Messages of love, peace and unity initially appear neutral; however, when contextualized in political turbulence, they become powerful acts of political activism. Any periods of political instability in the post-independence years have been rooted in partisan divides and party politics. Thus, street art that is visually removed from the political arena and does not reference such partisan politics appears to be apolitical at first glance, but it can simultaneously be seen as action taken.

Interestingly, the cultural symbols of identity featured in the 2012 street art are accompanied by visual and textual references to the Tour de Timor, a cycling competition and peace-building scheme that has taken place since 2008. The Tour de Timor is widely recognized as an important initiative that tackles numerous social and economic challenges of the post-independence state, and is in itself seen as a means of fostering national unity through sport. As such, in the wake of the 2012 post-election violence and in the weeks leading up to the cycling event that year, it is perhaps not surprising that it would be invoked in the art that followed. This chapter consequently examines how this contemporary sporting initiative was presented alongside symbols of an indigenous, cultural identity. In order to better understand the significance of these murals, it is necessary to first understand the nature of that identity and the origins of contemporary East Timorese street art. As a cultural product of the generation gap that emerged in the post-independence state, one cannot discuss street art without first contextualizing it within the early independence years, nation-building, and national identity construction.

East Timorese National Identity and Nation-Building

As a result of its long history of resisting foreign rule, the East Timorese nation identifies as one that has long suffered and fought to attain self-determination. It is this national identity, founded on the concepts of *funu* (struggle) and *terus* (suffering) in the name of independence, that has laid the foundations of post-conflict nation-building and that unites an inherently diverse people (Leach 2017; Arthur 2019).

Although this collective identity fosters powerful unifying bonds, the first decade of independence witnessed the emergence of numerous social divisions and conflicts in response to the challenges of state- and nation-building. One of the most prominent was the so-called 'generation gap', a divide along lines of cultural-linguistic differences, educational background, and recognized contributions to the national liberation struggle (Ramos-Gonçalves 2012a: 4). An older generation, raised under Portuguese colonialism, has been privileged as a result of its leadership of the national liberation struggle from Indonesia (1975–1999) and has subsequently held positions of state leadership since 2002. This so-called 'Generation of '75'[4] has institutionalized its Lusophone heritage and monopolized nation-building, constructing ideas of 'true' East Timorese-ness based on facets of their own identity (see Simonsen 2006). The younger Geração Foun, who grew up under Indonesia, have been marginalized from the nation-state as a result. Their linguistic capabilities in Bahasa Indonesia and their identification with aspects of Indonesian culture clash with the institutionalized heritage of their compatriots (see Leach 2003; Bexley 2011). This background is seen to delegitimize their membership of the nation because of the association with the most recent foreign occupier. Further, the Geração Foun's contributions to the independence struggle through various youth and student movements have been overshadowed by the political leadership of the resistance and its armed wing, the Forças Armadas para a Liberação Nacional do Timor Leste (Falintil), as the primary liberators of the nation (Bexley 2007: 86; Arnold 2009). Consequently, the Geração Foun has been faced with significant estrangement from their fellow East Timorese, coupled with limited future prospects in education and employment (see Jolliffe 2011).

The 'Generation of '75' has dominated national politics in the years following independence on the platform that their experience of leading the liberation struggle renders them suitable leaders in the present (da Silva 2008: 159–61). The institutionalization of a specific imagining of the national liberation struggle has consequently enabled this minority to enjoy continued legitimacy in the eyes of the population and, thus, electoral support (Kent 2011: 440–41). Parliamentary politics has been dominated by a select few former resistance leaders, and their support base draws on the respect that is widely held for those who suffered and led the fight for independence from Indonesia (see da Silva 2008: 161–67). In order to sustain popular support, the liberation struggle of the past is therefore often invoked in campaigning, in place of more prospective policies. As a result, diversity in political representation has been somewhat lacking, with few candidates to stand for the alienated, younger Geração Foun.[5]

Without adequate political representation or a formal platform in the post-independence state, the Geração Foun has turned to street art as a powerful representative and communicative tool. The under-represented can employ this typically illicit art form, often perceived as a 'voice for the voiceless' (Parkinson, cited in Storey 2013), to reach a large audience instantly. The messages in the murals are reactionary, and reflective of a highly politically-aware youth, and despite their difficult socio-economic and political circumstances, young muralists are positive and hopeful. Responding to the older generation's preoccupation with the past conflict and the struggle for independence, the young artists present an alternative viewpoint. The common themes, symbols and messages all project ideas of a positive, peaceful and prosperous life for their nation, and are largely focused on the future.

The fact that East Timorese street art typically communicates messages of peace, tolerance, stability, and national unity to a targeted audience is crucial. There is a sense of social responsibility felt by the artists towards their fellow East Timorese (Arthur 2019: 228), and this is evidenced in the content of their work during times of crisis and unrest. Artists from the Geração Foun make their voices heard and seek to have a calming influence on political tension, regardless of the nature of the crisis and despite the lack of a formal platform. The social and political critiques from the Geração Foun come to the fore and are made public, but in a positive and peaceful way.

Street art has emerged out of social and cultural conflicts, and crises of identification between generational groups. As a product of these divisions, it is interesting that it is during times of unrest that it becomes most visible. The two periods of political instability that took place in 2006 and 2012, and that saw much creativity in the streets, were very different. The 2006 Crisis was the worst period of violence since the end of the Indonesian occupation and saw an international peacekeeping intervention, whilst the 2012 post-election violence was troubling but it was resolved within a matter of days. Nonetheless, both periods were influenced by political divisions at state level, and both saw the capital city quickly covered in colour and positive imagery. It is not the scale of violence that prompts a reaction from street artists that is noteworthy but rather the fact that, at the first hint of disunity, the artists go out to promote peace and unity. Their 'go to' response to any violence is art promoting peace, as the following discussion will elucidate.

Turbulent Times: Periods of Political Instability in the Post-independence State

In order to fully grasp the significance of the street art that was produced in the wake of the 2012 parliamentary elections and subsequent violence, it is necessary to contextualize it and understand the precedent that had previously been set. Since the return to independence, the most significant period of political instability and violence was the so-called '2006 Crisis'. The crisis divided the nation along regional and political lines, posing a very real threat to the fragile peace and unity that had been established after 2002. In the worst period of violence since the Indonesian military left the territory, more than 150,000 people were internally displaced, thirty-eight were killed, and hundreds of homes were burnt down and destroyed over the course of two years (Goldsmith 2009: 122; Van der Auweraert 2012: 5).

The origins of the instability can be traced to tensions in governance at the state level, though a strike by members of the military in March 2006 is often cited as the first major event of the crisis (Richmond and Franks 2008: 185–86; Kingsbury 2007).[6] Hundreds of soldiers organized the strike to protest alleged discrimination that had taken place within the army. It was argued that older members of the military and those from the eastern regions of the country (known as *Lorosa'e*) had received preferential treatment, for example in relation to promotions, at the expense of soldiers from the west (*Loromonu*) (Grove et al. 2007). The regional divisions within the army were compounded by the allusions to respect gained through experience in warfare which, when contextualized in the recent past, relate to contributions to the national liberation struggle (see Leach 2017: 175–89; Arthur 2019: 23–25).[7] The social hierarchy that has been established since the return to independence, which places the older generation of resistance leaders and Falintil veterans at the top, was also felt to be present in the armed forces. Indeed, many of the older soldiers from the eastern districts had been Falintil guerrillas during the Indonesian occupation – a fact that contributed to their elevated status. Consequently, the soldiers on strike, known as 'the Petitioners', felt that not only were their career prospects limited but that the legitimacy of their membership in the national community had also been questioned, based on how their contributions to the liberation struggle were outwardly perceived (Grove et al. 2007; Arthur 2019: 23).

Within the same month, over six hundred of the striking soldiers were dismissed from service. Riots broke out, the armed police became involved, and the tense atmosphere escalated into widespread violence, civil disorder, and instability at the highest levels of governance. The East Timorese

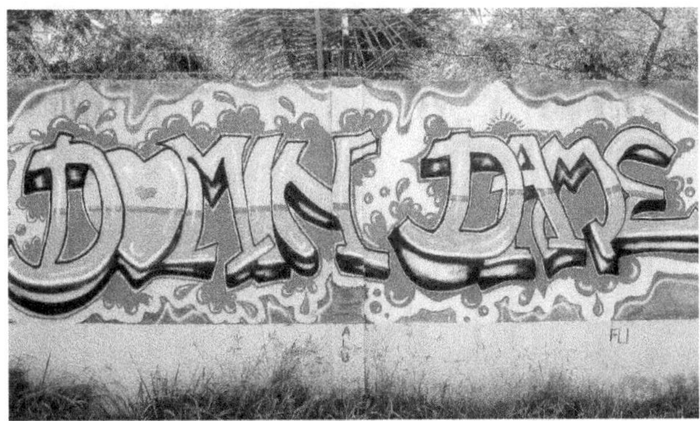

Figure 11.1 A piece from 2006 reading '*Domin Dame*' [Love Peace]. ©
Catherine E. Arthur.

government requested an Australian peacekeeping force in May 2006 following an open display of violence when members of the F-FDTL opened fire
on armed police, killing nine and seriously injuring over twenty (Goldsmith
2009: 121). This was followed by a United Nations Security Council decision to send in a new mission, the UN Mission in Timor (UNMIT), to
mitigate the unrest (Richmond and Franks 2008: 185). The violence of the
2006 Crisis affected the whole nation, from the hundreds of thousands of
displaced civilians to the state leadership. Before the internal conflict was
resolved in 2008, there had been two failed assassination attempts on the
lives of both the then president, Xanana Gusmão, and the acting prime minister, José Ramos-Horta (Babo-Soares 2012: 221–22).[8]

In the early months of the crisis, the response from artists of the Geração
Foun was practical, engaged and creative. A number of artists from the
Centro Arte Moris took to the streets of Dili to paint messages of peace,
national unity, and love. This was part of a project, designed by the artists
in collaboration with the East Timorese government,[9] that sought to diffuse
some tension and speak to the warring factions of their shared identity and
interests in a prosperous, peaceful future (Arthur 2019: 213–15).

The murals and pieces of street art of this project were typically brightly
coloured, the focus was very much on text, and messages emitted were
hopeful and positive. The language used was deliberately constructed to
present the young artists' ideas of national identity that transcends generational, regional and political divides, in calls for national unity through
messages of love (*domin*), peace (*paz, dame*) (Figure 11.1), and togetherness
(*Timor ida deit* [Only one Timor]; Figure 11.2) (Arthur 2015: 49–60).[10]

Figure 11.2 The image of a globe, covered in many different handprints, reading '*Timor 1 deit*' [Only one Timor], 2006. © Catherine E. Arthur.

Reflecting on the project that he had helped to instigate, then acting prime minister, José Ramos-Horta, noted:

> In 2006, whilst our country experienced the greatest social unrest since Independence … the young people involved [in the project] were given free reign to render the peaceful articulation of their hopes and desires, and while the text employed was direct and clear, the complete images were also beautiful; they brought some measure of light, colour and ultimately hope to streets [that had been] dark with foreboding at the time. (Ramos-Horta, cited in Parkinson 2010: 4–5)

At other points of crisis or political instability in the post-independence state, the response from the Geração Foun artists has been the same: to go out onto the streets and paint. Their works aim to bring about unity through common identification, as well as hope. This was evidenced in the graffiti and murals that appeared in the immediate aftermath of the 2012 parliamentary elections, the second to be held in East Timor since the return to independence.

The first elections of 2007 were conducted relatively successfully, despite the context of instability that lingered from the 2006 Crisis (Feijo 2012: 31–32). Although these elections had been monitored by the United Nations and deemed to be successful, the results revealed tensions between the two largest political parties: Prime Minister Xanana Gusmão's Congresso Nacional de Reconstrução de Timor-Leste (CNRT) party[11] and the Frente

Revolucionária de Timor-Leste Independente, or Fretilin.[12] Although Fretilin had secured the most votes, with 29 per cent of the mandate, it did not have a majority to form a government (da Silva 2008: 175). Gusmão and the CNRT then formed a coalition known as the Aliança de Maioria Parlamentar (AMP), which did not include Fretilin.[13] The AMP, led by Gusmão, was subsequently invited by the president to form the 2007 government (Leach 2017: 193). This perceived snub triggered ill feeling among Fretilin supporters, adding to an already tense political climate. Fortunately, the state leadership and Fretilin, acutely aware of the potential for violence, resolved to find a political solution to the issues, and further crisis was averted (ibid.).

The causes of discontent following the results of the 2007 parliamentary elections were somewhat mirrored in 2012. The electoral campaign period was again peaceful, characterized by the positivity and excitement with which the East Timorese people embrace democratic participation (Kingsbury 2012). The voter turnout was high across all districts, at an estimated 74.5 per cent (Feijo 2012: 48). However, once the votes had been counted and the results announced, the old discord between the CNRT and Fretilin reared its head. Gusmão's CNRT party secured 36.7 per cent of the vote and thirty seats in parliament, rendering it the largest party in 2012. Fretilin won 29.9 per cent of the mandate and twenty-five seats, which was an increase from its previous twenty-one seats (EUEOM 2012). Without an overwhelming majority, the CNRT was once again forced to form a coalition government, and it did so with the Partido Democrático (10.3 per cent, and eight seats) and Frenti-Mudança (3.1 per cent, and two seats) (Feijo 2012: 49–50).[14] Once again, Fretilin was excluded from the coalition government, meaning that the party faced a further five years outside of direct executive power.

Following the announcement of the new coalition government, indignant Fretilin supporters took to the streets of the capital and the traditional Fretilin strongholds of Viqueque and Bacau (Lopes and Morgan 2012; Feijo 2012: 52). The cause of the civil unrest and public disorder was, according to Fretilin supporters, the disrespectful and insulting comments made by the CNRT during the announcement of the new coalition, which had been broadcast live on television and radio. The violence lasted for several days, during which one person was killed, eight were injured (including four police officers), and dozens of cars and houses were either damaged or burnt out (Feijo 2012: 52; Leach 2013: 159).[15] Despite initial fears of further escalation, this period of post-election civil unrest was resolved within a matter of days.

In terms of the scale of violence, destruction, and loss of life, the unrest and political instability that followed the 2012 elections was far less serious than it had been in 2006. Indeed, the former was resolved very quickly, whereas the now infamous 2006 Crisis only subsided in 2008. The 2012 elections were largely successful, no peacekeeping forces were dispatched, and the UN presence that was still in East Timor at the time did not get involved – unlike in 2006. Nevertheless, of critical importance here is the initial response from street artists. In the days immediately following the 2012 election results, it was not clear whether or not the violence would escalate further. Indeed, there had been a precedent set for greater instability than actually transpired. It was during this period that the artists from Arte Moris went out into the streets of Dili and painted messages of peace and national unity in a call for calm.

When the national leadership publicly disagrees and political disputes are aired on a national level, a sense of insecurity and fears of instability inevitably arise. Regardless of the scale of violence or crisis, these artists see their role in the national community as a voice calling for peace when it seems to be threatened. Their art is their tool of advocacy for stability, utilizing public spaces and an alternative platform when the political elite and state leadership seem to be fractured and their relations tense. There is a clear sense of responsibility felt by members of the Geração Foun, who see themselves as having a vital role in the life and politics of the national community, despite having been alienated from the formal processes (Arthur 2019: 228). When contextualized in this way, the case studies of art that appeared in the wake of the 2012 post-election violence take on greater significance. The seemingly apolitical becomes political, and the positivity that typifies East Timorese street art is made more profound. Where the 2006 art project was heavily focused on text and communicative messages, the 2012 series of murals was more symbolic. An indigenous, cultural identity was invoked through traditional imagery, but alongside a more contemporary subject matter: the Tour de Timor.

Tour de Timor

In the post-election street art of 2012, an unusual theme was represented. This was the Tour de Timor, a five-day cycling competition inspired by the famous Tour de France, which is hosted in East Timor and open to international and national cyclists alike. The idea for a large-scale sporting competition was first implemented in 2004 with the Timor Challenge, which included canoeing and running as well as cycling. Following the great success of the Timor Challenge, a similar event was proposed for 2006, however it was cancelled as a result of the crisis. Two years later, in 2008, the Tour de Timor took place for the first time as part of the 'Dili City of Peace' campaign. This peacebuilding strategy sought to resolve the remaining issues of the 2006 Crisis and to overcome negative external perceptions of East Timor as having returned to the violence and insecurity of the past (Tour de Timor 2018).

Sport as a method for fostering peace in post-conflict contexts has been pursued by the UN, international non-governmental organizations and government partners for its numerous benefits, not only in relation to public health but to economic development, education, and peacebuilding (Kidd 2008: 373; Beutler 2008). Sport for Development and Peace (SDP) programmes have increased significantly in recent years on a global scale because of the perceived benefits. Indeed, in 2003 it was recommended that sports be supported as peacebuilding initiatives, and be better integrated into the Millennium Development Goals as set by the UN (Kidd 2008: 375–76).[16] It is perhaps not surprising, therefore, that in the worst period of violence since the return to independence, the East Timorese leadership looked to all available peacebuilding tools to address the conflict. The sporting event had been successful in 2004, and it provided an example of a peacebuilding initiative, without partisan associations, that could work.

During the 2006 Crisis, the divisions at the highest levels of government contributed to the atmosphere of insecurity and uncertainty that pervaded; consequently, any calls for peace and unity from the state leadership were perhaps perceived as hypocritical (Arthur 2019: 215). It is for this reason that alternative, non-state media were sought out to communicate with the East Timorese people and tackle the issues of disunity. These included the street art project with the Centro Arte Moris (Arthur 2015), and the 'Dili, City of Peace' campaign (which led to the creation of the Tour de Timor).

The mission statement of the Tour de Timor is clear in its advocacy of sport as a tool for peacebuilding: 'For Timor-Leste, sport is not just an exercise with social and health benefits, but a crucial tool in peace building, youth engagement, education, gender equality and economic development. In this way sporting events are also key to the well-being and livelihoods of the people of Asia's newest nation' (Tour de Timor 2018). The intentions behind the Tour de Timor cycling race are multifaceted and speak to wider social issues within peacebuilding and governance that remain pertinent in the post-independence state. On the official website, it is stated that: 'The Dili, City of Peace Campaign had environmental, peace building, poverty reduction and sporting events all simultaneously ongoing that were conducted in the capital and across the nation in all thirteen districts from 2008 until 2012' (ibid.). The objective of national unity through peacebuilding initiatives is underlined; it is suggested that without a connection across the thirteen districts, there could be no real national unity or peace. In primary research conducted in East Timor in 2013 on sport as a tool for social cohesion, Daniel Ahlm and Johanna Lindgren found that the Tour de Timor was perceived by local East Timorese as a positive example of fostering a sense of national unity across the districts. Moreover, the study found that the international aspect was seen as an effective way of presenting East Timor as a peaceful nation-state to the international community (Ahlm and Lindgren 2013: 38).

Given that voting patterns are played out by region and district in East Timor, this is an important factor to consider in the context of the partisan divisions of the 2006 Crisis and 2012 post-election violence. Irrespective of one's voting preferences, the Tour de Timor is a national scheme that has been widely acknowledged as being positive for both building peace within the national community and for fostering positive relations abroad. The fact that this sporting event has enjoyed support from both the East Timorese national community and external actors suggests that this has been a particularly successful peacebuilding initiative. It is perhaps for this reason that, in the weeks leading up to the 2012 competition, the Tour de Timor was invoked in the street art that followed the parliamentary elections of the same year.

The cycling event has itself become entwined with notions of peace and unity within the national imaginary, and its logo is therefore a symbol that has been given specific meaning by the artists in this way. The Tour de Timor logo is a triangle composed of red, white, yellow and black segments, mirroring the national flag of East Timor. In the following case studies, the logo is repeatedly incorporated into the murals, and the message that is emitted consolidates the connection between these ideals, framed within a uniquely East Timorese cultural identity.

Culture, Sport, Peace: Reconceptualizing an East Timorese National Identity in 2012

Within theories of nations and national identity, Ethnosymbolism posits that collective identification is possible through mythic, cultural artefacts and traditions, and this subsequently leads to national unity. As Anthony D. Smith summarizes, nations are 'cultural communities, whose members [are] united, if not made homogeneous, by common historical memories, myths, symbols and traditions' (Smith 1991: 11). By depicting cultural icons of precolonial Timor as a foundation of identity, the artists of the Geração Foun tap into a powerful source of symbolic power. Cultural symbols that represent such 'memories' and 'myths' are powerful, instigating positive

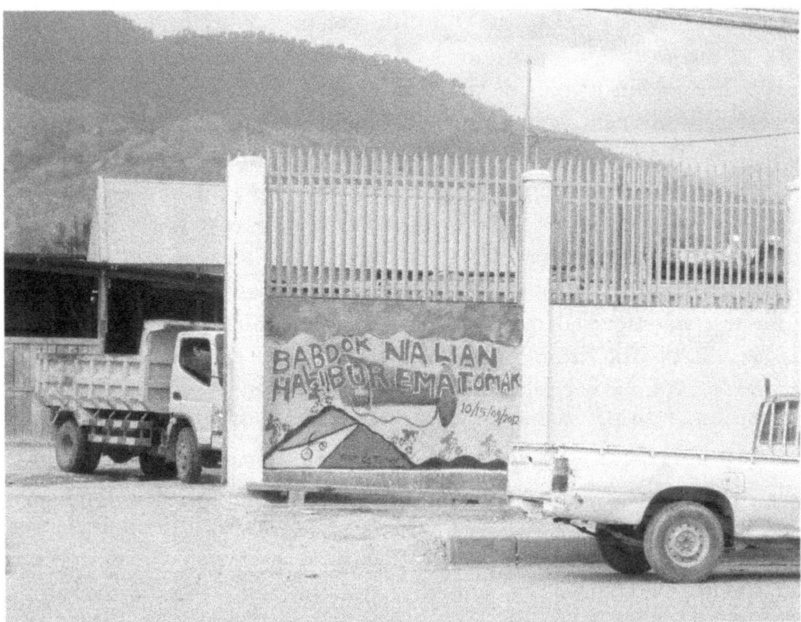

Figure 11.3 A piece in western Dili, reading '*Babdok nia lian halibur ema tomak*' [The sound of the babdok gathers the whole people together]. © Catherine E. Arthur.

identification as a nation with a shared heritage when evoked. This particular evocation simultaneously depoliticizes East Timorese nationalism, presenting an identity that is not defined by foreign occupation or the national liberation struggle (factors that have characterized nation-building and entrenched the generation gap). In doing so, the young artists' claims to nationhood and articulations of national identity can be legitimized, and by transcending the generational divide, greater national unity can be achieved. Indeed, the specific cultural images chosen for this series were perhaps incorporated precisely because they are not connected to party politics.[17] Focused primarily on images, several murals from the 2012 art series contained symbols of cultural identity and heritage, and pictorial references to a precolonial past.

The above photograph (Figure 11.3) was taken on 23 July 2012, one week after the CNRT party had announced its new coalition government, and thus mere days after the unrest had concluded. This mural-style piece was situated on a wall to the west of the capital, Dili, on a road leading out towards the Comoro area, traditionally a Fretilin stronghold and the site of much of the post-election violence (Lopes and Morgan 2012). This example is typical of East Timorese street art: the colours are bright, and are reflective of the artists' preference for bold, eye-catching images (Arthur 2019: 216). The colours of the Tour de Timor logo (and of the national flag) are especially prominent, connecting this art and message to the peacebuilding initiative. The connection to the Tour is further strengthened by the five stencilled cyclists that appear towards the bottom – cycling up and over the Tour de Timor logo itself – and by the textual reference to the cycling event.

At the centre of this piece is a depiction of the *babdok* (sometimes *baba dook*) and text. The *babdok* is a drum that has been integral to East Timorese traditional dances such as the *tebedai* for centuries (see Siapno 2012: 435).[18] The drum and *tebedai* dance are often used in ceremonial contexts and holiday celebrations. The text to accompany this image reads: '*Babdok nia lian halibur ema tomak*' [the sound of the *babdok* gathers the whole people together].[19] The depiction of a traditional drum invokes music and dancing that are widely known and celebrated as unique to the nation of East Timor, so much so that it needs to be preserved. Ethnomusicologist Ros Dunlop notes that the traditional musical instruments of East Timor are imbued with social and cultural significance, and that they constitute part of '[a] hidden culture, and its survival is precarious' (Dunlop 2013). Art scholar Leanor Veiga notes that ideas of a precolonial culture and heritage are central to artistic expressions of identity in post-independence East Timor. She asserts that many artists share a common desire to express their identity but look to a more distant past than that which typifies an institutionalized, resistance-era notion of 'true' East Timorese-ness: 'We look at these symbols … because in them lies *the true Timorese identity, which is prior to Portuguese times*' (cited in Veiga 2015: 92–93; emphasis added). The *babdok* thus becomes representative of not only traditional East Timorese music and dance, but also of this cultural side of a precolonial, indigenous national identity that is unanimously accepted and celebrated as 'true', and which does not discriminate along generational or partisan lines.

In this way, the image of a musical instrument can be understood as representative of a truly unifying East Timorese ethno-cultural heritage. Just as dancing and music are social activities that physically bring people together (literally in a circle for the *tebedai*), allusions to a national, ethno-cultural identity bring people together in imaginings of collective identity and nationhood. Within this sense of togetherness and unity, peace can be facilitated; if social divisions along generational, regional or partisan lines are causes of tension, then the celebration of commonality and identity is a logical means of resolving it. Allusions to fostering peace through cultural and recreational practices, such as music and dance, are further compounded by references to the Tour de Timor as a modern, successful internationally-recognized peacebuilding initiative. The art produced in 2012 offers insight into the creativity of East Timorese artists, who fuse the past with the present – precolonial culture with post-independence peacebuilding – under the common theme of national unity.

Veiga argues that 'despite the essentialism of this affirmation, the Timorese believe that it is important to look to the past to affirm their sense of identity' (Veiga 2015: 93). Crucially, artists from the Geração Foun look to represent a 'true' articulation of identity: one that predates any foreign occupation and that is depoliticized through a lack of association with official notions of nationalism and nation-building. Imaginings of a precolonial, 'true' East Timorese national identity is seemingly apolitical in that it predates all contemporary political differences and divisions. However, the act of painting such images in times of crisis is itself a political act by engaging and seeking to diffuse tensions. It is for this reason that cultural symbols such as the *babdok* (and the *Uma Lulik* and crocodile) appear in street art during this period of instability in East Timor; the young artists use these public spaces to express the national identity that they feel is 'true', to actively promote a more inclusive nationalism than the one promoted by the state, and to foster national unity and stability.

The image of the sacred house, or *Uma Lulik*, is another instantly recognizable cultural icon in East Timor. These *uma* are commonly found in rural areas but are universally recognized throughout the country; they are traditionally made from wood and bamboo, with thatched pyramidal roofs (see Figure 11.4). In the above image, the sacred house is a focal point, superimposed on the Tour de Timor logo and accompanied by the event name. The visual references to the Tour are clear in the small stencils of cyclists, as also seen in the previous example. The associations of the cycling competition with peacebuilding are made more explicit in the text, as the second letter of the word 'Tour' is presented similar to the famous CND peace symbol.[20] Surrounding these focal points are swirls of vibrant colours and a backdrop that resembles the mountainous landscape of East Timor. At first glance, this piece may seem to be a simple combination of cultural icons and a reference to a popular sport and peacebuilding initiative. However, upon closer analysis of the symbols within an East Timorese cultural context, they reveal significant insights into the motivations behind the piece, and a deeper understanding of identity and unity in post-independence East Timor.

Sacred houses have been important markers of kinship, clan, and ethnic identity since before the Portuguese colonized the half-island (see McWilliam 2005: 28).[21] For centuries, the *Uma Lulik* has been the site of ritual and the place where ancestral *lulik*s (sacred objects) are held.[22] Popular associations

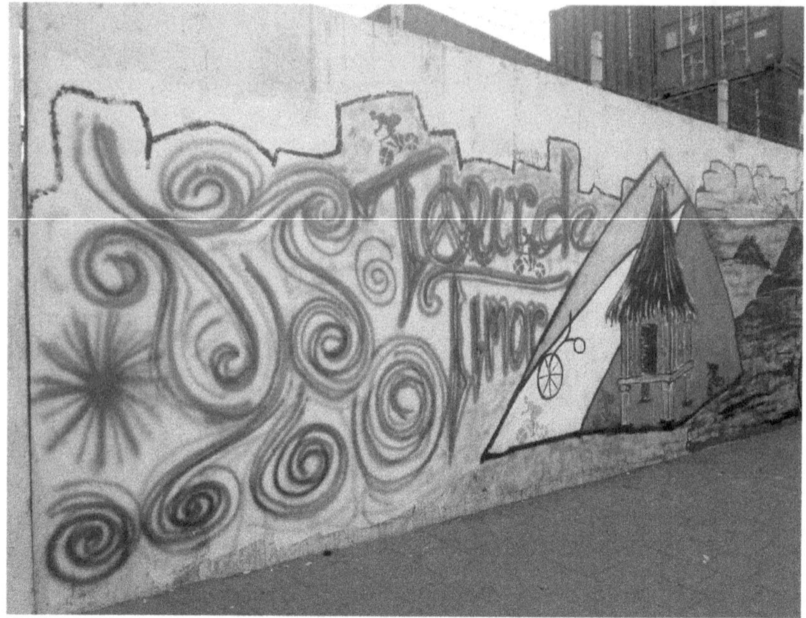

Figure 11.4 Piece in Dili city centre, depicting the traditional sacred house (*Uma Lulik*) and the Tour de Timor logo, 2012. © Catherine E. Arthur.

of the houses with spirituality connected to a unique East Timorese cosmology (see Bovensiepen 2011, 2015), combined with a sense of family and connectedness, have made the *Uma Lulik* a powerful symbol of cultural and national identity. The houses have become representative of a rich heritage of tradition and custom that remains untouched by foreign influence. Their symbolic power and popular appeal are attested to by their inclusion in posters, banners and symbols used by political parties in election campaigning as a strategy to garner votes (for example, see Arthur 2019: 185–89).

The contemporary significance of this cultural symbol has arguably increased in light of the recent past. Immediately following the 1999 UN-sponsored independence ballot, the Indonesian military and militia gangs waged a campaign of violence and destruction that saw 95 per cent of buildings, roads and homes in East Timor reduced to rubble (see Chopra 2000: 27; Chawla 2001: 2293). As part of this campaign, the traditional *Uma Lulik* houses were specifically targeted and burnt to the ground, with the ancestral sacred objects inside (McWilliam 2005: 28; Traub 2000: 80). Among the other acts of violence, the burning of the sacred houses in particular was an attack on the cultural heritage and identity that had distinguished the East Timorese people from the Indonesian occupiers – a primary argument in the case for independence. As Andrew McWilliam notes, the burning of the houses was 'yet another example of the desire to attack and erase a symbolic source of Timorese resistance' (McWilliam 2005: 28).

It is not therefore surprising that since self-determination was officially obtained in 2002, many communities across East Timor have rebuilt their *Uma Lulik*s (McWilliam 2005: 27–28; Bovensiepen 2015: 85–89). This has been a statement of affirmation at a grass-roots level of the continued importance of the houses to familial, ritual, social and cultural life, but also of their embodiment of aspects of East Timorese-ness. This cultural icon 'remains an important and central component of social and ethno-linguistic identity' (McWilliam 2005: 39). It was therefore no coincidence that the reconstruction of the houses took place at the same time that nation-building processes were underway.[23] Within the context of mass reconstruction of sacred houses across the country, together with processes of nation-building, the popular appeal and familiarity of this cultural symbol is evident. Pictorial representations of the *Uma Lulik* evoke notions of kinship within popular imaginings, alluding to the idea of the national community as family – a powerful nationalist trope.[24]

The significance of this symbol was reaffirmed in the street art from 2012, and, interestingly, its inclusion was not a new idea. In the 2006 project, the artists included this image in bright, colourful pieces that referred to national unity. Chris Parkinson's collection of street art from the period, *Peace of Wall*, includes an example of an *Uma Lulik* accompanied by the words: '*Timor messak ida deit. Cultura Timor*' [Timor is one. Timor culture] (Parkinson 2010: 163).[25] Parkinson's image from 2006 made the connection between the house and imaginings of nationhood and unity visible, and the accompanying text made it explicit. It was a timely reminder to a divided society in the midst of violence and crisis that there is a rich cultural heritage and identity that all East Timorese share, and through identification with it, national unity and peace are possible.

Consequently, when the *Uma Lulik* reappeared in the wave of street art that emerged following the 2012 parliamentary elections, the association had already been made in the popular imaginary. Once again, the positive sentiments and call for peace and unity in times of crisis and unrest are clear, presented creatively in imagery that is familiar to all, and integral to popular imaginings of identity and heritage. By depicting symbols from an indigenous, cultural identity, the artists of the Geração Foun again reassert imaginings of nationalism that they see as being more inclusive, whilst remaining 'true'. Allusions to precolonial traditions of Timor, in the *babdok* and *Uma Lulik*, are not related to foreign occupation or the national liberation struggle, and they precede all contemporary social divisions. Painted in times of political instability and crisis, these powerful symbols can diffuse tensions, and can appeal to all East Timorese across divisions of generation and party politics. Thus, in seemingly apolitical art, the young artists perform political activism that comes from the sense of social responsibility that they feel, despite their alienation from the nation-state.

The crocodile is a further symbolic representation of a mythic, precolonial culture and a 'truly' East Timorese heritage in street art. Whilst the symbolic meaning behind this image may not be immediately apparent to an international audience, the crocodile has very clear significance to the East Timorese national community in terms of creation myths and the origins of the island of Timor itself. There are various versions of the story in which the island of Timor was created (see McWilliam 2002: 10–12), each centred on the crocodile and invoking supernatural powers. As Amanda Wise attests, 'the crocodile is the most important symbol in the Timorese creation myth. The island of Timor is said to be shaped like a crocodile' (Wise 2006: 211). The most popular version of the origin myth, which is widely told to small children, recounts the tale of a crocodile who was sick and stranded on land.[26] Near death, the crocodile was saved by a little boy who returned him to the sea. The crocodile befriended the boy, and to repay his kindness, took the little boy on journeys across the sea to explore the world. When it came time for the crocodile to die naturally, he turned his body into a beautiful island for the young boy and his descendants to live on, as a token of gratitude and friendship (see ibid.). According to the myth, this constituted the creation of the island of Timor, and as such, this animal has become inextricably tied to an East Timorese cosmology, folklore, cultural heritage, and identity.[27]

In light of this, motivations for the use of the crocodile as a unifying symbol in times of division and instability is evident. Its appearance in the 2012 series of street art is logical alongside other ethno-cultural symbols that represent an indigenous, precolonial and 'true' East Timorese national identity. The photograph above (Figure 11.5), taken in 2012, depicts a large crocodile as the focal point. It sits on top of the text, '*Tour ba paz*' [tour to peace], and beneath the logo of the Tour de Timor. The backdrop consists of large swirls of aerosol spray paint in the colours red and yellow, alluding to the colours of the national flag, with blue beneath the text to represent the sea from whence the crocodile came.

The visual reference to the Tour de Timor associates the young artists with the state-sanctioned and internationally recognized peacebuilding initiative. Thus, even though they are not fully represented within national politics,

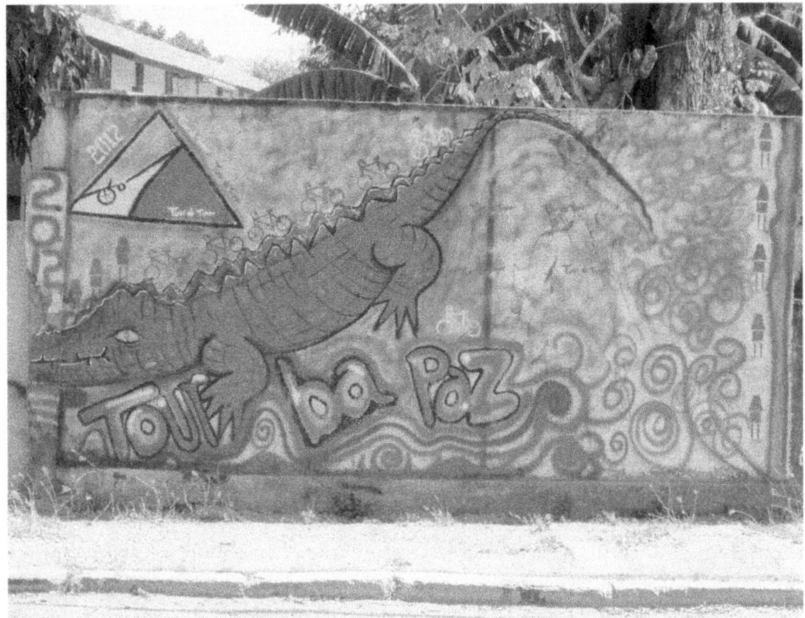

Figure 11.5 A piece featuring the Tour de Timor logo, an image of a crocodile and the words '*Tour ba Paz*' [Tour to peace], 2012. © Catherine E. Arthur.

the artists from the Geração Foun use public spaces to identify with the positive efforts towards peace that have taken place in the post-independence state. By appropriating cultural symbols and the Tour logo, they unofficially promote and support the initiative, and develop popular imaginings of peacebuilding, fusing them with icons of an ancient, cultural identity. Thus, visually distanced from national politics and partisan tensions, the artists are able to make an 'apolitical' statement. Embracing the responsibility that they feel as members of the national community, the Geração Foun artists actively and creatively communicate with their fellow East Timorese, and advocate for unity and stability at a time when the state leadership itself is fractured. By taking advantage of the instant and public nature of street art, the artists make their voice distinctive and heard.

Peace is possible when social divisions are overcome, and in the image of the crocodile it is possible to foster unity through widespread collective identification with this symbol. This is not the first time that the image of the crocodile has appeared alongside messages of peace in East Timorese street art. In Parkinson's *Peace of Wall*, he documents a mural of children sitting on the back of a crocodile, accompanied by the text: '*Hey, hare ba dame to'o tiha ona iha Timor Lorosa'e*' [Hey, look, peace has arrived in East Timor] (Parkinson 2010: 166).[28] The allusion to the creation myth is represented by the children sitting on the crocodile's back, reminding the audience that this animal then became their homeland. Again, the role of text in East Timorese street art is crucial to its impact and meaning, as it is a primary communicative tool for artists from the Geração Foun. The message announces that peace has finally arrived on the island, after a violent and difficult struggle for independence. Affirmative messages help to influence reality, and the inclusion of text facilitates the idea of Timor as a land of peace in the popular imaginary. Such images and text gained heightened significance when contextualized in the midst of crisis. The symbolic and cultural significance of this image, as a powerful unifying force, was great enough in the eyes of the artists for them to reproduce similar art in the 2012 post-election series.

Although the focus of the piece is again on the image, rather than text, there is much insight to be drawn from the short phrase painted. Considering the precedent set by the 2006 street art project, which largely focused on text, it is important to give this language critical attention because the messages presented in art are deliberately constructed with a specific, public audience in mind. The tagline is a play on words, where the word Timor has been replaced with the word for peace, '*paz*', and the Tour de Timor cycling event is given a new name. The significance of this wordplay is arguably twofold: first, it could simply be seen as promotion of the upcoming cycling tournament, but highlighting the nature of this peacebuilding initiative. Second, it could be understood as a more direct social commentary – a call for peace and a critique of those engaged in the post-election violence. The text suggests that the two words are interchangeable, that East Timor is an inherently peaceful place that has left behind its history of violence and conflict. For such a sentiment to appear in the streets of the capital city in the middle of riots is potent, and signifies a call for protestors to refrain from violence. It is a reminder that peace has become an important part of East Timorese-ness in the post-independence years (Arthur 2019: 171–73), and that anyone who identifies as such should act on this.

As a visual representation of an origin myth, the crocodile traces an East Timorese identity to its very beginnings, long before any foreign occupation, and thus it is a symbol that can be considered as 'truly' East Timorese. Its unifying power has great potential to transcend social and political divisions, and enable positive identification across the national community. As such, it was a powerful image to paint at a time when the fear of violence was very real following the elections.

Conclusion

Street art in post-conflict East Timor is unique in its message and use as a communicative and political tool. Adopted by artists from the younger Geração Foun, alienated from their fellow East Timorese by the exclusivist nation-building project that has entrenched the generation gap, street art offers them a public platform to have their voices heard. It enables them to publicly (re)construct and (re)present alternative notions of East Timorese-ness to the existing official, institutionalized nationalism – specifically, a precolonial, indigenous cultural identity that precedes all contemporary social divisions that have persisted in the post-independence state. This is not only an attempt to overcome the generational divide (and so to include their generational group within legitimate ideas of nationhood), but it is also an effective and creative way to call for national unity and peace. Furthermore, these artists demonstrate their willingness to act on a sense of social responsibility and use their work as a means of fostering peace and unity in this transitional society. It is arguably for this reason that street art activity peaks at times of political instability and crisis.

In 2006, the national political crisis saw the worst violence and unrest since the East Timorese nation regained its independence. In the initial months of this crisis, there was a street art project dedicated specifically to calming tensions, communicating messages of peace and unity, and trying to provide a voice of reason in the midst of the chaos. Similarly, in the post-election violence of 2012, and before it was clear how far the violence would escalate, the artists took to the street again. While the 2006 project was more focused on text and the written message, the art from 2012 was dedicated to representing cultural symbols of identity and heritage, combined with allusions to the Tour de Timor sporting event taking place that year. Such apolitical symbols of culture and sport were invoked in 2012 to foster unity and subsequently peace through common collective identification as simply East Timorese. The neutral nature of these symbols – the *babdok*, *Uma Lulik*, and the crocodile – is suggestive of a marginalized youth seeking to identify with those aspects of East Timorese culture and heritage that are not explicitly tied to state-sanctioned notions of nationalism (a root cause of the generation gap) in an attempt to overcome it. In this way, the street art scene in East Timor provides a vibrant visual representation of complex, ongoing processes of identity construction, nation-building, and social relations, especially in times of crisis when a clear message would perhaps otherwise be lost in the chaos.

Street art, in its various forms, is deserving of more rigorous analysis, and especially in post-conflict contexts. As a social and political commentary on an urban space, street art's ability to act as a potential indicator for increased tensions or periods of instability renders it a more useful and insightful tool than mere vandalism – or even art for art's sake. In post-conflict settings, it takes on a heightened importance and its additional communicative, representative and influential roles warrant further scholarly consideration. Apolitical art becomes political activism, especially within the context of crisis.

Catherine E. Arthur is a lecturer in peace and conflict studies at the Humanitarian and Conflict Response Institute at the University of Manchester. Her research areas include nations and nationalism; peace and conflict studies; postcolonial and post-conflict nation-building and reconstruction; political symbols and identity; ethno-nationalist conflict; and peacebuilding. Dr Arthur's regional expertise is particularly focused on East Timor and Northern Ireland.

Notes

1. In the power vacuum that followed Portuguese decolonization, there was a brief but bloody civil war. For a summary of this period, see Andrea Molnar (2010: 25–45) and Constâncio Pinto and Matthew Jardine (1997: 13–16).
2. The artists with whom I spoke during my fieldwork in Dili all identified as members of the Geração Foun in terms of their age and their cultural and educational backgrounds.
3. This information was gathered during my fieldwork and in personal interviews conducted with the artists in 2012. It should be noted that there is a marked absence of women in Dili's street art scene. Although one of the instigators of the so-called '*Movimentu Kultura*' (cultural movement) in East Timor, Maria Madeira is the sole East Timorese female artist of prominence who practices fine art rather than graffiti and urban art at the time of writing (Veiga 2015: 95). It should be noted, however, that the artists from this school have expressed a desire to continue teaching art and encouraging fellow East Timorese, including women: 'We will never stop and we will keep doing what we do. Hopefully we can influence more of our people, especially younger brothers and sisters, to also appreciate arts for the future of Timor-Leste' (Osme Gonçalves, cited in Hooi 2017).
4. This name has been given to the group of East Timorese who formed the national leadership in 1975, in the brief period of independence before the Indonesian invasion, and who went on to lead the resistance movement thereafter (see Ramos-Gonçalves 2012a).
5. Interestingly, in 2011 a small political party, KHUNTO (Kmanek Haburas Unidade Nasional Timor Oan), was formed by younger East Timorese to address this deficit. Although the party did not enjoy much electoral success initially (just below 3 per cent of votes in the 2012 parliamentary elections), KHUNTO won five seats in 2017 to stand for a 'disenfranchised youth' (see ABC 2017). Prior to KHUNTO,

it was thought that the Pártido Democrático was the political voice of the Geração Foun.

6. The military in East Timor is known as the Falintil-Forças da Defesa de Timor-Leste (F-FDTL), named after the armed wing of the resistance movement when under Indonesia.

7. Further, within an East Timorese cultural context, militarism or the ability to use violence is associated with notions of masculinity, strength and power (see Myrttinen 2009: 16–17).

8. José Ramos-Horta was appointed as acting prime minister following the resignation of the Fretilin premier, Mari Alkatiri, in 2006 in the midst of the crisis. Ramos-Horta was an independent candidate, though chosen by the then president, Gusmão.

9. To my knowledge, the East Timorese government had no influence over the content of the art. During my fieldwork interviews with some of the artists involved, I was told that they were given full autonomy, and that the limited involvement of the independent prime minister Ramos-Horta was from a non-partisan position.

10. These two images from 2006 were kindly shared with me by the artists at Centro Arte Moris.

11. The CNRT party was created by Gusmão in 2007.

12. Fretilin was the political wing of the resistance throughout the Indonesian occupation and it continues to be one of the biggest political parties in the post-independence state. The Fretilin government ruled from 2001 until 2007.

13. The AMP coalition was made up of Gusmão's CNRT party, the Partido Democrático (PD), the PSD, and the Associação Social Democrática Timorense (ASDT).

14. Frenti-Mudança was a very young party at this time, having only formed in 2011 after a small faction broke away from Fretilin. However, its leader had previously been prominent in national politics as the former deputy prime minister of the 2007 AMP coalition government (Feijo 2012: 49).

15. The one fatality of the violence was a young Fretilin supporter, killed by the police.

16. It is worth noting that numerous criticisms are levelled at Sport for Development and Peace initiatives for being ineffective, severely underfunded, poorly researched, and inconsistent in implementation, despite discourse and marketing that suggest the contrary (see Kidd 2008: 376–78; Hartmann and Kwauk 2011).

17. The crocodile is widely considered to be apolitical and not connected to generational markers of identity or partisan conflict, much like the symbol of the *Uma Lulik* and the *babdok*. Its neutrality as a symbol was underlined in 2001 when the crocodile was brought into a debate on the national flag of East Timor (see Wallis 2016: 88, 119; Leach 2017: 161; Arthur 2018: 243–46). Prior to independence there were debates within the Constitutional Commission, operating under the auspices of the United Nations Transitional Administration in East Timor (UNTAET) over which flag would become the official national symbol of the new nation-state. To avoid tensions between rival political parties and their agendas on nation-building, some minority groups suggested the crocodile as a neutral symbol to appear on the flag, representing tradition and cultural heritage (see Wallis 2016: 118–19; Arthur 2018: 244). Although this suggestion was ultimately not taken on, the idea of the crocodile was popular among some within the Constitutional Commission's hearings because of its political neutrality, its similarity in appearance to the outline land shape of Timor, and its centrality to East Timorese mythology (Wallis 2016: 199).

18. The *tebedai* dance can involve up to twenty people, both men and women, who beat the drum while moving forwards–backwards and left–right in a circle.
19. Translation my own.
20. This now internationally recognized symbol originated as the emblem of the Campaign for Nuclear Disarmament, which first mobilized in the late 1950s.
21. The house system of clan and familial organization is common to many other Austronesian and South East Asian societies (see Harrison 1993; Fox 2006; Hicks 2008).
22. For an overview of '*lulik*', East Timorese cosmology, and the importance of ancestral spirits and objects, see Trindade 2011, 2014; McWilliam, Palmer and Shepherd 2014; and Bovensiepen 2011, 2014, 2015.
23. Indeed, Kelly da Silva and Daniel Simião highlight that there has been significant state recognition of these 'icons of the vitality and cultural diversity of the Timorese identity' (da Silva and Simião 2012: 373), as well as among local clan groups.
24. For more on primordial notions of family connections in nationhood broadly, see, for example, Johnson 1986 and 1987.
25. Chris Parkinson is a professional photographer and scholar who has comprehensively documented street art in East Timor since 2006, and who interviewed numerous artists for his research, including *Peace of Wall*. This translation is his own.
26. This version of the story was published as a children's book in 2011 (Hughes 2011). This was part of the project *Myths and Murals*, a cross-cultural public art and literacy project run between Melbourne and East Timor. The focus of the project was fostering national identity and establishing connections between Australian and East Timorese artists, particularly those from the Centro Arte Moris.
27. The image of the crocodile has been commodified to be one of the most common symbols sold in tourist souvenirs in East Timor, postage stamps and company logos, rendering the image widely recognizable, and associated with the nation for both locals and visitors.
28. Translation by Chris Parkinson.

References

ABC News. 2017. 'Timor-Leste Election: "Disenfranchised Youth" Party Wins First Seats in Parliament', 24 July. Retrieved 5 March 2019 from https://www.abc.net.au/news/2017-07-23/disenfranchised-youth-party-wins-seats-in-timor-leste-election/8736032.

Ahlm, D., and J. Lindgren. 2013. 'Game, Set and Cohesion: A Case Study of Sport for Social Cohesion in Timor Leste'. Unpublished thesis, Linnaeus University, Sweden.

Arnold, M.B. 2009. '"Who is My Friend, Who is My Enemy?" Youth and Statebuilding in Timor-Leste'. *International Peacekeeping* 16(3): 379–92.

Arte Moris. n.d. https://www.facebook.com/ArteMorisTimorLeste. Retrieved 18 January 2019.

Arthur, C. 2015. 'Writing National Identity on the Wall: The *Geração Foun*, Street Art and Language Choices in Timor-Leste'. *Cadernos de Arte e Antropologia* 4(1): 41–63.

———. 2016. 'Painting their Past: Street Art, the *Geração Foun* and Representing Notions of "East Timorese-ness"'. *Sojourn – Journal of Social Issues in Southeast Asia (ISEAS)* 31(1): 173–206.

———. 2018. 'From Fretilin to Freedom: The Evolution of the Symbolism of Timor-Leste's National Flag'. *Journal of Southeast Asian Studies* 49 (2): 227–49.

———. 2019. *Political Symbols and National Identity in Timor-Leste*. Cham, Switzerland: Palgrave Macmillan.

Babo-Soares, D. 2012. 'Conflict and Violence in Post-Independence East Timor', in A. Suhrke and M. Berdal (eds), *The Peace In Between: Post-War Violence and Peacebuilding*. London: Routledge, pp. 211–26.

Beutler, I. 2008. 'Sport Serving Development and Peace: Achieving the Goals of the United Nations through Sport'. *Sport in Society* 11(4): 359–69.

Bexley, A. 2007. 'The *Geração Foun*, *Talitakum* and Indonesia: Media and Memory Politics in Timor Leste'. *Review of Indonesian and Malaysian Affairs* 41(1): 71–90.

———. 2011. 'Timor's Youth – from *Supermi* to Sojourns'. *Asian Currents* 75: 7–9.

Bovensiepen, J. 2011. 'Opening and Closing the Land: Land and Power in the Idaté Highlands', in Andrew McWilliam and Elizabeth G. Traube (eds), *Land and Life in Timor-Leste: Ethnographic Essays*. Canberra: Australian National University Press, pp. 47–60.

———. 2014. 'Lulik: Taboo, Animism, or Transgressive Sacred? An Exploration of Identity, Morality, and Power in Timor- Leste'. *Oceania* 84(2): 121–37.

———. 2015. *Land of Gold: Post-conflict Recovery and Cultural Revival in Independent Timor-Leste* (Ithaca, NY: Cornell Southeast Asia Program Publications)

Chawla, S. 2001. 'Shaping East Timor: A Dimension of United Nations Peacekeeping'. *Strategic Analysis*. 24(12): 2291–303.

Chopra, J. 2000. 'The UN's Kingdom of East Timor'. *Survival*. 42(3): 27–39.

Da Silva, K. 2008. 'Reciprocity, Recognition and Suffering: Political Mobilizers in Independent East Timor'. *VIBRANT – Vibrant Virtual Brazilian Anthropology* 5(2): 156–78.

Da Silva, K., and D. Simião. 2012. 'Coping with "Traditions": The Analysis of East Timorese Nation Building from the Perspective of a Certain Anthropology Made in Brazil'. *Vibrant* 9(1): 362–81.

Dunlop, R. 2013. 'The Traditional Musical Instruments of East Timor and their Place in the Social and Cultural Mores of East Timorese Society', in Tony Mitchell, Hollis Taylor and Andrew W. Hurley (eds), *Music and Environment Symposium Proceedings*. Sydney, NSW: University of Technology Sydney.

European Union Election Observation Mission (EUEOM). 2012. *Timor-Leste Final Report: Parliamentary Election 2012*. Retrieved Ace Project 24 August 2020 from http://ace project.org/ero-en/regions/pacific/TL/timor-leste-final-report-parliamentary-elec tions/at_download/file.

Feijo, R.G. 2012. 'Elections, Independence, Democracy: The 2012 Timorese Electoral Cycle in Context'. *Journal of Current Southeast Asian Affairs* 31(3): 29–57.

Ferrell, J. 1995. 'Urban Graffiti: Crime, Control and Resistance'. *Youth and Society* 27: 73–92.

Fox, J.J. 2006. 'Comparative Perspectives on Austronesian Houses: An Introductory Essay', in *Inside Austronesian Houses: Perspectives on Domestic Designs for Living*. Canberra: Australian National University E Press, pp. 1–30.

Goldsmith, A. 2009. '"It Wasn't Like Normal Policing": Voices of Australian Police Peacekeepers in Operation Serene, Timor-Leste 2006'. *Policing & Society* 19(2): 119–33.

Gómez, M.A. 1992. 'The Writing on Our Walls: Finding Solutions through Distinguishing Graffiti Art from Graffiti Vandalism'. *University of Michigan Journal for Law Reform* 26: 636–707.

Grove, N., et al. 2007. *Like Stepping Stones in the River: Youth Perspectives on the Crisis in Timor-Leste*. Dili: Plan Timor-Leste.

Harrison, S. 1993. 'The Commerce of Cultures in Melanesia'. *Man* 28(1): 139–58.

Hartmann, D., and C. Kwauk. 2011. 'Sport and Development: An Overview, Critique, and Reconstruction'. *Journal of Sport and Social Issues* 35(3): 284–305.

Hicks, D. 2008 'Afterword: Glimpses of Alternatives – The Uma Lulik of East Timor'. *Social Analysis* 52(1): 166–80.

Hooi, K.Y. 2017. 'How Arts Heal and Galvanise the Youth of Timor-Leste', *The Conversation*, 12 June 2017. Retrieved 21 August 2020 from https://theconversation .com/how-arts-heal-and-galvanise-the-youth-of-timor-leste-73927

Hughes, M. (ed.). 2011. *The Boy and the Crocodile*. Mulgrave, VIC: Affirm Press.

Johnson, G.R. 1986. 'Kin Selection, Socialization, and Patriotism: An Integrating Theory'. *Politics and the Life Sciences* 4: 127–40.

———. 1987. 'In the Name of the Fatherland: An Analysis of Kin Term Usage in Patriotic Speech and Literature'. *International Political Science Review* 8: 165–74.

Jolliffe, J. 2011. 'Postcolonial Blues: East Timor's Lost Generation'. *The Monthly: Australian Politics, Society and Culture* (March). Retrieved 9 May 2018 from http://www.the monthly.com.au/issue/2011/march/1301812693/jill-jolliffe/postcolonial-blues.

Kent, L. 2011. 'Local Memory Practices in East Timor: Disrupting Transitional Justice Narratives'. *International Journal of Transitional Justice* 5(3): 434–55.

Kidd, B. 2008. 'A New Social Movement: Sport for Development and Peace'. *Sport in Society* 11(4): 370–80.

Kingsbury, D. 2012. 'Democracy as Lulic?'. *Deakin Speaking: Deakin University Blog* (16 March). Retrieved 28 January 2019 from https://blogs.deakin.edu.au/ deakin-speaking/2012/03/16/democracy-as-lulic.

Kingsbury, D. 2007. 'Timor-Leste: The Harsh Reality after Independence'. *Southeast Asian Affairs* 1: 363–77.

Leach, M. 2002. 'Valorising the Resistance: National Identity and Collective Memory in East Timor's Constitution'. *Social Alternatives* 21(3): 43–47.

———. 2003. '"Privileged Ties": Young People Debating Language, Heritage and National Identity in East Timor'. *Portuguese Studies Review* 11(1): 137–50.

———. 2013. 'Timor-Leste in 2012: Beyond International Statebuilding?'. *Asian Survey* 53(1): 156–61.

———. 2017. *Nation-Building and National Identity in Timor-Leste*. London: Routledge.

Lopes, M., and J. Morgan. 2012. 'Violence in East Timor after Snub to Party', *East Timor Law and Justice Bulletin* (16 July). Retrieved 5 March 2019 from http://www.east timorlawandjusticebulletin.com/2012/07/violence-in-east-timor-after-snub-to.html

McWilliam, A. 2002. 'Timorese Seascapes: Perspectives on Customary Marine Tenures in East Timor'. *Asia Pacific Journal of Anthropology* 3(2): 6–32.

———. 2005. 'Houses of Resistance in East Timor: Structuring Sociality in the New Nation'. *Anthropological Forum* 15(1): 27–44.

McWilliam, A., L. Palmer and C. Shepherd. 2014. 'Lulik Encounters and Cultural Frictions in East Timor: Past and Present'. *The Australian Journal of Anthropology* 25(3): 304–20.

Molnar, A.K. 2010. *Timor Leste: Politics, History, and Culture.* London: Routledge.

Myrttinen, H. 2009. 'Poster Boys No More: Gender and Security Sector Reform in Timor-Leste'. *Geneva Centre for the Democratic Control of Armed Forces* 31: 1–40.

Parkinson, C. 2010. *Peace of Wall: Street Art from East Timor.* Melbourne: Affirm Press.

———. 2017. *Re: Marks from East Timor: A Field Guide to East Timor's Graffiti.* Master's dissertation, University of Melbourne.

Pinto, C., and M. Jardine. 1997. *East Timor's Unfinished Struggle: Inside the Timorese Resistance.* Boston, MA: South End Press.

Ramos-Gonçalves, M. 2012a. 'A Língua Portuguesa e o conflito intergeracional em Timor-Leste', in R. Teixeira e Silva et al. (eds), *III SIMELP: A formação de novas gerações de falantes de português no mundo.* Macau: Universidade de Macau, pp. 1–15.

———. 2012b. 'Para além do visível: Percepções de direitos humanos nos murais e graffiti de Timor-Leste', in Michael Leach et al. (eds), *Peskiza foun kona ba / Novas investigações sobre / New Research on / Penelitian Baru mengenai Timor-Leste.* Hawthorn, VIC: Swinburne Press, pp. 74–81.

———. 2013. 'Ideas of Human Rights in the Walls, Paintings and Graffiti of Timor-Leste', in the Humanities, Migrations and Peace Studies Group (NHUMEP) – Peace Studies Research Area, *P@x Online Bulletin* No. 22: 9–11.

Richmond, O.P., and J. Franks. 2008. 'Liberal Peacebuilding in Timor Leste: The Emperor's New Clothes?' *International Peacekeeping* 15(2): 185–200.

Siapno, J. 2012. 'Dance and Martial Arts in Timor Leste: The Performance of Resilience in a Post-Conflict Environment'. *Journal of Intercultural Studies* 33(4): 427–43.

Simonsen, S.G. 2006. 'The Authoritarian Temptation in East Timor: Nation-Building and the Need for Inclusive Governance'. *Asian Survey* 46(4): 575–96.

Smith, A.D. 1991. *National Identity.* London: Penguin Books.

Storey, T. 2013. 'Expressing the Legacy of Conflict: East Timorese Street Art', *The Culture Trip: East Timor* (March). Retrieved 1 March 2019 from http://theculturetrip.com/asia/east-timor/articles/expressing-the-legacy-of-conflict-east-timorese-street-art/

Tour de Timor. 2018. http://tourdetimor.com. Retrieved 13 February 2019.

Traub, J. 2000. 'Inventing East Timor'. *Foreign Affairs* 79(4): 74–89.

Trindade, J. 2011. 'Lulik: The Core of Timorese Values'. Paper presented at *Communicating New Research on Timor-Leste.* 3rd Timor-Leste Study Asscociation (TLSA) Conference on 30 June 2011, Dili, East Timor.

———. 2014. 'Matak-malirin, Tempu Rai-diak and Halerik: Expressions of What Timorese Longed for in Life'. *Buka Hatene Timor Leste Vol. II*: 55–59.

Van der Auweraert. 2012. 'Dealing with the 2006 Internal Displacement Crisis in Timor-Leste', in *Between Reparations and Humanitarian Policymaking: Case Studies on Transitional Justice and Displacement.* New York: International Centre for Transitional Justice/Brookings, pp. 1–23.

Veiga, L. 2015. 'Movimentu Kultura in Timor-Leste: Maria Madeira's "Agency"'. *Cadernos de Arte e Antropologia* 4(1): 85–101.

Wallis, J. 2016. *Constitution Making during State Building.* Cambridge: Cambridge University Press.

Wise, A. 2006. *Exile and Return among the East Timorese.* Philadelphia: University of Pennsylvania Press.

Chapter 12

Reigniting the Revolution

An Interview with Abu Malek Al-Shami

Hend F. Alawadhi and Julia Tulke

Street art can be a means to inspire people, to energize them, to raise spirits and generate morale. This is most pronounced at times of crisis, war, or revolution. Wars motivate governments and citizens to turn to street art in an attempt to inspire the citizenry.

—Lyman G. Chaffee, *Political Street Art*

The walls have always been breathing out our souls… leaving a trace wherever we go, and speaking out words that many are unable to say.

—Activists in Damascus, 2014

Introduction

The visual identity and cultural memory of the Syrian Revolution has, since its inception, been closely associated with the practice of street art and graffiti. In fact, it was an act of public writing that is commonly believed to have ignited the country's revolutionary movement when a group of teenagers scrawled the words 'Your turn, doctor' on the walls of a school building in the city of Dara'a in February 2011 (Wall 2016; Asher-Shapiro 2016; Tarabay 2018). Addressed to Syrian president Bashar al-Assad, a trained ophthalmologist, the slogan responded to the revolutionary momentum unfolding in the Arab world at the time, particularly the expulsion of Tunisian president Ben Ali and the resignation of Egyptian president Hosni Mubarak earlier that month. Two other slogans that appeared simultaneously on the

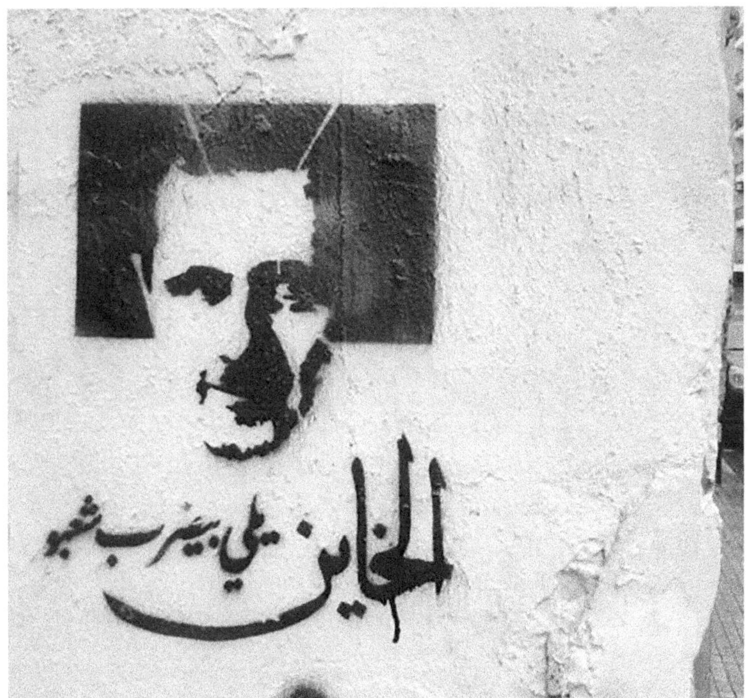

Figure 12.1 'A traitor is he who strikes his own people', unknown location, 2012. Creative Memory of the Syrian Revolution, Creative Commons, https://creativememory.org/en/archives/64797/a-traitor-is-he-who-beats-his-people/, cropped.

school's walls stated things even more explicitly, proclaiming 'The people want the fall of the regime', a slogan that had been used during both the Tunisian and the Egyptian revolutions, and 'Bashar, leave' (Bank 2014: 67; 'Creative Memory of the Syrian Revolution'). For the children, their act of public defiance resulted in several weeks of imprisonment and torture, sparking demonstrations across the country that eventually accumulated into the very uprising they had predicted. For Syria it was the beginning of a series of events that would result in a devastating war between al-Assad's military government, a heterogeneous revolutionary coalition lead by the Free Syrian Army (FSA), and Daesh, alongside myriad and variously aligned other factions and government forces.[1] In the context of this prolonged state of emergency, street art and graffiti remain a significant presence in everyday life in Syria, acts of meaning making in the face of crisis, death, and destruction.

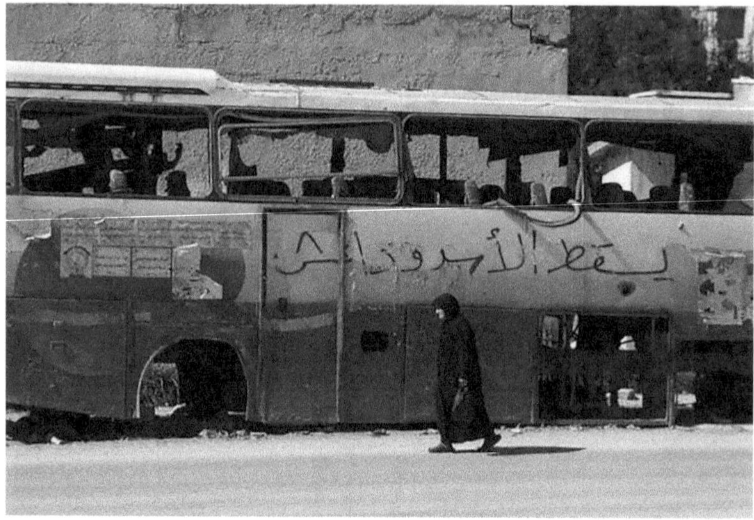

Figure 12.2 'Down with al-Assad and Daesh', Aleppo, 2015. Creative Memory of the Syrian Revolution, Creative Commons, https://creativememory.org/en/archives/93097/down-with-bashar-and-daash/.

Used primarily by activists and artists aligned with the Syrian Revolution, street art and graffiti form part of what Zaher Omareen has called a 'new grammar of dissent', which rejects the monolithic symbols and propaganda of the al-Assad regime in favour of a revolutionary aesthetics of the multitude, composed of a complex range of themes and approaches (Halasa, Omareen and Mahfoud 2014: 101). Political slogan writing has emerged as one of the most significant repertoires of such aesthetic contestation.[2] Explicitly oppositional statements such as those described above – most commonly directed at Bashar al-Assad, the government army, and Daesh (Figures 12.1 and 12.2) – remain ubiquitous, but many slogans engage with the Syrian crisis in more complex and poetic ways. A large body of writings distributed throughout cities all over Syria expresses a sustained commitment to the revolution in the face of the government's brutal military campaign, invoking motifs like freedom, dignity and resilience: 'Death before Humiliation', and 'We will not kneel' (Homs 2012); 'We stand strong no matter the damage' (Aleppo 2013); 'Destroy, destroy… we will rebuild' (Dara'a 2013); 'Freedom Will Prevail' (Idlib 2014); 'Building the country continues under al-Assad's barrels' (Aleppo 2015); 'We are not defeated, you did not win' (Homs 2017); and 'The revolution is an idea, and ideas don't die' (Idlib 2018).

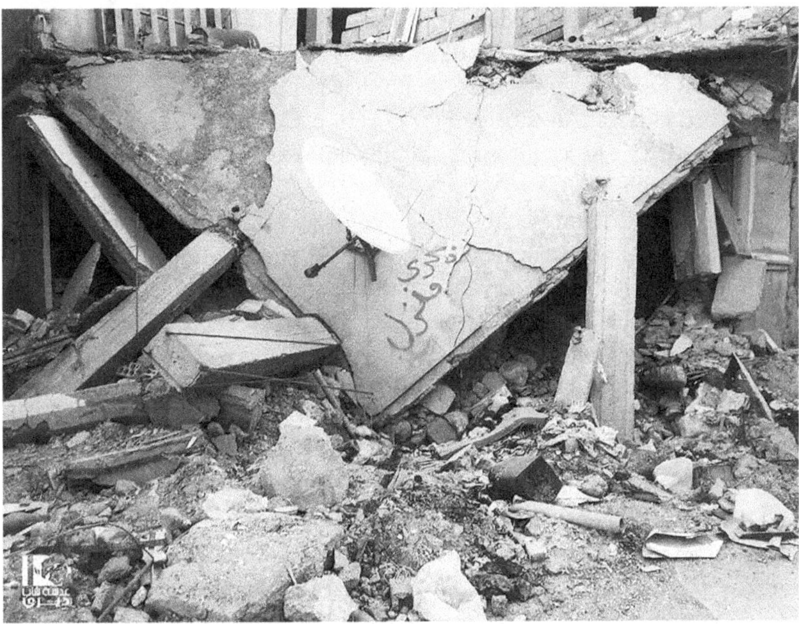

Figure 12.3 'Memory of a house', Deir ez-Zor, 2016. Creative Memory of the Syrian Revolution, Creative Commons, https://creativememory.org/en/archives/131806/memory-of-a-house/.

There have also been frequent solidarity campaigns that focus specifically on cities undergoing brutal periods of siege or attack, such as the chemical attack on Eastern Ghouta. Other works, often assuming the shape of more elaborate murals, honour those martyred as part of the revolutionary struggle – 'Our martyrs are the torch that lights our path to victory' (Aleppo 2014) – or commemorate the anniversary of the revolution. Some slogans have also directly responded to the mass emigration of Syrians, urging people to remain by stating, for example, 'Aleppo is more beautiful than Europe... Do not emigrate' (Aleppo 2015). Yet others signal to the significance of education and children's rights. Perhaps the most powerful set of slogans, however, departs from the explicitly political, instead taking on a more poetic, affectively saturated approach (Figure 12.3). Such works are often strategically embedded in the destroyed cityscape, occupying pieces of rubble or slabs of concrete hanging from the skeletal remains of bombed-out buildings, where they speak of recovery and return: 'One day, the war will be over... And I will go back to my poem' (Saraqib 2013); 'We were forced to leave, but we will leave our hearts here… we will return' (Homs 2013); 'When I leave, be sure that I did my best to stay' (Homs 2014); 'If the country has become a jungle you do not have to become an animal. Signed: A wretched citizen' (Al-Zabadani 2013); 'In a revolution, as in a novel, the most difficult part to invent is the end' (Saraqib 2017); and 'May we get well soon…' (Saraqib 2018).

Located at the intersection of the political and the poetic is the work of Abu Malek Al-Shami, a self-taught muralist and rebel fighter in the Free Syrian Army based in Darayya, a suburb of the Syrian capital Damascus.[3] Between 2014 and 2016, at a time when Darayya was besieged by government forces, Abu Malek produced over thirty artworks within the fragmented cityscape, from messages of resistance and witty political commentary on the Syrian regime, to memorials and works dealing with the affective impact of the ongoing crisis. Always signed *Darayya*, these murals simultaneously address a Syrian and an international public, and are deeply embedded in the broader visual ecology of revolutionary street art and graffiti described above. In the interview below, Abu Malek describes his involvement in the revolutionary struggle, the development of his creative practice during the siege of Darayya, as well as the trajectories and afterlives of his artworks.[4] We hope that his account will offer a meaningful addition to the scholarship on graffiti and street art of the so-called Arab Spring movements – which to date has disproportionately focused on the case of Egypt – and offer an engagement with the work of Abu Malek that moves beyond his previous representation in popular media as the 'Banksy of Syria'.[5] Our in-depth conversation with the artist furthermore serves as a point of departure to probe a number of broader questions related to the tactical significance of street art and graffiti in contexts of crisis, which will be elaborated in the conclusion.

Interview

Abu Malek Al-Shami (AM): I want to introduce myself. I am known as Abu Malek in Darayya. I am from Kafr Sousa in Damascus. I went to Darayya when running away from persecution and wanting to fight in the Free Syrian Army as a rebel. In 2013, Darayya had undergone a massive attack, and it was besieged. At that stage of the Syrian civil war, Darayya was witnessing a large massacre, and it was the closest city to my home town, Kafr Sousa. So in March 2013 I left my family, my studies and everything related to my everyday life hanging, and went to Darayya. I didn't know what was going to happen to me; I didn't know what could happen to me. But I knew that we would get rid of the regime and of the fear of being persecuted without reason, and would protect and defend the families in Darayya.

When I went I was still a high-school student. The exams would have been in June and I went to Darayya in March, so I couldn't have finished. When I got there I was really shocked. It looked very different from Kafr Sousa, which wasn't affected at all by the war. In comparison, Darayya was two-thirds destroyed. And most of its inhabitants had been evacuated due to the massacre and due to the presence of the regime. I was really shocked. I was inspired by the men who were there protecting the city, and I decided to remain, no matter what the consequences were going to be, even if we got wounded or killed. I remained there from March 2013 until we were forcibly evacuated in February 2016. We are now observing the second anniversary of our forced evacuation. When I entered initially, I entered as a fighter. I didn't have another job. The time of peaceful interventions was over – it was time to fight. In Kafr Sousa I had participated in peaceful protests, holding up signs that I had painted. It was then that I noticed that drawings could represent our needs in a way that was more aesthetic, in the best way possible. And I saw that people were using similar tactics to attract people's attention in other areas of Syria. We would embellish our signs with expressive drawings, which would lend them a beautiful angle, represent the city, and show that we are participating in the revolution in solidarity with the other cities and towns.

At the beginning of my time in Darayya a lot of changes were happening. The air raids were still ongoing, battles were ongoing. But after a few months, life somewhat returned to normal. Not completely, obviously – there was an embargo, no one could enter or exit. Even resources couldn't go in and out; all the roads were blocked. All the shops were closed, except for those families who had chosen to remain. But we woke up every day, we ate, we started to get more of a routine. But the resources were getting less and less. So we reduced our intake, so that we would cope with just the things we had. But life started to resemble some kind of normality.

Hend F. Alawadhi and Julia Tulke (HA/JT): This is how many months after you arrived?

AM: Approximately three months after I arrived – I think June/July 2013. Life started to be normal. So we needed to find a way to fill the spare time. Prior to that, all of our time had been consumed by defending and fighting, taking shifts. There was no spare time. But now we were confronted with it. So we started to think about activities that would occupy us – and we didn't have internet or mobile phones or ways to communicate with the world. So there were a lot of options. For me, I love drawing, so I started to

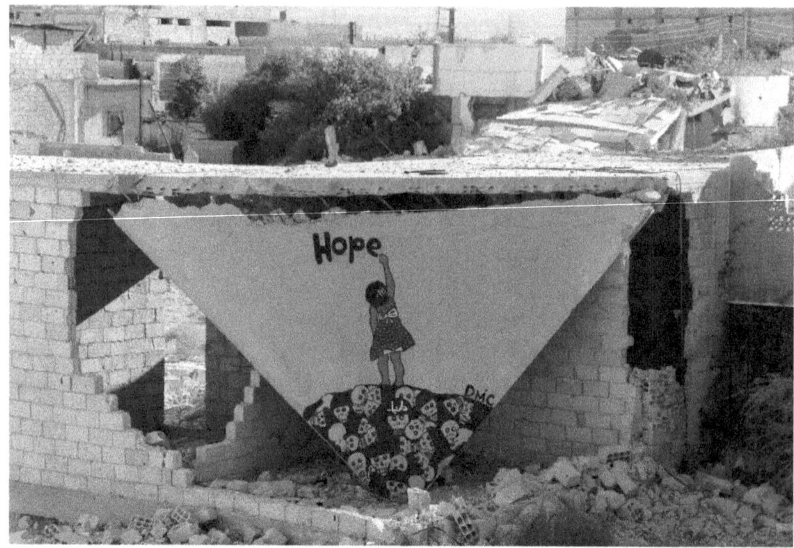

Figure 12.4 Abu Malek Al-Shami, 'Hope'. Photo courtesy of the artist.

beautify the place I was living in by drawing on the walls. Really simple draw-ings, and personal ones, things that I personally loved. I drew my rifle, politi-cal slogans, things related to the war. I drew symbolic things on the walls. So on one of those occasions there was a journalist called Majd Moadimani. He had been active in Darayya since the time when the protests had only been peaceful. So he saw the drawings that I did on the walls and he liked them, and he suggested that we should paint on the walls of Darayya. There were other cities where walls were being painted, and it gave the revolution an artistic side, which had been kind of overlooked in Darayya. And he told me that you could send a message with a drawing much more effectively than with a text or other means – better than speeches. There were many cities where this was being done, such as Homs, Aleppo and Saraqib, so many cities already had a creative practice on walls. I liked this idea. It was a good opportunity to paint something that would serve the revolution. In the beginning, the first point that we agreed on is that we would pick destroyed walls – whether still standing or falling down – as the canvas for our art. We wanted to do this for two reasons. First, we wanted to lend a sense of beauty to the destruction, and give life and colour to the devastation, and give hope to the people who still lived there (Figure 12.4); and second, to attract the attention of anyone who saw it. Anyone who would see the photos of the paintings and writings would feel that, despite the rubble, someone had decided to give it life, that life still persists in between the rubble and the death and destruction. In order to protect our identities, and with it our families, we chose to work anonymously, and independent of any organizations. We wanted to represent the revolution but we didn't want to represent a particular party. And this project didn't need any funding. We made use of the supplies that were already available in the city of Darayya. There was a good amount of colours and paint, not extensive, but the basic supplies that we needed to draw and paint with were available, even though it was using primary colours only. So we started, Majd and I. My first work was in July 2014. It was my first experience of painting on a wall, my first graffiti. To be honest, before the revolution, I was just a student who only drew in art class, and during the peaceful protests I only painted on cardboard signs. I never thought I would have to paint on walls, but now I had a desire to paint and draw on everything. So it was my first experience and I asked a lot of people and I took their advice – artists like Dialla Bursali, Hani Abbas, Mahmoud Salama, people painting in the revolution.

So the first painting was in July 2014. It was a challenge for me to paint on such a large scale, against such a destroyed backdrop, and in the name of the city, with an idea that could represent the reality of the revolution. So it was a big challenge – would I fail or would I succeed? I consulted a lot of friends and artists, and they gave me a lot of thoughts and suggestions. So I started to paint. The name of the artwork was 'Use Your Heart' (Figure 12.5). It has a soldier sitting, and a young girl teaching the soldier how to love. The soldier is shown entirely in dark green, carrying a weapon, and his figure was meant to represent any soldier, whether he was for or against the revolution. Any soldier in the world actually. And I was trying to express that whoever you are, before you take up arms and fight with them, you should learn from the more innocent. People took well to it. We wanted an angle that would be accessible to everyone and that would grab their attention: destroyed wall, clear colours, simple drawing. I was really invested in making a work that was not complicated, so that anyone from any culture, whether they're educated or not, whether they can read or not, a local or a Westerner who doesn't know Arabic, anyone following what was happening in Darayya, even if they don't know where Darayya is, could understand it. So thank God it was successful.

We started to think more about ideas, looking for specific events we would want to shed light on. We wanted to respond to ongoing events in a timely manner. We would pick an appropriate painting for an appropriate event and an appropriate time, so that the media would catch up on it also. This gave a lot of traction to the work. Through my time in Darayya, I painted thirty

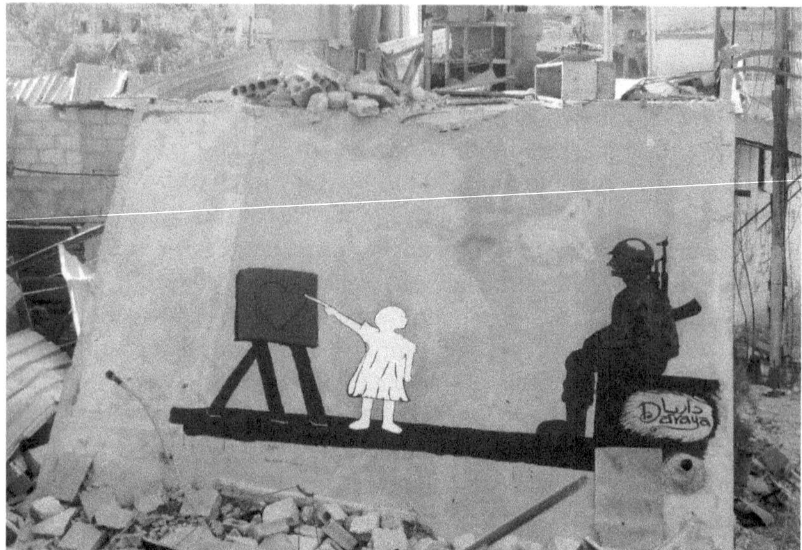

Figure 12.5 Abu Malek Al-Shami, 'Use Your Heart'. Photo courtesy of the artist.

murals at different times. Then I got wounded in my chest and I had to stop working for six months. Majd was martyred then, so I was practically alone.

Some people helped me, but not in the way that Majd had helped me before. Majd used to help me find an idea, places to paint, help me find supplies, finding the time to work, even help with documenting the process. He helped me with everything. When he was martyred in 2015, we had completed twenty-two works together. He had made me promise him, before he passed away, that if anything happened to him I would not stop painting, especially in Darayya. So when I started to get better and felt I could work again, I did my first work in January 2016. It was about the New Year, on 1 January 2016. That was my first work after getting wounded, and I continued to paint until the day that we were evacuated from Darayya. We faced a lot of challenges and problems. Some people were not receptive to the work. A few people told me that it was completely useless, that it wouldn't change anything, that it was a waste of time and a waste of paint. But a lot of people really encouraged me, and that support made me continue. I was worried that people were thinking: who is this guy scribbling on our houses after they've been destroyed.

I was worried that I would get negative reactions, but the majority were supportive. So I decided to continue with this work. I had other activities besides painting. I wasn't just a painter in Darayya – I had arrived as a fighter. But when I entered Darayya, I found that there were few men remaining. And the kind of men that were still there weren't professional fighters, they were mostly college students who had taken up arms. They were forced to defend their home town, to put their studies and life on hold, so that the city could stay alive. So I had activities with other people besides painting. We put together a library, collected from books found in destroyed homes. We set it up in a place that was somewhat secure, far away from raids, in the basement of a building. The library had fifteen thousand titles, and we categorized them. I wanted the people in Darayya to make use of it, to read, to educate themselves. This kind of activity was rare in those times. We would collect the books from places that were exposed to snipers and air raids. Of course this was dangerous. Most of the people who were helping were college students or recent graduates. There was an understanding that we needed to work on the cultural, scientific and artistic aspects of our day-to-day lives; we wanted to improve ourselves on these matters and to be the best people we could be. This was a positive thing in that area, especially in those times when there was a siege. We asked ourselves: how can we make best use of the siege? There's no food, no going in or out, and you're forced to stay. You can't surrender to the regime, which would mean that you'd either be shot or persecuted. So we had a lot of cultural gatherings and literary events, where we would discuss, and it had a positive effect on all of us.

HA/JT: Did these events last until you were evacuated?

AM: The cultural events started as soon as the battles and air raids lessened in intensity, but when the air raids started again in 2015, the events continued. We were still getting together. We would pick a book to read and we would discuss it; we would also discuss what needed to be done in Darayya. And these gatherings reflected positively on all of our souls. It gave us awareness – I don't know how to explain this to you, but it gave us hope.

HA/JT: Were there any women?

AM: There were women, but fewer, of course. Before the city was besieged we asked and helped families to leave the city, so a lot of women left. We told them that those who stayed would have an unknown fate, due to the siege and the military bombardment. The women who stayed were involved in teaching. They took care of the kid's education in Darayya. They wanted to stay because they didn't want an entire generation to miss out on education. They were completely dedicated to teaching children. The women were mostly also college students, which helped a lot. So we had a lot of support from the women in that sense. The men were involved in the action on the ground, fighting the regime, but the women were doing this essential work.

HA/JT: You mentioned that you kept your identity anonymous because of your family that was still in Kafr Sousa. But can you talk a little more about why you chose to sign your murals 'Darayya' instead of your own artist name?

AM: We chose to use the name of the city so that the work would not be tied to one person. Yes, I had a specific situation because of my family. But even if I had been from Darayya, I wouldn't have written my name. I didn't want any artwork to be connected to my person rather than the city and the name of the revolution. Whether it was on murals, or posters, or political signage, we avoided them being connected to a single person; we wanted them to be a collective work that had a revolutionary aspect to it. That's why it was all under Darayya's name.

HA/JT: In an interview published in 2016, you described the aim of your work, stating that 'there was a danger of people forgetting, forgetting about the struggle and forgetting the values that brought us here. There was a need to remind people exactly what they were fighting for, what this revolution meant' (Limoges 2016). How would you describe the state of the creative memory of the Syrian revolution now? What role can street art and graffiti play in this?

AM: In that interview, I was talking about one of the goals of painting, and one of the goals was to reignite the revolution. I started to paint in 2014 in Darayya, which had been exposed to military offensives since 2012, so by 2014 people's morale was low. They were always recovering from massacres, air raids, bombardment, persecution and then a suffocating siege, hunger and displacement. This made people forget. We forgot why we are fighting, what were the goals of the revolution. The regime was devastating us to the point of forgetting. So one of the goals of painting was to re-establish the aims of the revolution. What were the principles of this revolution, why did we go out, why did we take to the streets? What were the positive things that we did, and what were our mistakes? This renewed people's interest in the revolution. You see a work and you remember the noble goal of the revolution.

The images that we picked were chosen to affect the people who were still in the city. When I started to paint, I had a few points to consider. I wanted to affect the people who were still there, or the people who were outside, or both. And sometimes I would just reach out to the people in the city who had grown tired and weary of the situation, and had begun to lose their revolutionary impetus. So I would use the memory of the martyrs and detainees to remind them of the regime's crimes, the brutality of the regime. These paintings would allow the viewer to re-engage themselves with these things, and remind them why they were doing what they were doing. Where am I going and why did I remain in this city? What do I need to do now? These questions would allow people to re-engage themselves with the revolution. That is what I meant by we were forgetting. Long stretches of time were passing with non-stop struggle and pain. And through these simple drawings we were hoping that people would remind themselves to reconsider their position vis-à-vis the current situation, so that they would not forget the things that had happened in the city, the things that we had all been through. And correct their way of thinking.

HA/JT: In your opinion, do you think graffiti is making a difference?

AM: I think that in a certain period it made a huge difference. It was part of the battle that we were going through. The regime didn't fight us just with weapons, but psychologically, intellectually, with the siege, with fear, with hunger, with suppression. So in return we also had to fight in multiple ways, and one of these ways was to use colour. One of the things that meant a lot to me was that it was a way to communicate with the outside world. I was hoping, when they saw it, that someone, despite their struggle, was capable of using colour, that it would reflect life. Because I know, unfortunately, that Western media often represent us as barbarians – that we just want to fight without a goal, that we just like fighting for fighting's sake; that we like destruction, we like blood, and that we are content with the way things are. But on the contrary, it's quite the opposite. So in order for me to communicate a more truthful image, to counter the wrong image, I needed to use ways that would grab their attention, and I could do this through colour. I used colours that were full of life in a place that was almost dead, almost fully destroyed. This is how we could affect people who still had a conscience, still had some humanity and feeling. And I'm sure until now it has had a positive effect. So in Darayya, these paintings that were quite simple, only thirty murals, showed that Darayya wasn't like the other places. It didn't have internal conflict, people didn't have rifts against each other internally. We showed that we were able to live without Assad's regime. We showed that we could build ourselves, and work. We showed that we could run civil affairs, that we were aware of all aspects of life. We had the desire to keep on living, we did not want to die – unlike groups like Daesh, for example, who really didn't care if they died. We weren't like that, we wanted to live with dignity. So I considered that using this method – a simple painting with simple colours, which was easily exported to the outside world, especially the Western world – could garner sympathy that not a thousand speeches or politicians or video clips could. So yes, it had a very sensitive role in this struggle.

HA/JT: How did the works, the photos of works, get distributed? Was it through social media? How did the media catch on to you and your work?

AM: We relied on journalists, both local and international, who were following the revolution. We were invested in exporting our story globally, so we made it happen. We distributed images on our personal social media pages, such as Facebook. We also sent them to newspapers, and to well-known journalists, who we hoped would either spread the news further or write articles about us. We just alerted media that there was something going on here, and that they should be interested – and generally journalists are interested in the small details. Despite the fact that Darayya was being exposed to military bombardment, siege and constant struggle, there was still someone there painting on the walls. So they shed light on these kinds of things, and this helped us a lot. The fact that we were painting, despite everything, grabbed the attention of a lot of people who helped us to spread our story.

HA/JT: Are you still active, do you still paint where you are now?

AM: I'm in Idlib, in the north of Syria. I tried and I keep trying to go back to my artistic practice. But to be perfectly honest, things are really difficult here, very different from Darayya, in all aspects. To begin with, life here is relatively normal, despite what people think on the outside, that life has ceased in Syria. No, life is relatively normal here. The population here is also quite large. There is destruction, but it is confined to specific areas; not all areas are the same. There are certain areas that are known, for example, to be purely commercial areas. The area I'm in now is quite removed from reality, from the revolution.

In Darayya, the military would not interfere with civilians, they just wanted to protect the area. In Idlib, on the other hand, the military has adopted an authoritative approach to the space: I need permission to do anything. And since the area is open, you never know who is a spy, or working for the regime, or for Daesh, or generally who you can trust. I could be assassinated, kidnapped, exposed to danger if I was to openly pursue my work. Also, people here don't support these kinds of activities. They don't want to support any projects because they're afraid people may steal their money. Or they accuse us of taking the money to secretly fund the revolution. In the aftermath of the revolution, some people are really hard to deal with, they have very unexpected reactions, and I don't want to expose myself to that. So I am waiting, but I'm still looking for ideas and locations all the time. In the past two years in Idlib, I just haven't had the chance to work on new projects. I've resumed my studies, however, as I want to get my bachelor's degree in civil engineering. I'm also involved in intellectual activities, directed at students, similar to what we did in Darayya. I'm not sitting idle and waiting, I'm keeping busy and trying to improve myself, working on strategic things that will improve the living conditions in this city.

In all honesty, all of these things aren't stopping my creative energies. I'm not painting on walls but I'm still practising, working on small drawings on paper. We're also currently working on a project that commemorates those who were detained and martyred in Darayya – around a thousand people were executed there. So I'm preparing about ten paintings that depict the tortures of the regime, in addition to circulating the pictures of the martyrs. So things are happening. A few days ago I showed a large drawing I made a year ago for the anniversary of our forced evacuation from Darayya. So I haven't stopped drawing, even if I can't practise the same way I did in Darayya. It was an exceptional case – maybe it was an opportunity that will never repeat itself.

HA/JT: How did you distribute the work you just mentioned?

AM: I shared it on my personal Facebook page, and other pages belonging to activists from Darayya, as well as local news networks. Unfortunately, as long as I'm in Idlib, global agencies won't pay attention to us, they'll just focus on general news from Idlib. They overlook a lot of things. But that doesn't mean we stop working or producing creative works.

HA/JT: Can you tell us who is documenting this work, who is documenting your murals? Do you know if the murals you made in Darayya are still there?

AM: I don't know if they are. But personally I made sure to document my own work in high resolution formats, so I have my own archive. In some cases, when Majd was still alive, he would document all the stages of the drawing; sometimes he even took videos. But it depends. Sometimes we only managed to take a final photo if we were in a rush. It also depended on whether a certain news channel or outlet wanted more information or documentation of the process. So I have a copy of this archive, as well as another person in Darayya, who works in media. I never felt I should keep them to myself. I always wanted to share the images with anyone who asked me for them. It's a responsibility to send our message to the world by sharing our images with journalists and the media.

Conclusion

At once familiar and exceptional, the story of Abu Malek Al-Shami forms an ideal ground from which to engage with the objectives laid out by the editors of this volume: to examine the political potential of street art and graffiti in relation to contemporary landscapes of crisis, here understood with Lauren Berlant as an 'emergency in the reproduction of everyday life' (Berlant 2011). In order to do so, we will map Abu Malek's practice onto the

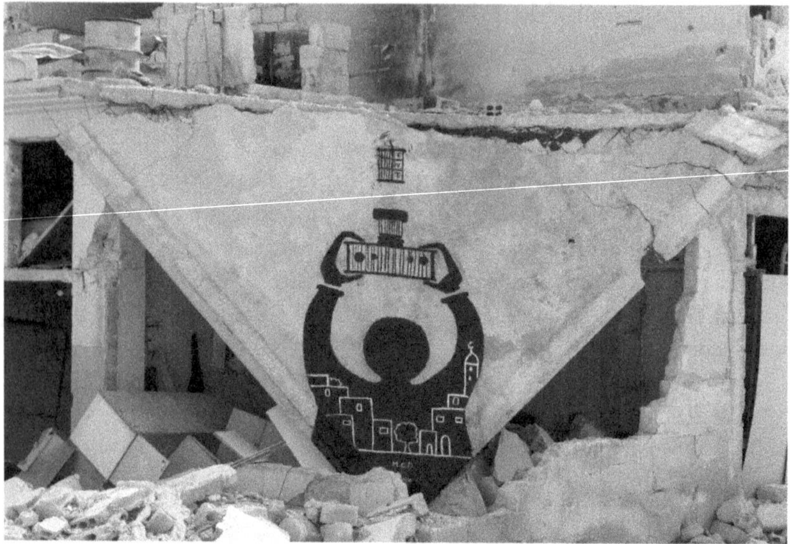

Figure 12.6 Abu Malek Al-Shami, Untitled. Photo courtesy of the artist.

three main aspects in which research on political street art and graffiti has located its potential to foster meaningful social change: its ability *to (re)claim space*, its commitment *to subvert hegemonic discourses* and the power relations they uphold, and its capacity *to reimagine social worlds*.

Abu Malek's work inhabits a very distinct spatial configuration: the streets of Darayya, a space marked by the ruin and destruction of war, a city besieged and evacuated of its population, a site where everyday life has largely been suspended. By staging creative interventions in this very context – adding murals to the bare facades of bombed out buildings, severed slabs of concrete, and piles of rubble – Abu Malek draws attention to the material conditions of everyday life in the city at war, while also defamiliarizing and resignifying the urban warscape. For the urban dwellers remaining in Darayya, he aims to imbue the city with a sense of hope and beauty, projecting visual traces of collective resilience onto the urban fabric. For the remote gaze of journalists and news consumers, he aims to disrupt the familiar image of destruction attached to the Syrian war, re-engaging the viewer with the state of exception. In so doing, he works against modes of representation that represent Syrians in active war zones as 'barbarians' content with the destruction of their county, instead drawing attention to the fact that 'life still persists between the rubble and the death and destruction'. As an affectively situated practice, Abu Malek's work not only recalls other instances of graffiti and street art created in the context of war and revolution,[6] but also aligns with a broader historical lineage of projects that engage with landscapes of crisis. A particular resonance can be found with projects that draw attention to the material and affective impact of urban renewal and transformation on the cityscape, such as the work of John Fekner and others in 1970s and 1980s New York City (John Fekner Research Archive), or Zhang Dali's *Dialogues* project in 1990s Beijing (Bruce 2010). These artists take urban ruins that have been abandoned, deemed unproductive, or slated for demolition as the basis for creative interventions that point beyond their mere economic value – or supposed lack thereof – gesturing towards their political potential as sites of affective attachment, collective memory, and resistance.

'Wars', cultural theorist Ella Chmielewska reminds us, 'are battles over symbols and over the right to write history' (Chmielewska 2008: 10). In a similar manner, Abu Malek frames his creative practice as a strategic tool in the struggle to 'represent the reality of the revolution' through a broad range of themes and issues. The Syrian war from here emerges as a polysemic event, at once ironic and tragic, exceptional and ordinary, revolutionary and oppressive. Abu Malek's murals in Darayya are always in dialogue with the war, engaged not only with current events, but also with hegemonic narratives that circulate globally in relation to Syria. Several of his pieces centre on the brutality of the Syrian government regime, thus critically engaging with the notion that Bashar al-Assad remains the legitimate leader of Syria. He particularly highlights the plight of journalists whose commitment to documenting the war in Syria comes at the cost of disproportionate exposure to injury and death (Reporters Without Borders). One work shows a machine gun and a camera facing each other, as if in battle. Another depicts the silhouette of a photographer, lens directed at the sky from where a barrel bomb is falling towards them (Figure 12.6). Another set of murals is explicitly aimed at maintaining the memory and presence of the Syrian revolution in the face of the ongoing war. One three-part series created in 2014 offers a didactic take on the ethics of the revolutionary project, as a young girl directs a soldier: 'Use your heart', 'Use your mind', 'Don't be a pawn'. Another wall shows the body of an FSA fighter standing on a hill, holding out for potential threats to a city laid out to his left. An inscription to his right reads: 'It doesn't matter to me when, how and why I die. What matters to me is that the revolutionaries remain, their cries filling the earth with noise so that oppression will not remain, standing on the bodies of the poor and the wretched'.

A revolutionary fighter first, and an artist second, Abu Malek orients his creative practice towards specific political objectives. Strategically using limited colours, simple and at times cartoon-like drawings, and clear messages,

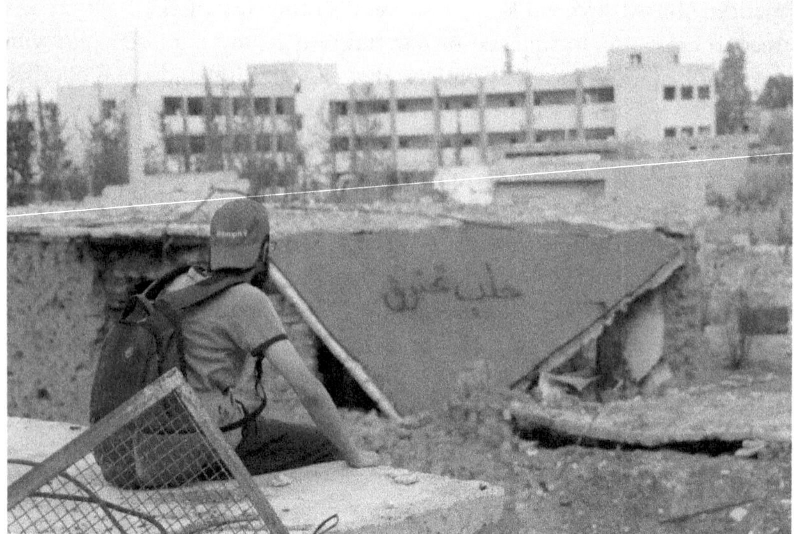

Figure 12.7 Abu Malek Al-Shami, 'Aleppo Is Burning'. Photo courtesy of the artist.

he distills his artwork to achieve the highest possible visual impact – 'so that anyone from any culture, whether they're educated or not, whether they can read or not, a local or a Westerner who doesn't know Arabic, anyone following what was happening in Darayya, even if they don't know where Darayya is, could understand it'.[7]

Notably, Abu Malek signs his murals Darayya, thus prompting the viewer to not read his work as the inner expression of an individual artist, but rather as part of a collective revolutionary endeavour.[8] The participatory aspects of his practice—he not only describes collaborating on artworks with his on-the-ground assistant Majd Moadimani, but also conferring with fellow revolutionary artists, and taking suggestions and comments from viewers both local and remote—sustain an idea of the revolution as an ongoing democratic dialogue, a project that continues to thrive in the face of destruction, siege and oppression. Beyond their encoded meanings and messages, Abu Malek's murals thus form part of a larger set of revolutionary practices aimed at reimagining the social world they inhabit, beyond its current state of crisis:

> We showed that we were able to live without Assad's regime. We showed that we could build ourselves and work. We showed that we could run

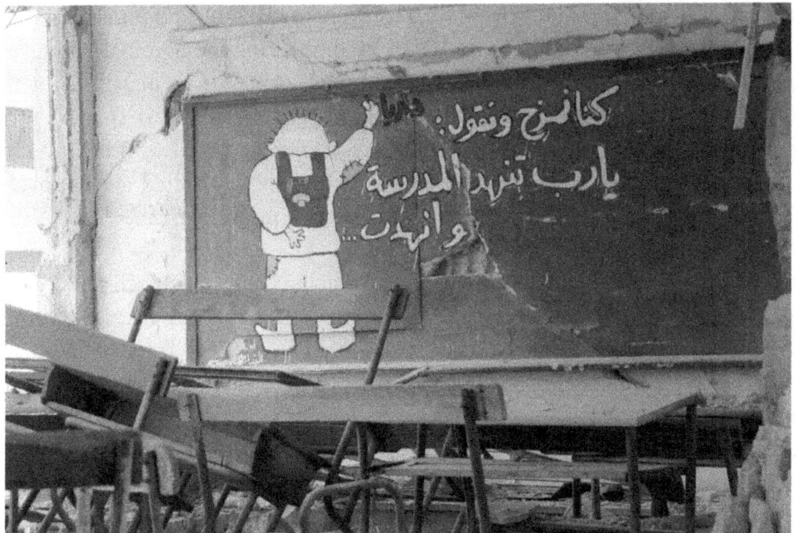

Figure 12.8. Abu Malek Al-Shami, 'We used to joke and say, God please destroy the school … and he did'. Photo courtesy of the artist.

civil affairs, that we were aware of all aspects of life. We had the desire to keep on living, we did not want to die – unlike groups like Daesh, for example, who really didn't care if they died. We weren't like that, we wanted to live with dignity.

Lastly, Abu Malek's murals also foster symbolic connections to other cities in Syria, as well as broader ecologies of resistance in the Arab world. In 2016, Abu Malek painted a wall in support of #Aleppoisburning, a social media campaign to raise awareness for the accelerating bombardment of the then rebel-held city by the government military (Jacoub 2016). As the campaign prompted people around the world to turn their social media profile photos red in solidarity with Aleppo, Abu Malek painted a concrete slab the same colour, adding the inscription 'Aleppo is burning' in Arabic, thus forging a connection not just between Darayya and Aleppo but also with transnational and virtual forms of solidarity (Figure 12.7). Another piece, painted in the rubble of a bombed out school classroom, features Handala, the famous cartoon figure created by Palestinian cartoonist Naji Al-Ali, a young boy typically depicted with his back to the viewer and his arms crossed in rejection, as he bears witness to the injustice inflicted upon the Palestinian people.[9] In Abu Malek's piece, the figure appears on a blackboard upon which he writes the words 'We used to joke and say, God please destroy the school … and he did' (Figure 12.8). By mobilizing the figure of Handala in the context of the Syrian crisis, Abu Malek strategically places his own struggle for autonomy and self-determination in relation to that of the Palestinian people. In so doing, Abu Malek projects a social world in which crises and struggles are not isolated events, but are connected across space and time through acts of solidarity and collective resistance.

Hend F. Alawadhi is an assistant professor at the College of Architecture in Kuwait University. She holds a doctorate in visual and cultural studies from the University of Rochester, NY, where her dissertation 'Tracing Trauma: Gender, Memory and Erasure in Contemporary Arab Cinema' earned the Susan B. Anthony Insititute for Gender, Sexuality and Women's Studies Dissertation Award. Hend's research interests centre on the history of the moving image in the Arab world, particularly as it relates to urban space and post-oil modernism in the Gulf. Her work also explores feminist media activism and the gendered representations of disability and illness in Arab media.

Julia Tulke is a PhD candidate in the graduate programme in visual and cultural studies at the University of Rochester, NY, where she was an Andrew W. Mellon Fellow in Digital Humanities from 2017 to 2019. Her research centres on the politics and poetics of space, with a particular focus on material landscapes of urban crisis as sites of cultural production and political intervention. She maintains a long-standing interest in political street art and graffiti as performative repertoires of protest. For her ongoing research project *Aesthetics of Crisis*, Julia has documented and examined street art and graffiti in Athens, Greece since 2013.

Notes

1. A detailed analysis of the complex network of actors involved in the Syrian conflict is beyond the scope of this contribution. For a more nuanced account of the context, trajectories and actors of the Syrian civil war, see: Yassin-Kashab and Al-Shami 2016; Van Dam 2017; al-Haj Saleh 2017; Abouzeid 2018; and Hisham and Crabapple 2018.
2. This observation and the slogans described in this section rely on the work of *The Creative Memory of the Syrian Revolution*, an online archive dedicated to documenting and enhancing the impact of the artistic Syrian resistance, including entries for caricatures, film, theatre, painting and many other genres of creative expression. At the time of writing this contribution, the site indexed 892 works of graffiti and street art created between 2011 and 2018. Every piece is documented photographically,

translated from Arabic into English, and contains information regarding geographical location, date of creation, and authorship. Within the graffiti archive, slogans emerged as the most ubiquitous form of expression, utilized mostly by activists. Murals and stencils, often assuming a more artistic approach, are less common yet are important creative repertoires. The importance of stencil making as a technique that allows for quick and anonymous dissemination (e.g. during the so-called Freedom Graffiti Week of 2012) is discussed in the edited volume *Syria Speaks* (Halasa, Omareen and Mahfoud 2014: 285; see also, Victoria and Albert Museum 2014).

3. Abu Malek Al-Shami is a chosen pseudonym, adopted in order to protect his family from the potential harm that may result from his status as an FSA fighter and muralist.

4. The interview was conducted on 29 August 2018 via Skype in Arabic, and translated from Arabic into English by Hend F. Alawadhi.

5. Throughout 2016, a number of interviews with Abu Malek Al-Shami appeared in different English-language online publications, three of which dub him 'the Banksy of Syria' (Irshaid 2016; Limoges 2016; Mobayed 2016). A more nuanced interview and description of his work that skirts this inappropriate comparison can be found at *Syria Direct* (Eddin 2016).

6. Most wartime graffiti and street art that has been documented assumes the form of soldier tagging, a self-referential marking of space. Perhaps the most iconic example of this is 'Kilroy was here', a tag that emerged prominently during the Second World War and has been attributed to a US-shipyard inspector, James J. Kilroy (Gastman and Neelon 2011: 36–39). In cases of occupation, graffiti and street art have also been used as means of communication by underground resistance groups in order to 'visually manifest a presence, … indicat[ing] to the regime and to the populace that there is an active opposition movement' (Chaffee 1993: 17). The role of graffiti and street art in moments of revolution has been examined extensively in relation to the Egyptian revolution of 2011 (Hamdy and Karl 2014).

7. Abu Malek's practice resonates with Lyman G. Chaffee's comments on the visual impact of political street art: 'Clarity in design is critical. Making a message simple and easy to grasp is paramount. It must be brief, clear and visible' (Chaffee 1993: 7).

8. Famous for having withstood a 4-year siege by the Russian-backed government military (2012–2016), the city of Darayya occupies an exceptional position in the symbolic geography of the Syrian revolution.

9. For more information on Naji Al-Ali and Handala, see http://www.handala.org/.

References

Abouzeid, R. 2018. *No Turning Back: Life, Loss, and Hope in Wartime Syria*. New York: W.W. Norton & Company.

'A Graffiti Campaign by Damascus' Free Men and Women on the Walls of the Capital 24-7-2014', *The Creative Memory of the Syrian Revolution*, 9 August 2014. Retrieved 12 April 2019 from https://creativememory.org/en/archives/65776/a-graffiti-campaign-by-damascus-freemen-on-the-walls-of-the-capital-24-7-2014-2/.

al-Haj Saleh, Y. 2017. *The Impossible Revolution: Making Sense of the Syrian Tragedy*. Chicago: Haymarket Books.

Asher-Shapiro, A. 2016. 'The Young Men Who Started Syria's Revolution Speak about Daraa, Where It All Began', *Vice News*, 15 March. Retrieved 12 April 2019 from https://news.vice.com/en_us/article/qv5eqb/the-young-men-who-started-syrias-revolution-speak-about-daraa-where-it-all-began.

Bank, C. 2014. 'Alshaab alsori aref tarekh [The Syrian People Know Their Way]: The Power of Persuasion', in M. Halasa, Z. Omareen and N. Mahfoud (eds), *Syria Speaks: Art and Culture from the Frontline*. London: Saqi Books, pp. 66–77.

Berlant, L. 2011. 'Austerity, Precarity, Awkwardness'. Paper presented at the Annual Meeting of the American Anthropological Association, Montreal, 2011. Retrieved 12 April 2019 from https://supervalentthought.files.wordpress.com/2011/12/berlant-aaa-2011final.pdf.

Bruce, C. 2010. 'Public Surfaces beyond the Great Wall: Communication and Graffiti Culture in China'. *InVisible Culture: An Electronic Journal for Visual Culture* 15. Retrieved Retrieved 12 April 2019 from https://ivc.lib.rochester.edu/public-surfaces-beyond-the-great-wall-communication-and-graffiti-culture-in-china/.

Chaffee, L.G. 1993. *Political Street Art: Popular Tools for Democratization in Hispanic Countries*. Westport, CT: Greenwood Press.

Chmielewska, E. 2008. 'Writing on the Ruins or Graffiti as a Design Gesture: On the Paradoxes of Lettering Place and History'. *Edinburgh Architecture Research* 31: 7–15.

'Creative Memory of the Syrian Revolution'. Retrieved 11 September 2019 from https://creativememory.org/.

Eddin, H. 2016. 'From One of Syria's Most-Bombed Cities, Street Art Sends the World a Message: "There is Always Something Beautiful, Despite All the Pain"', *Syria Direct*, 16 August. Retrieved 12 April 2019 from https://syriadirect.org/news/from-one-of-syria%e2%80%99s-most-bombed-cities-street-art-sends-the-world-a-message-%e2%80%98there-is-always-something-beautiful-waiting-for-us-despite-all-the-pain%e2%80%99/.

Gastman, R., and C. Neelon. 2011. *A History of American Graffiti*. New York: HarperCollins Publishers.

Halasa, M., Z. Omareen and N. Mahfoud (eds). 2014. 'Stenciling Martyrs: Graffiti Starts a Revolution', in *Syria Speaks: Art and Culture from the Frontline*. London: Saqi Books, pp. 284–90.

Hamdy, B., and D. Karl (eds). 2014. *Walls of Freedom: Street Art of the Egyptian Revolution*. Berlin: From Here to Fame Publishing.

Hisham, M., and M. Crabapple. 2018. *Brothers of the Gun: A Memoir of the Syrian War*. New York: One World.

Irshaid, F. 2016. 'In Pictures: How a Rebel Fighter Became "Syria's Banksy"', *BBC*, 13 October. Retrieved 12 April 2019 from https://www.bbc.com/news/magazine-37523340.

'It's Your Turn, Doctor', *The Creative Memory of the Syrian Revolution*, 25 March 2011. Retrieved 12 April 2019 from https://creativememory.org/en/archives/150713/its-your-turn-doctor/.

Jacoub, M. 2016. 'Aleppo is Burning', *Creative Resistance*, 27 May. Retrieved 12 April 2019 from http://creativeresistance.org/aleppo-is-burning/.

John Fekner Research Archive. 'Charlotte Street, South Bronx, NY, August 1980'. Retrieved 12 April 2019 from http://johnfekner.com/feknerArchive/?p=72.

Limoges, B. 2016. 'Meet the Banksy of Syria', *Middle East Eye*, 31 August. Retrieved 12 April 2019 from https://www.middleeasteye.net/in-depth/features/painting-dem ocratic-uprising-63328359.

Mobayed, T. 2016. 'Rebel Fighter By Day, Syrian Banksy By Night – This Is The Story of Abu Malik al-Shami', *MVSLIM*, 14 December. Retrieved 12 April 2019 from https://mvslim.com/the-syrian-banksy/.

Reporters Without Borders. 'Syria'. Retrieved 12 April 2019 from https://rsf.org/en/syria.

Tarabay, J. 2018. 'For Many Syrians, the Story of the War Began with Graffiti in Dara'a', *CNN*, 15 March. Retrieved 12 April 2019 from https://www.cnn.com/2018/03/15/middleeast/daraa-syria-seven-years-on-intl/index.html.

Van Dam, N. 2017. *Destroying a Nation: The Civil War in Syria*. London: I.B. Tauris.

Victoria and Albert Museum. 2014. 'Syrian Graffiti', *Vimeo Video*, 4:13, 4 December. Retrieved 12 April 2019 from https://vimeo.com/113619998.

Wall, P. 2016. 'Your Turn, Doctor', *Geographical Imaginations: Wars, Spaces, and Bodies*, 30 November. Retrieved 12 April 2019 from https://geographicalimaginations.com/2016/11/30/your-turn-doctor/.

Yassin-Kassab, R., and L. Al-Shami. 2016. *Burning Country: Syrians in Revolution and War*. London: Pluto Press.

A Public Crisis /
A Crisis of Publicness

Political Graffiti in the Post-coronavirus Age

Rafael Schacter

I write this Afterword from lockdown, from a crisis more prescient than the editors of this volume could ever have imagined, from an indeterminate period of globally spanning confinement the likes of which have rarely, if ever, been seen. Of course, I am very aware that a thousand essays are currently being written narrating an identical story, instrumentalizing our contemporary predicament to add grist to the scholarly mill. Yet, for us here, for the readers of this particular book at this particular time, the simultaneous prescience and pertinence of this moment of international crisis cannot be ignored.

This edited collection is situated, as editors Pavoni, Zaimakis and Campos declare in the Introduction, 'at the encounter between crisis …, urban space, and the visual expression of protest', triangulated at a point strangely attuned to the current condition of our COVID contagion. This is, of course, a health crisis first and foremost, a tragedy of a scale truly hard to envision, a tragedy in which absence[1] – the visual absence of the dead and dying, the physical absence of familial support at the time of most need, the material absence of personal protective equipment for front-line staff – has become the prevailing mode. Yet it is so too a public crisis that has formed a crisis of publicness, a crisis in which the quintessential site of protest, of debate, of urban life, has been (necessarily) evacuated, (forcibly) displaced, in order to protect ourselves *from* ourselves. We thus each today reside in the midst of an epidemiological emergency wherein the very notion of 'public' – both in social and spatial terms, both as people and place – has become stretched into an entirely new paradigm. We now have a public (public as people) existing solely in private. We now have a public (public as place) decanted of that which makes it exist. Where can citizenship occur if not in public? How can protest transpire, how can one's voice be heard, when the public – in both of its meanings – has become a profound danger in and of itself? The crisis that this pandemic has formed is thus one in which many of the concepts integral to this text have been both overwhelmed and accentuated, simultaneously put into question and given further prominence. It is in this way a crisis, as Pavoni, Zaimakis and Campos continue in the Introduction, not only in which the 'right to the city ... appears to be increasingly subtracted from urban inhabitants', but one in which the very way the city is 'managed and lived appears to be determined by global forces that escape our understanding, perception, and control'; a crisis that has become a 'filter through which reality is perceived, described, understood and, ultimately, contested'.

Whilst visual records of dissent are thus still discernible (see Figure 1 in Chapter 1, for example), and are in a strange way more conspicuous due to the stark emptiness of their surrounds, our very ability to articulate dissent has been sharply curtailed, at a time in which governmental response needs to be more keenly scrutinized than ever. Yet as the death tolls rise, seemingly inexorably (and as inexorably as the attendant economic pessimism), so too the power of the state comes to reveal itself ever more intimately to us. This is a crisis of welfare systems, a crisis in which an invisible disease can, in fact, make the hidden realities of our social structures more visible, in which the emptiness of our surrounds serves to highlight issues that were obscured yet already present. Who is it, then, on the frontline of the virus? It is of course the already marginalized, habitually subjugated groups who are forced to work under precarious circumstances – the underpaid, undervalued keyworkers who silently keep our city's and their inhabitants alive. There are thus very different lockdowns occurring. Those with secure incomes, safe homes, reliable networks, and those for whom regularity and stability is a luxury. Whilst we may all be in the same storm, as a recent meme related, we are certainly not all in the same boat. We can hence see how it is many of the already *existing* inequalities, the already extant urban crises of the twenty-first century – the increasing 'privatization and commodification of public space', the 'intensification of surveillance and social control', the escalating struggles of the 'housing crisis, social exclusion, austerity politics' (Chapter 1) – that the COVID crisis has come to intensify. It is a crisis in which the supposedly levelling force of the virus disproportionately attacks the spatially and racially marginalized,[2] a crisis in which those at the edge are pushed even further towards it, a crisis in which the health of our publics is more precarious today than ever.

Here in this book, however, written before COVID-19 even existed, we are talking primarily about graffiti, about an explicitly political aesthetic, a tool of grass-roots urban activism linked to social movements and collective action. Here we are talking about what seems as a bygone age of the public sphere, about a practice in which solidarity is formed through aesthetic/discursive means, in which statements act not as imperatives, but enjoinders towards a community of hidden others. Here we are talking about a certain politics of visibility in which a community comes into existence through the existence of the very texts themselves. So how do the various authors in this text explore these particular relationships, the relationships between crisis, the city, and protest? Split into three parts – 'street activism and visual protest' (Part I), 'anti-gentrification protests' (Part II), and sites of 'political turmoil, regime transformations and revolutions' (Part III) – the essays uncover an array of equally ethnographic and conceptual specifics that help to clarify and elucidate this tripartite bond. From Jonna Tolonen's exploration of street art in Spain during the 2010s – a 'fight against gentrification … for a fair minimum wage, … for justice for Franco's victims' (Chapter 2), to Jeffrey Ian Ross's examination of anti-Trump graffiti in Washington DC, a site in which it 'feels like the entire city is trying to resist' (Chapter 5); from Dobratz and Waldner's investigation of post-WW2 graffiti in Berlin, which analyses how graffiti comes to 'intersect with the political crises surrounding the division and reunification of Germany' (Chapter 7), to Pafsanias Karathanasis's analysis of stencil graffiti in Nicosia – the 'visualized and spatialized results of … sociopolitical change' (Chapter 8); from Cláudia Madeira et al.'s consideration of post-revolution murals in Portugal, in which the city is understood both as a place of 'visibility and passage' and a 'resource for political expression' (Chapter 10), to Catherine Arthur's study of street art in East Timor, where these images act to 'foster national unity and stability' during times of political flux (Chapter 11); and from Yiannis Zaimakis and Leonidas Oikonomakis's comparative analysis of activist images in two South American and South European states, which sees them as 'affective and effective means to creatively express sociopolitical content' (Chapter 3), to Hend Alawadhi and Julia Tulke's moving interview with the Syrian artist Abu Malek Al-Shami, which highlights his work's ability to '*(re)claim space*' and '*reimagine social worlds*' (Chapter 12), the text provides us with a range of highly situated, contextualized and localized accounts that deliver us the thick descriptions necessary to truly understand a city's texture and intimacy.

Other chapters, however, take up the methodological baton. Konstantinos Avramidis and Myrto Tsilimpounidi, for example, argue for the notion of 'periegesis' (meaning both a 'tour and a geographical description'), a tool to map the 'social, political and urban context' and one that underscores the relationship between movement and the temporality of space (Chapter 1). Other contributors focus on particular thematic issues: from Anna Giulia Della Puppa on the heritage industry and urban regeneration (Chapter 9), to Andrea Pavoni on vandalism on monumentalism (Chapter 6), and to Javiera Manzi et al. on differing patterns of production and circulation emergent from a range of graphical techniques (Chapter 4).

Yet whatever their geographical or theoretical focus, each of the chapters underscores the way that political graffiti can help us to 'understand the subtext of a city without resorting to mainstream accounts or official histories' (Dobratz and Waldner in Chapter 7). They highlight – returning to Pavoni, Zaimakis and Campos – the way in which 'aesthetics has grown into a key context in which urban politics is expressed, repressed and fought', as much as the way the city has always been a site where 'regulation, governance and control coexist with extended patches of darkness, invisibility and resistance' (Introduction). Political graffiti is thus located in a particularly privileged site. It is an aesthetic that can both reveal and recreate the political structure of our public spheres, an aesthetic that can influence and cohere, show and tell. Yet for our editors, the key site of conflict remains that of progressing out of the bind of contemporary crisis, of both '*critically* re-imagining our present ... away from the linear path that the narrative of crisis seemingly forces us into', as much as discovering how to 'turn the passive enduring of ... crisis into the active imagining of alternative, *critical times*' (Introduction).

So, returning once more to the present moment in which I write, how is it that we can become active rather than passive citizens of the coronavirus? How can we critically reimagine the particular path of the crisis that we are currently set upon? If the crisis has evacuated the city, absenting us of the traditional *space* of protest, where is the site of reimagination, where is the site for activity today? These questions, I feel, take us back to the core issue of what we believe political graffiti really affords (or rather afford*ed*). What does/did it endow us? What does/did it secure?

Beyond everything, it is graffiti's peculiar double-sidedness that I believe is key – its status as both practice and image, order and ornament, social and spatial, ritual and visual (Schacter 2014). Is it not its ability to depict and reveal relationships (as much as to create those relationships itself), to materialize sociality and affectivity, that could be seen as its true aesthetic? The simultaneous reaching outwards to a community of others and the creation of a community itself; the formation of community *through* direct address and the direct address formed through community; the commonality visible *through* the image and the image visible *through* commonality – is it not this status as a truly *common* image that is key? It is that which is 'public, shared by all or many' (from Latin *communis*). That which is 'belonging to all, owned or used jointly' (from Old French *comun*). Perhaps it is graffiti as common*s*, as that which exists – as Pavoni discusses in his chapter – not just as a revered *space* but as a modality of solidarity and sociality, that is key. It is that which is created and that endures as practice, as a vast, material entanglement of the 'tangible and intangible bodies, relations, and practices that produce a city' (Chapter 6). It is the everyday acts of dialogue and debate, the mundane, minor acts, that bind life together. Graffiti as common image, as both spatial and social act, as both order and ornament, does something very particular for a very particular moment. It speaks to the city at a time when it most needs speech. It holds tight to an idea of the urban with the social firmly at its centre. It returns us to art before the age of Art, to art as that which forms an aesthetic community. It returns us to an image working beyond itself, to pure words, pure discourse, to the magnitude of the marginal, the power of the peripheral. Yet how, to get back to the question, can this double-sidedness, the representational and communal politics that political graffiti engages, be itself engaged during our current days of crisis?

For me, this question is best approached via two, highly juxtaposed scales: those of the hyperlocal and the hypermediated. In the first instance, over recent months we have seen the explosion of local mutual-aid groups all over the UK (and internationally too, of course). These are grass-roots organizations seeking to support and aid the most vulnerable – be that physically, mentally, socially or economically. They are highly localized collectives seeking to create solidarity during these crisis times. Whether volunteering to drive neighbours to hospital, to pick up medicine or shopping, to provide household essentials, to support with home-education, or simply to act as a reassuring voice on the end of the phone, these groups brought communities together, reasserting the strength of neighbourly relations, building connectivity and active engagement in formerly politically passive, socially isolated locales. These are also innately egalitarian assemblages: they are non-hierarchical and non-bureaucratic, operating through shared leadership and cooperative decision making, with membership free and open to all. Where the state has pulled away, communities have mobilized. Sharing ancestral links to groups such as medieval guilds, to working men's clubs and fraternal societies – collectives whose dense rituals created long-lasting solidarities, support networks and aesthetic confederacies (Schacter 2014) – here embodied action is solidarity; orthopraxy rather than orthodoxy is thus key. Here it is the doing, the action, the participation that counts, fidelity emergent through action not words. As such, within these groups, the very inability to *be* public, the public *absence*, has created a new ecology of private individuals performing together politically, creating commonality beyond national, religious and ethnic boundaries, beyond status, hierarchy, gender and race. These are groups reimagining a form of localism (rather than nationalism) that can endure and persist beyond our current calamity – a web of care, of progressive (rather than popular) politics. Moreover, amidst the peak of the pandemic, these groups are already deliberating how to continue to engage with the inequalities that the coronavirus crisis has exacerbated beyond this time of 'crisis'. The grass-roots politics discussed in this volume thus still persists, albeit now enabled and facilitated through *digital* means. Here, then, we can begin to think about the digital not only as a tool of enablement but as a tool of sustainability for the public sphere, and the digital commons as a potential site of reimagination, of subtext, of vernacularity itself.[3]

We are a species for whom companionship and community is essential, for whom cooperation, rather than competition, is the primary mode. Community must still be built, social ties still lubricated, and, as such, the digital has today become the space where being together *must* occur. We thus speak to kin on Facetime; we Houseparty with friends; we teach over Teams; we attend lectures on Periscope; we rave on Instagram Live. We even bury our dead on Zoom. Rituals thus continue, commitments are reaffirmed. We remain socially intimate whilst physically distant.[4] Yet we also go beyond this, not just replicating but supplementing, broadening the physical public, using the power of the digital to go beyond the concrete. The WhatsApp and Facebook groups that make these mutual-aid groups possible, the Excel spreadsheets and public Google Docs, thus become incredibly powerful via their absolute mundanity. They are not 'sexy', not bombastic.[5] They are ordinary and everyday. Yet as discussed by the anthropologist Chris Kelty, we can think about such digitally formed groups as *recursive* publics, publics that that have been brought together 'in ways that were not possible before the internet' (Kelty 2008: 2), publics that are 'constituted by a shared concern for maintaining the means of association through which they come together as a public', that 'exist independent of, and as a check on, constituted forms of power' (ibid.: 1). These publics are recursive, however, in that it is the making and maintenance of these publics that becomes key to the existence of the publics themselves. The infrastructure formed through and by the digital can thus not only be seen to express a particular moral order (non-hierarchical, open, egalitarian), but their existence as structures that also enable the 'circulation, archiving, movement, and modifiability of our enunciations' (ibid.: 7) must be seen as key to the perpetuation and potential of the publics themselves. Mobilization with the context of this crisis can thus be seen, in many ways, as spectacularly unspectacular. And yet, perhaps because of this, the social imaginaries that these digitally enabled publics create can be seen to come closer to the utopian ideal of a physical public than our cities may have ever truly reached. The polis, as Arendt famously argued, is not a location but *a mode of organization*, one that arises 'out of acting and speaking together' (Arendt 1958: 198), that emerges when 'words are not used to veil intentions but to disclose realities', when 'deeds are not used to violate and destroy but to establish relations and create new realities' (ibid.: 200). Perhaps the digital can, in this way, elude many of the endemic structural issues of the city, the privileges and exclusions that are so often occluded. Perhaps its simplicity, its normativity, its *banality*, can circumnavigate this, built to belong to all, to be used jointly, to be in common.

Like political graffiti then, this modality of the digital can be seen to form community through its address itself, through its ingress into the public, its appearance in the public realm. Like political graffiti it is visible yet works through its mundanity, not spectacularity. It makes no grand claims (which will never be fulfilled) but rather functions to formulate new relations as well as upholding old ones, to materialize community through a particular ethic of care, through a minor, vernacular modality. It activates not through a representation of the *self* (like, one could argue, much political activism and classical graffiti), but through becoming diffuse and distributed. Here then, we could think about a certain politics of scale. The extravagant is now impossible; we cannot climb Everest to save the rainforests, or run a marathon every day for a week to highlight climate change. But we *can* act, in a myriad of unexciting yet critical ways. The crisis the coronavirus has engendered, the public crisis and the crisis of publicness, is thus one in which our enforced passivity has come, in many ways, to create a new form of activity: to connect to our communities through geographically located and technologically enabled means; to force us to reimagine the future beyond (the) crisis. Of course, nothing can replicate the feeling of physical presence, the way in which 'collective actions collect the space itself, gather the pavement, and animate and organize the architecture' (Butler 2011), and I pray that our public spaces will soon be returned to with an extra vigour that this period of renunciation has bestowed. Yet during a time in which political, economic and spatial divisions of our urban worlds are becoming once more exacerbated, it is to the efficacy of political graffiti that we can once more look. Can its sheer visibility, its ability to force one to encounter other positions, other possibilities, continue to be harnessed outside of our physical publics? Can its pure commonality, its ability to create bonds of allegiance, to create grass-roots community, be engaged through the digital? Can this crisis, indeed, be one that refuses the return to normality *of* crisis?[6]

Rafael Schacter is a lecturer in anthropology and material culture at University College London. He works on public art and global art, curating and writing widely in both these areas. He has published three books: *Street to Studio* (Lund Humphries, 2018), the award-winning *World Atlas of Street Art and Graffiti* (Yale University Press, 2013), and *Ornament and Order: Graffiti, Street Art and the Parergon* (Ashgate/Routledge, 2014). He most recently curated the exhibition Motions of this Kind at the Brunei Gallery (SOAS, 2019), and has previously curated at the Tate Modern (for the Street Art Walking Tour exhibition in 2008), Somerset House (the exhibitions Futurismo Ancestral, Mapping the City, and Venturing Beyond, in 2014, 2015 and 2016 respectively), amongst other national and international projects in Mexico, Madrid, Manila and beyond.

Notes

1. Like most people reading this, I too have highly personal narratives to tell, yet still feel strangely, uncomfortably disassociated from events, absented from their reality.
2. See for example the geographies of park closure in London, let alone the disparities of death rate for BAME communities.
3. Much of the initial optimism concerning the progressive potential of digital has largely been harshly curtailed over the last decade. We have seen, for example: the increasing use of political disinformation campaigns emergent through social media (let alone the political right's astonishing engagement with meme culture); firm evidence that the internet both enables and propels inequality; the endemic racism and problematization of the algorithm; the exacerbation of the internet as an echo chamber; and the swifter burn-out of digital activism (and activists) in comparison to the slower, more drawn-out mode of its traditional counterpart. Beyond this, we can also see the way in which many of the core issues affecting the *physical* public sphere have morphed directly into their digital counterparts: the increasing commodification and corporate control of digital space; the spiralling of digital surveillance; the escalation of digital exclusion. It would be a huge ask for any of these issues to be suddenly surpassed. Yet whilst caution and pessimism are crucial, the post-coronavirus age has opened up space for hope.
4. Anthropologists in particular have been vehement in their desire to change the term 'social distancing' to 'physical distancing'. We must be socially intimate and physical distant to survive the rigours and isolation of quarantine.
5. The surge of individuals using 3-D printing to make PPE at home for medical usage (in what has been termed the 'citizen supply chain'), for example, is thus fantastic, and in many ways does act as a positive example of the opening up of the production process that the digital has enabled; but it is not, in fact, too dissimilar to those sewing facemasks – albeit with a 'sexy' digital twist.
6. To be clear, I am not sure if I really believe this myself, despite wanting to. At the very least, however, it is somewhere to start from.

References

Arendt, H. 1958. *The Human Condition*. Chicago: University of Chicago Press.
Butler, J. 2011. *Bodies in Alliance and the Politics of the Street*. Transversal.
Kelty, C.M. 2008. *Two Bits: The Cultural Significance of Free Software*. Durham, NC: Duke University Press.
Schacter, R. 2014. *Ornament and Order: Graffiti, Street Art and the Parergon*. Aldershot: Ashgate.

Index